THE SOCIAL ANTHROPOLOGY OF AFRICA:
AN INTRODUCTION

THE SOCIAL ANTHROPOLOGY OF AFRICA:

AN INTRODUCTION

M. Angulu Onwuejeogwu

Senior Lecturer in Anthropology
University of Benin

LONDON
HEINEMANN
IBADAN · NAIROBI · LUSAKA

 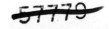

Heinemann Educational Books Ltd
48 Charles Street, London WIX 8AH
P.M.B. 5205 Ibadan · P.O. Box 45314 Nairobi
P.O. Box 3966 Lusaka
EDINBURGH MELBOURNE TORONTO AUCKLAND
SINGAPORE HONG KONG KUALA LUMPUR NEW DELHI

ISBN 0 435 89700 4 (Cased)
ISBN 0 435 89701 2 (Paper)

Printed in Great Britain by
Cox & Wyman Ltd, London, Fakenham and Reading
Set in Intertype Baskerville

To
African Peoples
The Nigerian Federal Government
The Midwest State Military Government
My Parents and Guardians: Nonyeluobi, Afadiazi, Ffozia, Mbekwute
My UCL Teachers: Professor Ford, Professor Barnicot, Professor Douglas, Dr. Kaberry, Professor Lewis
My Wife: Onyetugo

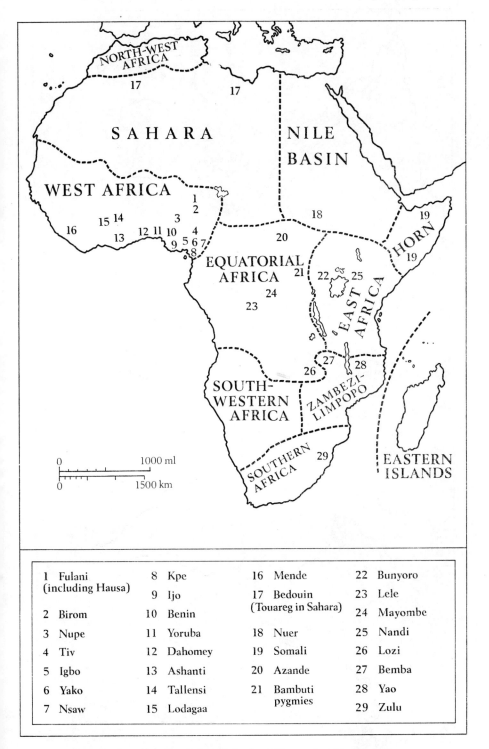

NORTH-WEST AFRICA

17

17

SAHARA

NILE BASIN

WEST AFRICA

1
2

15 14
16
13 12 11 10 4
9 5 6 7
8

3

18

20

19

HORN

19

EQUATORIAL AFRICA

21

22

25

24

23

EAST AFRICA

27
26

28

SOUTH-WESTERN AFRICA

ZAMBEZI-LIMPOPO

0   1000 ml

0   1500 km

SOUTHERN AFRICA

29

EASTERN ISLANDS

1	Fulani (including Hausa)	8	Kpe	16	Mende	22	Bunyoro
		9	Ijo	17	Bedouin (Touareg in Sahara)	23	Lele
2	Birom	10	Benin			24	Mayombe
3	Nupe	11	Yoruba	18	Nuer	25	Nandi
4	Tiv	12	Dahomey	19	Somali	26	Lozi
5	Igbo	13	Ashanti	20	Azande	27	Bemba
6	Yako	14	Tallensi	21	Bambuti pygmies	28	Yao
7	Nsaw	15	Lodagaa			29	Zulu

MAP I   *The approximate location of the societies in Africa mentioned in this book*

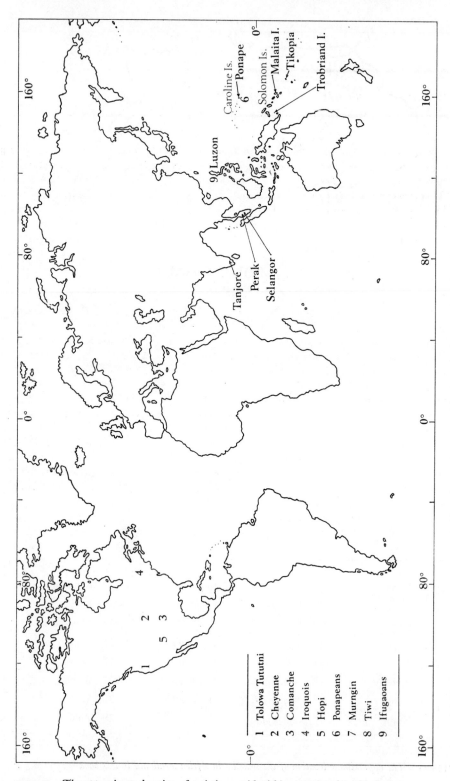

Caroline Is.
Ponape
Solomon Is.
Malaita I.
Tikopia
Trobriand I.
6
9 Luzon
8
7
Tanjore
Perak
Selangor
4
2
3
5
1

1 Tolowa Tututni
2 Cheyenne
3 Comanche
4 Iroquois
5 Hopi
6 Ponapeans
7 Murngin
8 Tiwi
9 Ifugaoans

160° 80° 0° 80° 160°
160° 80° 0° 80° 160°
0°
0°

MAP 2 *The approximate location of societies outside Africa mentioned in this book*

ACKNOWLEDGEMENTS

This book has profited in many ways from the brotherhood, companionship, and friendship of several persons endowed with the rare gifts of sympathy and generosity. Here I can only mention some: Agnes and Vincent Okonkwo, Austin Okonkwo, Caro Nwankwo, Feli Omezi, Philo and John Isichie, Obi and Adim. Elueze, Ben Akunne, Professor and Mrs T. Shaw, Dr V. Low, Peter and Pat Okonji, Paul and Terry Adiasor and, last but not the least, Austin Odita's family. I owe all of them my deepest gratitude.

I wish to explain why this book is dedicated to peoples, institutions and persons. First it is dedicated to African peoples because it is primarily about their cultures.

I dedicate it to the Federal Nigerian Government who awarded me a scholarship to study for a first degree in anthropology (1961–1965) and to the Midwest Military Government who also awarded me a scholarship for a post-graduate degree in anthropology.

It is dedicated to four persons who influenced my early life making it possible for me to appreciate the equality of human cultures at a time when colonialism and imperialism were deeply eroding and down-grading African cultures. The first was my late father Nonyeluobi Onwuejeogwu whose keen interest in traditional music, dance and folklore enkindled my childhood imagination. Then my mother, the daughter of Efozia. She has a fantastic memory for recalling kinship relationships. She knows the kinship network of any important adult in Ibusa, a town of up to 50,000 persons. Next was my mother's brother, Dibia Efozia who spearheaded the formation of many cultural associations in Jos between 1930–1950. I lived with him towards the end of this period and was his letter-writer. At an early age he confronted me with the problem of translating Hausa or Igbo into English. Lastly, is my master and friend Pat Mbekwute of Isseke, Ihiala. He was a teacher at Jos and Agyavagu, Northern Nigeria. He took great delight in decorating his sitting room with beautiful works of art which he acquired from his Birom, Arago and Hausa friends. He would say: 'A person's personality is rooted in his culture.' All these people had profound influence on my young mind.

I dedicate it also to my teachers at University College, London for the part they played in making me a professional anthropologist. Although I do not agree with all their views on the role of an anthropologist in society I find some of their theoretical approaches exciting and stimulating.

This book is also specially dedicated to my wife whom I wish to mention last, for emphasis, because she continues to bear the burden of caring and loving during the long years of my work both in London and in Nigeria.

In writing a book of this nature there are other peripheral influences which are equally important. I must mention here that for over five years I benefited from the ideas of many of my colleagues in the Institute of African Studies, University of Ibadan. I am grateful to the Director, Professor R. G. Armstrong, whose concept of ethnography transcends the field notebook system. He always insists on tape recording and filming living cultures. Professor E. J. Alagoa and Dr B. Awe are great optimists concerning the historical potentialities of oral traditions. Mr S. O.

Babayemi and Val Olayemi are enthusiasts in historical reconstruction and the oral literature of Africa respectively. They have all contributed to opening my mind to a new panorama of African cultures. I am grateful for the shared experience of working with them and learning about African cultures.

Beyond the walls of African Studies three people have been very helpful. Professor Thurstan Shaw, the founder of the Archaeology Department at the University of Ibadan, who allowed me to use the Igbo-Ukwu photographs and all the facilities available in his department. Dr O. Otite and Dr I. Nzimiro were always saying kind words of encouragement that pushed me ahead. I am grateful to them all.

The making of a book is the handwork of many people working in co-operation or in isolation unknown to one another. I wish to thank all who contributed in one form or the other to the production of this book. I am especially grateful to E. O. Ohaegbu, of the Institute of African Studies who typed from the rough original handwritten scripts and Caroline Nwankwo, my field assistant, who cross-checked every page for errors and omissions.

The following read the manuscript in its very early state and I profited immensely from their criticisms: Dr O. Onoge, Sociology Department, University of Ibadan; E. Emenanjo, now of the Oxford University Press, Ibadan; W. Nwaegbe, English Department, University of Nigeria, Calabar Campus. I am, indeed, indebted to them and also to J. E. Ikem, of the University of Ibadan Library whose personal guidance in the use of the library facilities accelerated my work.

These acknowledgements cannot be regarded as complete without expressing my thanks to the staff of Heinemann in Nigeria, especially Aig Higo and Tunji Akande and those in London, especially James Currey and Elizabeth Ledermann. Their concept of a business relationship transcends the impersonal system of bureaucracy described by Max Weber. Lastly, I extend my appreciation to Mrs P. N. Butler for her editorial suggestions.

My humble desire is to bring to all African peoples, and those genuinely interested in them, African cultural experiences in the context of the equality of all human experiences. A book of this nature cannot claim to be free from blemishes, minor or major. I accept full responsibility wherever such blemishes occur.

M. Angulu Onwuejeogwu

CONTENTS

PART ONE: CULTURE AND SOCIETY

xi

PART TWO: KINSHIP AND MARRIAGE

PART FOUR: ECONOMIC ACTIVITIES

PART FIVE: RELIGION, COSMOLOGY & ETHICS

ILLUSTRATIONS

MAPS

FIGURES

TABLES

PROLOGUE

As the world moves into the last quarter of the twentieth century, it is emerging into a type of gigantic society – a global society. The making of this global society, imperfect as it is, has been possible because of several interacting factors: the development of international mass media and of fast means of communication and transportation, the rapid growth of international economic and political inter-dependence; the increase both in the number and quality of international associa-tions, organizations and institutions, and the expansion and universality of intellectualism, academicism and morality.

As this positive movement towards a global society pushes ahead, a strong negative politico–economic undercurrent splits the global society into four divisions: the first-world peoples made up of the USSR and USA; the second-world peoples consisting of most European countries, China and Japan and their satellites; the third-world peoples comprising the independent African countries, the Arab and Asian countries; and those of the fourth-world, the Australian aborigines, the blacks in Rhodesia and South Africa, and the Red Indian tribes of Canada and the USA.

The present political and economic struggle that exists amongst the countries that constitute the global society is both a conscious and an unconscious effort to transform these divisions into a gigantic class system. The mobility of countries within this global structure is determined by the techno–economic and techno–political level attained by member countries.

There is a conscious effort by those countries that have acquired advanced technological knowledge to hide the key secrets of technology from those countries that have not acquired it or are just acquiring it. Similarly, there is a conscious effort by those countries that are just acquiring the advanced technological know-ledge to search for the treasure island where the key secrets of technology are hidden.

The third-world peoples in Africa and Asia have been subjected for centuries to the material and intellectual attitudes to life of the first-world and the second-world peoples. They recite the philosophy and ideologies of these peoples as if they are infallible. Above all, they have learnt to use most of their technological products without knowing how to make them.

Pre-colonial African countries were small-scale producing units. Industrial colonialism transformed them into industrial consuming units. Hence the preoccu-pation of most members of the African élite is how to make enough money to buy a car, a radio, woollen suits, sewing machines, etc. They do not worry about how these things are made.

The major problem facing the peoples of the third world is probably not poverty, as the first-world and second-world peoples want them to believe. Their problem is the sociological problem of changing over – in the midst of the technological hide-and-seek which is internationally organized – from an industrially orientated consuming unit to an industrially orientated producing unit.

The third-world peoples have to realize that they have been subjected to only a part of the total cultures of the first-world and second-world peoples. Culture being what it is, it is impossible for them to acquire the total cultures of these peoples. If the third-world and fourth-world peoples have to depend for their entire development on the part cultures of others, they are doomed to stagnation. Their greatest period of cultural dynamism and development will come when they are able to generate a healthy dialogue between their total cultures which are at their own doorstep and the part cultures they have acquired from others.

But they cannot create a condition for such a healthy dialogue if they do not fully comprehend the nature and character of their total cultures, which I will henceforth refer to as 'traditional cultures'.

The third-world peoples have a contribution to make to world civilization, but it cannot come out of the part cultures they have acquired from the peoples of the first and second world. It will come partly from what they are able to build up from materials obtained mainly from their traditional cultures and partly from the part cultures of others.

Interest in traditional African cultures and societies transcends the wearing of African traditional costumes. It should be a positive effort to understand and appreciate Africa. Most African universities have a section devoted to the study of African cultures and societies. Perhaps it is prestigious to have one, since after all every respectable European university does.

One can argue that some of the African élite have yet to understand the fullness of African cultures and societies. What happens in Nigerian universities is a case in point. Some of these universities are communities where students as well as a large number of the teaching staff live on huge campuses. There are big and fairly self-contained communities of the African élite living side by side with some Europeans and Asians. For example in Ibadan University, the Institute of African Studies is situated almost in the centre of the campus. Functionally, this Institute is a link between the European-orientated intellectual life which the university is pursuing and the traditional African-orientated intellectual life, of which little is known, since its centres are in the villages where it is swiftly undergoing very rapid changes.

By 1971 the impact which the Institute of African Studies at the University of Ibadan had made on the total life of Ibadan University community was significant but minimal. One of the major reasons for this is probably the calibre of over 90 per cent of the Nigerian members of staff, who from their colonial training and mission education, like most élite elsewhere in Africa, have deep in them a negative attitude towards African cultures. To most of these people, a piece of African art is a piece of *juju* wood or a bronze object which Europeans only admire out of curiosity. To the more money-minded, such a piece is an object to be sold to European antique dealers. To them traditional African music is a cacophony of barbarous pagan noise and traditional African drama or dances are forms of incoherent or grotesque pagan displays. Although most of the Ibadan élite spend their summer holidays in Europe visiting squares, gardens, parks and even museums, in their home country they have no interest in taking their families to watch an African play staged say in the Institute of African Studies, or elsewhere in the campus, or in the town or nearby village. It is true that up to 1975 Ibadan had no museum, and it is still a bitter fact that apart from the few collections of African material cultures displayed in the front of the Institute of African Studies and in some of the halls, Ibadan University has none either. But this is not an excuse, for very few members of the staff have raised even a feeble cry about this affair, and these few are members of the Institute.

I will attempt to show that African studies and the appreciation of African cultures should be an integral aspect of our total education if ever Africans south of the Sahara are to contribute anything to world civilization. I am not very sure that Africa or any continent of the world will astound the world with any more critical technological inventions. The point is that it is unlikely that future technological inventions will be critical, since the needs of the present world have taken a different turn. These statements may be considered as serious errors of fact, but they are not so to persons who admire the technical know-how involved in landing a man on the moon, yet are unable to see how it is relevant to solving some of the basic human problems such as famine, flood, war and disease.

In textbooks may be found the fundamental principles which will help in the maintenance of technological products, but not in the making of these products. During the Nigerian civil war, the secessionist scientists produced rockets. One of the scientists said that they tried out the textbook instructions and the rockets did not move an inch. Then they abandoned the instructions and tried other ways; at last the rocket moved a few yards and then a few miles. Africans have to generate a great deal of imagination and initiative in order to understand the technological secrets of the twentieth century.

Indeed Africa's contribution to world civilization will probably take two major directions: evolving more effective and efficient methods of organizing and promoting industrial technology, which should eventually result in an increase of yield *per capita*; and working out a means of neutralizing the dominant position of the peoples of the first and second worlds, whose international attitude towards peaceful coexistence endangers world peace, because of their possession of atomic secrets.

The bulk of the peoples who make up the first and second world became decommunalized long before they became technically industrialized. Their methods of technological organization and their concepts of peace are fashioned on the basis either of a highly individualist society or an extreme communist society. Such societies seem only to be able to cope with the inventions of technology, and seem unable to organize effectively the technological problems connected with world peace. The persistent downward trend in industrial relationships in Europe and America, and the duplicity and dishonesty that mark Western and Eastern diplomacy, are indications that these systems have ceased to be positively effective.

It seems probable that only certain societies, in which there is a balance between 'communalism' and 'individualism', can provide the ingredients for building a society based on modern industrial technology and with a concern for the problems of world peace. Such societies can be found in Africa, and there are a few in Asia.

The African societies which can realize such objectives are those able to use the human material around them effectively, that is, by developing creative minds. It is clear to me that the present generation of the African élite who are educated and nurtured in colonial traditions do not have creative minds. They are full of the contradictions and challenges generated by the sudden contact of two cultural systems. For example, in one breath, Africans talk of the African personality, and in another breath they discard those things that make them African. They want their children to be proud of being African but are reluctant to teach their children their first language. They speak foreign languages to their children in their homes. They rationalize this contradiction by saying that they want to give their children a sound education. To them the ability to speak fluent English or French at an early age constitutes a sound education. Useful as any language is, it is only an aspect of knowledge used for communication. It never occurs to them that their children would learn faster about their environment in the language spoken by their people and that foreign languages should be a second language.

It is my belief, based on observation, that past generations of Africans had creative minds. For example, the makers and users of the Nri bronzes (called the Igbo-Ukwu bronzes), the Benin bronzes and the Bida bronzes, and the carvers of Congo masks, possessed such minds. Past generations of people who developed the African songs and chants in the indigenous languages also had great creative minds. The village farmers who compose poems, or talk on drums, or perform in masks, have more creative minds than some modern African professors in literature or music who spend their time reciting and chanting Chaucer or listening to Beethoven. The village medicine man who mixes herbs and roots for his patients and patiently observes his reactions and progress before trying out another mixture, has a better mind than the physician who is satisfied by prescribing formulae invented four thousand miles away by his European colleagues. The rural blacksmith who fashions out a hoe, a knife or a cutlass is more creative than the African engineer, trained in London or Moscow, who simply repeats hackneyed theories which have no relevance to the problems inherent in his society, and spends his time maintaining and repairing machines and engines made in London or the United States.

Between the present members of the élite and the past there is a big cultural and social hiatus. The traditions of the past from which they should have drawn inspiration were shattered by the slave trade and colonialism. Today they consider it necessary first to learn about only the part cultures of the traditions of Europe. But they cannot comprehend the depth of these foreign traditions, because they are difficult to comprehend from outside by mere imitation. One must be born or nurtured in a tradition to understand it profoundly. If Africans are determined to make an impact on world civilization they must first understand their own traditions and then combine them with the foreign imported traditions to produce a hybrid one with its own vigour. Africans must also by education try to develop creative minds, for only thus can there be achievements in scientific fields.

The general trend in African countries is to build colleges of science and technology without considering how to get the best results from them. Such colleges could be built all over Africa but if no clever people attend them, the efforts will be to no avail. Great scientists and industrialists do not emerge out of a vacuum. They are born with first-rate creative minds and turn their energies towards specific scientific fields.

African children cannot develop creative minds without using imagination, which cannot emerge out of emptiness, but must be built out of the raw cultural materials around. These raw materials are to be found in traditional languages, music, arts, drama, science, technology – in short, in the African traditional cultures and society that mould every part of their minds.

Most of the African élite of the present generation do not have creative minds, because their imagination was atrophied during the formative period of their lives by several factors beyond their control. They lost touch with the past; and they can only begin now to take the first steps towards re-establishing contact. They must begin to take a serious and genuine interest in African cultures and societies and teach and accustom their children to their own traditions as well as the traditions of other cultures, so that by the end of this century the new generation should start to have its first crop of excellent minds.

This is why African studies should be taken seriously. The centres of African studies should be at the forefront in this struggle. They should provide the facilities for a more scientific study of African cultures and traditions. All African universities and colleges of science and technology should include courses in African studies to encourage the students' development to be based on the traditions in which they are nurtured.

The quality and character of the future African personality depend on how well these studies are able to bridge the cultural hiatus by effectively influencing the present élite and, more especially, their children who will become the Africans of tomorrow.

It is the cognizance of these sociological facts that has led me to write this social anthropology book using mainly African source materials, and a few Asian and American sources that are similar to the African ones.

This book is written to satisfy mainly the needs of students in all faculties in African universities and higher colleges of education, science, arts, technology as well as military colleges, irrespective of whether they are reading social sciences or not.

It may be useful to lecturers and teachers whose essential task should be to impart a balanced education to the next generation of African students. It is believed that probably the most satisfactory way the coming generation of Africans can best serve Africa and the world as a whole is by first understanding the cultural content which constitutes the total superstructure of their personality.

Furthermore, it is also designed to give some specialized information to both civil and military administrators, civil servants and businessmen, who, although Africans, as a result of their involvement in Western cultures have failed sufficiently to appreciate the richness in creativity and the context of African cultures in terms of modernization and industrialization.

Social anthropology is part of a larger subject, the study of man. It is concerned with the study of man as a member of society with culture and social organization. The social anthropology of African peoples is a study of the society of these peoples. It embraces their forms of social organization, social structure and institutions, which are still living realities in the sense that they exist today in one form or the other and they influence the thinking and behaviour of the élite.

I wish to make some explanatory comments on the methodology adopted in organizing and presenting the subject matter of this book. The first is that I realize that many anthropology books on the peoples I have used as examples are not only copious and difficult to read and to understand but also difficult to find in libraries in Africa and Asia.

Because of this, I have selected and written on fifty-nine topics which I judge to be central to social anthropology. These topics are grouped into five parts. Part One deals with some general theories of culture and society; Part Two deals with kinship and marriage; Part Three deals with politics, law and order; Part Four deals with economic activities, and Part Five deals with religion, cosmology and ethics. Each Part has a short introduction before its constituent chapters. The topics in each chapter are grouped around a set of themes. To a large extent I have summarized the important facts on each topic discussed as recorded by the authors who studied the peoples used in the examples. I have closely followed their methods of presentation and language, and added some critical comments of my own.

Most of my examples are taken from Africa, but I have gone farther afield to include some from outside Africa in order to give the reader a broader and deeper perspective into certain problems common to both African and non-African cultures.

It is hoped that in the future these topics may be elaborated, modified and re-organized to meet the needs of other readers, taking into account any constructive criticisms and suggestions which may be made.

This is not an apology. Because of the type of arrangement and examples cited it was not possible for the sequence from chapter to chapter to be a continuous and coherent overview, since in reality human society is not continuous and coherent –

although some anthropologists have tried to show the opposite. Furthermore, I have tried to be sufficiently detailed to satisfy the needs of those who wish to know more about certain societies. Thus in some cases, where I describe a people twice or more when discussing various topics, I repeat certain important aspects of their organization because I envisage the possibility that readers will study one topic only.

The case studies cited are quite ordinary and commonplace to the professional anthropologist, but they may look strange to the readers I have in mind while writing this book. Hence I have avoided over-systematized analyses of social systems and institutions characteristic of advanced anthropological studies. Rather I have adopted the descriptive, comparative and analytic methods based on both functional and structural analysis.

In the Appendices will be found a brief section explaining the signs used for describing kinship models in anthropological works, followed by a glossary of anthropological terms to help the reader understand some of those used in describing culture and society and abruptly introduced during discussion or analysis. Concepts introduced in the main body of the book are also explained in the glossary.

At the end of the chapters there are lists of works consulted. Many of the topics discussed are followed by suggestions for further reading arranged in order of importance. I have added these lists for two main reasons: to stimulate further reading and critical understanding, and to acknowledge the work of the authors of the books and articles used and quoted.

I have included selected photographs of creative arts in metal, wood and clay of some of the traditional African peoples used as examples in this book. Five of these photographs belong to the Igbo-Ukwu art of the Nri culture in Eastern Nigeria.

I hope by this display to generate amongst Africans a spontaneous aesthetic interest in and appreciation of African art forms, dance, music and drama.

I write mostly in the ethnographic present because my aim is to illustrate the traditional patterns which form the bedrock of present-day ones. Many changes have taken place but the basic patterns still remain lively in the rural areas. Indeed, the problems of social change in Africa will need another book. Hence no such theme is included in this book except in the Epilogue.

Part One

CULTURE & SOCIETY

1 *Some westernized African women and men wear traditional African dresses during traditional ceremonials. This dress was worn by Igbo women who were successful in their marriages*

CHAPTER 1

Some Theories
of Culture and Society

I *An Introduction to*
some Theories of Culture and Society

The social anthropologist, formerly the student of small-scale societies, generally uses different techniques of study from the sociologist, formerly the student of large-scale societies. But it is possible for each to use the techniques of the other or to study what has been the traditional field of the other.

In the nineteenth century anthropologists built their theories from the incomplete reports of early travellers, colonial administrators and missionaries. About 1883 Franz Boas visited Baffinland and there he did what may be considered to be the first systematic anthropological fieldwork. In 1898 Professor A. C. Haddon studied the islanders living in the Torres Strait in Melanesia. He stayed there for about six months with his team studying their culture, physique and mental capabilities.

Thus fieldwork technique started in the nineteenth century. However, by the beginning of the twentieth century when Bronslaw Malinowski studied the Trobriand Islanders in Melanesia for over three years and Radcliffe-Brown studied the Andamanese Islanders, the technique of living inside a society and studying it extensively began.

It is now a traditionally accepted method that anthropologists should spend at least a year in the field studying the culture of a people. Each study helps to add to our knowledge of human society by contributing something to existing theories about culture and society.

Three theories about culture and society have been put forward by both scholars of anthropology and sociology. They are the evolutionary theory, the diffusionist theory and the sociological theory.

The evolutionary theory assumes that complex societies develop out of simple ones. Some evolutionists argue that the so-called primitive societies that still exist today are survivals from the past. Max Muller and MacLennan were among the earliest evolutionists.

By the end of the nineteenth century a number of scholars had begun to attack the evolutionists. They argued that evolution alone cannot account for all the differences between 'primitive' or small-scale societies. They became interested, as did F. F. Graebner for example, in the distribution of cultural traits and elements, which means they hoped to find out how cultural traits had diffused from a common origin or origins. These diffusionists were condemned mainly for atomizing culture into elements.

In the nineteenth century Emile Durkheim, a French sociologist, began to study society as a unit whose different parts are related. He is now regarded as the father of the sociological approach.

The anthropologist studying a community lives in the community; he participates and observes what is going on around. He asks questions, such as about the economy, the kinship, the political system and the religion of the community. He investigates how new ideas come about and how old ones are abandoned.

Small-scale societies are changing rapidly and anthropologists have started to use the techniques they developed in the study of small-scale societies to study segments of modern and more complex communities. Anthropologists are therefore not anachronistic in Africa; in fact they ought to know more about the development of African cultures and societies than other social scientists. But the trend is that social anthropologists and sociologists are joining together in some of the methods they are using and in the type of problems they are trying to solve.

Some African cultures and civilizations have vanished because there were no 'written records' to tell us about them, but archaeologists by careful excavation and study of ancient remains are able to reconstruct them with the aid of ethnographic data collected by anthropologists. Similarly historians are able to tell us about what happened in the past in Africa, by collecting and carefully using oral traditions and by cross-checking their data with archaeological, anthropological, linguistic and other data available.

The topics discussed in this section include some of the methods anthropologists have developed, by fieldwork and careful observation of what people say, think and do, by critical analysis of their observations and by open dialogue about the quality of the major conceptual tools they use in studying and analysing cultures and societies of all kinds.

II *The Concepts of Culture and Society*

Three main groups of anthropologists have come to be established during the development of 'culture' and 'society' as concepts in the study of social science. These consist of:

1. Anthropologists who define culture as all-embracing, including society. One of the chief proponents of this view was Malinowski.
2. Anthropologists who dichotomize between society and culture, for example, Radcliffe-Brown, Evans-Pritchard, Leach, most of the British and some American anthropologists.
3. Anthropologists who steer a middle course by accepting that society and culture are two aspects of social realities viewed from different dimensions: that of relationship and grouping, and that of action and behaviour. The chief advocates of this approach are Bateson and Nadel, and Lévi-Strauss, a French anthropologist.

Before discussing the validity of these views, it will be useful to turn first to Lévi-Strauss's statement that society appeared before culture, because it obliquely refers to the evolutionary development of culture and society and also because its implication has very significant bearing on the reason why different views are held by anthropologists.

Kroeber, an American, was one of the earliest anthropologists to say that societies do exist without culture and that culture marks human from other animal societies. He holds that in the main it is men's culture that directs the kind of life they can lead. The cultural determinism of Kroeber has been rightly challenged. Kroeber pointed out that culture and society are arbitrary concepts, and as actual phenomena are interwoven and difficult to disentangle. He postulated a truism in the study of man : no society, no culture; no culture, no society. By this he was emphasizing the uniqueness of human society as opposed to that of other animal species.

Leslie White in his evolutionary approach to culture holds that man is the only living species that has culture. Culture, he says, depends upon 'symboling' which he defines as the 'ability to originate and bestow meaning upon a thing and ability to grasp and appreciate such meaning'. Man, he says, is the only animal that can distinguish 'water' from 'holy water'. This is due to man's ability to symbol which is fully expressed in articulate speech. The transition from anthropoid society to human social organization was made possible by the emergence of the faculty of symboling.

Symboling made the development of culture possible; it also made human society unique and different from other types of animal societies. It is clear from this reasoning that human society is different from that of ants or anthropoid apes; it is a type of society based on the ability to use symbols.

How far is it valid to say that culture is closer to the material world than society? The bees and the ants have no culture but they have a network of social interaction. The same is true of a group of gibbons, gorillas or baboons.

Physical anthropologists have shown that a group of baboons, although largely sexual, sometimes defends a fruit tree, a 'territory', against another group, of gibbon. Their temporary interaction at such moments is purely materialist.

Students of insects have shown that bees or ants do interact; thus, the 'workers' in the anthill interact only when performing an 'economic' function, for example, when transporting and distributing food, or when repairing the anthill. These activities which give rise to a network of interaction are materialist in all respects.

If these examples are accepted, then we have before us examples of societies without culture and yet close to the material world. It is therefore invalid to postulate, as Lévi-Strauss did, that culture is closer to the material world than society, unless he meant that society is a more abstract notion than culture, which can consist of a mere enumeration of material things.

Of course it is clear that material things like tools, motor cars, etc., can never be made without people interacting in a special relationship, having similar beliefs and ideals.

One can argue that even though society originates before culture, it is as near to the material world as to culture. It is therefore narrow to define culture in terms of material things. Ideas and beliefs must be included, otherwise it is not true to say that animals have no culture since some make use of sticks and stones as tools, or fashion them into specific structures.

It is difficult to locate any living species that does not have some symbols. Similarly one cannot say that a society can exist without symbols.. Groups of gibbons, gorillas, ants or bees use symbols when they are interacting. Lévi-Strauss is incorrect when he says that culture depends more completely on symbols than society. Both culture and society depend on certain types of symbols. Thus one can distinguish those symbols that are important for interaction in any type of society, and those which are necessary for the development of the human type of culture. Society and culture, therefore, both depend completely on symbols, but the levels are different. Culture probably depends on 'symboling', to use White's word, while society depends on 'symbolic codes'.

It is clear that it is useful to treat culture and society conceptually as two aspects of human phenomena. They are abstractions, conceptual entities, and ought not to be treated as real things.

One need not declare, as Leach does: 'I am a social anthropologist, and I am concerned with the social structure of Kachin society . . . as far as I am concerned, the cultural situation is a given factor, it is a product and an accident of history.' In his book *The Political Systems of Highland Burma,* he says that the Kachin concepts of property and ownership are paramountly important for his general argument because they provide the categories in terms of which social relations are linked with economic facts. He says: 'The power relations in any society must be based upon the control of real goods and the primary sources of production.' In short, he is saying that certain types of social relations are based on cultural realities. The control of real goods and the primary sources of production is a cultural situation which is far from being a given factor or an accident of history. Every chapter of Leach's book about Kachin social structure is really a classic demonstration of how culture and society are interwoven.

It is therefore futile to pretend that culture and society are two polar conceptual tools. Hence when discussing them it seems valid to follow Bateson and Nadel's approaches.

A short examination of the concepts of culture and society may now be attempted. Tylor defined culture as: 'the complex whole which includes knowledge, belief, art, morals, law, custom and any other capabilities and habits acquired by man as a member of society'. Kroeber defined it as 'the mass of learned and transmitted motor reactions, habits, techniques, ideas and values and the behaviour they induce'.

By these definitions, and if one also accepts the view that the network of relationships unique among human beings are habits and behaviours that are acquired, society is part of culture.

Let us examine Leach's structuralist definition: 'culture emphasizes the component of accumulated resources, immaterial as well as material, which the people inherit, employ, transmute, and add to, and transmit.'

The British parliamentary system of democracy, a type of relationship, is a part of British immaterial resources, accumulated, transmuted and transmitted from generation to generation by the British people. Thus if Leach's definition is applied here, this relationship is a culture; of course it is. This example simply shows that pragmatically society and culture are indistinguishable, although conceptually they are distinct.

Since culture is a concept it can be considered from various operational aspects: firstly as having traits and complexes originating through innovation and spreading through diffusion, thus having a geographical distribution; secondly, as having patterns, structure and function; thirdly, as static or dynamic, as a continuum and as symbolic. It may be treated as a whole or as made up of systems and sub-systems. None of these has been found to be effective on its own for understanding cultural realities.

The concept of society has been chiefly developed by sociologists. Anthropologists have adopted it, and some, especially the British social anthropologists, have made it their central theme in analysing group behaviour.

Society may be defined as an aggregate network of social relationships of a group or groups.

As a concept society is far broader in scope than culture. A society may be made up of a handful of people and it may embrace a huge number of people. Modern civilization may be called the 'great society'.

In a small homogeneous group the concept of a society becomes more meaningful and demonstrable than in a more diversified population having different types of social systems.

6

Society has been conceptualized as static, dynamic, structural and functional. The validity of any type of approach is a matter of what one is looking for.

Society and culture may or may not be co-terminous, but both are in fact aspects of the same phenomenon. The essential relations between the concepts lead to the frequent use of a compound term 'socio-cultural' as applied to group behaviour.

It seems that the concept of culture as all-embracing is the most useful one. In this case human society is an aspect of culture. It is possible to abstract and study relationships just as it is possible to abstract and study the material things of a people without much stress on anything else. In my view, society as a concept, in the human situation, is one aspect of the immaterial cultures of man. Accepting this view does not make one cease to be a social anthropologist. It simply means that a social anthropologist is one who studies that aspect of the immaterial culture of man that deals with interactions. By so viewing it the danger of losing sight of other aspects of culture is minimized.

III *The Concepts of the 'Primitive' Society and the 'Advanced' Society*

At a very early date European observers and writers used words like 'savages', 'barbarous', 'primitive', 'pagans', 'heathen', to describe other cultures in the Americas, Africa, Asia and the islands in the Pacific Ocean. Then the word 'primitive' meant simple and the word heathen meant unpolished, not civilized, of low mentality. But as colonialism and imperialism gained ground the word 'primitive' took on a different meaning. The Germans saw the Bushmen as subhuman inferior beings. The Australian whites regarded the Australian aborigines as human beings with very low intelligence. The white South Africans see the black Zulu as inferior beings who should always be their servants. Some Englishmen regard Africans as monkeys, or dirty smelling pigs. Some North American whites regard the American blacks as second-rate citizens. It is obvious that in the history of racial tension it is always the white people, some of whom are colonialists, who regard peoples of other cultures as inferior, dirty pigs, monkeys, subhuman beings, savages, primitives, heathens. This may be regarded as one of the appalling failures of Western civilization.

In the 1960s when many African countries began to achieve political independence and colonial rulers began to give way to African rulers, the concept of the superiority of the white peoples began to alter in both form and content. Adjectives such as 'small-scale', 'non-technological', 'under-developed', began to occur in various literatures to describe these societies. In order not to annoy Africans, many Europeans now talk of 'developing countries'.

Social scientists must put aside sentiment and face the realities of social facts. When two extreme societies such as the Eskimo or Hottentots on the one hand and the British or Japanese on the other hand are studied, basic differences will be seen, of which the major ones may be set out as follows:

Eskimo or Hottentot	*British or Japanese*
1. No developed technique of writing.	1. Developed technique of writing.
2. Rudimentary technology.	2. Developed technology.
3. Low output.	3. High output.

7

Eskimo or Hottentot	*British or Japanese*
4. Low density of population.	4. High density of population.
5. Little specialization.	5. High scope of specialization.
6. Homogeneous production.	6. Diversified production.
7. Low ratio of capital to consumer goods.	7. High ratio of capital to consumer goods.
8. Distribution is chiefly non-market, and the monetary sector is undeveloped.	8. Distribution is chiefly by market and the monetary sector is developed.
9. Mainly multi-interest social organization, in which status-holding and wealth-holding are congruent. Status and roles are mainly ascribed.	9. Mainly single-interest social organization, in which wealth and status are held separately. Status and roles are mainly achieved. (Multi-interest occurs in Japan.)
10. Unspecialized political and legal institutions.	10. Specialized political and legal institutions.

Eskimo or Hottentot society is frequently referred to as primitive, small-scale, non-technological, or non-literate. Some large-scale societies may have a rudimentary technology with all its economic and social consequences. It is also possible for a literate society with a rudimentary technology to exist, and a small-scale society with an advanced technology. Since these variations occur, the terms small-scale and non-literate may not be inclusive. The two most inclusive terms are primitive and non-technological. As shown above, the word 'primitive' is loaded with meaning derived from unfortunate white–black race relations. The term 'non-technological' seems to put all the emphasis on technology, and so might be misleading.

Those who wish to sidetrack the issue avoid the use of the word 'primitive'; instead they use words like 'simpler', 'non-technological'. Those who do not mind stick to the word 'primitive', because it is a technical term which ought not to have additional connotations of inferiority. It is also a relative term, for one society may be 'primitive' in a technological way while another is not. For example, Britain's space technology is primitive compared to that of the USA. Similarly, the industrial technology of Nigeria is primitive compared to that of Britain. In 1910 Japan's industrial technology was primitive compared with Britain or Germany, but in 1970 Britain was primitive in certain technological fields compared with Japan.

Development in rituals, philosophy, arts, etc., is not included in the comparison above because they cannot be described in relative terms, but are subjective and immeasurable. Technological development, however, has a direct influence on economic, social and political behaviour and may be subjected to statistical analysis. It seems that the words 'primitive' and 'advanced' may be used to describe only certain aspects of a society. It may not be advisable to use them to describe a society as a whole. Thus if one refers to Igbo economy as 'primitive', one is thinking of the state of its technology and its economic consequences. The concept of 'primitive' implies a continuum of a certain aspect of societies at different levels of technological advancement. In such a continuum, a !Kung society is placed at one pole, a Nigerian society will be placed near the middle, while a British or Japanese society will be at the other pole, without any implication of respective evolutionary development.

IV *The Concepts of*
Culture Area and Culture Pattern

The concept of the culture area was invented by American anthropologists, of whom Wissler was the most important. He thought that the basic units of culture were culture traits, which cluster together to form culture complexes, which in their turn cluster together in an area giving rise to a culture area.

A culture area is therefore a geographical area occupied by peoples whose cultures exhibit a significant degree of similarity with each other as well as a significant degree of dissimilarity with the cultures of others. The concept of the culture area is like the concept of geographical regions, because it is based on the premise that cultures reflect geographical conditions. This does not mean that culture areas do coincide in every detail with geographical regions, for man has control over his environment and its effect is not exclusive.

A culture area is also a shorthand way of describing the way of life of thousands of peoples in a whole continent. In Africa there are over a thousand ethnic groups, each having its own culture, but these have been broadly divided into ten culture areas, namely: Hottentot, Bushman, East African cattle, Western cattle, the Congo, the Guinea Coast, the East Horn, East Sudan, West Sudan, Egyptian, Mediterranean. Each of these areas may still be subdivided into sub-culture areas. With this simple classification system it is possible to give the approximate geographical distribution of groups of African cultures belonging to the same type.

The continent of North America has been divided into fourteen culture areas, namely Arctic, Sub-Arctic, Northwest Coast, Plateau, Plains, Prairies, East, California, Great Basin, Baja California, Oasis, Northeast Mexico, Meso-America, Circum-Caribbean.

Culture areas are delineated by categorizing cultures according to standard classifications such as techniques, physical environment, religion, language, and saying that those that are similar and closely related belong to one culture area. In this respect a culture area is also a statistical concept since the important characteristics have been documented and plotted on a map.

The boundaries of such areas on maps would give a false impression by showing a sharp break between culture areas; in reality cultures bordering each other overlap. It is erroneous to assume that the centre of a culture area is also its core. The culture-core of a complex could be statistically determined, but it would be a dangerous exercise, particularly when the culture is considered as a totality, because of the continuous shifting character of people and cultures.

On the whole the concept of the culture area is a useful generalization and device for teaching. Thus when we talk of the Plain Indian culture area we think straightaway of the American Indians – the Blackfoot, Crow, Sioux, Cheyenne, Comanche, etc. – who rode horses, ate buffalo meat and lived in conical tipis.

Wissler's concept of the culture area has been criticized for atomizing culture into disjointed elements and traits. However, it may be a good museum technique for recording and displaying material culture. The concept is also linked with the idea of the universal culture pattern, which may be defined as a general outline that will fit all cultures. Wissler gives nine headings under which all the facts of culture may be listed: speech, material traits, art, knowledge, religion, society, property, government, war. The number of these headings could of course be increased.

9

Wissler's American colleagues felt that there were limitations in his universal culture pattern. Thus Kröeber introduced the term 'systematic pattern' to mean 'a system or complex of cultural material that has proved its utility as a system and therefore tends to cohere and persist as a unit'. He says that total-culture patterns deal with culture wholes, and style patterns are ways of achieving effectiveness by choosing one line or procedure and sticking to it.

Edward Sapir, whose major work is in the field of linguistics, regards behaviour as an unconscious patterning and culture as an abstracted configuration of idea and action patterns with different meanings for each individual. Sapir's work inspired a whole generation of anthropologists, for example, Ruth Benedict, who extends to all individuals within a culture qualities which psychologists attribute to individuals. Thus the Pueblos culture makes each of them extrovert, while the Zuni culture makes them introverts.

These configurations, according to Kroeber, are cultural items, whose interrelations are such that one is necessary for the continuation of the others. On the other hand Benedict sees them as single values into which culture moulds the individual.

Kluckhohn, in an attempt to refine and reduce the gamut of terms introduced by configurationists, suggests that traits are grouped into patterns which may be considered generalizations of behaviour, that is, overt regularities noted by observation, and that configurations are generalizations which define covert regularities. He also says that generalizations referring to total-culture characteristics represent the integration of the culture.

One fact becomes very obvious when the concept of pattern and configuration in America and the concept of function and structure in Europe are considered, and that is that they all refer to forms at different levels of analysis. Pattern refers to forms of culture, configuration to the psychological forms conditioned by culture, function and structure to forms of social relationships.

V The Parts played by Innovation and Diffusion in Culture Change

Raymond Firth in his essay, 'Comment on Dynamic Theory in Social Anthropology', writes that at least three types of conceptual approach seem to have been involved in the study of the dynamics of culture change:

1. The approach advocated by Fortes in which the forces of repetitive change operate in an unaltered social system, as illustrated in the dynamics of Tale clanship and lineage.
2. The approach advocated by Malinowski, which stresses that the operation of change results in both immediate or partial disintegration of the existing society, finally leading to the creation of a new form which is the blending of old and new elements. (His full theory will be sketched later on.)
3. Worsley's approach, which assumes that change is the result of forces of opposition and that changes of a revolutionary kind are inevitable – a typical Marxist approach.

Professor Firth ignores American anthropologists' approaches: the evolutionary one advocated by L. White and M. D. Sahlin, and the diffusionist one spearheaded by Dixon, Kroeber and Boas.

The second approach is popular among those who call themselves historicalists. Historicalists consider that the minimum unit of culture that may be isolated by observation in time and space is a trait. Interrelated traits group into a trait-complex. The historic nature of culture involves invention and diffusion which result in a distribution of cultural elements at any one time into cultures or well-defined culture areas.

American anthropologists were influenced by the type of material they handled, such as the distribution of the Sun dance among the Indians, the diffusion of the horse complex and the spread of tobacco smoking from the New World to Europe.

Dixon in his book *The Building of Cultures* says that the origins of culture are based on discovery and invention. Thus the diversity of human culture is to be explained mostly by invention and partly by diffusion.

Wissler defined diffusion as the transfer of elements from one culture to another and called the process natural, based on chance contacts, and organized, when purposively transferred. Kroeber classifies the type of diffusion into contact diffusion and idea diffusion and stresses the processs of cultural extinction.

Early anthropological writers laid much stress on invention. Later students of culture change introduced a wider term, 'innovation'. This term not only stresses the original inventor but also emphasizes the fact that there are innovators who experiment within cultural systems.

Some anthropologists recently suggested that initial acts of discovery or invention should be called primary innovation, and initial acts of adoption into another cultural system might be called secondary innovation. The refinement of terminology is not a defect but a symptom of a developing science.

However, this method of dealing with culture change was vehemently criticized by Malinowski who studied the changes which had taken place in Africa. This is the crux of the difference between the approach of Kroeber and Dixon and that of Malinowski.

Malinowski dismissed all diffusionist, historicalist, approaches based on culture element distributions. He branded them incapable of scientific control and said they were frivolous. How far was Malinowski justified in making such a criticism and how far should we listen to his 'grandfatherly' advice? To answer these questions we have to examine his approach to the study of social change more critically.

In his book *The Dynamics of Culture Change* edited by Phyllis Kaberry and published after his death, he revealed his theory of culture.

He based his theory on his early concept of need and the cultural whole. He postulated that the process of cultural change is based on the interaction of institutions. Thus European institutions and systems interact with those of the Africans. Both institutions impinge on each other, and the impact produces conflict, co-operation and compromise, and the result is the emergence of a new African culture.

He maintains that there are five basic factors which govern the scientific study of the processes in Africa (and elsewhere). These are :

1. The influence of the white man, his interests and intentions.
2. The processes of culture contact and change.
3. The surviving forms of tradition.
4. The reconstructed past.
5. The new factor of spontaneous African reaction.

Several anthropologists have criticized Malinowski's approach. Radcliffe-Brown pointed out that culture change is not due to the interaction of cultures but to the interaction of individuals and groups within an established social structure which is itself in the process of change.

It should be explained that Malinowski was Polish by birth and because he had experienced sudden cultural changes in Poland he was very sympathetic with the African situation. He wrote more as an anthropological prophet of Africa than as a theorist. The Polish and African cultural changes were strong stereotypes for him. He fell into the same trap as Kroeber and other American anthropologists about the spread of the horse complex among the American Indians.

Malinowski's concept of the transformation of culture based on organized systems is valid in some cases, for instance, Lord Lugard's indirect rule in Africa, which is a blending of new institutions with African traditional systems. But it does not explain cultural facts such as the introduction or acquisition of new technology in a society, the well-known spread of tobacco smoking from America to Europe, tea drinking from Asia to Europe, the adoption of foreign words into a language. Similarly Radcliffe-Brown's structural approach, based on the theory that situations are created in which individuals are forced to enter into new social relationships, does not explain these phenomena either, although it is useful in many other cases.

It seems, therefore, that the historicalist diffusionist approach has to be accepted in order to explain certain phenomena. When tobacco smoking is diffused it is simply as an element of culture, not as an institution as such, and its diffusion may not even effect structural changes. Even where the acquiring of a technique causes structural change, what we are dealing with are two different phenomena, the causes and the effects. We need two different methods to analyse the two.

When applying the diffusionist approach care should be taken not to treat cultural elements as transferable in units mechanically from one culture to another. Diffused elements are likely to undergo complicated changes of structure and function as they enter new cultural settings.

Furthermore, social changes can be viewed as changes in value systems. At this level it is difficult to account for such changes only in terms of structural changes or the clash of institutions. Here again the diffusionist theory of change may be of great use.

It seems that the methods discussed above are valid and useful in their different ways. The validity of each depends on what level and types of change in culture are being analysed. Therefore, contrary to Malinowski's advice, one may consider seriously some aspects of the historicalist approach to the diffusion of traits and complexes, for its utility depends on the type of material being dealt with.

BIBLIOGRAPHY

SECTION II
Works consulted

BATESON, G. *Naven: a survey of the problems suggested by a composite picture of the culture of a New Guinea tribe drawn from three points of view* (Cambridge: Cambridge University Press, 1936; New York: Macmillan, 1937)

DIXON, R. B. *The Building of Cultures* (New York: Charles Scribners, 1928)

EVANS-PRITCHARD, E. E. *Social Anthropology* (London: Cohen & West, 1951)

KROEBER, A. L. *Anthropology Today* (Cambridge: Cambridge University Press, 1953; Chicago: University of Chicago Press, 1953)
—— *Configurations of Culture Growth* (Berkeley and Los Angeles: University of California Press, 1944)
LEACH, E. R. *Political Systems of Highland Burma* (London: London School of Economics and Political Science, 1954)
LÉVI-STRAUSS, C. *Structural Anthropology*, translated by C. Jacobson and B. G. Schoepf (New York: Doubleday, 1967; London: Allen Lane, Penguin Press, 1968)
NADEL, S. F. *The Foundations of Social Anthropology* (London: Cohen & West, 1951)
RADCLIFFE-BROWN, A. R. *Structure and Function in Primitive Society* (London: Cohen & West, 1952)
WHITE, L. A. *The Evolution of Culture* (New York: McGraw-Hill, 1959)

SECTION III
Works consulted
ABEGGLEN, J. C. *The Japanese Factory*: Aspects of its Social Organization (India: Asia Publishing House, 1959)
AMIN, S. *Neo-Colonialism in West Africa* (Harmondsworth: Penguin, 1973)
BANTON, M. P. *The Coloured Quarter: Negro immigrants in an English city* (London: Cape, 1955)
BEARDSLEY, R. K., I. W. Hall and R. E. Ward *Village Japan* (Chicago: University of Chicago Press, 1969)
BETEILLE, A. (ed.) *Social Inequality* (Harmondsworth: Penguin, 1969), especially parts 8 and 9
DANIEL, W. W. *Racial Discrimination in England* (Harmondsworth: Penguin, 1968)
FORDE, D. *Habitat, Economy and Society* (London: Methuen, 1946)
FOSTER, G. *Traditional Cultures and the Impact of Technological Change* (New York: Harper, 1962)
HAYS, H. R. *From Ape to Angel* (London: Methuen, 1959)
KLINEBERG, O. *Race Differences* (New York: Harper, 1935)
LITTLE, K. L. *Negroes in Britain: a Study of Racial Relations in England* (London: Routledge & Kegan Paul, 1974)
MACRAE, D. G. *Ideology and Society* (London: Heinemann, 1961)
MORANT, G. M. *The Significance of Racial Differences* (Paris: UNESCO, 1952)
MYRDAL, G. *An American Dilemma: the Negro Problem and Modern Democracy* (New York: Harper, 1944)
PATTERSON, S. *Colour and Culture in South Africa* (London: Routledge & Kegan Paul, 1953)
TYLOR, E. B. *Primitive Culture* (London: Murray, 1891)
VERNON, P. E. 'Race and Intelligence' in P. Mason (ed.), *Man, Race and Darwin*, paper read at a joint conference of R.A.I. and I.R.R., 1960
MARSHALL, L. '!Kung Bushman Bands' *Africa* 1960 (30) No. 4

SECTION IV
Works consulted
BENEDIG, R. *Patterns of Culture* (New York: New American Library, Mentor Book, 1959) (original 1934)
DRIVER, H. E. *Indians of North America* (Chicago: University of Chicago Press, 1964)
KLUCKHOHN, C. and A. M. HENRY. 'Personality Formation: the Determinants', in *Personality in Nature, Society and Culture*, C. Kluckhohn and H. A. Murray (eds.) (New York: Kropf, 1948; London: Cape, 1949)
KROEBER, A. L. *Anthropology Today* (Cambridge: Cambridge University Press, 1953; Chicago: University of Chicago Press, 1953)
LÉVI-STRAUSS, C. *Structural Anthropology*, translated by C. Jacobson and B. G. Schoepf (New York: Doubleday, 1967; London: Allen Lane, Penguin Press, 1968)
MALINOWSKI, B. *A Scientific Theory of Culture and Other Essays* (Chapel Hill: University of North Carolina Pess, 1944; London: Oxford University Press, 1944)
MURDOCK, G. P. *Africa – Its Peoples and Their Culture History* (New York: McGraw Hill, 1959)

RADCLIFFE-BROWN, A. R. *Structure and Function in Primitive Society* (Cohen & West, 1952)

SAPIR, E. *Language* (New York: Harcourt Brace, 1921)

WISSLER, C. (F. Boas, ed.) *Man and Culture* (Boston: D. C. Heath, 1938; London: Harrap, 1923)

SECTION V
Works consulted

BOAS, F. 'Evolution or Diffusion?', *American Anthropologist* (1924), 26

DIXON, R. B. *The Building of Cultures* (New York: Charles Scribners, 1928)

FIRTH, R. W. 'Comment on "Dynamic Theory" in Social Anthropology', in *Essays on Social Organization and Values* (London: Athlone Press, 1964)

KROEBER, A. L. *Anthropology Today* (Cambridge: Cambridge University Press; Chicago: University of Chicago Press, 1953)

—— *Configurations of Culture Growth* (Berkeley and Los Angeles: University of California Press, 1944)

MALINOWSKI, B. (P. M. Kaberry, ed.) *The Dynamics of Culture Change, an Inquiry into Race Relations in Africa* (New Haven: Yale University Press, 1948; London: Oxford University Press, 1948)

RADCLIFFE-BROWN, A. R. *Structure and Function in Primitive Society* (London: Cohen & West, 1952)

SAHLIN, M. D. and SERVICE, E. R. (eds.) *Evolution and Culture* (Ann Arbor: University of Michigan Press, 1960)

WHITE, L. A. *The Evolution of Culture* (New York: McGraw-Hill, 1959)

Suggestions for further reading

BAILEY, F. G. *Politics and Social Change* (Bombay: Oxford University Press, 1963)

FIRTH, R. W. *Social Change in Tikopia* (London: Allen & Unwin, 1959)

MEAD, M. *New Lives for Old: Cultural transformation – Manus, 1928–1953* (London: Gollancz, 1956)

REDFIELD, R. *A Village That Chose Progress* (Chicago: University of Chicago Press, 1950)

CHAPTER 2

The Concepts of Social Structure, Function, Status, and Role, and Cultural Education

I *A Brief Survey of the Functional and Structural Approach in Anthropology*

The late nineteenth-century approach and the early twentieth-century approach to the study of social systems have been named evolutionism and diffusionism respectively. The advocates of evolutionism, best represented by Muller, MacLennan, Morgan and Tylor were interested in the origin and development of culture. The diffusionists decried the evolutionists' approach, holding the view that culture, of which social systems are only part and parcel, is the product of a historical process. Boas, Kroeber and Wissler, all Americans, are exponents of this school of thought.

Quite recently Leslie White and others have advocated the revival of the evolutionary approach. These neo-evolutionists, as some call them, argue that 'culture advances as the amount of energy harnessed per capita per year increases, or as the efficiency or economy of the means of controlling energy is increased, or both'. Leslie White thinks that the technological component of culture is the fundamental determinant of a general evolution.

Sahlin, another advocate of the evolutionist approach, views it as 'a movement in the direction of increasing utilization of the earth's resources'. He thinks that the evolutionary approach of the study of culture complements the structural approach.

At the beginning of this century two British scholars put forward what is generally called the functional and structural approach to the analysis of culture.

The first of these was Malinowski, who condemned the old historical and evolutionist attitudes. Malinowski's preoccupation was with the study of culture as a totality. He introduced a new principle, now called functionalism, which attempts to explain the parts institutions play within the interrelated whole of a culture. According to this, the institutions of a culture operate to satisfy the needs of the individuals and that of the society as a whole. Thus Malinowski's argument is that every aspect of culture has a function, the satisfaction of needs. He distinguishes three levels of needs, namely, primary, instrumental and integrative. By primary needs he means biological needs such as sex and feeding; by instrumental needs he means those institutions such as economic, legal and educational, which help to achieve the primary needs, and by integrative needs he means those that help the society to cohere, such as religion, magic and play. One of the weaknesses of this theory is that it subsumes every aspect of culture to the satisfaction of wants.

Malinowski was a superb fieldworker who emphasized the importance of empirical and participant observations. He developed his theory of reciprocity while studying the Trobriand Islanders, but he was so obsessed by it that he came to regard almost everything as law in his analysis of social sanctions.

Just at the time that Malinowski was developing his concept of function which neglected forms, Radcliffe-Brown was developing another approach, which stressed forms. It is now called the structural approach. As a matter of fact it was not a very new approach to sociological analysis, since it was a remodelling of Durkheim's ideas. While Malinowski dealt with culture, Radcliffe-Brown dealt with social relationships. He saw the ceremonials of the Andamanese as functionally contributing to the maintenance of social structure, that is, as a mechanism of social integration. To him function meant the 'contribution which a partial activity makes to the total activity of which it is a part'.

Radcliffe-Brown's concept of function is based on analogy with an organism. When he talks of social morphology he is referring to social structure; social physiology means how the social structure functions; social evolution means how social structure changes, and social condition refers to the 'health' of the society. Above all, Radcliffe-Brown, unlike Malinowski, believes in diachronic as well as synchronic studies of society. Diachronic study means studying society in time and space, though it is doubtful whether by this Radcliffe-Brown means the culture history of the society, while synchronic refers to how the society is at present.

The functional and structural approaches have been subjected to very strong criticisms, some useful, some useless. Some critics have argued that it is wrong to look at society as a living organism, because the structure of a living organism does not change, although society does. Other critics say that the concept of social structure has led to the 'fallacy of misplaced concreteness', that is an error arising from assuming that one's abstraction of a social situation reflects social reality in all details.

As shown earlier on, Malinowski's theme was culture, whereas Radcliffe-Brown's was society. Nadel, however, has pointed out that the concept of society may be viewed from two angles: that of action, such as kinship and economics, and that of groupings such as family, clan. He also says that there are some social and cultural facts which fall outside the social and cultural scheme: these he refers to as 'action-autonomous'.

Other social scientists such as Talcot-Parsons and Lévi-Strauss have made great contributions towards elaborating the concepts of function and structure. Talcot-Parsons, a sociologist, has argued that they are interrelated and that a change in structure will affect function. This approach gives a more dynamic flavour to the study of social structure.

Lévi-Strauss's structural approach is partly based on Sapir's and partly on Troubetzkoy's linguistic approach. Troubetzkoy says that structural linguistics are based on four operations: the study of the unconscious linguistic structure; the treatment of terms not as isolates but as set of relations; the study of the structure of a system, and the discovering of 'general laws'. Lévi-Strauss, following this approach, considers that social structure is distinct from empirical reality. 'Social relations consist of the raw materials out of which models making up the social structure are built,' he argues. It is a method applied to the study of social relations, that is, it is a model.

Between the time of Malinowski and the present day, the word 'function' has been used in various ways to mean:

1. The satisfaction of human needs.
2. The modification of human needs.

3. The elaboration of human needs.
4. The moulding and training of human beings.
5. The integration of groups of human beings.
6. The interdependence of culture elements.
7. The relationship between elements of culture.
8. The principles of operation of partial system.
9. The maintenance of the *status quo.*
10. The synchronic cause and effect within a culture.
11. The diachronic cause and effect of a culture.

Similarly, between the time of Radcliffe-Brown and the present day, anthropologists have used the word 'structure' to mean:

1. The morphology of society, its social structure.
2. The morphology of culture, its cultural structure.
3. The model of social relations.
4. The patterns of behaviour.
5. The patterns of culture.

When reading any anthropological literature it is important to understand what approach an author has adopted and why, how the author justifies his approach, and how the approach has led to more understanding of society and culture.

II *How Functional Significance Constitutes an Explanation of an Institution*

Anthropologists and sociologists have used the word 'function' in several ways, most of which fall under one of these three main groups of definitions:

1. Following Radcliffe-Brown, function is defined either as a relation of interdependence, such as a relationship, to maintain the *status quo,* or as a relationship between the elements of culture.
2. Following Malinowski, function is defined as the orientation towards given ends, such as the direct or indirect satisfaction of human needs, the socialization and moulding of human beings, the integration of a group.
3 Following Bateson, function is defined as the whole interplay of the synchronic cause and effect within a culture. Such relationships fall into five classes: structural, affective, ethological, ideological and sociological. This definition of function is interesting because it is a conglomeration of the cultural postulates of Malinowski, Radcliffe-Brown and Benedict.

What is meant by explanation in an anthropological sense? 'Explanation' means adding a meaning to something by relating it to another existing 'something' so that it ceases to be isolated. It can be said that explanation gives and adds meaning to existence. There are various methods of explanation which are logically valid as long as certain basic principles are kept in mind.

1. Description.
2. Reference to antecedent events.
3. Reference to a mediating factor.
4. Reference to an end or purpose.
5. Reference to a general law, class, or principle.

An attempt will be made here to illustrate how such explanations demonstrate functional significance and how functional significance constitutes an explanation of an institution.

Every description employs general terms which are only abstractions. In describing an institution the anthropologist is explaining the working and the functioning of its component parts in a generalized fashion. Thus when Huntingford described the age organization of the Nandi he was at the same time explaining the function of the age organization in Nandi society. Such an explanation is of a generalized type, for each item needs further analysis.

Explanation in terms of antecedent events constitutes a more historical approach. Thus the military institutions of the Comanche can best be understood by reference to their social organization before they acquired the horse. In order to explain the institution of the British cabinet system one has to know its historical development from the time of Walpole. Certain institutions are as they are because of historical reasons. In this case the role of the institution in history becomes a functional explanation of the institution.

Explaining an institution in terms of mediating factors means explaining it in terms of other factors. Thus Durkheim explained the occurrence of suicide by referring to other social factors. This is a kind of relation of interdependence and is thus a functional approach similar to Radcliffe-Brown's.

The meaning of explaining an institution in terms of its purpose and end is self-evident. Malinowski explained institutions in terms of needs. So also Forde explained Yako ceremonials in terms of integration and cohesion, in which case his method was Radcliffe-Brown's. Such purposeful actions tend to be repetitive and standardized. Thus standardization and function go hand in hand. Standardized interrelated actions may be regarded as a cultural pattern.

When an institution is studied and grouped or classified with other previously known institutions in terms of a general law or principle it can be considered as explained. Thus, when Mauss classified the Potlatch and Kula as general cases of prestation, their sociological implication became more obvious. This type of explanation is an oblique way of referring to its function. The function of Kula can be regarded as based on reciprocity and status differentiation, and so rather political and social than economical.

The emotional aspects of institutions are more difficult to verify. Benedict's description of the Dobuan culture as introvert and that of the Pueblos as extrovert is really a functional explanation in terms of end and purpose, since the goal is achieved by the Dobuans and Pueblos being nurtured in their respective types of culture.

To show that an institution has a function helps to understand it, however this is demonstrated. Nevertheless, except for Radcliffe-Brown's extreme supporters who assume that institutions exist in order to fulfil the demonstrable effects, it does not tell us how or why the institution came about. This requires a knowledge of antecedent events and external factors, that is, an adaptive historical approach.

III *Status and Role in Social Relationships*

The concept of status and role has its basic foundation in social relationships, for wherever and whenever animate beings, of any order, interact reciprocally the notion of rights and duties comes into operation. This is significantly so of human relationships. Thus if A and B interact socially A's duty to B defines B's rights;

conversely, B's duty defines A's rights. The matter is not as simple and straight-forward as this, since complications will result when A has to act as A1, A2, A3, etc., in different social contexts.

Sir Henry Maine, an authority in comparative jurisprudence, postulated as early as 1871 the differences between 'primitive' and 'advanced' societies. He considered that kinship constituted the earliest bond of human societies and was characteristic of 'primitive' societies, whilst in 'civilized' societies the territorial bond was the criterion for membership.

Maine further argued that, 'the movement of progressive societies has hitherto been a movement from status to contract'. In 'primitive' peoples, on the other hand, the roles which the individual performs are based on status, that is, determined at birth. Thus one is born royal, commoner, or slave; one is either a senior or a junior among one's kin. In this respect individual abilities are not among the considerations. In 'advanced' societies, roles are mainly achieved by contract, that is by free agreement based on the capabilities of the individual.

Maine's ideas have been challenged by Lowie and Schapera, although some have been adopted and reformulated by Linton, Nadel, Goodenough and Banton. Not one of these writers entirely agrees with each other on the definition of the concepts of roles and status.

Linton was one of the first social scientists to systematize the concept of status and role. He defined status as: 'the polar position . . . in patterns of reciprocal behaviour'. The polar position consists of rights and duties. Thus status has a double connotation: a position in the social structure occupied by a person, and a collection of rights and duties which the position confers on the person. He went on to define role as 'the dynamic aspect of a status' and argued that status may be achieved or ascribed.

This was indeed a reformation of Maine's ideas. Linton's division of status mirrors Maine's division of societies into those defined by status and those defined by contract. The difference is that Maine refers to the classification of all societies while Linton refers to statuses in any one society.

The main error in Maine's argument is that he saw the principles of kinship and residence as separate criteria for the allocation of political roles, whilst he also saw status and contract as two exclusive principles in both time and space. This brings us back to Linton's ascribed and achieved status, which is sociologically limited because it is impossible to think of any one status that is wholly achieved and indeed very few that are entirely ascribed.

Banton, in his book *Roles: An Introduction to the Study of Social Relations*, rejects Linton's definition of the word status. He says that status should be left to mean 'the condition of belonging to a particular class of persons'. He defines role as: 'sets of rights and obligations'. Thus Banton's meaning of role is similar to Linton's second meaning of status.

However, this confusion creates an analytic vacuum. For example, why are positions in the social structure usually named in cultures? That is, why is a person called a teacher in one context, and a president in another? Linton gave status a double meaning precisely in order to distinguish these positions.

Goodenough did something towards filling this vacuum when he introduced the concept of 'social identity' to mean almost the same thing as Linton's second meaning of status. Goodenough defined social identity as: 'an aspect of self that makes a difference in how one's rights and duties distribute to specific others'. He defines status as 'combinations of right and duty' and role as the aggregate of one's composite statuses.

Goodenough's approach follows Linton, whereas Banton's was rather a departure from him. The terminology of Linton, Goodenough and Banton (not to speak of Nadel, Merton and Talcot-Parsons) consists of words and phrases such as 'social identity', 'status', 'role', 'ascribed', 'achieved'. Here are some examples from West Africa that may make this battle of conceptual remodelling clearer.

Among the Yoruba, Benin, Kalabari and some Igbo, a person who has been initiated into certain associations may during certain occasions 'carry the masque'. Let us examine the status and roles of such a person in his society. The person may be a father, a farmer, a warrior and also a local leader. In different social contexts, he is identified as occupying a specific social position which has specific rights and duties attached to it. Thus as a father, farmer, warrior, leader, or masquerader, he is occupying specific social positions which are linguistically differentiated. Such positions may be referred to by using Goodenough's terminology of 'social identity'. But while Goodenough talks of social identity for all types of identities, it may be useful also to talk of social identities, political identities, economic identities and ritual identities, thus specifying the nature of the identity. Where it is not possible to be specific, one may speak of an all-purpose identity.

Each identity has attached to it specific rights and duties which shall be called roles. Thus a person as a father, farmer, leader, warrior, or masquerader, is assuming different identities which enable him to perform different roles in different social contexts with a minimum of conflict. The degree of conflict of roles will be equivalent to the degree of the effectiveness of the identity assumed. Thus as a father and a farmer, the former a social identity and the latter an economic identity, the conflict of roles should be greater than that between a father and a masquerader, the former of which is a social identity and the latter a ritual one. This is because the uniform of the identity of the masquerader is visually extremely effective. This enables him to act the role of a spirit or an ancestor without making a significant conflict with his role as a father. However, the roles of both farmer and father overlap, and as well the visual signs or uniform used to separate these identities are ineffective.

It should be made clear that identities and roles are two different social phenomena, even though both are as two sides of a coin. One can assume an identity without performing the role associated with the identity while a role may be performed by another person who does not pretend to assume the identity. This is true among the Hausa. The king, the *Sarki,* may confer a political title on an individual whom he may restrain from discharging the roles associated with the identity. The *Sarki* will authorize another person, who does not at all identify himself as the holder of the title, to perform the role associated with the title. Thus a person will be the *Galadima,* which is a political identity, only in name while another person performs the role of the *Galadima* without identifying himself as the *Galadima.*

My definition of role, similar to that of Banton, is the collection of rights and duties associated with one specific identity. My concept of status, different from that of Banton and Goodenough, is the sum total of one's roles in one's society.

In some societies status is arranged in a hierarchial order, which may be divided into broad groups called classes or castes. The degree of flexibility with which members of a society may change their social identities and so their roles and status will determine whether or not the society is a class or a caste society. A caste system like that of India is where status mobility, that is moving from one set of roles to another, is very rigid. If status mobility is comparatively fluid, the society will be a class society similar to that of the Hausa. If it is very fluid and unpredictable, it would be an egalitarian society like that of some Igbo or Tiv.

IV *The Range of Institutions to be Considered in the Study of Education in Non-Literate Societies*

Since Margaret Mead directed the attention of anthropologists to the study of child care and training in non-literate societies, the question of traditional education in non-literate societies has been seen to be important. This is especially so when a Western system of education is introduced into these societies, and makes cultural education, a process which helps to bridge the gap between the past and present, an imperative necessity. The growth of psychological anthropology and the interest of psychoanalysts in the use of anthropological materials for cross-cultural analysis have given the study of socialization and education a new dimension.

If by institution we mean a standardized mode of co-activity 'regularly' performed by a group of persons in a society and orientated towards achieving an implicit or explicit purpose, then there are many institutions which must be taken into account in a study of education in non-literate societies.

The range of such institutions is not only various but also variable even within one society. In some societies education is a never-ending process which runs from the cradle to the grave. This is clearly illustrated among the Tiwi of Australia. In some, a short initiation ceremony is the only formal lesson; the others are given informally during the process of growing and living with members of the society. Myths, legends, folktales, genealogical charters are recited in songs. Music and arts, ritual and ceremonials, and play activities, are other ways in which the individual is socialized and educated. Club-houses, female houses and family associations are other specialized institutions.

The processes of child-training in different societies provide diverse sets of values. Even when the same unit in a different society undertakes the education of its members, emphasis is laid on different fields. Thus the Yurok fathers would stress thrift and sexual restraint, while the Comanche fathers would stress bravery.

The institution of the family unit is basic for the education of the younger ones in all societies, but more so in small-scale ones. In some societies the father is the centre of authority and affection; this clash of role places both child and father in a psychological conflict. Among the Tallensi the father has to avoid his eldest son; they do not eat together, and this conflict, expressed in avoidance, is related to a child's succession to his father's position. Among the Hausa the father and eldest son need not live together. This clash of interest is avoided in some matrilineally organized societies where the father has little or no authority over his children. The centre of authority then is the mother's brother.

The mother and other members of the family play their own parts in educating the children. The education of girls is usually left to the mother who teaches them how to cook and perform domestic work, for instance, among the Igbo of Nigeria. Among the Fulani the eldest brother teaches the younger ones how to herd cattle and obey their seniors. The family is an important organ in the education of its members.

Kinship is also important. In societies organized in patrilineages, like some of the Igbo, the term 'father' may be applied to all males of one's father's generation in the lineage. These males are persons who are authorized culturally to discipline all persons called 'children'. Similarly all females of one's mother's generation are authorized to discipline all persons called 'daughters'. Thus members of the extended family have their part to play in the training of the child.

21

Age-grades, associations and secret societies are common to many societies. These institutions socialize and educate the coming generation. Among the Nandi and Kipsigis the age-grades are organized into seven sets. There are elaborate ceremonies before one is initiated into the warriors' grade. Special 'lectures' and 'lessons' in tribal folklore and rules of conduct are given during the seclusion periods. The new members are drilled in hardship to demonstrate the type of warrior life they will be expected to live in future. Among the Mende, the junior grade of the *Poro* is a 'school' where non-initiates are educated in tribal activities and the responsibilities of adult life. The women have their own secret society called the *Saude* where they are trained in domestic activities, and which also controls the sexual codes of conduct of the Mende people. Among the Mumbuti pygmies of Ituri forest the women have their association called the *Alima* and the men have theirs called the *Lusumba*. The women's association has an elaborate initiation ceremony in which the girls are taught and educated in their tribal values of womanhood.

2   *A new generation of African children dancing traditional dance in front of a microphone*

In some societies polygamy and delayed marriage are means of domesticating junior and younger wives. Thus among the Tiwi, a man marries when he is about thirty-five or forty years old. His first wife must be a widow of over fifty, who is experienced in food gathering and home management. After this the man marries younger wives who may be between ten and twelve years old. The old wife becomes the director and teacher of the younger wives. She teaches them how to forage and collect fruits, insects, etc. She watches them and acts as a spy, thus controlling their moral conduct. Similarly among the Igbo all wives of a lineage are expected to help in the domestication of newly married wives.

In some state-organized societies children are recruited into various associations and are required to be present during ceremonials and rituals. Through these formal activities they gradually understudy and learn about the activities of their seniors. This happens among the Benin where all children are recruited into one of the palace associations and are promoted to the highest hierarchy of chiefs according to their ability.

In some societies informal activities such as moonlight play, entertainment and regular rituals are the ways children learn about the society. In Igbo society children are taught stories which convey the morals and values of their society. Songs and poems, riddles and rhymes, are memorized; in some of them, the names of animals, the varieties of yam, animals and genealogies, etc., are recited. Through such informal yet institutionalized procedures children learn about nature and society.

In some societies, like the Hausa, children are expected to follow the trade of their father or nearest relation. In this case the father or relation's duty is to begin from an early period to educate the child in his trade. Some societies have guilds that control specific trades. Children are recruited into these various guilds which act as 'schools' in the education of members. This is common among the Habe, Nupe and Awka-Igbo of Nigeria.

Among the Murngin, children are initiated at the age of seven into the mysteries of the totem. This is only the beginning of a lifetime's ritual education. When one is married one is initiated into other higher mysteries and after a while into another higher grade, and so on until one reaches the top. By this gradual process the elders of the clan control the 'academic' qualifications required; in this case the general behaviour of the individual in the camp, his secretiveness and his sense of responsibility are put to the test. The elders may refuse to initiate someone who is below standard.

The learning process is a cultural activity that enables society to pass down its store of accumulated knowledge from generation to generation. It can be both formal and informal.

V *The Main Cultural Factors Affecting the Present Status of Women in Some Non-Western Societies*

The main factors which determine or affect the status of women are various. They may be listed as: biological, cultural and ideological, political, economic and technological, ritual and marital.

It is quite obvious that even in western societies women are exempted from certain types of job for biological reasons. The same is true in some non-western societies. The basis of this exemption is that women at certain periods of their lives are unfit for the performance of certain work. Thus among some Western Igbo, women are not allowed to do certain types of farm work such as clearing the heavy forest and firing it. These biological facts are ritualized in some societies. The exemption of women from such hard work means they have no access to the most productive task of the economy, and this limitation to the wealth they can accumulate affects their political and social scope.

Mansa-Musa of the Songhai Empire visited the Arab world during his rule in the fifteenth century. On his return he introduced the purdah system of secluding 'married women'. The custom spread all over the Sudan and today is an important influence on the status of women in Hausa land. It must be pointed out that it is not a religious observation imposed by Islam, even though conservative Islam does regard it as a religious duty. The purdah system in West Africa is a result of innovation and is now institutionalized. The exclusion of women from social activities means exclusion from economic and political ambition.

In some societies women do not take part in politics at all; in others women may take part. In the nineteenth century in Dahomey women took an active part in politics. Every officer of the state had a woman counterpart who acted as a spy reporting to the king all the doings of the male officers. Women were recruited into the army and made up a strong fighting unit in the Dahomeyan military organization. Among the Ashanti, the office of the King's mother occurs at all levels of their organization and it is influential. Among the Iroquois, women dominated the councils and wielded great influence. Among the Lovedu a woman is always the ruler but the general status of women is not higher than that of men. Among the Mende the women had their own independent secret society which they could manipulate to gain some political influence. They in fact controlled the sexual code of conduct of the society and could impose fines on men who had infringed the rules.

In most small-scale societies women are so occupied with the home economy that they have little or no time to accumulate wealth outside the domestic domain. They are therefore very influential in the home, and less so outside. Among the Nsaw, women are the controllers of agriculture. The husband does the hard farm work and the wife does the planting and weeding. The farm produce is controlled by her, and the husband does the trading, especially externally. The woman thus has to obtain all she wants and sell everything through her husband. Women are 'farmers' because of religious beliefs about fertility: since women are fertile they alone should do the farm work. Women are therefore looked upon with high esteem.

Among the Tiwi, women are debarred from carving, which is the job of elderly men who carve the ritual spears which are the symbols of prestige. Nevertheless, women are influential and powerful in the domestic sphere because the household depends on them for their daily bread. They are expert foragers and collectors of food. A man without a wife has to depend on another household, which lowers his prestige. The interdependence of men and women is remarkable in Tiwi society.

Among the Yoruba, women have long been fairly independent of their husbands because they are engaged in trading. This accumulation of wealth by women, which enables them to increase their status in society at least in the domestic sphere, is also very obvious among the Nupe. The Nupe woman is economically independent and the Nupe husband depends on her financially. The Nupe men resent this state of affairs, and this is fully expressed in their belief in witchcraft, for only women are witches.

In some societies women have gained their status ritually. Fertility is associated with 'sacredness' and 'pollution'. When women are young and can still bear children they are regarded as 'sacred' and 'defiling'; that which is 'sacred' is 'defiling'. After their menopause they are regarded as 'men' and are accorded great social mystical respect. This is seen among the Zulu where certain women are great prophets, and among the Balinese where such women play a major role in spirit possession.

In most matrilineally organized societies women have greater freedom than in patrilineally organized ones. This 'freedom' is associated with the prevalence of divorce. In a matrilineally organized society certain rights, such as those over the children, are not transferred during marriage. The children belong to the same lineage as their mother. The locus of effective authority is usually not the 'father' but the 'mother's brother'. The father has little or limited authority over his children and wife. Divorce can easily be got. In such societies the status of women tends to be higher than in a patrilineally organized society, at least in the domestic domain.

In some patrilineally organized societies, however, such as the Okrika Ijo, women have a greater 'freedom' than among some Igbo, for example. The Okrika Ijo have two forms of marriage. One involves the transfer of small bride wealth and there is no transfer of rights *in genetricem*. Children of such marriages remain members of their mother's lineage. The wife has 'freedom' in that she can even take a lover or go back to her lineage without ceremony. The second form of marriage involves the transfer of big wealth and the transfer of rights *in genetricem*. The woman is less free in this second form.

Among the Hausa there are several forms of marriage: the form determines status. A woman who is married according to the '*Kulle*' or '*purdah*' is held in greater 'respect' than a woman who has entered into one of the other forms of marriage. Here freedom and 'status' are opposed. This is also true among some Igbo of Eastern Nigeria where the smaller the bride wealth the lesser the status of the woman, the bigger the greater. Also the number of children a woman bears and their sex enhances her 'status'.

The variations of factors are many, but these factors are not isolated but inter-related to make a complicated pattern of cause and effect in the social framework. The status of women in any society is basically relative. For example, what is considered as enhancing status in one society may be considered as lowering it in another one. Thus, cross-cultural comparison of the status of women seems a futile exercise.

BIBLIOGRAPHY

SECTION I
Works consulted

BOAS, F. 'Methods of Ethnology', *American Anthropologist* (1920), 22
—— 'Evolution or Diffusion?', *American Anthropologist* (1924), 26
—— *General Anthropology* (London: Harrap, 1939)
DURKHEIM, E. *The Elementary Forms of Religious Life*, translated by J. W. Swain (London: Allen & Unwin, 1961)
—— *Rules of Sociological Method* (8th ed.), translated by S. A. Solevay and J. H. Mueller (New York: Free Press, 1964)
FIRTH, R. W. 'Function' in W. L. Thomas Jr. (ed.), *Yearbook of Anthropology* (New York: Wenner-Green Foundation for Anthropological Research, 1955)
KROEBER, A. L. *Anthropology Today* (Cambridge: Cambridge University Press, 1953; Chicago: University of Chicago Press, 1953)
—— 'The Basic and Secondary Patterns of Social Structure', *Journal of Royal Anthropological Society* (1938) 68.
LÉVI-STRAUSS, C. *Structural Anthropology*, translated by C. Jacobson and B. G. Schoepf (New York: Doubleday, 1967; London: Allen Lane, Penguin Press, 1968)
MALINOWSKI, B. *A Scientific Theory of Culture and Other Essays* (Chapel Hill: University of North Carolina Press, 1944; London: Oxford University Press, 1944)
MORGAN, L. H. *Ancient Society* (New York: World Publishing Company, 1877)
NADEL, S. F. *The Foundations of Social Anthropology* (London: Cohen & West, 1951)
PARSONS, T. *The Structure of Social Action: a study in social theory with special reference to a group of recent European writers* (New York: McGraw-Hill, 1937)

RADCLIFFE-BROWN, A. R. *The Andaman Islanders* (Cambridge: Cambridge University Press, 1922)

—— *Structure and Function in Primitive Society* (London: Cohen & West, 1952)

SAHLIN, M. D. and SERVICE, E. R. (eds.) *Evolution and Culture* (Ann Arbor: University of Michigan Press, 1960)

SAPIR, E. (D. G. Mandelbaum, ed.) *Culture, Language and Personality* (Berkeley: University of California Press, 1962)

TYLOR, E. B. *Primitive Culture* (London: Murray, 1891)

WHITE, L. A. *The Evolution of Culture* (New York: McGraw-Hill, 1959)

WISSLER, C. (F. Boas, ed.) *Man and Culture* (Boston: D. C. Heath, 1938; London: Harrap, 1923)

SECTION II
Works consulted

BATESON, G. *Naven* . . . (Cambridge: Cambridge University Press, 1936; New York: Macmillan, 1937)

BEATTIE, J. H. M. *Other Cultures, Aims, Methods and Achievements in Social Anthropology* (London: Cohen & West, 1964)

BENEDICT, R. *Patterns of Culture* (London: Routledge & Kegan Paul, 1934)

FORDE, D. *Yako Studies* (London: Oxford University Press, 1964)

LLEWELLYN, K. N. and HOEBEL, E. A. 'The Political Organization and Law-Ways of the Comanche Indians', *Memoirs American Anthropological* (1940), 54

MALINOWSKI, B. *A Scientific Theory of Culture and Other Essays* (Chapel Hill: University of North Carolina Press, 1944; London: Oxford University Press, 1944

MAUSS, M. *The Gift*, translated by I. Cunnison (London: Cohen & West, 1954)

RADCLIFFE-BROWN, A. R. *Structure and Function in Primitive Society* (London: Cohen & West, 1952)

SECTION III
Works consulted

BANTON, M. P. *Roles: An Introduction to the Study of Social Relations* (London: Tavistock Publications, 1955)

GOODENOUGH, W. 'Rethinking "Status" and "Role"' in the *Relevance of Models for Social Anthropology*, A.S.A. Monographs, 1, M. P. Banton (ed.) (London: Tavistock Publications, 1965)

LINTON, R. M. *The Study of Man* (New York: Appleton, 1936)

LOWIE, R. H. *The Origin of the State* (New York: Russell & Russell, 1962)

MAINE, H. *Ancient Law* (London: John Murray, 1861)

NADEL, S. F. *The Theory of Social Structure* (London: Cohen & West, 1957)

SMITH, M. G. *The Government of Zazzau, 1800–1950* (London: Oxford University Press, 1960)

SECTION IV
Works consulted

ARDENER, E. W. 'Lineage and Locality among the Mba-Ise Ibo', *Africa* (1959), 29, 2

BRADBURY, R. E. *The Benin Kingdom and the Edo-Speaking Peoples of S.W. Nigeria*, Ethnographic Survey of Africa, West Africa, Part 13 (London: International African Institute, 1957)

FORTES, M. *The Dynamics of Clanship among the Tallensi* (London: Oxford University Press, 1945)

GREEN, M. M. *Ibo Village Affairs* (London: Sidgwick & Jackson, 1948)

HART, C. W. M. and PILLING, A. R. *The Tiwi of North Australia* (New York: Holt, Rinehart & Winston, 1960)

HUNTINGFORD, G. W. B. *The Nandi of Kenya, Tribal Control in a Pastoral Society* (London: Routledge & Kegan Paul, 1953)

LITTLE, K. L. *The Mende of Sierra Leone* (London: Routledge & Kegan Paul, 1951)

LLEWELLYN, K. N. and HOEBEL, E. A. 'The Political Organization of Law-Ways of the Comanche Indians', 1940 (See under Section II)

MEAD, M. *Coming of Age in Samoa* (New York: Morrow, 1928; London: Jonathan Cape, 1928)

NADEL, S. F. *A Black Byzantium* (London: Oxford University Press, 1942)

PERISTIANY, J. G. *The Social Institutions of the Kipsigis* (London: Routledge & Kegan Paul 1939)

SMITH, M. *Baba of Karo* (London: Faber, 1954)

SMITH, M. G. *The Economy of Hausa Communities of Zaria* (London: HMSO, 1955)

STENNING, D. J. *Savannah Nomads* (London: Oxford University Press, 1959)

TURNBILL, C. M. 'Initiation among the Bambuti Pygmies of the Central Ituri', in *Cultures and Societies of Africa*, Ottenberg, S. and P. (eds.) (New York: Random House, 1960)

WARNER, W. L. *A Black Civilization: a Study of an Australian Tribe* (New York: Harper, 1937)

SECTION V
Works consulted

BASCOM, W. 'The Esusu: a Credit Institution of the Yoruba', *J.R.A.I.* (1952), 82

BOHANNAN, L. 'Dahomean Marriage: a Revaluation', *Africa* (1949), 19

COKER, G. B. A. *Family Property Among the Yoruba* (London: Sweet & Maxwell, 1958)

FAGE, J. D. *A History of West Africa* (Cambridge: Cambridge University Press, 1969)

GLUCKMAN, M. 'The Kingdom of the Zulu', in *African Political Systems*, M. Forbes and E. E. Evans-Pritchard (eds.) (London: (Oxford University Press, 1940)

GREEN, M. M. *Ibo Village Affairs* London: Sidgwick & Jackson, 1947)

HART, C. W. M. and PILLING, A. R. *The Tiwi of North Australia* (New York: Holt Rinehart & Winston, 1960)

HERSKOVITS, M. J. *Dahomey: an Ancient West African Kingdom* (New York: J. J. Augustin, 1938)

KABERRY, P. *Women of the Grassfields* (London: HMSO, 1952)

KRIGE, E. J. and J. D. *The Realm of a Rain Queen* (London: Oxford University Press, 1943)

LINTON, R. M. *The Study of Man* (New York: Appleton, 1936)

LITTLE, K. L. 'The Changing Position of Women in the Sierra Leone Protectorate', *Africa* (1948), 18

—— *The Mende of Sierra Leone* (London: Routledge & Kegan Paul, 1951)

McCALL, D. 'Trade and Role of the Wife in a Modern West African Town in Southall.', (ed.); *Social Change in Modern Africa* (London: Oxford University Press, 1959)

MORGAN, L. H. *League of the Iroquois* (reprint of 1851 edition) (New York: Corinth Books, 1962)

NADEL, S. F. 'Witchcraft and Anti-Witchcraft in Nupe Society', *Africa* (1935), 8

—— *A Black Byzantium* (London: Oxford University Press, 1942)

NOON, J. A. 'The Law and Government of the Grand Iroquois', (New York: Viking Fund Publication in Anthropology (1949), 12)

ONWUEJEOGWU, M. A. 'The Cult of the *Bori* Spirits among the Hausa', *Man in Africa* (London Tavistock Publications, 1969)

OTTENBERG, P. 'The Changing Economic Position of Women among the Afikpo Ibo', in *Continuity and Change in African Cultures*, W. R. Bascom and M. J. Herskovits (eds.) (Chicago: University of Chicago Press, 1959)

RATTRAY, R. S. *Ashanti* (Oxford: Clarendon Press, 1923)

SMITH, M. *Baba of Karo* (London: Faber, 1954)

SMITH, M. G. *The Economy of Hausa Communities of Zaria* (London: HMSO, 1955)

WILLIAMSON, K. R. M. 'Changes in the Marriage System of the Okrika Ijo', *Africa* (1962), 32, 1

CHAPTER 3

Some Aspects of Inter-Disciplinary Cooperation in the Study of Culture

I Problems of Origin: the Fulani of Northern Nigeria

Early ethnographers and historians usually traced the origin of most African peoples and most of what they considered respectable West African culture complexes, such as that of kingship, to Egypt or Africa north of the Sahara. This approach is based on three factors. Firstly, most of the European cultural heritage has been derived from Mediterranean civilization. Secondly, Europeans used to be biased about the ability of Africans. Thirdly, most African oral traditions refer to Eastern origins.

Since this last factor still influences not only European but also African writers, it should be pointed out that oral traditions of origin do not always refer to accurate historical facts; this is true of some Igbo. Such claims are generally related obliquely to other historical events that occurred in the recent past. For example, the Onitsha and Aboh peoples of the Lower Niger basin claim Benin origin. A study of their genealogical charter and their social and political organization strongly suggests that they might have migrated from the Agbor area during the Agbor and Benin expansion. At Agbor an autonomous Igbo kingdom lying between Benin and the River Niger flourished before the Benin expansion eastward.

Attempts to resolve problems of origin should involve the cooperation of scholars of different disciplines. This will be illustrated below in a brief attempt to trace the origin of the Fulani of Northern Nigeria.

THE HISTORICAL SOURCE (BASED ON ORAL TRADITIONS)

There are many conflicting accounts about the origin of the Fulani and how they migrated into the Sudan. Sultan Bello argued that the Fulani had an Arabic origin and that they used to speak a language called Fulfulbe.

Sir Richmond Palmer suggested that the Fulani proper were the result of marriages between Arabs and Berbers and that they might have come from an area south of Marrakesh. L. Tauxier thought that the Fulani were a branch of a red Hamitic race which lived first in East Africa. They migrated in an anti-clockwise movement touching the foothills of southern Morocco, then Tukrur and the Senegal Basin to mix with the Serer and Wolof.

Roland Oliver and J. D. Fage argue that the Fulani were non-negroid who have intermarried with the Negroes, and so they should be regarded as negroid.

THE LINGUISTIC SOURCE

Roland Oliver and J. D. Fage hold that the Fulani language is close to that of the Tucolor of the Lower Senegal, a people whom the Fulani had closely been associated with until about the fourteenth century. Greenberg says that the Fulani language closely resembles that of the Serer, a language spoken in Senegal and more remotely connected with Wolof. Westermann grouped the Fulani language into the northern sub-group of the Western Atlantic section of the West Sudanic family. Both Greenberg and Westermann agree that the Fulani langauge is non-Hamitic, and Greenberg thinks it is non-Hamito-Semitic.

THE SOCIAL ANTHROPOLOGICAL SOURCE

Two well-known English studies of the pastoral Fulani are those of D. J. Stenning and C. E. Hopen. From them it is clear that the Fulani are sociologically of three types: the pastoral Fulani, the Fulanin-gida (town) and the semi-pastoral Fulani. As social anthropologists Stenning and Hopen do not deal with the problem of origin, but they do tell us about the pastoral Fulani by examining their various institutions, their population movements, and the mutual interdependence of the people and their cattle. Stenning holds that the Fulani became widely distributed in the Western Sudan through three types of population movement, transhumance, migratory drift and migration, which have been going on for over eight centuries. He argues very strongly that: 'There is no doubt, on both ethnological and sociological evidence, that the gross movement of Fulani has been west to east within the zebu cattle-keeping zone of the savanna belt of the Western Sudan. The natural conditions of this zone, in which there are few topographical barriers, has facilitated the cumulative progress of migratory drift and migration.'

THE PHYSICAL ANTHROPOLOGICAL SOURCE

An important English study of the blood groups of the cattle Fulani has been done by Blumberg, Ikin and Mourant. The blood groups show a high frequency of the N gene, O gene and cDe gene, suggesting a relationship with the Berber and Tuaregs. The cDe frequency is lower than in any other African population so far tested from south of the Sahara, other than the Tuaregs. However, the cap gene frequency is similar to that found in Africans and not at all near to the high frequency found among the Berbers and Tuaregs. In this respect they show affinity with the Mediterranean rather than a Berber admixture.

Garlick, Ikin and Robert's unpublished work shows a cDe chromosome frequency of 55 per cent, representing a more negroid trend than Blumberg, Ikin and Mourant, who recorded 45 per cent. They also found a higher cDe frequency of 10 per cent, suggesting connections with other Nigerian tribes and with the Belgian Congo. The MNS frequencies showed a high N; this supports the theory of Berber admixture.

It must be mentioned that any peculiar genetic traits shown by the Fulani are marked only among the cattle Fulani, whose mode of life, social isolation and inbreeding might have resulted in the occurrence of genetic drift or natural selection. The Fulanin-gida, the settled Fulani who have intermarried with the Negro, are indistinguishable from their Negro relations. The Fulanin-gida may be considered as a kind of genetic bridge linking the Negro gene-pool with the cattle Fulani gene-pool since they marry both the Negroes and the cattle Fulani, a process that might have started many centuries ago and is becoming increasingly common.

Until more systematic work is done on various Fulani groups and other West African peoples, analysis of their characteristics must be incomplete. However from the scanty data above two important facts emerge: the Fulani are not unique; they show Mediterranean, Berber and Negro traits.

29

57779

ARCHAEOLOGICAL EVIDENCE

Rock paintings in the Sahara desert show that the desert was occupied by pastoral nomads. Some cattle Fulani customs and cattle complexes are regarded similar to those of the inhabitants of Tassili, as depicted by the rock paintings. However, this evidence is weak.

REMARKS

There is no evidence to show that the Fulani migrated from Asia or elsewhere. It is sufficient to argue, as the information reveals, that the Fulani might have been one of the early tribes to settle in the west of the Western Sudan. It was there, probably, that they picked up the Berber and Mediterranean traits shown by the blood group tests, and it was there that they began to mix with their Negro neighbours. They moved southwards and eastwards slowly mixing with the agricultural Negroes through whose territory the Fulani grazed their cattle.

Some began to settle in urban areas and became Muslims, keeping their ties through marriage with their pastoral relations. These settled Fulani gradually developed into an élite group, the Fulanin-gida. They were allowed to lead their own lives and gradually began to take an interest in urban politics.

The Fulanin-gida became a dominant group in the eighteenth and nineteenth centuries when the Sudan was politically and economically unstable, and when direct Arab and northern African influence was insignificant.

This Fulani élite was able to mobilize followers, because it controlled, at least indirectly, the only stable wealth of the Sudan during the eighteenth and nineteenth centuries. This wealth was livestock, especially cattle. Furthermore, as a minority element less involved in Western Sudan state politics, they devoted themselves to Islamic learning which embraced political and theological studies. As the Sudanic states became more complex and bureaucratic, the kings began to employ Muslim officers, at first mostly Arabs and Moors, but later the Fulanin-gida. It is therefore not surprising that by the eighteenth century Fulani Mallams had assumed positions of influence in the various states of the Sudan (with the exception of Bornu).

As the Sudanic civilization gradually declined during the eighteenth and nineteenth centuries, the Fulani élite was able to appeal to the frustrated inhabitants whose lives were pestered with fear of slavery, wars, maladministration, and the general instability of the state system. Hence between 1725 to 1870 there were about eight major revolts in the Western Sudan.

The Fulani Jihads can be sociologically regarded as one great millenarian movement which swept the Sudan off balance. It had taken about two centuries to build up the political and sociological conditions necessary for this movement to be successful; thus, when it came, it took not only a millenarian but also a reformative character which ended in the time of European colonization.

This is not to ignore the religious motivation characteristic of the Jihads, the individual ability and leadership shown by the Fulanin-gida, and the discipline which Islam inculcated in the army of the Jihads. Similarly, the Jihads would not have been so successful if the Fulani leaders had not been able to strike at the right sociological moment.

The tracing of origin does not tell us much except where a people come from. Our interest in a people should transcend the knowledge of their origin; we want to know about their customs, heritage and way of life. The recent trend in modern scholarship is less concern with the tracing of origin as a central theme in research.

(For more detailed accounts of the Fulani, see Chapter 8, Section III, and Chapter 16, Section I.)

II *The Importance of Historical Knowledge for an Understanding of the Contemporary Significance of an Institution*

Much has been written in anthropology about the use of historical knowledge, and some anthropologists indeed call themselves historians of a special type.

By the early twentieth century the anthropologists who called themselves 'historicalists' were saying that the study of anthropology meant focusing attention on unique or specific objects and events in time and space. They considered that each culture was a result of historical growth. The study of traits, complexes, invention, diffusion and the distribution of culture was historical. For example, Wissler drew and defined the culture areas of North America by postulating cultural patterns which could be geographically defined. However, this approach does not explain the nature of institutions, it simply shows that a trait exists here or there. It does not help towards understanding the contemporary significance of the institutions which make up the cultural area. As a historical approach, it is valid in its own right, but it does not go far enough in explaining the nature of any institution.

Evolutionist anthropologists, such as Morgan, L. White and Sahlin, consider that culture evolves; thus present institutions are results of an evolutionary process determined by ecology, culture contact and diffusion.

Sahlin, for example, used the evolutionary theory to try to explain the segmentary lineage system of the Tiv. His theory is that it is a social means of intrusion and competition in an already occupied ecological niche. This sounds more like a functional ecological interpretation than an evolutionary principle.

L. White, more adventurous than Sahlin, showed how among some Australians the Kariera type of marriage evolved into the Arunta type. He argues that this change was due to changes in the modes of subsistence and offence and defence. This approach, demonstrating how and why one institution evolves into another, is useful as a historical exercise, but the hypothesis on which it is formulated cannot be tested or verified. One simply has to believe or not believe White. This weakness makes the theory of cultural evolution vulnerable to criticism.

Among British anthropologists, who are mostly functionalists and structuralists, there has been in the past a long argument about the status of history in the discipline. Malinowski, for example, held the extreme view that the past is irrelevant to a functional study of culture.

Radcliffe-Brown's emphasis on diachronic study seems to point to the usefulness of history, but his structural principle is too rigid to tolerate the change which is characteristic of history. He draws a distinction between history and anthropology by maintaining that anthropology is a science in which it is attempted to formulate laws. Sociology is a natural science in which the object is the formulation of social laws.

Evans-Pritchard decries Radcliffe-Brown's approach; his view is that social anthropology is an art and not a natural science, and that it has more in common with branches of historical scholarship than with natural science. It seeks patterns rather than laws. For him history alone provides a satisfactory situation in which to test the hypothesis of functional anthropology and give a fuller understanding of an institution. Evans-Pritchard drew much from history in his analysis of the social institution of the Azande. The history of the conquest of each kingdom revealed the nature and character of the Azande kingship and social stratification.

M. G. Smith, R. E. Bradbury and P. Hill have demonstrated how historical knowledge is essential for the understanding of institutions. Smith described the Fulani conquest of the Habe of Zaria in 1808, and how the Habe king fled and established himself at Abuja, where he set up a similar system of government as formerly at Zaria. The Fulani conquerors of Zaria established a new system of government based on the old Habe system. By comparing the two systems of government, Smith was able to illustrate how this institution of kingship developed in time and space. He described the Habe kingship as a limited monarchy, and the Fulani as an autocracy. He supported his theory by illustrating the structural and functional similarities and dissimilarities of the two governmental systems.

Bradbury studied the Benin and compared them with the Oyo. He showed how Benin and Oyo derived their kingship from Ife, and how both differ in their principles of succession, associational organization, pattern of settlement and lineage organization. His historical approach made these variations more meaningful.

West African states and their various institutions cannot be understood without a knowledge of their historical background; indeed, this is true of any society. Historical knowledge gives depth to the understanding of an institution but does not explain its every aspect. History may show how and why an institution was established but it may or may not be able to provide an explanation of why an institution takes a different function. Where it does, it throws more light on the function.

The anthropologist does most of his work in pre-literate societies. He cannot understand the present institutions of these societies without understanding their history. He can help the historian – and himself, for that matter – by studying cultural survivals, their 'origin', comparing different societies derived from a common origin and the degrees of complexity and similarity in two adjacent cultures. But he should remember that historical knowledge has its limitations. Since the system which he is trying to understand is a temporal unit, it includes continuity and change alike, and so requires a combined synchronic and diachronic analysis. It is therefore useless to argue against the usefulness of history for understanding the contemporary significance of an institution, if by history we mean the knowledge of some past occurrence which is related to any particular anthropological problem.

III *The Use of Ethnographic Data in Archaeological Interpretations*

There is abundant evidence to support the thesis that over half a million years ago the evolution of man had reached a stage in which he was able to fashion tools. By the Upper Pleistocene he had probably started to think in the abstract, as is evident from Aurignacian-Madgalenian cave art. Through the Mesolithic, Neolithic and Iron Ages to the present day we see man developing complex material and immaterial cultures. Only the later part of man's adventure in this universe is documented by written history, and documents contain both inaccurate and contradictory acounts. The task of the archaeologist is to interpret every aspect of man's past activities. In this respect an archaeologist is a type of cultural anthropologist.

The one great problem facing the archaeologist is not so much the ability to make interpretations as to validate them. An interpretation that is not validated with substantial evidence is subject to queries; at most such an interpretation is looked upon as mere speculation, and at the least as one of those fanciful dreams accredited to imaginative archaeologists. The archaeologist's main task is therefore to elevate his interpretations from mere fable or speculation to real history.

One of the basic assumptions in archaeology is that man is a social animal. In living together in groups he has basic needs to satisfy. The satisfaction of his basic needs is generally ecologically and culturally conditioned. His actions and activities are motivated and so usually directed towards certain goals. This assumption enables archaeologists to make certain convincing interpretations. Another archaeological assumption is that man always leaves marks of his motives on the things which he makes and uses. In this way archaeologists attempt to interpret man's past by piecing together his remains and reading meaning into them.

To do this archaeologists should have a basic knowledge of geology, botany, biology and zoology, and a working knowledge of anthropology and ethnography. They are generally well informed in primitive technology, and are prepared to increase their archaeological techniques by working with other scientists, such as physicists, chemists, geographers, historians, linguists, anthropologists and geologists. Their ability to coordinate the contributions of other sciences in interpreting man's past is probably the only sure way they can validate their interpretations.

The culture of man in all its entirety may be divided into four main categories: technological, sociological, ideological, attitudinal. Therefore archaeological interpretation should describe man's activities in these areas. Let us examine each of these categories and explore their inherent possibilities as well as their limitations.

Technological interpretation seems to be the simplest. The archaeologist can reconstruct the settlement pattern and economic life of the people who used the materials by applying his knowledge of primitive technology, ethnographic parallels, and the climate and ecology of the period. The limitation here is that only very few objects usually survive and their function may have been quite different from the archaeologist's 'guess'.

How an object was made is a pointer to organizational principles underlying activities. Bronze, for example, is an alloy of copper and tin. It implies smelting which in its turn implies the application of great heat. It also implies techniques of acquiring metals. Each of the above processes – mining, trading, smelting, division of labour, specialization – is a locus around which several types of activities concentrate. It is the task of the archaeologist to investigate these activities and show how they are related to one another and to the whole economic, social, ritual and political life of the people 'studied', or rather, reconstructed.

The archaeologist's sociological interpretations are inferences from the material remains of a settlement site and graves about the nature of the homestead, the settlement pattern, the distribution of wealth in the society, and possibly the political system of the people.

The quality and quantity of remains available usually limit the archaeologist's ability to interpret. Added to this difficulty are the known facts that human beings both have diverse ways of doing any one thing and can do different things in ways which leave similar material traces. These limitations reduce the archaeologist's ability to frame his interpretation in any specific way, so that he has to make generalizations.

The interpretation of man's attitudinal and ideological configuration is the most difficult of all. For example, it is now accepted that the Upper Paleolithic cave art of Western Europe makes sense if it is considered that it is motivated by ritual impulses. But one has to be careful in interpreting phenomena as ritual. They may simply mean man's expression of his fears, hopes and/or admiration of the universe in which he lived, without any implication of the existence of a deity or a force; or they may be, in his view, purely practical. Before interpreting any phenomenon as ritual, that is an expression of the existence of a power or force or deity, it should be seen to occur in a syndrome. Thus flexed burial alone does not suggest anything ritual even if it occurs in fifty graves. It simply implies a mode of burial common to a people. But when flexed burial, use of ochre, and a special type of grave goods are associated in one or more burials, all three together may be regarded as a syndrome suggesting a ritual ideology. However, the reason may still be difficult to pin down.

The archaeologist seeks to reconstruct past cultures and to describe as fully as possible a former culture from the remains found in ruins and refuse left by its inhabitants. Stratigraphy, typology, association and synchronism are his basic tools, as well as the help from scientific techniques. He usually phrases his interpretations in broad generalizations, even about graves, raided villages and burnt down houses, which seem to be more specific.

His task is to make the past live again. He needs imagination and common sense but he must not be extravagant in using them. He should realize that in dealing with man's social, political, economic and ideological systems he is dealing with very abstract and fluid concepts that cannot leave all their marks on the scanty materials available. Furthermore, he should not forget that the basis of his assumption in interpreting man's past is that he has not changed in his basic modes of life and thought; these are assumed to be developing in a multilineal progression through the ages, with some cases of deterioration. If this assumption is proved to be erroneous then archaeologists will have to rethink the whole problem of interpretation.

IV *The Use of Archaeological Data in Anthropological Interpretations and Reconstruction of the Distant Past*

Anthropologists, like archaeologists, are also faced with the problem of interpreting or explaining cultural and social facts. They do this in various ways, such as by description, reference to antecedent events, reference to a mediating factor, reference to an end or purpose, and reference to a general law, class, or principle. In order to interpret extant cultures and social systems with reference to the past, an anthropologist has to rely mostly on oral tradition scientifically cross-checked and processed; and/or on written documents describing the cultures or social systems of hundreds or thousands of years ago if they are available; and/or on information obtained from scientific archaeology.

Written documents do not occur in all cultures and they do not contain all the facts. Some of the facts have been recorded incorrectly, or have undergone changes as a result of continuous modifications and alterations by generations of writers, reporters and reviewers. Here again archaeology helps to find out more exactly about past recorded events and cultures. For example, the archaeological work in Jerusalem has thrown more light on the development of Judaism and Christianity as recorded in the Bible.

Indeed, archaeologists have successfully made scientific reconstructions of the cultures of the Near East from the Palaeolithic era, 9000 BC, through the Meso-lithic, Pre-Pottery Neolithic, Pottery Neolithic, Early Chalcolithic, Late Chalcolithic, to the Early Bronze age, 3000 BC, which is regarded as the beginning of the historical period in Egypt and Sumer. Similar work has been done for Europe and Asia. Gordon Childe's books, such as *The Dawn of European Civilization*, and S. Piggott's *Prehistoric India to 1000 BC* are typical examples of what archaeology can do to bring to light buried and unknown cultures and civilizations. *The History of Mankind, Cultural and Scientific Development* (Part 1, Volume 1) by Jacquetta Hawkes and Sir Leonard Woolley is an attempt to piece into a coherent whole the cultures and civilizations of the prehistory of man which, they say, started when 'Our species, homo sapiens, emerged into full humanity during the Pleistocene age.'

Such works have been made possible because archaeologists have unearthed acres of ancient habitations and have interpreted their finds into a meaningful system of cultural wholes which make sense when compared with extant cultures that are studied and recorded by both professional and amateur anthropologists.

In Africa south of the Sahara, however, there are no written records of any great antiquity. Here, archaeological data are not only useful for cross-checking some facts in the oral traditions of peoples, but they also constitute the only scientific method of ascertaining the near true nature and character of extinct and forgotten cultures.

It is ridiculous to think that anthropologists or archaeologists working in Africa are enemies of African society. On the contrary the archaeologist's task is to find out more about Africa's past cultures, from which their present ones have emerged, and the anthropologist's task is to study, record and analyse the present cultures and social systems. It is believed that a scientific articulation of the past and the present will probably help Africa to develop a distinctive African personality that will propel her into a new and vigorous future.

From my three years' fieldwork experience, I am convinced that archaeologists and anthropologists working in Africa have both social and moral responsibilities towards the people they have studied. The discharge of these social responsibilities can best be achieved through cooperation and sincerity of purpose based on extending the horizon of their work beyond the university walls by presenting to the people studied some aspects of the work done.

Chapter 4, on the Nri Study, is an example of the use of available archaeological data in an anthropological interpretation and reconstruction of the past.

BIBLIOGRAPHY

SECTION I
Works consulted and further reading

BLUMBERG, B., IKIN, E. W. and MOURANT, A. E. 'The Blood Groups of Pastoral Fulani', *American Journal of Physical Anthropology* (June 1961), N. S. 19, 2

GARLICK, J. P., IKIN, E. W. and ROBERT, D. F. unpublished work, quoted by Blumberg, Ikin and Mourant, 1961

GREENBERG, J. H. 'Studies in African Linguistic Classification' revised as 'The Languages of Africans', Part II, *International Journal of American Linguistics* (January 1963), 29, 1

HOPEN, C. E. *The Pastoral Fulbe Family in Gwandu* (London: 1958)

LHOTE, H. *The Search for the Tassili Frescoes* (London: Hutchinson; New York: Dutton, 1959)

OLIVER, R. A. and FAGE, J. D. *A Short History of Africa* (Harmondsworth: Penguin Books, 1962)

ONWUEJEOGWU, M. A. 'An Outline Account of the Dawn of Igbo Civilization in the Igbo Culture Area', *Journal of the Odinani Museum, Nri* (March 1972), 1, 1

PALMER, H. R. *Sudanese Memoirs* (Lagos: Government Printer, 1928) (3 vols.) 'Western Sudan History' in *Journal of African Society* (1916), 15, 59

ST CROIX, F. W. de *The Fulani of Northern Nigeria* (Lagos: 1944)

STENNING, D. J. *Savannah Nomads* (London: Oxford University Press, 1959)

TAUXIER, L. *Moeurs et histoire des Peuls* (Paris: Payot, 1937)

WESTERMANN, D. *The African Today*, translated by A. H. Brodrick (London: Hutchinson, 1934)

SECTION II

Works consulted and further reading

BOAS, F. 'Evolution or Diffusion?', *American Anthropology* (1924), 26

BRADBURY, R. E. 'The Kingdom of Benin,' in *West African Kingdoms in the Nineteenth Century*, D. Forde and P. M. Kaberry (eds.) (London: Oxford University Press, 1967)

EVANS-PRITCHARD, E. E. 'Anthropology and History', in *Essays in Social Anthropology* (London: Faber & Faber, 1962)

HILL, P. *The Migrant Cocoa-Farmer of Southern Ghana: a Study in Rural Capitalism* (Cambridge: Cambridge University Press, 1963)

KROEBER, A. L. *The Nature of Culture* (Chicago: University of Chicago Press, 1952)

LÉVI-STRAUSS, C. *Structural Anthropology*, translated by C. Jacobson and B. G. Schoepf (London: Allen Lane, Penguin Press, 1968)

RADCLIFFE-BROWN, A. R. *Structure and Function in Primitive Society* (London: Cohen & West, 1952)

SAHLIN, M. D. 'The Segmentary Lineage: An Organization of Predatory Expansion', *American Anthropology* (1961), 63

SCHAPERA, I. 'Should Anthropologists be Historians?', *Journal of the Royal Anthropological Society*, 1952

SMITH, M. G. *The Government of Zazzau 1800–1950* (London: Oxford University Press, 1960)

WHITE, L. A. *The Evolution of Culture* (New York: McGraw-Hill, 1959)

—— *The Science of Culture: a Study of Man and Civilization* (New York: Farrar, Straus & Giroux, 1969)

WISSLER, C. *Man and Culture* (New York: Thomas Y. Crowell, 1923)

SECTION III

Works consulted and further reading

BORDES, F. *The Old Stone Age*, translated by J. E. Anderson (London: Weidenfeld & Nicolson, 1968)

CHILDE, V. G. *The Dawn of European Civilisation* (London: Routledge & Kegan Paul, 1959)

CLARK, G. *World Prehistory: a New Outline* (Cambridge: Cambridge University Press, 1969)

CLARK, G. and PIGGOTT, S. *Prehistoric Societies* (London: Hutchinson, 1965)

COLE, S. *The Prehistory of East Africa* (London: Weidenfeld & Nicolson, 1964)

DAVIES, O. *West Africa Before the Europeans: Archaeology and Prehistory* (London: Methuen, 1967)

LEAKEY, L. S. B. *Adam's Ancestors* (London: Methuen, 1934)

——*Stone Age Africa* (London: Oxford University Press, 1936)

——*Olduvai George, 1951–61* (Cambridge Cambridge: University Press, 1965)

PYDDOKE, E. *Stratification for the Archaeologists* (London: Phoenix House, 1961)

—— *The Scientist and Archaeology* (London: Phoenix House, 1963)

PIGGOTT, S. *Prehistoric India to 1000 BC* (Harmondsworth: Penguin Books, 1950)

UCKO, P. J. and ROSENFELD, A. *Palaeolithic Cave Art* (London: Weidenfeld & Nicolson, 1967)

WASHBURN, S. L. (ed) *Social Life of Early Man* (New York: Wenner & Gren, 1961)

SECTION IV
Works consulted and further reading

CHILDE, V. G. *The Dawn of European Civilisation* (London: Routledge & Kegan Paul, 1959)

CLARK, G. *World Prehistory: a New Outline* (Cambridge: Cambridge University Press, 1969)

HAWKES, J. and WOOLLEY, L. *History of Mankind, Cultural and Scientific Development* (UNESCO) (London: Allen & Unwin, 1963), Vol. 1

PIGGOTT, S. *Prehistoric India to 1000 BC* (Harmondsworth: Penguin, 1950)

37

CHAPTER 4

The Nri Study

Prior to Professor Shaw's excavation at Igbo-Ukwu, very little was known about the nature and character of Nri hegemony in South-Eastern Nigeria. Nri activities were always described by observers and scholars of early this century as 'priestly', 'sacred', etc. The archaeological work of Igbo-Ukwu reveals that a highly organized system of both sacred kingship and chiefly functionaries had reached an advanced development in the forest zone of South-Eastern Nigeria in the East Central State about the ninth century AD.

I *Who Are the Nri People?*

The Nri are Igbo people, traditionally farmers, traders and ritualists. Nowadays many are private businessmen and government workers. Their population was about 10,000 in 1967. For a more detailed account of the Igbo, see Chapter 9, Section II, and Chapter 16, Section II.)

They live in three wards, formerly villages, called Agukwu, Diodo and Akamkpisi. The wards consist of segmentary patrilineages of various depth and span. Generally, between three and four levels of patrilineages occur: the maximal, major, minor and minimal. The minimal lineage is the smallest unit of political importance. Each level of lineage has a temple called *Obu* dedicated to its founding ancestor after whom the lineage is named. Thus, members of a minimal lineage whose founding ancestor was a man called Ochogu, supposed to have lived five generations ago from the present living elders, are called the children of Ochogu, Umu Ochogu, and this minimal lineage has a temple called the temple of Ochogu, *Obu Ochogu Ogboo*. The minimal lineages consist also of various lineages and extended families, each having its temple and named after its founder. These lineages below the minimal are only important in the domestic organization.

The various levels of lineages are also territorial units in the sense that they occupy a tract of land. They are also corporate units in that they own a common temple and land and have a common role to perform in the interest of the ward or Nri town as a whole.

These lineages are under the headship of both the elders and *ozo* titled men. The *ozo* title is an achieved status which gives the holder both ritual and political rights to assume the position of leadership in the lineages to which he belongs and in Nri town.

Nri town has a sacred king, who is regarded as a spirit, *mmuo*, called Eze Nri. Traditionally he rules Nri town through his two state councils called *Nzemabua* and *Ndi Nze*, and an association of women called *Illimmadunate*.

Nri town has been ruled by fourteen kings. The present king is the fifteenth. Kingship circulates among three maximal lineages and within two or three minimal lineages. An interregnum of a period of not less than seven years is allowed to intervene between two reigns.

In the past, Eze Nri had ritual and some political control over many Igbo settlements. The external affairs of Nri were administered by the state officials and other men who had taken the *ichi* title.

The Nri state system and the ritual hegemony were not based on the use of military force, for Nri never had a military or police organization. The Nri system of control was based on the propagation of the ritual ideology that Eze Nri had mystical powers and that Nri men and Nri towns were sacred. To achieve this control, Nri titled men spread out all over a large proportion of Igbo land, especially in the northern parts of Igbo land, and lived in these settlements as agents of Eze Nri. In some settlements they became the chiefs and priests. Nri became a centre of a ritual hegemony for many centuries until 1911, when the British took over the administration and banned the activities of Eze Nri.

Below is a reconstruction of the external political system of Nri between the tenth century AD and 1911.

II *The Sources of Reconstruction*

As mentioned above the external political system of Nri is now a thing of the past. Thus reconstruction is based on deductions obtained from the following sources.[1]

1. My personal observations of the present attitude of most Igbo peoples towards Nri people and Nri town.[2]
2. Information obtained from Nri elders.[3]
3. Information obtained from elders of Nri lineages in other Igbo towns.[4]
4. Information obtained from elders of other non-Nri settlements that were formerly under Eze Nri's influence. (See note 2.)
5. Intelligence reports written between 1910 and 1934 by some British administrators.[5]
6. Records of Nri people by early writers, such as Equiano (1789), John Adam (1825) and Baikie (1856).
7. Records of scholars, such as Major Leonard (1895–1906), Northcote Thomas, a government anthropologist (1910–14), Talbot (1921), Meek (1931), Jeffreys (1934).
8. Records of missionaries such as Rev. Father Duhaze (1906), Bishop Shanahan (1906–20), G. T. Basden (1910–20).
9. Facts based on the genealogical and ethnographical data collected by me about the distribution of Nri lineages and Nri culture in Igbo land.
10. Facts and evidence based on the distribution and interpretation of the material cultures of Igbo-Ukwu and Ezira archaeological finds and the ethnographic material in Odinani Museum, Nri.
11. Events recorded in the Bight of Benin and Biafra between 1500 and 1900.
12. Linguistic evidence.

It is likely that when the facts are pieced together, one cross-checking the other, and the Nri social structure and the belief system as an on-going process are seen in their full context, the picture that will emerge will tell a fairly reliable story.[6] Of course, reliability lessens as one moves from the most recent to the most distant past.

III The Major Problems of Reconstruction

There are several ways of reconstructing a past culture whose major systems are still on-going and which has abundant ethnographic and archaeological material. The method I have adopted is as follows:

1. Making an intensive and extensive study of the existing culture of the area.
2. Studying the systems in terms of the most recent past and noting the links holding the present and the most recent past.
3. Reconstructing the distant past with all past fragmentary evidence obtained and seeking for links between the distant past and the most recent past and the present.
4. Interpreting the most recent past in terms of the links with the present and interpreting the distant past in terms of its links with the most recent past.
5. Seeing the whole system as a continuous process from the past to the present, or as a discontinuous process, depending on the nature of the evidence available.
6. Leaving the interpretation open to further investigation and reinterpretation in the light of evidence yet unknown.

The problem to be considered seriously in reconstructing Nri external political system between the ninth century AD and 1911 is that of change, especially in the symbolic field, since the system is sustained by the ritual manipulation of symbols. By symbols I mean the use of concrete and/or abstract imagery to express concrete or abstract ideas and emotions; also the use of concrete or abstract imagery to express a wider and general ideal world of which the one we live in is an imperfect representation.

A field study of the major culture complexes and traits found in the Igbo-Ukwu finds was made by me between 1966 and 1967. I selected three elders between the ages of sixty and seventy from six Igbo towns to look at ten selected photographs of the Igbo-Ukwu objects, to identify them and give the use of the objects. The elders had never seen these pictures before and I did not give them any indication about the nature of the subjects of the pictures other than that they were traditional things.[7] The result obtained has been quantified as shown in Table 1, from which it is clear that the Nri and Oreri elders had the highest scores.

Amongst the present Nri people the *ichi* title is associated with parallel marks cut on the face with small curved iron blades and the ritual egg competition that follows. The *ozo* title is associated with several types of staff paraphernalia, with the tying of cords on the two ankles, and the elephant tusk and bronze bells. The Nri title is associated with a sacred kingship; the king wears a copper or bronze anklet on both feet and beads on his wristlets. He is believed to have mystical control over flies, bees, yam beetles and locusts, and his greatness is associated with animals such as the leopard and elephant. Each category of people in Nri keep certain special taboos; all keep a common taboo of not eating snails or some monkeys and not killing or harming pythons. The breaking of taboo is an abomination that is purified by using the ram or the head of a ram and eggs.

The Eze Nri were buried sitting on a stool. Decorated pottery and wooden bowls of various sizes and shapes are used for the rituals associated with the supernatural beings, *alusi*, and dead ancestors, *mmuo*. Horses are connected with the achievement of prestige and are traded from the north through Nsukka.

TABLE I

The identification of Igbo-Ukwu Finds by Elders

Subjects	Identification (per cent)	Use (per cent)	Remarks
Nri elders	90	80	Identified all the objects and associated them with the Nri title
Oreri elders	65	78	Identified most of the objects and associated them with the Nri title
Awka elders	80	25	Identified some and associated them with the *ozo* title
Igbo-Ukwu	51	30	Identified the bronze bell and animal heads, and *ichi* marked faces
Okwulobia	9	9	Identified the bronze bells only
Aguleri	25	–	Identified the bells and pottery and associated them with the *ozo* title

In the Igbo-Ukwu finds, we find the occurrence of bronze objects marked with *ichi*, various objects described as staff heads, human figures with anklets and *ichi* marks, elephant tusks, bronze objects which depict flies, beetles, grasshoppers' (possibly locust) eggs, heads of animals such as leopards, elephants, rams, monkeys, snails, pythons. There are also thousands of pottery sherds and some whole pieces, and a most important burial chamber in which the occupant was buried sitting in the midst of rich grave goods that included beads.

A comparative study of the culture traits that occur in Igbo-Ukwu with those that occur in the extant cultures of Nri shows that they can be classified under five broad headings: those associated with the Nri title; the *ozo* title; the *ichi* title; the rituals of *alusi* and *mmuo*; status and prestige.

The links between the Igbo-Ukwu objects and present day belief systems are illustrated in Table 2. How does one account for these links. Are they accidental? In answering these questions one must bear in mind that the extant culture is still flourishing near the very spot where the archaeological finds described above were buried.

The *ichi* marks on the face of living Nri men may be taken as an example to demonstrate the linkage. *Ichi* marks are crucial in the Nri title system because without taking that title one cannot take the *ozo* title, and without taking the *ozo* title one cannot take the Nri title. Furthermore *ichi* is a mark of royalty made on the face of human beings as well as on objects such as walls, wood and metal.

The objects, including three bronzes, excavated by Shaw at Igbo-Ukwu dated *c*. AD 850 have *ichi* marks on them. Those excavated by Hartle at Ezira and carbon-14 dated at AD 1495 have *ichi* marks on them. Equiano, who was born in Igbo land around 1745, associated *ichi* marks with persons exercising political office. John Adam (1823) associated *ichi* marks with persons of some high political status in Igbo land. Baikie (1856) associated *ichi* marks with persons of high respect in

TABLE 2

Links between Igbo-Ukwu and the present Nri culture

Culture trait on Igbo-Ukwu finds	Connections with extant cultures of Nri				
	Nri title	*Ozo* title	*Ichi* title	Other rituals	Prestige
1. Sitting burial	x	–	–	–	–
2. Coiled python	–	–	–	x	–
3. Coiled snake with egg in mouth	–	–	–	x	–
4. Snail shell	–	–	–	x	–
5. *Ichi* marks on faces	–	–	x	x	x
6. *Ichi* marks on things	x	x	x	x	x
7. Marks around navel	–	–	–	–	x
8. Rope anklets on legs	–	x	–	–	–
9. Bronze anklets	x	–	–	–	–
10. Wristlets	–	–	–	–	x
11. Grasshoppers (locusts)	x	–	–	–	–
12. Beetles (yam beetles)	x	–	–	–	–
13. Flies	x	–	–	–	–
14. Birds (some species)	x	–	–	–	–
15. Tortoise	–	–	–	x	–
16. Roped pot	x	x	–	x	x
17. Pottery types (others)	x	x	–	x	x
18. Bronze bowls	x	–	–	x	–
19. Fans	x	x	–	–	x

Igbo land. These archaeological finds show that morphologically the *ichi* marks have not undergone any major radical change. Probably also the idea they express might not have changed much, since they have remained constant since Equiano's time and he was not describing the end of a period.

This is not surprising because Nri oral traditions, and those of other Igbo towns east of the Niger, exhibit a conspicuous absence of events or episodes leading to radical changes. On the whole the Igbo culture area was comparatively less disturbed than the rest of the west coast of Africa until the later part of the eighteenth century. Even then the disturbances were not of the type in which a new influx of immigrants brings radical ideas to alter the existing ideas and social structure.[8] Nri is therefore probably a society whose culture had undergone minimal changes during the past thousand years. The structure, depth and span of Nri genealogies support this view which I have tried to establish by using combined archaeological, written and ethnographical evidence. Thus, just as the form and style of *ichi* marks remained relatively constant in time and space, so also probably has the symbolic expression conveyed by the *ichi* marks. (See author's thesis on Nri in works consulted.)

It is very important to note that the most disturbed period in West Africa has been from about 1750: first of all, the slave trade, followed by the growth of militant states, industrialization, colonialism, anti-colonialism and independence. During

Culture trait on Igbo-Ukwu finds	Connections with extant cultures of Nri				
	Nri title	*Ozo* title	*Ichi* title	Other rituals	Prestige
20. Elephant tusk	x	x	–	x	x
21. Iron blades	–	x	–	x	–
22. Bronze head of leopard	x	–	–	x	–
23. Bronze head of elephant	x	–	–	x	–
24. Bronze eggs	–	–	x	x	–
25. Bronze head of rams	–	–	–	x	–
26. Bronze head of horses	–	–	–	x	x
27. Staff heads	x	x	–	x	x
28. Coiled iron	–	–	–	x	x
29. Beads	x	x	–	x	x
30. Double-headed human figure	–	–	–	x	–
31. Bronze bells	x	x	–	x	–
32. Man on horseback	–	–	–	–	x
33. Burial Chamber	x	x	–	–	–
34. Raised platform	x	x	–	x	–
35. Fish	–	–	–	x	–
36. Monkeys	–	–	–	x	–

this period, however, the form and idea relationships expressed by *ichi* marks have remained relatively constant. This has been proven.

From the indirect evidence available it seems that no major changes took place before Equiano's time. The oral tradition and history of Nri shows, as I have already said, that Nri has been ruled by fifteen Eze Nri. Evidence based on Nri genealogy collected by me and transformed into a time chart shows that between about 1745 and the present day, Nri has been occupied by four Eze Nri, the twelfth to fifteenth in succession. The first eleven ruled before Equiano's time. According to cultural history, the heyday of the kingdom was between the third and the eleventh rulers. It is very likely that the form and idea relationships associated with *ichi* marks were developed during the heyday of the Nri kingdom. It is very likely that what Equiano described was an on-going process that was gradually on the decline not in form or expression but in its extent and degree of control based at Nri.

A parallel outside Nri may be cited to illustrate how major symbolisms central to a system do not change so radically. The Eucharist is central to the doctrine of Roman Catholics. It is the doctrine of the Real Presence of the Body and Blood of Christ under the appearance of bread and wine. The Eucharist is symbolized in form as a fish and some round loaves of bread, or as a round host suspended on the top of a chalice. This form and idea relationship in the Eucharist has remained constant from the Middle Ages to this day. Catholic records show that the form and idea relationships of their central doctrines have remained constant in spite of the great upheavals in the Catholic church whose history has been directly tied up with European politics. The barbarian invasions, the Renaissance, the Reformation, the age of exploration, the age of colonization, the age of industrialization span over 1500 years, yet the symbolic meaning of the Eucharist has remained relatively constant. This is not because of the existence of written records, for we know of many symbolic forms that have been recorded but have changed, but because the symbolism central to the existence of a system must remain constant to sustain the system.

The evidence before me for the Nri supports the view that the form and idea relationships of symbols central to Nri political and ritual systems, with special reference to the *ichi*, *ozo* and *Nri* titles, have remained sufficiently constant to warrant a valid reconstruction of the system at most back to the tenth century AD, supported by fragments of the past as contained in Nri oral tradition and in the dispersal of Nri lineages in Igbo land, and as revealed by archaeological finds and some early documents. The piecing together of all this evidence may be done in the light of the present and the most recent cultures of the Nri in particular and of the Igbo in general. New evidence may, of course, necessitate reworking the reconstruction.

IV *The Ritual Basis and Character of the Hegemony*

All evidence indicates that the establishment of Nri hegemony and its ascendance in Igbo land in the past was based on the effective manipulation of the religious ideologies, doctrines and symbolisms by Nri men. In Nri religious ideology bloodshed is the greatest abomination on earth. Spears, clubs, bows and arrows, cutlasses, hoes are transformed into ritual objects. Only the gun is not ritualized, maybe because it was introduced later. The taboo and the abominations associated with bloodshed were one of the major factors inhibiting the development of militarism.

The occurrence of Nri lineages in an area of over 4500 square miles in the northern sector of the Igbo culture area, indicates that a proliferation of Nri lineages from Nri to these areas did occur sometimes in the past. Since the genealogies of these lineages vary in depth, they appear to support the oral tradition of these lineages that says that they might have left Nri at different times. The political and ritual activities of Nri lineages in Igbo settlements were connected with the *ozo* title, the cleansing of abominations, promoting general fertility, especially yam growth, abrogating old and enforcing new rules of taboo and abominations, and restoring peace.

Nri men were therefore invited to these villages by the people through their leaders. Such an invitation and its acceptance were sealed by a ritual oath between the leaders of the settlement and any Nri man who represented Eze Nri. Settlements under this type of agreement were regarded as owing certain types of allegiance to Eze Nri. They identified themselves with Nri by observing some of the major rites of taboo and abominations prescribed by Nri. The Nri men consecrated their priests and gave the insignia of office, *ofo*, to their *ozo* men. The settlements, apart from paying the Nri officers, sent annual tributes to Eze Nri, and nearby ones also sent their leaders and representatives to Nri town once a year for a New Year ceremony, *Igu Aro*, in Eze Nri's palace. At the end of the ceremony the Eze Nri gave them the yam medicine and the blessing of fertility and longevity.

Nri men resident in the settlements were the eyes and ears of Eze Nri, who manipulated many aspects of the internal and external affairs of these settlements through them and through visiting Nri. They sent information backwards and

3   *The Eze Nri, Nrijimofo II, is flanked by members of Umu Diana lineage during a ceremonial in Nri, eastern Nigeria. Beside the iron gong is his regent, Prince Ruben Tabansi*

forwards to Eze Nri's palace by a secret 'language' which is still spoken among Nri elders.

Eze Nri had no army to enforce his will, for militarism was inhibited by the doctrine of the abomination of shedding of human blood. Nevertheless, Eze Nri could impose his will effectively by threatening to use or actually using what were considered as mystical forces. Eze Nri could curse or declare anathema on any settlement that flouted his authority. Nri men would at once spread horrifying and shocking news about the settlement all over Igbo land. In some extreme cases the Nri men in the village would withdraw to other neighbouring settlements. The settlement would be in a state of ritual blockade and siege. The markets would close down because neighbouring towns would boycott attending a market in a town that was under a ritual curse by Eze Nri. In due course of time the settlement would be forced to come to terms with Eze Nri, and negotiations would begin. Conditions for peace would be given and if they were fulfilled the ritual curse would be lifted and the news would spread.

Another important feature of Nri hegemony was the struggle between Igbo settlements for the economic control of markets and ritual control of cults. Every autonomous settlement in Igbo land had four market days. Groups of settlements in an area of about fifty square miles attended the markets of one another. One of Eze Nri's major powers was his ability to help build up a market or cause its dissolution. Several neighbouring towns competing for the control of markets in their area would submit their claims to Eze Nri. The success of a town depended on how the political game was played in Nri. When Eze Nri had decided, he announced his decision. Nri men would spread this news. It became law to attend the market of the town that won the appeal. The others were closed down or remained local markets.

Another important feature of the system was that Eze Nri could step in and stop two towns fighting and then finally settle the dispute. Northcote Thomas, the government anthropologist, first made this observation in 1910, but said that he saw no dispute referred to Eze Nri. Of course he did not stay long enough, but in any case it would have been difficult to observe because by 1910 the British had established native court areas in Awka Division and Nri town was grouped within the Agulu court area.[9] M. D. W. Jeffreys also noticed Eze Nri's powers in this area: 'It was pointed out that he might act as a peace-maker if fighting occurred between two towns. He could send for the elders of the two towns and endeavour to settle the dispute.'[10]

My investigation also showed that in the past Eze Nri settled disputes between towns. According to one of my informants, 'Nri people could not stop towns from fighting if they wanted to fight. We only made peace when war had begun. Eze Nri would send Nri men accompanied with Eze's dwarf to stop the fighting and to start peace negotiation. During my father's time Eze Nri stopped the fighting between Ichi and Ojoto, Oba and Ojoto, Umuoji and Oba, Abatete and Uke, Ojeto and Uke.' Some elders in these towns seemed to accept the fact that Eze Nri was the only person who had been able to stop fighting between towns in the past.

During my fieldwork in 1968 Eze Nri sent for the elders of Umuleri and Aguleri who had been quarrelling and fighting over a piece of land. The decision of the Privy Council did not stop the fighting, because both sides had killed one another. So all social activities between them had stopped before the announcement of the Privy Council decision, which was rejected by one of the parties. Eze Nri sent his agents and the dwarf to make peace and I accompanied them. First the abomination of killing was purified by the performance of the purification ritual by a Nri man, and thus the association between the two towns was reopened. The land dispute was heard and judgment was about to be given when the Nigerian civil war broke out.

This system of control of settlements did not involve control over the day-to-day running of the government of settlements. Each settlement managed its internal affairs according to its customs and traditions. Only matters related to taboo and abominations, the interpretation of customs and traditions, long-standing disputes within the towns or between towns were submitted to Eze Nri, who was regarded as the supreme head.

V *External Policies and the Economic Basis*

The external policy of Nri was based on a deliberate, well-planned and carefully executed method of moving into Igbo settlements, indoctrinating the political élite there in the ideologies of the mystical supremacy of Eze Nri and the mystical power of Nri men, and persuading them to enter into alliance with Eze Nri in order to obtain materially the benefits of his mystical protection. There would follow a long period of control and manipulation. The relationship between Nri and these settlements took various forms.

In some towns the leadership was vested in the *ozo* men. Eze Nri by controlling the *ozo* men through his agents had a measure of control over certain of the political, ritual and economic activities of these settlements. Towns very near Nri fell into this category, for example, Nimo, Enugu-Ukwu, Enugu-Agidi, Nnawfia, Awka, Adazi, Agulu, Oraukwu, Abacha, Abagana.[11]

Other towns had chiefs. Eze Nri had control over the conferring of the *ozo* title and the coronation of these chiefs. But the day-to-day government of the town was under the control of the chief and his councillors. Some of the new Aro settlements, such as Ufuma and Ajalli, fell into this category.

In some settlements resident Nri lineages dominated the politics. In this case the Eze Nri had a measure of control through the leaders of these lineages. Towns like Abatete and those towns in the Nsukka area such as Ehalumona came under this category.

Some towns set up a political system of the Nri type with or without an Eze and became completely autonomous after some time. Some, however, still accepted Eze Nri as the fount of authority, such as Ogboli-Ibusa, Ogboli-Issele-Ukwu, probably Agbor in its early stages, Owo, Uteh, Okpanam, Asaba, Illah, Aballa, Akuku.

Nri men regularly moved from one settlement to the other, as ritualists, diplomats and agents of Eze Nri, or as traders. They were paid for some of the ritual or political duties they performed. For example, Nri men were paid for every *ozo* man they installed outside Nri, and a part of the payment was sent to Eze Nri. These ritualist diplomats were also traders. They traded their stocks of ritual and social objects and iron. The Peace of Nri enabled inter-settlement trade to flourish.

Old iron cutlasses and hoes were used by the Nri people in performing the rites of cleansing abomination and purification of the settlements. The client had to provide these items and after the rites the Nri man took them away. Iron was essential for the making of agricultural tools and ritual spears for the *ozo* titles. In this respect Nri people controlled an important source of iron supply in the area under their control.

The traditional Igbo economy was mainly based on yam culture and palm produce. Yam required not only fertile land but also skill and patience to nurse the vines into producing a handsome yield. Communities that depended solely on yam not only for subsistence but also as a source of wealth had to rely partly on their accumulated skill and knowledge and partly on the mystical forces that supplemented those aspects of knowledge that were beyond their control. The doctrine which Nri men spread all over Igbo land with regard to the yam cult was convincing. The yam cult, called *ifejioku*, was controlled by Eze Nri, whose power was also substantiated by the existence of a powerful oracle called *Agbala Nze Nri* in Nri town. This oracle is said to be the oldest in Igbo land. Igbo men from various settlements consulted it and got results that puzzled them and, because of its accuracy, it reinforced the Nri claims of controlling mystical forces. Markets and the markets rituals were also firmly under Nri control.

The belief that Nri was a great ritual centre, the path through which the spirits of the dead went to spirit land, and that its king was mystically great and powerful, were central in the building of the Nri hegemony. (For Nri cults, especially the *Ikenga* cult, see Chapter 21, Section II.)

VI *The Character of the Nri External Control System*

I have shown that the administrative and entrepreneurial activities of Nri involved a high degree of control being established over the patterns of ritual, economic and ideological organization, and projected into other Igbo settlements. To achieve this a system of control, which mirrored the non-military character of Nri, was developed. The characteristics of this system were as follows. There was an elaborate hierarchically arranged title system achievable by any individual. Through this process the individual was gradually socialized in Nri rituals and administrative techniques. To control the system a hierarchy of a political official élite was developed: the Eze Nri, *Nzemabua*, *Ndi Nze* and *ichi* titled men. The chief external officials were the *ichi* titled men. The system was based on the proliferation of Nri lineages as a method of occupying Igbo settlements before indoctrination and domination. The settlements were indoctrinated in the ritual and political ideology that Eze Nri was sacred and had mystical powers which could be beneficial materially. Nri itinerant agents, ritualists and traders went to the old Igbo settlements and persuaded their political élites to enrol and remain loyal to Eze Nri. Loyalty was achieved by controlling the *ozo* title and obeying and keeping the taboo and abomination codes of conduct. A secret language was developed, used only by Nri men, so that information could pass between the political élite in the Nri palace and Nri men outside. A complex code of rules and regulations was set up to guide the conduct of Nri men officiating outside Nri.

Technically this process of building and sustaining a political hegemony was limited by a number of factors, such as the absence of an adequate supply of Nri manpower available to cover the settlements within the hegemony; the problems of an interregnum and the state of the internal politics of Nri; the spatial distribution of the settlements; the ecological limitations of communication which consisted of trekking through bush paths; and the inability to maintain the belief system that sustained the ties between Nri and the settlements. And also the inability to cope with new ideas, new opportunities and aggression by armed forces.

VII *The Nri and Oreri Relationship*

Nri tradition holds that the Oreri people left Diodo during a crisis in the reign of Nri Namoke. This seems to corroborate with a similar version current in Oreri.[12]

My study of the Oreri social structure and political system shows that they have three maximal lineages: Umu Nri Agu, Umu Nnakwa and Umu Nri Ezula. The founders of these three maximal lineages were regarded as the sons of Avo, who was himself regarded as the brother of the founder of Nri. Avo fled from Nri after a disagreement and founded Oreri which is only about ten miles south-west of Nri and is now bounded by Adazi Enu town on the north, Igbo-Ukwu on the south, Agulu-Uzo-Igbo on the east and Ichida on the west.

It seems likely that a second wave of Nri immigrants led by Nri Agu, who abandoned the Nri throne in the sixteenth century, also settled in Oreri, Oraukwu and across the Niger, to found some of the Nri lineages in the West Igbo area at Ogboli-Ibusa, Ogwashi-Ukwu and Ogboli-Issele-Ukwu.[13]

The political system developed in Oreri was similar in many respects to that in Nri. It was based on a sacred kingship called Nri that manipulated the *ozo* title and the religious symbols in order to achieve political cohesion and economic viability and dominance amongst people whose basic social structure consisted of segmentary patrilineages.

A comparative study of the political system of Oreri and Nri will not be attempted here, but it is important to note that in Oreri the *okpala* title is highly elaborated, while in Nri it is not a title but a social status defined by birth. The Nri kingship has a deep and long connection with Aguleri, while that of Oreri has not, and this may be attributed to the fact that it is a state that developed out of Nri.

Map 3 shows the extent of Nri and Oreri hegemony at their apogee. It is clear that the Nri sphere encompassed that of Oreri, but each avoided encroaching. By the middle of the nineteenth century the Oreri sphere of influence had almost ceased to exist and the relationship between Oreri and some towns within its sphere had degenerated to that of hostility and mistrust caused by the slave trade. However, those towns under Nri, especially those around Nri, still kept their ties with Nri, as was described by Major Leonard, until a little after the advent of the British.

Igbo-Ukwu and Oreri towns belong to the same cultural milieu, but all the evidence indicates that the objects, although archaeologically baptized Igbo-Ukwu, were probably associated with Oreri ancestors. The fact that the culture traits depicted on the objects are associated with the *ozo* complex and are found in most parts of Igbo land, suggests that we are dealing with a pan-Igbo culture. Indeed about 90 per cent of the sixty important Igbo towns that I visited claimed that Nri people from Agukwu conferred these titles on them; about 10 per cent claimed that Oreri had conferred the titles, and these towns were around Oreri. Not one town pointed to Igbo-Ukwu. This does not mean that Igbo-Ukwu people are completely ignorant of the use of these objects, but it means that they are not responsible for the pan-Igbo development of the culture depicted on the objects or by the objects.

VIII *The Decline and Collapse*

According to Nri political history the heyday of Nri hegemony was before the reign of Eze Nri, Alike and Nri Apia, who probably reigned jointly during the late seventeenth and early eighteenth centuries, using genealogical dating.

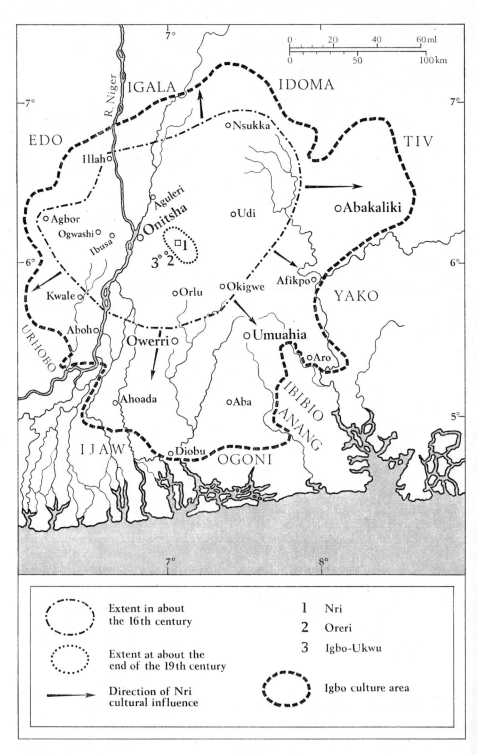

MAP 3   *The approximate extent of the Nri hegemony*

Its ebb was during the later part of the nineteenth century, as recorded by Major Leonard.

At the beginning the hegemony appears to have included a few settlements around Nri such as Enugu-Uku, Nneofia, Enugu-Agidi, Amanuke and Awka. At its zenith it included places such as Owa, Ogboli-Issele-Ukwu, Ogwashi-Ukwu, Ogboli-Ibusa, Igbouzo, Asaba, Abala, Illah, part of Urlu, Okigwe and Nsukka areas, Udi areas, and settlements around Nri such as Nimo, Adazi, Agulu, Nise, Oraukwu, Nneni, Nnewi and Ifite. Between 1896 and 1911, according to Major Leonard, it included settlements near and around Nri, such as Isuama, Agbaja, Enugu-Agidi, Enugu-Ukwu, Ezi-Owelle, Abacha, Achalla, Abagana, Nime, Ifite, Abatete, Nibo, Awka, Nise, Agulu, Adazi, Umuoji, Agidi, Obosi (Major Leonard: 1906) (Map 3).

The coming of Europeans to the coast of Biafra around the late sixteenth century resulted in the introduction of new crops like cassava in Igbo land. Hence cassava was never ritualized by the Nri. Cassava was an effective substitute for yam as a means of subsistence, but it was not an effective substitute for wealth. The gradual spread of cassava into the area under Nri hegemony in the seventeenth and eighteenth centuries gradually undermined the dependence of settlements on the power of Eze Nri over fertility and famine.

Just at the time that cassava was establishing itself as a stable food in Igbo land the transatlantic trade in palm produce and ivory, and later in human beings, began. This resulted in the liberation of the Igbo traditional economy from its ritualized anchorage at Nri. Many Igbo settlements joined in the trade and new settlements which never came under Nri were founded. One of these new settlements was Aro Chukwu. By the later eighteenth and nineteenth centuries the Aro were fully involved in the slave trade. They built a monopoly of the trade and established new settlements deep in the heart of Igbo land. They planted most of their settlements at the periphery of areas bordering on the Nri sphere of influence and began to operate in these areas. The Aro also used the paramilitary age-grade organization of the Abam, Ada and Ohaffia, and the cult of the Aro oracle to obtain their merchandise of human beings. Eze Nri Enweleani did all he could to discourage the raiding activities organized by Okolie Ijome of Ndikelionwu, and failed.

During the seventeenth and eighteenth centuries the Agbor and Benin influence began to be felt on the western flank of the Nri hegemony. The movement of peoples following the Adigwe-Ezechima crisis in Agbor and the Benin attack on Ubulu-Uku between 1750 and 1755 was eastward, and with them new ideas flowed rapidly into the area under Nri. New settlements like Onitsha and Oguta were founded around this period; they never came under Nri hegemony, but were subjected to the Nri cultural influence. Similarly during the eighteenth and nineteenth centuries the Igala began to push north-eastwards into the Nsukka area, the northern limit of Nri hegemony. Eha Alumona, Nsukka Asadu and other towns under Nri hegemony fell under the Igala militarized administration.

At the beginning of this century, between 1907 and 1910, the Roman Catholics and the church missionaries began to establish schools and churches in Igbo land with a vigour unheard of in Nigeria. Nri was one of the first targets, for it was considered by the Catholics as 'the citadel' of 'Satan'. By 1906 there were 130 children in the Catholic school in Nri, and 70 and 80 at Isingwu and Umuoji respectively. Thus Christianity and Western education helped to erode the system.[14]

By 1906 the British had taken over the administration of Igbo land, and in 1911 they banned the Nri system. Hence little was known of the system which I have here attempted to reconstruct. For a detailed account and analysis of the Nri political system, see my thesis in works consulted.)

NOTES

1 Evidence from one source is used to cross-check the evidence from other sources.
2 I lived in Nri town for about three years and visited up to sixty other Igbo towns in the Igbo culture area during this period to conduct surveys and make cross-checks of facts.
3 Persons like Anumba, Nwaokoye, Odenigbo, the Eze Nri, Nrijiofo II, Akunne, Anumba, Atnanya, Okeke Okonkwo, who participated in the tail-end of the system as adults or as adolescents.
4 Nri lineages in such towns like Ute, Owa, Isselukwu, Ibusa, Ogwashi-Ukwu, Asaba, Illah, Akuku, Aballa,Nnobi, Oraukwu, Adazi, Mba-ukwu, Umuleri, Enugu-ukwu, Enugu-Agidi, Nneofia, Ehalumona in Nsukka, and in Orlu.
5 See works consulted. Read *An Outline History of Nri, 10th century AD to 1972*, by M. A. Onwuejeogwu (see works consulted).
6 This exercise was carried out before the publication of *The Igbo-Ukwu* by T. Shaw (see works consulted). Since its publication some of the élites have started to interpret and reinterpret the symbolic meanings of the culture traits depicted on the objects. A feedback process seems to have begun in the towns.
7 See bibliography.
8 The movement of peoples from Agbor and Benin that resulted to the establishment of Onitsha, Oguta, Aboh, etc., did not alter the existing social order, although new ideas slipped in. The variants of *ichi* marks found on the bronze objects are still found on the faces of the people of Umana and Ebenebe, areas formerly under Eze influence.
9 Thomas, p. 52. See bibliography.
10 Jeffreys, Chapter X. See bibliography.
11 Some élite members of these towns, because of the present-day struggle for the political autonomy of towns and ignorance of the facts, may swear that their towns were never under Eze Nri. But some of the elders will readily not only support the view, but will give the full story, if they are interviewed privately.
12 There is a version that claimed autochthony for Oreri. It could be that certain Igbo people were there before the influx of Nri immigrants. There is no doubt that Nri immigrants moved into Oreri, since there is a chain of Nri lineages all the way from Nri through Adazi, Oraukwu, Nnobi and Oreri. All these lineages claim to have migrated from Nri.
13 This explains why Umu Nri Agu lineages occur in some of these towns.
14 Father Duhaze, 1906, in *Bishop Shanahan* by J. P. Jordan (see bibliography).

BIBLIOGRAPHY

Works consulted
ADAM, J. *Remarks on the Country Form . . . Inhabitants* (London: 1923), pp. 124–5
AFIGBO, A. E. *The Warrant Chiefs: Indirect rule in S.E. Nigeria 1891–1929* (London: Longman, 1972)
ANADI, I. C. K. *Our History and Cultural Heritage and the Oreri Genealogical Chart* (Onitsha: Tabansi Press 1967)
BAIKIE, W. D. *Narrative of an Exploring Voyage in 1854* (London: John Murray 1856)
BASDEN, G. T. *Among the Ibos of Nigeria* (London: Seeley, Service & Co 1921)
CROWDER, M. *West Africa under Colonial Rule* (London: Hutchinson, 1968)
EKECHI, F. K. *Missionary Enterprise and Rivalry in Igbo Land 1857–1940* (London: Frank Cass, 1971)
EQUIANO, O. *The Interesting Narrative of the Life of Olaudah Equiano etc.* (London: 1789)

HARTLE, D. 'Archaeology in Eastern Nigeria', *Nigerian Magazine* (June 1967), 93.

IDIGO, M. C. M. *The History of Aguleri* (Yaba, Nigeria, 1955)

IDUWE, A. E. *A Short History of Agbor*, unpublished, 1970

ILOZUE, E. O. *The Umuoji Cultural Heritage* (Onitsha: Tabansi Press, 1972)

JEFFREYS, M. D. W. *A Report on Nri*, unpublished Ph.D. thesis, 1934

JORDAN, J. P. *Bishop Shanadan of Southern Nigeria* (Dublin: Clonmore, 1949)

MEEK, C. K. *Intelligence report, 1930 Enugu, SP 6810/400.*

—— *An Ethnographical Report on the Peoples of the Nsukka Division – Onitsha Province*, 1931

ONWUEJEOGWU, M. A. *An Outline History of Nri, 10th century AD to 1972*, in Symposium Leo Frobenius, Deutsche UNESCO Commission, Cologne, West Germany, 1974

—— *The Political Organization of Nri, South-Eastern Nigeria*, unpublished M.Phil. thesis (London University, 1974)

—— 'A Short History of Odinani Museum, Nri', in *Journal of the Odinani Museum* (March 1972), 1

SHAW, T. *The Igbo-Ukwu* (London: Faber & Faber, 1970), vols. 1 & 2

TALBOT, P. A. *The Peoples of Southern Nigeria* (London: Oxford University Press, 1926), vols. 2, 3.

THOMAS, N. W. *Anthropological Report on the Ibo-Speaking Peoples of Nigeria* (London: Harrison & Sons, 1926), Part I 1913, Part II 1914

VAUX, H. *On the Asab Clana – Asaba Division*, in Nigerian Archives, Ibadan University, 1936

Part Two
KINSHIP & MARRIAGE

4 *Wooden figure (Zulu, South Africa)*

CHAPTER 5

Kinship Terminology and Social Groupings

I *An Introduction to Kinship*

When anthropologists discuss kinship they are more concerned with the social behaviour it generates than with the biological facts.

There are two important ways of looking at kinship. As a human being one has relationships with people one refers to as father, mother, sister or brother. The relationship between the person and his parents and siblings is the most elementary kinship system. One's father and mother are related to other members of a similar elementary family and as this extends, a complicated pattern of relationships emerges. This elementary model can be represented as in Figure 1.

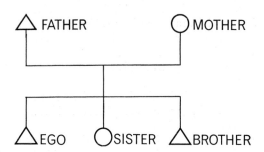

FATHER   MOTHER

EGO   SISTER   BROTHER

FIGURE 1   *Model of a simple family*

But this system of elementary kinship ties does not occur in all societies. In some societies, the role of the father is played down and he is regarded as mother's husband. As far as 'ego' is concerned his relationship with his father is a social fact based on the 'alliance' or 'marriage' between his mother and her male spouse.

Another way of looking at kinship is to regard oneself as a member of a set of siblings, that is, brothers and sisters. This situation arises from a man's socially accepted union (marriage or alliance) with a woman. But the man also belongs to a set of siblings and the woman belongs to another set of siblings. As a result of a socially accepted union, a third set of siblings is born which is related to the two other sets. These three sets may also be related to other sets in different ways, and thus another complicated pattern of relationships emerges. This model can be represented as in Figure 2.

The biological facts of kinship may (or may not exist) in all human societies, but these facts are socially and culturally defined. To put it bluntly, one may ask: how does a person know that he is the biological child of his father? The answer is that a man he calls his father and a woman he calls his mother agree to accept this fact and make him believe it, through a social process. But suppose (and such cases are very frequent), the person's mother was conceived by another man and she never told her husband, then the person's belief in his biological relationship with his father is incorrect, but the social fact still remains that the person is considered for social reasons child of his parents.

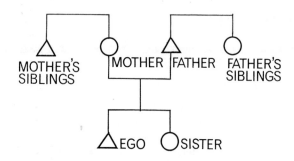

FIGURE 2   *Model of a simple family and father's and mother's siblings*

Kinship is, therefore, a socially accepted fact based on biological assumptions which may be real or unreal. It is because kinship is a social fact that it is referred to as a cultural product. Cultural situations differ from one place to the other; hence kinship systems differ. For example, Europeans have developed only two systems, bilateral and a limited type of patrilineal. Africans have four major systems: patrilineal, matrilineal, combined patrilineal and matrilineal called double unilineal, and bilateral. (See Appendix 2.)

The heterogeneous systems of kinship that are found in African countries such as in Nigeria, Ghana and Mali, generate complex situations in the social, economic, political and moral lives of the people.

The topics here are designed to help the reader understand the nature and character of some of the social problems arising from kinship relations that face those people who in the course of their careers serve and work for Africa in any part of Africa.

Kinship can be both a positive and a negative force in the dynamics of social, economic and political development, but it is not the system of kinship that is negative or positive, but the way the system is operated. Thus nepotism and tribalism which have their roots in kinship may be positive or negative factors towards development. When a president of the United States of America appointed his brother Attorney-General, it was not considered nepotism, because other factors dominated the appointment and it was exceptional. In this case kinship was a positive force that helped to accelerate the process of decision-taking in the appointment of state officials.

Similarly, if the Kipsigis or the Igbo use their age-grade system or town's union, respectively, to build a road or a maternity clinic the kinship force that drives them into such action is positive. If on the other hand the Rhodesian whites or the Hausa Fulani appoint only whites or Hausa Fulani respectively, to offices in the government in which the white Rhodesians or Hausa Fulani are dominant, the kinship force that drives them into such action may be considered negative. The Rhodesian appointments follow the line of skin colour and may be described as racism, while those of the Hausa Fulani follow the line of tribe and may be described as tribalism. Both are negative actions based on kinship.

Africans working for Africa in any capacity should understand the mechanics of kinship in the country they are working. Attempts should not be made to destroy kinship, because they would not only be futile but would also generate destructive counter-reaction. Force or violence cannot help to resolve the negative problems of kinship. When it is subjected as a social reality to other social realities, such as the acquisition of new ideas, it takes on new forms. If the positive forces of kinship which lie dormant and untapped in African systems of kinship are fully understood and properly directed, a tremendous source of energy for economic, political and social development may be released.

II Ways in which Kinship Terminology Reflects Social Groupings: the Lozi and the Zulu

Every society can be conceived as a structure within which people interact and coordinate in comparative harmony or disharmony. People are linked together by convergence of interest and sentiment and they are disjointed by divergence, but in the midst of these centripetal or centrifugal tendencies, society is able to sustain itself owing to the systematic functioning of several factors in the structure. Two media of interactions exist: between individuals, and between groups. Group interaction may be achieved either through the formation of associations, clubs, etc., in which membership is not based on any real or supposed blood relations; or through the formation of groups related by blood, real or fictitious. Here we are concerned with the latter.

Two persons are kin when one is descended from the other or when they are both descended from a common ancestor. Kinship therefore means a relationship actually or putatively traced through parent-child or sibling relations which are recognized for social purposes. Kinship terminology refers to the words used by relatives of different kinds to describe or address each other.

Kinship terminology may be of various types, such as: descriptive, classificatory, descriptive-classificatory. In a descriptive terminology few specific terms for relatives of the first and second order and other relatives are indicated by compounds of these specific terms, e.g. mother's brother. A classificatory terminology is one in which the terms used for lineal relatives are used for collateral relatives, e.g. father's brother is called 'father'. It must be pointed out that some systems are neither descriptive nor classificatory, e.g. the English terminology and that of the Timne of Sierra Leone.

The classificatory terminology has certain characteristics. Apart from using lineal terms collaterally it emphasizes the unity and solidarity of the sibling group, of the lineage group, and of the affine group. It may also lay emphasis on generation.

Kinship cannot sustain itself without marriage, because marriage is one important way of creating kinship. But marriage causes a disequilibrium in the family in all societies. However, the practice of preferential marriage, joking relations, the avoidance of exogamy and endogamy, rules of incest, etc., help to maintain equilibrium.

Kinship is also based on descent, and so one of its characters is the way descent is recognized and reckoned. There are four chief systems for the recognition of descent. The first is called cognatic or bilateral, whereby filiation is traced through both parents. This system impedes the formation of a corporate group beyond the family group, because such a great number of persons is involved. In order to forge a corporate group or an open group from this system several methods have to be used, such as the concepts of sib, stock, cousinage. The purpose of these concepts is to limit the number of persons ego will regard as close relatives for practical social purposes. (See Figs. 12 and 13.)

The second is the unilineal system, where filiation is either through the father's or through the mother's lineage. Patrilineal (also called agnatic) or matrilineal groups emerge from this system. In a patrilineal group where exogamy is practised the children of the women of the lineage are not considered as members of the lineage, while in a matrilineal group the children of the men of the lineage are not considered as members of the lineage. (See Figs. 10 and 11.)

It is clear that a corporate group beyond the family group could be formed from a unilineal system. Some groups such as clans, sub-clans, moieties, etc., are all different degrees of arrangements of kin groups based on the unilineal principle.

The double unilineal system is another method of filiation and reckoning descent; here ego is a member of a patrilineage in certain social contexts and a member of a matrilineage in another one. The classic example are the Yakö of Nigeria. This system creates two different types of lineage corporate groups in a given society (see Chapter 6, III for the Yakö).

It may be useful to mention the ambilateral system as the fourth method of filiation – with some caution. By this method ego may filiate into either of his parent's lineages. The creation of a corporate group depends on which side ego filiates. Here are some examples of how kinship terminology reflects social groupings.

The Lozi of Zambia, studied by Gluckman, are organized into a powerful kingdom and dwell mainly in the flood plains of the Upper Zambezi River. They build their villages on 'mounds' that stand above the waters of the floods. In summer they migrate to the flood plains and after the flood they come back to their permanent homes on the mounds. They have two types of villages: royal and titled villages, peopled by persons of different tribes and numbering between ten and a hundred; agnatic villages, peopled by a core of agnates and kinsmen numbering from five to ten people.

They have developed a bilateral system of kinship with a paternal bias. They have no clans, for no corporate unilineal group of kinsmen exists among the Lozi. Every child has a right to make its home in the village of either of its mother's parents and to inherit there. Only royal people can trace their descent from Mboo, the founder of the Lozi kingdom. Kinship links are important for commoners in order to define membership of a village, which is a corporate group of kindred that has lasted from the beginning of Lozi history. Descent-names provide the reference for common origin by blood, so that by whatever links cognates are united they express their kinship by citing any of the eight descent-names. Each descent-name refers to an ancestral village on one of the mounds. The possession of a descent-name enables a man to point to his ancestral village.

The Lozi bilateral system is reflected in their kinship terminology. They use the classificatory system and they distinguish sex in their terminology. A strict three-generational principle is maintained. Thus ego calls all relations of his generation sisters or brothers according to sex; those of his parents are called fathers or mothers, but above that everybody is 'grand'. Similarly he calls his children and all in their generation sons or daughters, below that all are grandchildren. This principle is extended to the spouse's relatives except to the mother-in-law and father-in-law.

The behaviour pattern coincides with the terminology, but mother's brother and sister's son call each other 'fellow husband', etc. These fall in the sphere of relation of familiarity called the joking-relation. In all lines, except the purely patrilineal, the Lozi allow marriages where a distant genealogical connection can be traced, for that helps to renew the relationship. (See also Chapter 17, Section I.)

The Zulu are garden cultivators and pastoralists in south-east Africa. They live in small villages inhabited by groups of agnates and their wives. Members of a number of villages are often related to one another by patrilineal ties, thus forming a group within a lineage system in which a genealogically senior headman is recognized. As the village grows, it splits into patrilineal branches which establish independent villages within the lineage land area. The Zulu are organized in a powerful kingdom. (For religious movements among the Zulu, see Chapter 23, Section II.)

The kinship system and terminology reflect the unity and solidarity of both the sibling and lineage group, which in this case is the patrilineage group. The terminology combines the classificatory and descriptive system. The chief characteristics are as follows. Relatives of the father's and mother's sides are clearly distinguished. The father's brothers are fathers and his sisters are 'female fathers'. The mother's sisters are mothers and her brothers are 'male mothers'. In the grandparents' generation the same terms are used on both sides to distinguish male from female. A man calls all siblings' and uncles' children of both sexes in his lineage brothers or sisters. Children of all siblings and uncles are called 'child' and all their children are grandchildren. Cross-cousins are called by another term. Marriage is not allowed with any member of one's father's or mother's clan or with anyone who shares a common grandparent. The relationships of affines are marked by restraint and avoidance.

The Lozi kinship terminology reflects their bilateral system in which either a patrilineal or a matrilineal group, or both, cannot be formed. The only kin group is the family with some near cognates, thus nearness of cognatic relationship, and not membership of a unilineal kin group, is emphasized. The Lozi village, which is a corporate group of kindred, is not formed with a unilineal core, but is based on the descent-name concept and residence, by which cognates are linked; or it is formed by the king. The Zulu, who are patrilineal, are grouped into patrilineages and clans. A man's rights of inheritance reside only in his agnatic lineage. For purposes of inheritance the Zulu are more interested in their distant patrilineal relationships than in those people in close relationships in other lines.

The basic difference between the Lozi and Zulu system is that because the Lozi system is bilateral, a corporate group cannot be formed save by the application of other principles, in this case the choice of descent-name and residence. The Zulu are patrilineal and so have corporate groups based on the fact of patrilineality. In the application of kinship terminology the Lozi terms refer to a wide circle of relations, which is consistent with its bilateral outlook. The Zulu kinship terminology, on the other hand, emphasizes the unity of patrilineages by having specific terms for specific relations within specific groups.

BIBLIOGRAPHY

SECTION II

Works consulted

GLUCKMAN, M. 'Kinship and marriage among the Lozi of Northern Rhodesia and the Zulu of Natal', in *African Systems of Kinship and Marriage*, A. R. Radcliffe-Brown and D. Forde (eds.) (London: Oxford University Press, 1950)

RADCLIFFE-BROWN, A. R. 'Introduction' to *African Systems of Kinship and Marriage*, A. R. Radcliffe-Brown and D. Forde (eds.) (London: Oxford University Press, 1950)

—— *Structure and Function in Primitive Society* (London: Cohen & West, 1952)

Suggestions for further reading

FIRTH, R. *Two Studies of Kinship in London* (London: Athlone Press, 1956)

FORTES, M. *Kinship and the Social Order: the Legacy of Lewis Henry Morgan* (London: Routledge & Kegan Paul, 1969)

FREEMAN, D. 'The Concept of the Kindred', *J.R.A.I.* (1961), 91

NAKANE, C. *Kinship and Economic Organisation in Rural Japan* (London: Athlone Press, 1967)

CHAPTER 6

Unilineal Systems and Social Groupings

I *The Patterns of Relationships Established in a Society with a Patrilineal Descent System: the Nuer of the Southern Sudan*

The Nuer are Nilotic pastoralists keeping cattle in the savannah country near the Upper Nile in Africa. (The population was between 200 000 and 300 000 when Evans-Pritchard studied them.) They are organized patrilineally, that is, descent is reckoned exclusively through males. (See Fig. 10.) They are divided into a number of tribes, and live in scattered villages on mounds during the rainy seasons; during the dry season they leave their villages and reside in large waterside camps. The cattle of a camp are watered and pastured together and different families take it in turn to provide herdsmen. Hunting, fishing and other dry-season activities are done collectively. Inter- and intra-village interaction is greater in the dry season.

Each village is a corporate group of 80–100 persons and is identified with a dominant agnatic lineage of the dominant clan; attached to these dominant lineages are cognates, affines and strangers. The lineages provide networks of kinship ties. In order to understand the pattern of relationships established through descent and complementary filiation, Nuer types of marriage and other types of parent–child relationships will be described.

ORDINARY NUER MARRIAGE
This is a union between a man and a woman instituted by transferring cattle and other goods. The ideal procedure is for the groom's paternal kin, aided in some cases by his maternal kin, to give forty cattle to the bride's paternal kin, who in turn distribute the cattle to the appropriate persons. (For a full description of the bride-gift, see Chapter 8, Section I.)

Marriage is not permitted between clansfolk, close cognates, close natural kinsfolk, close kinsfolk by adoption, close affines, and persons who stand to one another as fathers and daughters in the age-set system. Clan exogamy is stated in terms of clan symbols.

Cattle transfer during marriage has many implications. The compound family keeps only twenty beasts while the remaining twenty are shared equally between the maternal and paternal kin. When the full brother of the bride, according to custom, marries, all those who received his sister's cattle will contribute to his aid. The cattle-gift therefore has a cementing effect between the two families and within the kin group it is an expression of kinship ties. The two families by giving and accepting have created a new pattern of relationships and behaviour fully expressed in the avoidance between bride and father-in-law. Relationships between a father's brother and his brother's daughter and that between brother and brother, and brother and sister, are fully expressed.

The bride does not join her husband until she has had her first child, who is regarded as the child of the maternal as well as the paternal kin. The child bridges the two kin groups. It is only at this stage that all rights in a woman are fully transferred to the husband and to the husband's kin through the husband.

Ideally a Nuer family is polygynous within this group, and outside it kinship relations are translated into the idiom of cattle.

Some patterns of social relations are established as a result of an ordinary Nuer marriage. These will be described below.

The Husband–Wife Relationship
At first the wife stays in her parents' home and is occasionally visited by her husband. After the birth of the first child and when it has been weaned, the husband builds his wife a hut in his father's homestead facing the family kraal. It is not until a child has been born that the husband is accepted by his wife's people as one of themselves. Until this happens the husband continues to live the life he lived before marriage, that of a bachelor with his younger brothers in their father's byre.

When the wife returns to her husband's home she makes a mud windshield and the spirit of his lineage comes to dwell there. The husband's father tells him to build a byre and gives him a few cows to start a herd.

A woman must obey her husband, but a Nuer knows it is difficult to ill-treat a wife, because kinsmen would certainly intervene on her behalf.

The Co-Wife
In a polygamous family the relations between husband and wife are complicated by the husband's relations with his other wives. The first wife has no special status. Nuer insist on equality of status for the wives. Children are impressed to obey their mother's co-wife or wives and call them mother. A husband is expected to be fair in order for there to be a smooth relationship between his wives and children alike.

The Parent–Child Relationship
The care of small children falls to the mother, but fathers are also proud of their children. The affection of the father for his children is striking in Nuer land.

Daughters grow up under the direction of their mothers. Fathers take little interest in the affairs of their daughters. Their only concern is to get them properly married.

Boys are trained by their fathers and members of their patrilineage. Young men submit to their fathers.

The first son, who is a bridge between the mother's and father's kin group in the Nuer social system, never uses the spoon of his father or mother, and he is always brought up by his maternal grandparents or his maternal uncle. This eldest child is the keystone of the marriage. Although he belongs to his father's lineage, because he is the child of the cattle, the claim of his mother's people to their daughter's child is recognized in their right to bring the child up in their home. He represents the physical symbol of relationship between the two kin groups.

Siblings
Full brothers are expected to love one another. Paternal half-brothers always insist on their rights but try to dodge their obligations. The breaking of lineages and the dispersal of paternal kin are results of quarrels between half-brothers. They usually

drift apart after the death of their father or after they are married. A man, before his death, may direct how his herd is to be divided among his sons. If he does not do this the whole herd is left until all the sons are married. What remains of it may then be divided among them at a family council.

When one of the brothers wants to marry, the different paternal kin collect their customary share of cattle. All who share a bride's cattle must contribute their own quota during her brother's marriage.

A brother keeps an eye on his sister; he knows who is courting her and may intervene to protect her from someone without cattle. In doing this he is really protecting his own economic interest.

Wife and Husband Kin

A wife enters her new home as the mother of a child of her husband's lineage. She is a part of her husband's group but she still belongs to her own family and lineage. Her father pays compensation to her husband if she misbehaves.

Avoidances are observed before the birth of her first child, but afterwards they are gradually discarded. Thus the older she becomes and the more children she has, the more freely she moves with her husband's kin. She is the wife of his patrilineage and may be taken by her husband's brother or kinsman in levirate.

Husband; Father-in-Law; Mother-in-Law

A son-in-law respects his parents-in-law by hiding his nakedness in their presence from the day he asks for their daughter's hand in marriage. They must not visit one another when they are sick. A man's attitude to his mother-in-law consists of avoidance and shyness.

Brothers-in-law and fathers-in-law do ask husbands directly for what they want. The rules of avoidance and respect apply to the kinsfolk of the wife and of her parents' generation.

As the relationship with the wife increases, in terms of the number of children she bears, the obligation on the part of her husband to observe these rules lessens and may altogether cease, when the wife's father and maternal uncle pay beasts to enable them to eat in their son-in-law's home. All relations cease after a legal divorce.

OTHER FORMS OF 'MARRIAGE'

The Nuer recognize other forms of 'marriage' and unions and these generate new patterns of social relations. The most significant and general aspect of these marriages and unions are that the *pater* (social father) and *genitor* (biological father) are different. However, once the *pater* is established, behaviour patterns take the form of ordinary marriage.

Woman to Woman 'Marriage'

The woman 'husband' 'marries' her 'wife' in exactly the same way as a man. When the marriage rites have been completed the woman 'husband' gets a male kinsman or friend to beget children by her 'wife' and assist her. When the daughters of the marriage are married, the *genitor* will receive the cow of begetting. The woman 'husband' is the legal 'husband' and regarded as the *pater* and all rights over the wife and children are vested in her.

Ghost Marriage

Among the Nuer it is considered bad to die without heirs. If a man dies without a legal male heir a kinsman or his sister's son if he has 'inherited' cattle from his mother's brother, will marry a wife to his name and all the children of such a marriage become the dead man's legal children. Here again the *pater* and *genitor* are different, but the legal and social recognitions emphasize the rights of the *pater*.

It is evident that a complicated pattern of social relationships is established between the actors in this type of marriage.

Levirate

If a man dies, the widow is taken by his brother or closest kinsman. All children born are legally and socially considered the children of the dead man and when the daughters of such a union marry, the *genitor* is only entitled to the cattle of begetting. Sororate is practised by the Nuer, but it depends on the goodwill between the families concerned. (See glossary for sororate.)

Widow Concubinage

Widows at times may refuse to live with their husband's kin. Since divorce has not been granted, they may take lovers. All children of such unions are children of the late husband and their kin, although the *genitors* are entitled to the cattle of begetting.

Married Woman Concubinage

It may happen that a woman is not willing to remain with the husband after the birth of the first child and her family is not in a position to return the cattle. The husband may have to give up his claim. If the wife goes to live with another man in another district, all children of this union are children of the *pater* not of the *genitor*.

Unmarried Woman Concubinage

Nuer women and maidens are usually strong-minded. An unmarried woman may live alone and have children, who may suffer the reproach of bastardy. She may never get support from her lineage, and the man living with her has no right over her children. But the man can legitimize any child she may bear by him, by giving four or six cattle for each child to the woman's family. He may, if both agree, give fewer cattle to the woman's parents, and by going through the nuptial rights he can become the legal husband.

From the discussion above, we have seen that the Nuer 'family' has variants of which each one is set into the social pattern. When the *genitor* is the *pater* a familiar pattern, which is regular, emerges, but when the *pater* is different from the *genitor* another pattern of behaviour arises in which the *pater* is socially upheld.

THE KINSHIP STRUCTURE OF THE NUER

It has already been noted that the Nuer are patrilineal. To a Nuer his parents and siblings are not his kin but members of his family. His kin are those people related to him patrilineally or matrilineally. In the arrangement of categories and in the attention paid to them, there is a recognized balance between the kin on the father's side and those on the mother's side. The emphasis laid on the patrilineal side makes it a descent group which is corporate in the sense that inheritance of cattle is from father to son or brother to brother, that is, within the patrilineage.

However, the matrilineality is also stressed. This relation is shown between the first child and his mother's kin, especially the maternal uncle.

The maternal uncle gives all assistance to his sister's son. He is always gentle and

5 *Mayombe mother (Mayombe, Central Africa)*

kind to him. However, the sister's son can never inherit from the maternal uncle. Only rights and duties connect them. This relationship is marked by special observances. The curse of a maternal uncle is believed to be among the worse. This relationship is called complementary filiation.

The distribution of cattle during the marriage of the bride has already been mentioned. The marriage gift and cattle are distributed among the following categories of kin: the father's brother, the father's sister, the mother's brother, the mother's sister, the father's father, the mother's father, the father's mother and the mother's mother.

When a man is killed, the cattle transferred by the murderer, apart from those reserved for marrying a wife to the name of the dead man, are divided among the same set of kin named above.

In the past, it was the duty of the paternal kin to help a man, avenge his death if he was killed, and marry a wife to his name. A man who wronged a kinsman was shamed and might incur a curse.

We can sum up what has been said as follows. Descent, complementary filiation and marriage establish a complicated pattern of social relationships among the Nuer. Each relationship is tied up with rights and duties emanating from different social sources. Kinship and marriage are two separate aspects of Nuer social life, but each supplements the other and each has its own established pattern in the complicated network of social relationships.

The Nuer lineage system is segmentary but within this system the most effective group is a core of agnates dwelling in a village under the 'Bull', who is the head. The principle of tracing descent through males is upheld. Females may be included in the genealogy, but they are then regarded as males. Thus the definition of patrilineal descent should include the reckoning of descent through 'females' regarded as males. Adopted children or persons suffer no disability, for they are incorporated into the agnatic lineage. Evans-Pritchard holds the view that the Nuer agnatic principle is unchallenged. I myself, using data from his record, feel that it is challengeable. I feel that it has a flexible structure which can incorporate foreign elements and graft female branches into a structure supposed to be an agnatic lineage.

The Nuer have various ways of arranging marriages. Each way initiates a special type of relationship which is expressed in the kinship idiom. Kinship is therefore 'created' and may be 'cut', that is broken, when it interferes with marriage, which creates new and nearer kin.

There are various categories of relationships in the system, of which the following are paramount: between siblings, husband and wife or wives, first son and mother's brother, brother's son and daughters and father's brother, in-laws.

The relationship between siblings may be explained as the result of common parentage whose behaviour has been orientated towards a common interest – cattle. This interest in cattle is the main factor which divides half-brothers.

The relationship of husband and wife is at first one of respect and avoidance, but with the birth of the first child, the marriage becomes stabilized and the relationship one of familiarity.

Co-wives are regarded as equal and everything is done by the husband to maintain the autonomy of each one. In short, co-wives are related to one another through the husband; children are made to call the co-wife of their mother, mother. This is an extension of the solidarity of the sibling group.

The relationship between the first son and mother's brother may be explained in this way. Marriage affects the bride's lineage because it breaks the unity of the sibling group and the woman is incorporated into another agnatic group. This incorporation implies loss of rights and status in her agnatic lineage. The son of such a woman bridges the gap between the two agnatic groups and represents not only a symbol but in reality his mother. As a reality he claims his mother's rights and as a symbol his mother's status. All these he get in a limited form, because his claims are mediated by his mother, who after all has limited rights according to agnatic principles. To make his rights legal, not moral, a cow is always given to the mother's brother during the marriage of his sister's daughter. This also helps to explain why boys always protect the interests of their sisters.

The relationship between ego and father's brother is based on the extension of the solidarity of the sibling group. He is not a counterpart of the mother's brother, for his rights and duties emanate from a different source, the one who takes the place of a father.

All these relationships are interwoven with the economic, social, political and religious activities of the Nuer.

II *The Patterns of Relationships Established in a Society with a Matrilineal Descent System: the Lele of Central Africa*

The Lele (studied by Mary Douglas) live in dispersed village settlements in Central Africa between the Loange and Kasai Rivers. In about 1948 the population was about 26 000, with a density of four persons per square mile.) They are agriculturalists practising shifting cultivation. Owing to poor soil and inadequate farming techniques, production is very low. Wealth consists of raffia cloth and camwood.

Among the Lele, the matrilineal system, the principle of reckoning descent through females, is upheld ideologically. There are no matrilineages concentrated in any given locality. The residence pattern is such that brothers, sisters and mothers live in different villages from one another. This pattern is further complicated by economic, social and personal interests. (See Fig. 11.)

The Lele have matrilineal exogamous clans, but they have no interest in genealogical relations and they have no matrilineages similar to those found among the Ashanti or Mayombe who have similar systems.

How then do the Lele organize themselves in the absence of the matrilineages which are frequently a characteristic of matrilineal descent? The answer, according to Mary Douglas, is in the concepts of village and clan.

The most important social unit is the village which has a name and a population of up to 170 persons. The pattern of settlement is one of groups of villages which are united to one another by alliance; each group is autonomous. Each village has its chief which is a semi-hereditary post in so far as that one of the original clans which founded the village has the right to appoint its senior member to the office. In a group of related villages the descendants of the clan which led the immigrant party remain dominant and attempts are deliberately made to have at least one such member in each village, because it is believed that evil may befall a village which has lost its physical association with its founding clan. A mystical relationship, devoid of any special privilege, links the founding clan with other clans in the village.

The dominant clans of a village constitute its permanent core, while other members of other clans attach themselves to it at different times.

Villages, although independent, ally with other villages in war, and so on. Such alliances are based on three principles: that of common origin when fission of one village produces dispersed 'brother' villages; that of proximity when enemy villages become neighbours and peace is usually sealed with ritual; and that of pawnship and marriage (see page 71 for pawnship).

The clan is a corporate group which has some political functions. Without the clan organization the full operation of blood debts and pawnship might never be a reality. The recognition of a common descent, which is never expressed genealogically, gives a person the right to claim a blood debt, imposes responsibility on clans for the misdeeds of any of its members, and makes effective residence in any village easier. Pawns are considered the 'property' of the clan and can only be effectively claimed by appealing to the village.

A clan, although dispersed, has its core identifiable as the dominant clan in at least one of the many villages. This is because the members always have a local concentration of older members; they tend to dominate numerically and socially in a village which their ancestors helped to found. Thus a village is usually named after the foremost of its founding clans and the men of this clan usually occupy the rectangular houses in the village. The village heads are always the oldest male members. These heads hold many cult positions in the village. Members of the *Pangolin* cult, for example, are exclusively from the founding clans of the village: these are men who married women of another founding clan and have had two children of opposite sexes by their respective wives. This is a case where cult, marriage and descent maintain the foundation on which the village is built.

The most effective groups at any given moment are local clan sections that make up the village of which the dominant section, which is the founding clan, provides the village head. The older men of a clan section effectively control the supply of women belonging to the clan section, and by so doing the younger generation of men has to wait until about age thirty-five to get married. This delayed marriage is compensated for by the institution of the village wife and the freedom accorded to youths by the nature of their authority system which allows them to change their allegiance and residence at will. Since the clan sections are distributed among the villages, a youth is welcomed into any section of his clan that happens to be in a village where he wishes to reside. The clan section is only made up of between three and five men, including strangers, and members may be dispersed around the village. This group is not an economic unit, but it shares rights to wives and wealth. The possessions, debts, claims and widows of a dead man revert to his local clan section over which matrilineal relatives residing nearby have priority. Thus we have a group with a concept of common descent, which although corporate in terms of owning property is yet dispersed. The effect of dispersed residence is to reduce the degree of friction resulting from a dyadic relationship. This is compatible with Lele political organization in which authority is diffused.

In each village two or more clans are recognized as 'owners' of the village. So also for the Lele as a whole one clan is regarded as 'owner' of Lele. This ownership is based on a mystical belief. The clan that is supposed to own Lele is called *Tundu* and others are called *Wongo*. Members of this so to speak aristocratic clan are always addressed as *Kumu*. The relationship between a *Tundu* and a *Wongo* is informal.

When the head of a *Tunda* village visits a friendly *Wongo* village he receives gifts of raffia from members of each corner-hut. He sits in the middle of the village and addresses the villagers reminding them of the dignity of the *Tundu* and the rights and duties that are involved. At the end of his visit every man in the village gives him a raffia cloth. They escort him home to his village and he takes one of his own daughters or grand-daughters and presents her to the loyal village as their future wife. The daughter of such a wife, according to their rules of preferred marriage, is for her grandfather. Thus two villages play the role of father-in-law and son-in-law in alternate generations.

The aristocratic clan has certain prerogatives which it maintains not by force but by generous reciprocity and control of the insignia worn by the sons-in-law of villages. This is done by secret purchase of the insignia. The rights of the aristocratic clan are supported by the claim that they are descended from Woto, the mythical hero, first ancestor of the tribe. This descent makes them stand between God and man. Men reach God through their mediation but they themselves speak directly to God. They are also credited with the control of powerful sorcery.

We can sum up by saying that the whole political and social organization of the Lele is based on an ideology of a mystical descent from the clan to the village level. At each level marriage and filiation with its reciprocal rights and duties tend to strengthen the newer bonds thus created. Here is therefore a situation where 26 000 people are without either political personnel and authority or a defined lineage system. All the same, by applying a matrilineal descent ideology for closer relations and a mystical descent ideology for distant relations, and propped up by marriage ties and the institution of pawnship, they have maintained comparative cohesion in their social and political organization.

Pawnship, marriage and blood debts are intricately linked together in Lele society. Killing a man from another village is a matter of blood vengeance between villages and not one to be dealt with between clans. The method of settling blood debts through the village seems to be one of the factors that gives it its corporate quality. Blood debts are based on the principle of a life for a life, as interpreted in the institution called *bukolomo,* translated as 'pawnship'. A pawn is a woman or one of her matrilineal descendants who is transferred in perpetuity in settlement of a blood debt. The pawn and her descendants have semi-servile status. They depend on their lords for protection and they owe him certain services. They are not slaves since they are still full members of their clan and are fully protected, for no action can be taken against them without the permission of their clans; anyone who kills a pawn must pay blood compensation both to the master and to the clan – a full life to each. But two rights are transferred when a clanswoman or her daughter is offered in settlement of a blood debt. The first is the right to give in marriage both her and her female matrilineal descendants. The second is to use her or her female matrilineal descendents to settle further blood debts. This latter right has to be exercised with the consent of the pawn's clan, to which a fee must be paid.

Before the implications of pawnship can be fully appreciated it is essential to understand Lele marriage. The Lele recognize two types of marriage and family life. In the first the wife may be called 'private'. It is a preferred marriage by which a man marries a wife or wives who must be of a different clan and preferably his daughter's daughter. His children do not belong to his own clan, but he has rights as the man on the spot to allocate his daughters in marriage, that is, marriage is virilocal. Preferred marriage gives the father of daughters prestige in his own clan. He has a say in the disposal of marriageable girls, and he can offer his daughter's daughters to individual clansmen if he likes. But his right as a father of his daughters is limited by the similar rights of his daughter's mother's father. The final result of their separate claims is a compromise – a fair share of daughters between the two claimants, and the others used in settling blood debts.

By the rule of preferred marriage, a grandfather is expected to marry his granddaughters. These wives become the co-wives of their grandmother. Co-wives are expected to be partners, but there may be strained relations. We are also told that sisters, mothers and daughters often live together in peace and cooperation. All these are not contradictory statements; they express the contradictory roles a Lele woman has to play, which she does by readjustment.

Thus where there is only one daughter to a marriage the daughter goes to the mother's father, while the father waits till the next generation of women to claim his daughter's daughter.

One point must be made clear. The maternal clan B is never compensated with women except for the initial bride-gift. Thus clans A and C continue to get women from B while clan B loses women. This apparent loss is compensated for by marriage from other clans.

There is no inequality between those clans giving wives and those who are receiving, except in the case of the aristocratic clans.

Since girls are born outside their clan, that is, in the village of their father, and married into another clan, one would expect sisters to be dispersed and have little contact with their brothers who change residence frequently. But women tend to congregate in one area. They resist moving very far from their mothers or sisters, because of the strong attachments between mothers, sisters and daughters, and because they like to cooperate in labour. Also, fish ponds are handed down from mother to daughter or sister.

The dominance of fathers over matriclans in the share of women is very significant. A man with many sons-in-law will have sufficient labour to help him. The elders of clans and villages always cajole young men to join them and the only bait they use is the prospect of giving their daughters to the young men, since men of the senior generation control the stock of women, and the younger men have to solicit for a share. This state of affairs would normally lead to open conflict, but such conflicts are held in check by the institutional mechanisms such as the village wife, and the concepts of sexual pollution, avoidance and sorcery.

It seems that the Lele provide their young men with village wives to soften the rigour of long bachelorhood. This is the second form of marriage. A village wife belongs to men of a particular age-set of a village and her children belong to the village. Both the village wife and children are honoured and given great respect. In Lele society, monogamy, polygamy and polyandry are practised, and at the same time adultery is fully recognized. The system works harmoniously because of the rules of sex pollution and avoidance.

Peace is essential for the continuation of village, clan and family life. Quarrels in a village spoil the hunt, so confessions and fines are made before a hunt in order to appease God. This is the village idea of peace. The village suffers when the family is not at peace for hunts will be unfavourable and people may begin to quit the village. To avoid this, personal quarrels are resolved before the village goes to hunt. Thus by applying the sanction of the hunt, the family is restrained from quarrels. A husband and wife are both expected to live in peace with one another and with their neighbours. They are bound to stay with one another in sickness and in health. Polygamists are supposed to treat their wives with fairness. There is a strict sex dichotomy between the husband's and wife's rights and duties. Each is expected to play his or her role satisfactorily, for instance a wife must cook – except with good reason.

The crops which a wife harvests are under her control and her husband must never dip into her store without her permission. This rule applies to everything that belongs to the woman. Only her brothers can store with her.

Lele ideas of sex pollution control the sexual life of the family. Illicit sexual intercourse is dangerous to married life because it endangers the lives of both husband and wives, as well as the children. If a man is sick and his wife commits adultery he will get worse. If a woman conceives, her safe delivery depends on whether she or her husband or her co-wife has committed adultery; their adultery would endanger the life of the newly born child. Sex pollution is equally applied to the village wife, who is given great respect, as well as her husbands when she is pregnant. Owing to the fear of the evil of sex pollution some fathers refuse to let their daughters join the honourable ranks of village wives on the plea that village husbands are careless about keeping the regulations and so endanger their daughter's lives.

There is strict avoidance between sisters and brothers. A woman avoids her sons, her son-in-law, and to some extent her father. The avoidance relation practised by women is in line with the doctrine that men should use women in building up their prestige. In return women are helped and protected.

In spite of this, women do control to some extent the mobility of men. They resist moving far from any of their female relations, especially their mothers. Girls are supposed not to hide any secrets from their mothers, even their extramarital adventures. Mothers also avoid all their daughters' lovers. This is compatible with the sanctions of sex pollution and avoidance. Thus if a girl (or woman) is sex-polluted she has to confide it to her mother who consults a diviner to avert the mystical danger her daughter is exposed to.

Brothers tend to cooperate less than sisters. Fathers and sons do quarrel and separate to live in different villages. On the whole a man avoids his elder brother, his mother's brother and father, and his wife's father and mother, and mother's brother. He goes to any of his relations for aid, starting with the closest ones. A son-in-law is expected to respect his father-in-law; he owes perpetual service while his marriage exists to him and to his mother-in-law.

Village children are usually better off. They are well cared for. The village looks after its children with great lavishness although it may split in rivalry for the village wives.

The village in-law has great obligations and services to discharge, which he carries out with his age-mates. The village wife and village in-law stand in a special relationship to the village. They enjoy a kind of diplomatic immunity. If two villages are fighting, one the man's and the other his wife's, the man may intervene and demand a truce. He may be sent to the other village to negotiate at a time when tension is high. Village wives are sometimes also ambassadors of peace. If two villages have been fighting, one of them may send its village wives on a 'diplomatic' mission to the other. When they arrive, they are treated well and sleep with the men of their choice. Next morning they discuss the outstanding quarrels and then are escorted home having created the goodwill for peace negotiations to start in earnest – a kind of preliminary negotiation before a 'summit meeting', as it were !

The relationship between a mother's brother and sister's son is rather obscure, and probably insignificant. The mother's brother who is avoided gets the back and a haunch of a large animal killed by his sister's son, and he is expected to help his sister's son. He never has rights of life and death over his sister's children, as among the Yao or Bemba, and never claims them, as among the Ashanti. He is just a mother's brother to be avoided and respected with gifts of meat.

Certain persons are bound to play contradictory roles in Lele society. Owing to the dispersed nature of the clans, the same clan may be in different warring villages. In this case clan members are not expected to kill one another. This is a clash between clan solidarity and village solidarity.

The status of a *Tunda* woman is different from that of an ordinary woman. The rule of clan exogamy requires her to marry commoners, yet she cannot be subordinate to her commoner husbands. Usually she is a village wife because this helps to reduce the conflict in the role, but she is a village wife of a freer type and chooses a house husband who is regarded as a begetter of chiefs. The husband, contrary to Lele sexual etiquette, is tabooed on pain of capital punishment not to have sexual intercourse with any other woman. When the woman has conceived she restricts herself, for fear of sex pollution, to the men she has known since her last confinement. She goes to her *Tundu* village to bear her child.

To sum up some of the major points raised, it is safe to say that among the Lele the pattern of social relationships established through descent is based on the concept of matrilineality fully expressed in clan organization. Marriage is conceived as a mechanism of widening the field of inter- and intra-clan relationships and of increasing one's network of relations. The Lele father is interested in his daughters, for he has a say in the disposal of his marriageable daughters even though he belongs to a different clan from them. The father's right is challengeable by his daughter's mother's father who also has a right to the disposal of his daughter's daughter.

Complementary filiation seems to be of no social significance in Lele society. Neither the father's brother nor the mother's brother has any significant role to play with regard to his brother's daughter or his sister's daughter respectively.

In the absence of any centralized political authority, peace and stability are achieved by limiting those personal interactions which are the source of friction. This is done by adopting a series of avoidance relationships and the 'fear' of sex pollution, which are, therefore, systems of ordering people's social life to achieve some kind of pattern, order and harmony.

(For methods of distribution and a description of the economy, see Chapter 17, Section III.)

III *The Patterns of Relationships Established in a Society with a Double Unilineal Descent System: the Yakö of Nigeria*

D. Forde studied the Yakö, who are of a semi-Bantu linguistic group. (Their population in 1935 was about 20 000.) They live in five compact independent village settlements situated at distances of from three to six miles from each other, 120 miles up and to the east of the Cross River in Eastern Nigeria. They have a system of a double descent kin-group organization, that is, they have developed both patrilineal and matrilineal kin-groups.

The country lies in the northern part of the forest belt of Southern Nigeria. Rain falls all the year round, amounting to about eighty inches, with the temperature up to 79°. The most rainfall occurs between April and October and the least between November and March. The natural vegetation is dense tropical forest rich in palms, coconut trees and several timber-producing trees. The soil is fertile and men and women cultivate yam. Women also grow other subsidiary crops such as coco-yams, beans, maize and cassava between yam-hills. They are subsistence farmers, practising shifting cultivation and intercropping, though they do trade in oil palm produce.

(For more information about farming and land-holding, see Chapter 17, Section I.)

Umor village (which had a population of 11 000 in 1935) is the largest of the Yakö villages. Starting with the smallest unit, the elementary family is the nucleus of the Yakö household. However, some of the older men have more than one wife, and where this occurs, that is, in polygynous households, every wife has a right to occupy a separate house provided by her husband and has personal property of food supplies and other domestic equipment. A man with his wife or wives constitutes a single farming unit and each wife has her own rights and duties.

Each family dwells in a larger group of patrilineal relatives and their wives. This larger group of patrilineages of between fifteen and thirty adult men who are kinsmen under a senior man called 'our father', collectively holds rights to a section of the village site and to tracts of farmland in the surrounding country. 'Our father', arbitrates in disputes among the lineages and is their leader in affairs with other groups. The ritual head of the patriclan is in charge of the shrine and presides over the informal meetings of recognized elders and notables of the lineages. He also arbitrates in disputes, initiates the boys into the *Ebiabu*, and organizes other ritual ceremonies. His influence and effectiveness depend on the strength of his personality, the religious sanctions at his disposal and the support of the clan elders.

The patrilineages form larger groups or patriclans which are also territorially compact. These patrilineages do claim a common descent in time of peace, but when disputes over dwelling sites or farmland arise, the separateness of the lineages is emphasized. The various component lineages claim particular tracts of house land and farmland according to established principles of seniority and the principle of the first to use the land. Patriclans are grouped into wards. Wards are not based on kinship ties but on territory. There are four wards in Umor, each of which is made up of between five and eleven patriclans with 50–200 adults.

There are other groups of matrilineal kin, which are not territorially delimited. Since residence is patrilocal, the members of a matriclan are dispersed among the patriclan territories of the village, and a handful may be living in other villages. Apart from full siblings, the persons composing the patrikin and matrikin of each individual are normally distinct.

Kinship between the lineages is not generally traced genealogically and the clans do not claim a common descent. There is no ancestor cult. The wards translate their 'oneness' territorially. The patriclans and the wards are products of a long process of fission and fusion alternatively or simultaneously.

The distribution of fixed property rights corresponds to the organization of social groupings; both are related to land usage. Umor is a large compact village settlement covering an area of nearly a quarter of a square mile, and it is economically and territorially autonomous, having its own independent local political organization. Umor village has a territory of 47 square miles with a density of 230 people per square mile (1935 figure). There are 4–5 square miles of unfarmed forest on the eastern border and a square mile of uncultivated swamp land in the north-west. The remainder, about 40 square miles, is criss-crossed by farming paths which lead to farmland and other villages. About 18 square miles are cleared for cultivation and only 4 square miles are actually cultivated in any one year.

The village territory is divided into four wards and each ward owns its own territory or land which it defends jealously as one whole. The ward land is divided up among patrilineal kin groups. A man can migrate from his own patriclan area and go to live in the area of another patriclan; he can also obtain temporary rights to make a farm in the land of another kin group.

A man is entitled to a piece of farmland when he marries; he firstly receives a part of his father's farmland. It is the father who takes on a new piece of farmland which is unoccupied.

The patrilineages of a clan live together on a territory. There are family rights to build and land with its trees is inheritable from father to son, though they be used under certain conditions. Each patriclan has a square, a shrine and a common house which are owned in common. Trees are acquired through patrilineal kin groups.

The individual's claims to land and economic resources are established within the patrilineal kin group. The matrilineal kin groups claim all movable property, and raffia palms. Although matrilineal kin have no farming rights on land, the general economic activities of the group are controlled by the priests of the matriclan who are in charge of the shrines and the fertility cults (see Chapter 17, Section I).

(For Yakö associations, see Chapter 10, Section III.)

BIBLIOGRAPHY

SECTION I
Works consulted
EVANS-PRITCHARD, E. E. *Kinship and Marriage among the Nuer* (Oxford: Clarendon Press, 1951)

Suggestions for further reading
ARDENER, E. W. 'Lineage and Locality among the Mba-Ise Ibo', *Africa* (1959), 292
BOHANNAN, P. *Tiv Farm and Settlement* (London: HMSO, 1955)
FORTES, M. *The Web of Kinship Among the Tallensi* (London: Oxford University Press, 1949)
FREEDMAN, M. *Lineage Organization in South-eastern China* (London: Athlone Press, 1958)
STENNING, D. J. *Savannah Nomads* (London: Oxford University Press, 1959)

SECTION II
Works consulted

DOUGLAS, M. *The Lele of the Kasai* (London: Oxford University Press, 1963)

Suggestions for further reading
FORTES, M. 'The Structure of Unilineal Descent Groups', *American Anthropologist* (1953)
—— 'Descent, Filiation and Affinity: A Rejoinder to Dr. Leach'. *Man* (1959)
RADCLIFFE-BROWN, A. R. and D. FORDE (eds.) *African Systems of Kinship and Marriage* (London: Oxford University Press, 1950)

SECTION III
Works consulted
FORDE, D. 'Land and Labour in a Cross River Village', *Geographical Journal* (1937), 90, 1
—— 'Double descent among the Yakö' in *African Systems of Kinship and Marriage*, A. R. Radcliffe-Brown and D. Forde (eds.) (London: Oxford University Press, 1950)
—— *Yakö Studies* (London: Oxford University Press, 1964)

Suggestions for further reading
GOODY, J. R. 'Fission of Domestic Groups among the Lodagaba', in *The Developmental Cycle in Domestic Groups*, J. R. Goody (ed.) (London: Cambridge University Press, 1958)
NADEL, S. F. 'Dual descent in the Nuba Hills' in *African Systems of Kinship and Marriage*, A. R. Radcliffe-Brown and D. Forde (eds.) (London: Oxford University Press, 1950)

CHAPTER 7

Non-Unilineal Systems and
Social Groupings

I *The Patterns of Relationships Established in a Bilateral System and the Differences between a Bilateral and a Double Unilineal System*

Descent is a socially recognized connection between a person and his or her fore-bears either through the father or the mother. After birth one has various modes of filiation into social groups. For purpose of analytic studies there are many possible ways, outlined below, of tracing filiation; this list is not an exhaustive one.

1. Matrilateral filiation in which the role of the father is absent, e.g. among the Nayas.
2. Matrilateral filiation with patrilateral complementary filiation, e.g. the Bemba or Trobrianders.
3. Patrilateral filiation in which the matrilateral group is similar to the patrilateral, due to endogamy, e.g. the Bedouin.
4. Patrilateral filiation with matrilateral complementary filiation, e.g. the Zulu and some Igbo.
5. Double unilineal filiation in which the patrilateral and matrilateral groups are both property-holding units, e.g. the Yakö and Lodagaba.
6. Double unilineal filiation in which only the patrilateral or matrilateral group is a property-holding unit, e.g. the Lowiili.
7. Bilateral filiation, in which filiation is through both parents, e.g. the Ifugao, Lozi, Hausa and Kalinga.

The task here is to show the difference between the double unilineal and bilateral systems and the patterns of relationships generally characteristic of the bilateral system.

The Kalinga are groups dwelling in the north-central portion of northern Luzon in the Philippines. They grow rice on terraced fields on the mountainsides. (The population when studied was 25 000 with an average density of three people per square mile.)

Kalinga society is organized primarily on the bilateral principle and secondarily on a territorial unit called a 'region' which consists of certain villages with their lands within defined boundaries. The family is the most effective unit and is made up of a man, his wife and children. The economic unit is the household made up of the simple family and other dependants. Polygamy is not practised, but concubinage is frequent. The property of each spouse is regarded as individually owned; it consists of land, water and heirlooms which are inherited by the children. If the marriage is childless the property reverts to the partners' respective kin after their death. (See Figs. 12 and 13.)

For ego, Kalinga kinship consists of the descendants of his eight pairs of great-great-grandparents: this includes his siblings, his parents, and his first, second and third cousins on both sides. This means that the kin of any individual consists of the kin of his parents minus their third cousins. Only brothers and sisters have the same kin; after they have married their affinal groups are different. Also ego's kin is a group of unrelated persons of whom in any instance some may act on his behalf and some be neutral.

In this system all one's kin are never corporate groups in the sense that they are land- or status-owning units. Among the Kalinga the elementary family is the land-owning unit, although one's nearest kin, up to the first cousin, may have vested interests in one's land, since it is a matter of disgrace for it to slip into another unit – although it does after a sale. This category of cognates defined above is referred to as kindred. The Kalinga kindreds function socially for blood vengeance, collective responsibility and, very important, for the sharing of meat.

In this type of ordering of kinship there are several centrifugal and centripetal forces operating. If ego kills a person of another kindred, members of that kindred may take vengeance on ego's kindred up to the third cousin; thus this range of cousins would be forced to pull towards ego. Also some of the kindred may object to contributing to the business of a distant relative, although they may not object to sharing with him when the going is favourable. In theory, the kindred includes the third cousins, but in practice the tendency is towards a narrower range; for example, marriage between second cousins is frequent. Here the range is restricted to first cousins. In meat distribution, only influential second cousins may be included. It is therefore clear that the Kalinga kindred is a very variable social unit.

The fluidity of the kindred as an instrument of group organization is apparent among the Kalinga in the development of their quasi-territorial units called regions. These regions are weak in so far as domestic and internal affairs are concerned but strong with respect to external affairs. These regions are under the control of *Pangats,* peace-makers.

Among the Kalinga wealth tends to accumulate in the hands of a few individuals from generation to generation. The result is the stratification of the society into the poor, the rich, the wealthy aristocrats and the *Pangats* who exercise functions that are political. The distinctions are not rigidly applied, since a man can work hard and become a *Pangat.* Also there is a class of specialists called 'go-betweens' whose duties are to mediate between people or groups in all negotiations. The rise of the wealthy class, the territorial development with *Pangats* at the helm, the rise of the professional 'go-betweens', all reflect the secondary importance of the kindred.

The chief characteristics of the Kalinga bilateral system can be summed up thus. It is a wider method of creating kinship relations without forming a corporate group. However, in order to form an action group based on kindred, secondary means are applied, that is, in this case, the principle of cousinage and in a wider sense the idea of regionalization. In this system both parents can transmit wealth which tends to accumulate in certain families, thus giving rise to a stratified society. Some of the people in the upper class act as agents in the region. The inability of a bilateral system to give rise to the formation of a large and lasting corporate group which would give minimum security to the family units might have given rise to the formation of other various groupings which do not interfere with the autonomy and independence of the sibling group or the elementary family, which is the only effective corporate group the system can create.

We now turn to the Lowiili who live on the banks of the Black Volta in northern Ghana and the Ivory Coast. (The population was about 2 335 in 1931 with a population density of 100 per square mile.) They are mixed agriculturalists who keep some cattle and grow guinea-corn, millet, maize, groundnuts and some yam. They also keep sheep, goats and poultry.

The simplest dwelling group consists of an elementary monogamous family, although about 25 per cent are polygynous. Marriage is virilocal and married women have rights to use their husband's land. A group of agnates dwells in a compound under a compound head who is the oldest as well as the custodian of the ancestor shrine. Such a compound may harbour four males, five females and seven children. The compound joint families are split into closer groups of male agnates for purpose of production and consumption called farming-groups.

Some seven or more large compounds situated about 100 yards apart consist a patrilineage. These lineages are shallow in depth but form a corporate group in that they own land jointly and have a lineage shrine under the head of a senior member. The continuity of the lineages through time and space is expressed jointly during funerals, rituals, marriages and the inheritance of land and widows.

Dispersed patrilineages, having one earth shrine and claiming a common descent, form a clan-sector. Some clan-sectors claiming a common descent and sharing a common name amalgamate into clans. These clans are not corporate groups in the sense that members or representatives act jointly. The unity of the clan arises from the concept of a common descent, prohibition against marrying in, and prohibition from killing clan members which is an unpardonable offence.

The Lowiili have another descent group traced through women. The uterine descent group of the greatest extent is the matriclan of which there are four. Individuals in a neighbouring settlement can establish a matriclan or matrilineage relationship. The matriclan has only a ritual function. It has no property to transmit, only membership.

The Lodagaba are neighbours of the Lowiili and have a similar organization save in one aspect. They live in the orchard bush country within the Niger bend and are also agriculturalists. (Their population density was eighty-one people per square mile at the time of the study.) Their social organization is similar to that of the Lowiili. The chief difference is that both the matrilineal and the patrilineal groups are property-holding groups. Thus the Lodagaba child not only filiates with both his matrilineage and his patrilineage, but he also inherits immovable property such as land from his patrilineage and movable property such as grain and money from his matrilineage.

The double unilineal inheritance system has produced some pronounced differences between the Lodagaba and Lowiili. According to Goody, the major differences are as follows: the relationship between the mother's brother and the sister's son tends to be one of hostility with the Lodagaba and cordiality with the Lowiili. The father–son relation is cordial among the Lodagaba and tense among the Lowiili. The farming group, that is, the productive group, is smaller among the Lodagaba than among the Lowiili, because fission of the elementary family takes place at an early period. Thus the situation is avoided whereby in the event of the father's death the wealth accumulated jointly might be inherited by a member of another group.

The social organization of the Kalinga is based on a bilateral system, and the Lowiili and Lodagaba have a double unilineal system. The chief differences between the two systems are as follows.

The first difference is *structural*. The Kalinga kinship system is based on tracing relations through both parents. This means that with ego at the centre relations constantly ramify on both sides towards the periphery, thus including a huge number of persons. The Lodagaba kinship group is traced through males for one purpose and through females for another purpose. This tends to narrow the number of persons involved in any given line. Because of the structural implications the Kalinga bilateral system cannot give rise to the formation of a corporate group beyond the elementary family. In order to produce such a corporate group they have applied other secondary principles such as cousinage, regions and class. With the Lodagaba the double unilineal system forms two corporate groups, the patrilineal and the matrilineal. No secondary extraneous method is applied to support the kinship system.

The second difference is both *functional* and *sociological*. Because of the structural 'defect' of the bilateral system in corporate group formation, except for the elementary family, the concept of continuity dies away when the elementary family vanishes during its normal cycle. But the Lodagaba dual unilineal system, on both sides, lasts through time, and a sense of continuity, depth and permanence is shown in their common interest in land, in their earth shrine and ancestor cult. The Kalinga family transmits land to its offspring, and this is regarded as parents' property, while with the Lodagaba it is the ancestors' property that is inherited.

In the bilateral system the concept of the mother's brother is non-existent; he is just a kinsman. This concept, however, is highly developed among the Lodagaba because the mother's brother is the visible link in one's female line.

Another difference is in the system of marriage. The Kalinga, in order to fashion a group that may last, encourage marriage between second cousins, who in another context are regarded as kin. The inheritance system, which invests both parents' property on the children or returns it to the kin, inhibits polygamy and encourages concubinage. The Lodagaba are usually polygynous and they practise clan exogamy; wife inheritance is common.

The Kalinga woman inherits land and also transmits it. The Lodagaba woman can neither inherit nor transmit land; she can only own and transmit movable wealth.

Lastly, the political and social organization of the Lodagaba is geared almost entirely to reflect their unilineal kinship structure. That of the Kalinga, on the other hand, depends partly on a kindred structure strengthened by other secondary structures. The Lodagaba society is unstratified while that of the Kalinga is. This is because achieved roles and statuses are significant in bilateralism. In Africa the Hausa and Lozi have a bilateral system.

II *The Patterns of Relationships Established in a Society with an Ambilineal System: the Malaita of the Pacific Ocean*

The Malaita Islanders of the Pacific Ocean were studied by H. I. Hogbin. They are predominantly of Melanesian stock. (In 1933 the population was 93 415, of which over 40 000 were concentrated on the island of Malaita and the others in other islands.) The island is about 1 500 square miles in area. There are two peoples occupying the island: the saltwater people who are chiefly fishermen, and the bush people who are agriculturalists, with whom we are dealing here.

These people reckon descent through either parent. This is called an ambilineal system. This system has not yet been recorded in Africa, but it occurs among some other inhabitants of Pacific islands.

They do not live in villages but in isolated homesteads occupied by three or four brothers or other close relatives and their families. A few large homesteads may contain as many as thirty persons, but the average number is between twelve and fifteen.

Husband and wife have separate dwellings and always sleep apart. The elementary family is the nucleus of the domestic unit which works in its garden and superintends its piggery. Pigs are important in Malaita culture.

The principal social unit is the district group of between thirty and eighty people who trace their descent from a common ancestor and regard ties through males and females as of equal importance. The district is a discrete territory with its boundaries demarcated by mountain ridges and streams; it varies in size from one to three square miles. The district comes together under its own leader to carry out communal work such as clearing land for new gardens, during the death of a priest, and avenging wrongs committed by outsiders. Also members take pride in their local traditions and refer to themselves by the name of the districts they occupy. Leadership is attained by a man who is able to give a big feast within the district. Thus men try to outdo one another, relying not only on their ability but also on their relatives, especially those living in the district.

All the members of a district group have at least one ancestor. The elders can enumerate their forebears through thirteen generations. The majority, however, reckon relationship only through males. For instance, of the five branches in Uala district, only one traces descent from a woman.

At death a person is buried in one of the sacred groves of the area where his house is situated, and his descendants offer sacrifices at intervals near the grave. Since the number of ancestors, from whom one is descended directly though males or through males and females, increases with every generation and since marriages outside the district are frequent, a person who wishes to worship all his forebears has to make sacrifices in many different places, in any of which he may reside. Hogbin does not suggest why people prefer to live in one place rather than in another, but he says that in practice people restrict the number of graves by choosing those near the districts in which they reside. He also adds that Malaita are patrilaterally biased and the general tendency for all is to reside where one's father formerly resided. The exception would be some crisis when one might decide to join one's mother's relatives. From the system of leadership I conclude that, apart from the graves, the factors that finally influence a person to settle in a district are twofold: the number of close relatives who will be ready to cooperate at the initial stage; and the availability of suitable land for cultivation and pig-keeping. An individual is related through his progenitors to the persons living in all the places where he has the potential right of residence.

An individual can have up to two hundred relatives genealogically related, but these never form an effective group. They are people to whom one owes certain obligations and from whom one can claim certain rights. Of these people the most effective ones are those who live in the same neighbourhood in a district.

A person is allowed to marry anyone except his first cousins and those within the immediate family circle. In about two-thirds of the marriages, the partners come from different districts. If this is the case, the sons have the right to erect their dwellings and make gardens in the territories of either of their parents.

It should be clear that the Malaita do not have a unilineal system. Firth would call their system ambilineal as distinct from bilateral, whilst Murdock would classify it as ambilineal, a type of cognatic system in which the bilateral and what he calls the quasi-matrilineal and quasi-patrilineal fall in the same class. Firth puts forward seven major criteria normally involved in the demarcation of descent groups whether unilineal or not. Of the seven he maintains that four of these, when considered with regard to their operational significance, provide closure for bilateral descent group membership and help to create a typology of bilateral groups. These four are generation depth, lineality, point of attachment and rule of residence.

The Malaita system does not limit the generation depth. What is necessary is the ability to remember that one's ancestor ever lived in an area, and this should be socially recognized by the district's chronicle. Once this is done, a person may claim land for dwelling and cultivation and in return he worships the spirit of his ancestor buried in the near-by grove and keeps the laws of the district. A person often lives near his father's relatives, and this is convenient because it means that when moving to a new district the relatives there will vouch, in case of argument, that his forebears had lived and died there and were buried in one of the groves. The limit in this case, therefore, is the memory.

Malaita genealogy, apart from being paternally biased, is in theory multilineal. But in practice a person can only dwell either with those he is related to on the father's side, or with those he is related to on the mother's side. This gives it its ambilineal nature.

The point of attachment is primarily through males, but may be through females. This is also optative in that effective membership is only possible in one at any given moment. However, choice does not exclude someone from the other group.

The Malaita district is undoubtedly a descent group. Whether it is fictional or not does not matter; what does matter is that the people accept that they are descended from a common ancestor. This concept of common descent gives them cohesion and purpose. Firth's term 'optative' does not reveal the implications in Malaita's ambilineality, so I will adopt Murdock's term 'optative non-exclusive'. It is more suitable because some ambilineal systems do not permit plural membership once choice of affiliation has been made. That of Malaita does allow active membership in one and passive and potential membership in the other. In other words, residence activates membership while absenteeism inactivates membership but does not make it lapse or close. The districts may be called major ramages while the sub-sections of very large districts may be called minor ramages. These ramages are not kindreds, for they are not composed of persons related to a particular individual bilaterally, that is, they are not ego-oriented but ancestor-based.

Murdock suggests that non-unilineal kin groups should be classified as cognatic under which heading he distinguishes three types, as mentioned above. He further differentiates bilateral from ambilineal by assigning to each certain criteria. To the ambilineal type he assigns the following characteristics: ambilineal descent groups, monogamy, extension of marriage prohibitions to all second as well as first cousins, avuncular terminology of the Hawaiian type, and ambilocal residence with matrilocality or patrilocality dominant.

If the Malaita material is examined using these criteria, it turns out that the system falls within the classification of ambilineality since filiation in each successive generation is acquired through either parent. Membership in districts or ramages is optative non-exclusive. Monogamy seems to be the rule with few exceptions. A person can marry anyone beyond the range of his first cousins. Sibling terms are applied to cousins and the kinship terminology is of the generation type. Residence is ambilocal but patrilocality is dominant.

Another interesting theory was that of Goodenough. He seems to have accepted Murdock's reconstructed characteristics of cognatic systems. He also suggested two propositions which are relevant. One was that in Malayo–Polynesian societies land ownership is vested in kin groups, thus meeting the problem of land distribution in the face of constant fluctuations in kin group size. Secondly, in areas where there is an abundance of land bilocal residence is no longer functionally advantageous and so unilocal residence rules can and do develop; the large islands of Melanesia provide conditions of this sort. Two implications are important here. One is that a non-unilineal system is one method of solving conflict arising from land scarcity, which is difficult to solve in unilineal systems. The other is that the Melanesian cases are transitional cases of development from non-unilineal to unilineal systems.

The Malaita are Melanesian with a population density of about forty persons per square mile including the saltwater people, and about twenty-six per square mile if only the bush people are considered. Before deciding whether a population is dense or sparse, several factors have to be taken into account such as the mode of subsistence and land usage, which we do not completely know for the Malaita. We can only say that twenty-six per square mile, in a culture where status is based on land produce and the ability to give it out generously, is relatively dense. Even then land disputes are not entirely uncommon, and do occasionally occur between districts. So here we have a relatively densely populated people with bilocal residence rules. This seems to fall outside Goodenough's scheme, and there is no evidence of a change taking place from bilateral to unilineal.

To sum up, the Malaita have an ambilineal descent system which emphasizes patrilocal residence, although within the patrilocal groups several choices are open to an individual apart from his matrilineal relatives. Residence, granted consanguinity, determines his right to use and own land. Filiation to any descent group is unrestricted at any given time. But the residence rule pins a person down to a definite area, and during that period he cannot effectively claim rights in other areas. Other factors, such as the number of close relatives and availability of suitable land around, apart from the location of the forefathers' graves, influence the choice of permanent residence. The districts are major ramages and are descent groups. Descent groups may therefore exist where a unilineal kin group does not form the core of the residence pattern. The relationship between land use and the descent system is obscure, but it cannot represent a phase in a change from bilateral to unilineal.

BIBLIOGRAPHY

SECTION I
Works consulted

BARTON, R. F. *The Kalingas, Their Institutions and Customs, Law* (Chicago: University of Chicago Press, 1949)

GOODY, J. R. 'Fission of Domestic Groups among the Lodagaba', in *The Developmental Cycle in Domestic Groups*, J. R. Goody (ed.) (Cambridge: Cambridge University Press, 1958)

—— *The Social Organization of the Lowiili* (London: HMSO, 1959)

Suggestions for further reading

FREEMAN, J. D. 'The Family System of the Iban of Bornea', in *The Developmental Cycle in Domestic Groups*, J. R. Goody (ed.) (Cambridge: Cambridge University Press, 1958)

GOODY, J. R. 'The Classification of Double Descent Systems', *Current Anthropology* (Feb. 1961)

HARRIS, R. 'The Political Significance of Double Unilineal Descent', *Journal of Royal Anthropological Society* (1962), 92

SECTION II

Works consulted

FIRTH, R. 'A Note on Descent Groups in Polynesia', *Man* (1957), b, 57 (2)

GOODENOUGH, W. H. 'A Problem of Malayo-Polynesian Social Organization', *American Anthropologist* (1955), 57

HOGBIN, H. I. *Experiments in Civilization, the Effects of European Culture on a Native Community of the Solomon Islands* (London: Routledge, 1939)

MURDOCK, G. P. 'Cognatic Forms of Social Organization' in *Social Structure in South-east Asia*, G. P. Murdock (ed.) (Viking Fund Publication in Anthropology, 29) (Chicago: Quadrangle Books 1960; London: Tavistock Publications, 1960)

——*Social Structure* (New York: Macmillan, 1949)

CHAPTER 8

Marriage and the Family, and their Stability

I *The Social Significance of the Transfer of Gifts at Marriage: the Nuer of the Southern Sudan*

Bride-price, marriage-payments, bride-purchase, etc., are all phrases which have been adopted at one time or another by observers to describe services and/or goods given by a groom to his bride's family before a union is socially recognized. It has by now been established that such a custom is not 'purchase' because an economic purchase ends after the final transaction without any residual obligation while, as will be shown, bride-gift transfer generates a never-ending current of obligations and counter-obligations.

The word bride-gift will be used here, instead of 'bride-wealth transfer', because the former more nearly denotes the residual obligations and the elaborate formalities that such gift-giving implies, while the latter exaggerates the quantity of the goods by calling it wealth, and the word 'transfer' blurs the behaviour patterns that accompany the giving.

The bride-gift has various characteristics, of which a few follow here. There must be a giving end and a receiving end and both of these may be groups of people. The acceptance of the gift by the receiving end means acceptance of certain obligations. Services and non-economic goods may form part and parcel of the things given. The giving of gifts and rendering of services may continue as long as the marriage continues. The gift is fixed by custom, but may fluctuate in economic terms depending on some factors such as the availability of suitable brides and change in people's attitude towards wealth. The birth of children tends to initiate new sets of relationships and behaviour patterns that go a long way to stabilize the union. Divorce strains and breaks the established patterns, so that part or whole of the gift has to be refunded; thus the new situation is socially and legally recognized. As Evans-Pritchard said, the bride-gift 'is a technique for creating new social relations of durability and frequency between persons . . . a mechanism by which the marriage group comes into being.' With these facts in mind we may now examine the significance of the transfer of bride-gift among the Nuer.

The ideal family for a Nuer is the polygynous type; outside the group kinship relations are translated into the idiom of cattle. What happens before a 'family' comes into being? The Nuer have several methods ranging from simple marriage to concubinage, and each differs from one another in the way the negotiation is backed by cattle and ritual or not. The forms of marriage among the Nuer and the importance of cattle transfer have been fully discussed in Chapter 6, Section I.

Apart from marriage, the situations created by divorce and homicide also throw light on our understanding of the significance of the bride-gift. Evans-Pritchard says that divorce is uncommon among the Nuer, and if it does happen it is usually at the preliminary stage of the marriage when the bride is still in her parents' home waiting for the birth of the first child.

If divorce takes place at an early stage when no child has been conceived, all the cattle except the cow of the 'hair' and 'skirt' must be returned, unless they have died a natural death. Wise parents never distribute the cattle until this stage has been passed. If the bride dies after the first birth, only the cattle due to her extra-family kinsmen are returned; if she dies after having two children no cattle are returned. If she leaves her husband after the birth of her first child the man may claim all his cattle less six, which gives him legal rights over the child, or he may allow her to bear children for him outside wedlock. The laws governing divorce and the returning of the gifts depend on the relationship between the families.

The situation created by homicide is relevant, because the ideal compensation is forty cattle, just as for marriage. These cattle are used for marrying a wife for the dead man – ghost marriage. If a Nuer kills his wife he is not expected to pay compensation. Evans-Pritchard does not say what happens if a wife kills the husband, but we can suppose that she does not pay compensation, since she can stay and have children for the name of her dead husband.

Some conclusions may be drawn about the significance of the bride-gift at marriage. It is an effective machinery for creating new relationships and acquiring new statuses and roles whereby new patterns of behaviour are set up between two unrelated families. The change of roles and statuses disturbs the existing structure; the bride-gift tends to establish a new equilibrium by giving confidence to the losing end.

Several rights are transferred to the husband with the bride-gift. These are rights *in genetricem*, that is, rights over her sexual, domestic and economic services. The wife gets rights of co-residence in the man's lineage. The transfer of these rights is expressed and symbolized in the goods given. For example, the cow of the 'hair' and 'skirt' refers to sexual rights; the mother's spear refers to domestic services. The bride-gifts are backed by ritual ceremonies in which the solidarity and unity of the lineage are expressed.

Marriage can never be created and legalized without the giving of cattle, for this legitimizes the children. That is why all children conceived outside wedlock legally belong to the *pater* and not to the *genitor*. When the customary gift-giving is completed a jural stability is established. The conjugal stability may be shaky but it becomes stronger after the birth of the first child and subsequent children. Divorce may happen before the birth of the first child, but it is unlikely afterwards. The birth of children must be one of the stabilizing factors in Nuer marriage. Thus the most significant feature of the bride-gift is the way it legitimizes children in a given lineage. This is clear from ghost marriage, widow concubinage and unmarried woman concubinage.

Finally, jural stability is achieved by the bride-gift, so there can be no conjugal stability without first legal or jural stability in Nuer society. Both jural and conjugal stability can lapse at almost the same time. However, jural stability can continue long after conjugal stability has collapsed, as is shown in married woman concubinage. It is common practice for paternal kinsmen to exert some pressure on both sides to help to stabilize a marriage.

II *The Problems of Residence and Family Authority in a Matrilineal Descent System: the Mayombe, the Bemba, the Yao of Central Africa*

Matrilineal descent is a system whereby descent is reckoned through females. It also implies the transmission of authority, inheritance and succession through females. It does not, however, imply that females do inherit, although in some cases females can inherit where no brother or sister's son exists. Immediately a male appears in the next generation he inherits, so that it may be said that female inheritors are 'trustees'.

The Bantu of Central Africa have a matrilineal descent system which makes them distinct from other Bantu. They believe that blood passes through the woman and not through the man, therefore it is the duty of every woman to bear children for her lineage, in most cases through a legally constituted husband.

The Mayombe are Bantu inhabiting the Lower Congo. They are small-scale agriculturalists farming fertile land with considerable forest wealth. (The population density was twenty per square mile at the time of the study.) Small stock such as goats and sheep are kept and used for the marriage gift. In the past there were three social strata in the society: chiefs, freemen and slaves.

The Mayombe also believe that blood passes through the woman to her children. The children therefore belong to their mother's matrilineal clan. The people live in small local groups called *Muumu*, that is villages, each of which is composed of a group of brothers with their wives, widowed sisters, sister's sons and unmarried daughters. A number of villages occupying a district is called a *Dinkanda* which is exogamous. Two or more *Dinkanda* combine to form a *Muila* which is an exogamous clan. The Mayombe have nine clans.

Any free-born Mayombe belongs to his or her matrilineal group. Slave children used to belong to their father's matrilineage. Descendants of immigrants attached to a chief are of the chief's clan.

After giving the bride-gift (valued in 1948 at £9), a man takes his wife to his matriclan without further delay. It takes a man about six years or more to accumulate the bride-gift, but normally he is aided by his matrilineage. Since children of the union are of the wife's clan, it seems that the bride-gift gives a husband rights over the sexual services of, and virilocal residence with, the wife. A woman in her husband's village is looked upon as a stranger and she is paid for any work she does that is outside the customary prescription. She contributes to her own lineage by sending her quota to her brother from time to time. The husband has rights over the children before 'puberty', but the mother's brother may remove them at any time. When the children are adolescent they go to live with their mother's senior brother who has 'totalitarian' authority over them.

The family structure of a village is composed of brothers and their wives who are strangers, sister's sons and daughters, and old widowed sisters. This is a corporate group owning land in common and other liquid assets under the administration and jurisdiction of the mother's senior brother.

The question of residence and authority is solved in three ways. Marriage is virilocal, for the giving of the bride-gift by the husband allows him to claim sexual and domestic services and the co-residential rights of the wife. However, rights *in genetricem* and some of the wife's economic services are claimed by the wife's senior brother for the matrilineage. So a husband has limited rights and control over the wife. The children are sent back to their mother's brother at adolescence, but before then they are fairly under the control of their father. The Mayombe boy in his life cycle has two residences the villages of his father and his mother's brother. The Mayombe girl has three: the villages of her father, her mother's brother and her husband. The Mayombe are a typical example of a matrilineally organized society with virilocal marriage and authority fully vested, with few exceptions, in the mother's brother.

Another group is the Bemba of Zambia. They have a matrilineal system. Their economy is poor and soil is infertile. They practise shifting cultivation on a basis of four to seven years, at the end of which they shift their village to another site. This and several other factors affect the stability of the family composition and that of the village as a whole. (The population density was four persons per square mile in 1934.) They have no inheritable wealth, so that the economic importance of the mother's brother to his sister's children is minimal.

A Bemba man gives a series of gifts and services to his parents-in-law over a long period. He lives with his wife in her matriclan and after three or four years, when the total bride-gift has amounted to £3 (1934 figure), he may remove his wife to his matriclan. However the wife, or even her parents, may resist this. In practice, the ability to remove one's wife depends on the success of the marriage and the personality of the individual.

A Bemba man starts his marital life in his wife's village. If he is able to remove his wife and gain sufficient dependants to convince his chief to grant him permission to start a new community, he becomes the head of that group. If he is unable, he goes to his matrilineage or to his father. A Bemba village is made up of a father and his wife, his daughters and their husbands, his grand-daughters, widowed sisters, and their daughters and husbands.

Among the Bemba, residence is at first uxorilocal, then virilocal or neo-local, depending on the influence of the husband. The authority and rights over the wife fluctuate with the type of residence he is able to establish, and residence is influenced by ecology and the agricultural cultivation practices.

It seems that a Bemba father has little authority or control in the early years of his marriage, but that he gains more in later years. The authority over the children is divided between the father and the mother's brother, depending on residence. On the whole, the maternal uncles' rights are indisputable although they find it difficult to attract their sisters' sons, because they have no tangible wealth for them to inherit except status, which they can obtain even if they are residing away from them. In this respect a Bemba child contrasts strongly with a Mayombe child who is attracted by his mother's brother's wealth.

The Bemba girl during her lifetime has one or two residences : her father's and later her husband's. Her brothers are separated during manhood in their quest for a wife and may never join again.

The Yao of Malawi were formerly traders who traded with the Arabs for two hundred years. At present they are farmers and live in dispersed settlements. (The population density in the 1930s was 19–53 persons per square mile.)

A Yao belongs to his matriclan. Marriage has to be validated by two witnesses, and it seems as if marriage gifts and services are not of much importance. A Yao senior brother lives in his wife's village until he is called by his sisters to be the village head. He is installed head of a sororal family after a ceremony. He takes his wife with him to his village, so that marriage becomes virilocal. He is in charge of his wife's children, his sister's children and his sisters. He treats his children according to the customary code. In the past when men were great traders and always absent from home, the eldest sister had great authority over the family, although her brother was the caretaker and owner of the village.

In this society marriage is uxorilocal for younger brothers, and uxorilocal and virilocal for elder brothers. Since the core of a residential unit is an elder brother as the head man, his sisters and their husbands and married daughters, it is clear that the influence of the mother's brother is overwhelming.

A Yao boy has two residences in his life cycle: with his matrilineage and with his wife's matrilineage. A girl has only one residence throughout her life, her matrilineage.

The residence problem of any matrilineal descent system arises from the application and recognition of descent through the women and at the same time the encouragement of the rule of exogamous marriage. The matrilineage attempts to keep the loyalty of sisters and their children within the group and at the same time stipulates that the husband should be from another group. All this results in problems of residence and clashes of authority between the husband and the mother's brother. These problems may be minimized by cross-cousin marriage (or slave marriage, formerly) as among the Mayombe.

The Mayombe adopted the fraternal extended family system to solve these problems. By this, sisters are married out and children returned to their lineage at puberty. Thus virilocal marriage makes it possible for brothers to live together and exercise full authority over the community except for their wives and children.

The Yao and Bemba have adopted a method of combining virilocal and uxorilocal marriages and by so doing the authority of the father and the mother's brother ebbs and flows. It is important to stress that the system whereby a senior brother is made the head man of the village results in clashes between brothers, which may lead to the disintegration of the village.

It may be noted here that other matrilineal societies have solved the same problem by various methods. Thus the Nayar of Malabar eliminate the role of father, and the Hopi of North America adopt the visiting brother system.

III *Marriage Stability in a Small-Scale Society: the Fulani of Northern Nigeria*

According to Stenning, among the pastoral Fulani there are various ways a family can come into being: by betrothal marriage, contract marriage, gift marriage, widow inheritance and married woman concubinage. The development of a simple family begins when an infant boy is born and given a name and a calf is set aside for him. At ten he is circumcized, and becomes a herd boy. More calves are allocated to him as he grows up. Since he has the nucleus of a herd and every herd must have its dairy woman, he is betrothed to an infant girl who should preferably be his patrilateral cross-cousin or parallel cousin. This marriage is marked by the transfer to the bride's parents of two bulls, of which one is slaughtered and meat distributed within the two lineage groups concerned.

The new bride joins her husband who dwells in his father's homestead. She goes back to her father's home for the birth of the first child and on her return after two years she takes up residence in this distinct family with a distinct homestead and herd. If the husband marries another wife during this period a ceremonial expression of conflict is held in which the first wife whips the new wife. The state of affairs between the two wives and their children is that of constant jealousy and tension which may end in the breaking up of one of the marriages.

The new family depends on the parent family for about five years or more, because it has not sufficient cattle and also because the father controls the loan and aids which are channelled through agnatic ties. When the last son inherits the last cattle of his father, the parents retire to his homestead till death. They are at this last stage economically and socially dead.

It is evident that at an early stage the position of the new family is shaky and may never be formed at all if no children are born. Even when it is formed it needs the support of parents and the agnatic lineage group for a considerable length of time, especially in time of disaster. The kinship ties are strengthened by the need to support the family and the herd. The unit of cooperation is the agnatic lineage group. (For more information about the lineage arrangements, see Chapter 16, Section I.) This group consists of householders, which arrange the marriages of their daughters, for the group is endogamous.

The settlement pattern of the pastoral Fulani is intimately connected with their habitat and mode of life. (For a detailed description, see Chapter 16, Section I.)

Contract marriage has several meanings, but among the pastoral Fulani, it describes a marriage made by a man on his own responsibility; or a marriage in which the partners have previously undergone betrothal marriage with others; or a marriage in which they are not virgins. Contract marriage is not as ceremonious as betrothal marriage and the partners are not usually in the same order of clansfolk as in betrothal marriage. A bull may be transferred and some payments made to settle any previous marriage of the bride.

In gift marriage the bride-gift is not given, although the marriage is solemnized by Muslim rites. The bride is given as a gift to the bridegroom who may give a return gift (not a bride-gift) as a sign of gratitude. Gift marriage has a double function: to give security to those who are at a disadvantage in marital affairs, for instance, a girl pregnant before marriage; or it may be a form of tribute, by which a Fulani seeks security in a political unit to which he is a newcomer, or for which he wishes to gain some benefits.

Widow inheritance depends on the rights of the lineage group in the fertility of its women. A young brother is bound to take over the wife or wives of his dead brother, even for a short period. Other eligible kinsmen of the dead man may make their claim if the brothers are unwilling or if he has none. There is no feast and no marriage payment made. If a widow declines to be inherited, she may marry a man of her own choice and in this case, if she is childless, the senior claimant in her dead husband's lineage may claim cattle equivalent to those slaughtered at the various stages of the betrothal marriage. Whether a widow chooses to be inherited or not depends upon her age, the number, age and sex of her children, and her past relationship with members of her husband's group.

Finally, there is 'escape' marriage, which may throw some light on to the nature of their marriage and its stability. This marriage is one in which the previous union has not been properly dissolved by any authority or by payment of compensation or by a declaration of release. A woman or a betrothed girl may leave her husband and marry someone else without any formal divorce. The new husband takes her off to a new home far away from the first husband's house, slaughters a cow, and the matter is ended. In their eyes this is a new and valid marriage, like a marriage arranged by betrothal. It is a mechanism for avoiding betrothal marriage, and in this respect may be regarded as a safety-valve which helps to reduce the tension and strain within the family and lineage group resulting from betrothal marriage.

Furthermore, the woman may quite possibly grow tired of her new husband after a time, and either return to her first husband or take a third in the same way as she took the second. There is no limit to the number she can take except that her action may soon turn public opinion against her, and sooner or later she will have no suitors.

The Fulani hold the view that in the past divorce was rare and that it is common and easier now. Their attitude is that marriage, like other social relationships, must be carried on with patience and fortitude. The most common grounds for the divorce of a woman are: real or assumed barrenness; incompatibility with her co-wives; insubordination to her husband; acts which bring her into public disrepute; adultery with a kinsman. The common grounds for the divorce of a man are: a husband's sale of cattle to buy luxurious goods or to curry favour with chiefs or officials; long absences on unnecessary visits; inconsiderate choices of camp-sites at long distances from water supplies or markets; favouring a co-wife; and meanness. On the whole men can initiate divorce more easily than women, because men are able to manipulate loopholes in their institutions more effectively than women. Also women are more dependent on their lineage group than men.

The stability and the easiness to obtain divorce in the types of marriages considered above may be summed up thus:

TABLE 3

Types of marriage, stability and divorce among the Fulani

Types of marriage	Stability scale	Divorce rate
Betrothal	Stable	Very low earlier Low now
Widow	Stable	Low
Contract	Fairly stable	High
Gift	Unstable	High
'Forced' marriage	Very unstable	Very high

It is evident from the above that the most stable type of marriage is the betrothal, followed by the widow marriage, which is virtually based on betrothal marriage. The questions before us are: why are there such wide variations in Fulani marriage types? Why is betrothal marriage more stable than 'escape' marriage? Why is there a regular gradation in terms of stability? Finally, can the reasons deduced here be applicable to other societies, and if so to what extent?

The significant thing about Fulani marriage is the nature of the groups that contract the marriage. In betrothal marriage the contract is between two lineages with their heads as chief witnesses to the marriage. The bride and bridegroom are subsequently under constant pressure from these effective groups to keep the terms of the contract. The marriage gift is shared only within these two closed groups and thus they accept certain moral and legal responsibilities. For example, if the female spouse is dissatisfied and wants a divorce, she has only one effective group to appeal to, which is her lineage group, which really negotiated the marriage. Her lineage, of course, is committed to see that the marriage is successful, and so will put up a strong opposition to her wishes. The group will also make very genuine efforts to get the male spouse's lineage group to bring pressure to bear on the male spouse to persuade him to relax. Thus sometimes the matter is settled amicably. But where the conciliatory attempts fail or are prolonged the female spouse has only one alternative, which is to leave her husband and contract an 'escape' marriage. This has only become possible in recent times since the lineage group has lost its control because of political, religious and even economic factors.

As noted above, the contract entered into in the other forms of marriages is between individuals or between an individual and a lineage group. The absence of lineage groups acting as watchdogs over the marriages exposes them to the vagaries of individual temperaments. Hence 'escape' marriage, which is virtually a marriage contract entered into by two individuals without involving any group, is characterized by instability.

Hopen in his book about the Gwandu Fulani points out that they maintain that when most people are betrothed to and married their cousins, there is much solidarity between siblings of both sexes, because of the marriages of their children; and between husband and wife there is also affection, because of the kinship of their parents. Since parents of both spouses live in the same village they intervene in the disputes between spouses and so try to preserve the conjugal and jural bond of the marriages.

To sum up, the stability of marriage among the pastoral or cattle Fulani depends on the following. One is the fulfilment of the purpose for which marriage is contracted. This is tied up with the birth of a child and the viability of the family at its initial stage. Another is the nature of the contract, that is, what groups arrange and support the contract. If it is a person-to-person contract the marriage is liable to be shaky and unstable. If it is between groups, then the stability of the marriage depends on the constitution and structure of the groups. Thus two effective groups tend to give an optimum stability to marriage.

Other economic and political factors modify the effectiveness of the marriage group. The bride-gift may or may not have a significant part to play in stabilizing marriage. In societies like that of the Fulani where the marriage gift is essential before the marriage can be socially recognized, its function is mainly to create the marriage and legitimize the children of the union. A bride may in fact delay her divorce because she has no means of refunding the gifts, but in this case jural instability has already set in, because the marriage bond has started to break, and separation may ensue. The refund of the bride-gift sounds the end of the marriage, that is, it represents the legal form of what we call divorce.

BIBLIOGRAPHY

SECTION I

Works consulted
EVANS-PRITCHARD, E. E. *Kinship and Marriage among the Nuer* (Oxford: Clarendon Press, 1961)
SCHNEIDER, D. 'A Review of Kinship and Marriage among the Nuer', in *American Anthropology* (1953)

Suggestions for further reading
EVANS-PRITCHARD, E. E. 'The Social Character of Bride-Wealth', *Man* (1934), 194
—— Correspondence on 'Bride-Wealth and the Stability of Marriage' in *Man* (1953), 75, 122, 223, 279; *Man* (1954), 96, 97, 153

SECTION II
Works consulted
RICHARDS, A. I. 'Some Types of Family Structure amongst the Central Bantu' in *African Systems of Kinship and Marriage*, A. R. Radcliffe-Brown and D. Forde (eds.) (London: Oxford University Press, 1950)

Suggestions for further reading
FORDE, D. 'Hopi Agriculture and Land Ownership', *J.R.A.I.* (1931), 41
FORTES, M. 'Kinship and Marriage among the Ashanti', in *African Systems of Kinship and Marriage* A. R. Radcliffe-Brown and D. Forde (eds.) (London: Oxford University Press, 1950)
GOUGH, K. 'Changing Kinship Usages in the Setting of Political and Economic Change among the Nayars of Malabar', *J.R.A.I.*, (1952), 82
MALINOWSKI, B. *Sex and Repression in Savage Society* (London: Routledge & Kegan Paul, 1953)
TITIEV, M. 'The Influence of Common Residence on the Unilateral Classification of Kindred', *American Anthropologist* (1943), 45: 5111–30

SECTION III
Works consulted
HOPEN, C. E. *The Pastoral Fulbe Family of Gwandu* (London: Oxford University Press, 1959)
STENNING, D. J. *Household Viability among the Pastoral Fulani*, in Cambridge Papers in Social Anthropology, No. 1, J. R. Goody (ed.) (London: Cambridge University Press, 1958)
—— *Savannah Nomads* (London: Oxford University Press, 1959)

Suggestions for further reading
EVANS-PRITCHARD, E. E. 'The Social Character of Bride-Wealth', *Man* (1934), 194
GOUGH, E. K. 'The Nayars and the Definition of Marriage', *J.R.A.I.* (1959), 89
LEACH, E. R. 'Aspects of Bride-Wealth and Marriage Stability among the Kachin and Lakhar', in *Rethinking Anthropology* (London: Athlone Press, 1961)
Correspondence on 'Bride-Wealth and the Stability of Marriage' in *Man* (1953), 75, 122, 223, 279; *Man* (1954), 96, 97, 153

CHAPTER 9

Some Problems Arising
from Kinship Studies

I *The Nature of Double Unilineal Descent:*
the Kpe (Bakweri) of Southern Cameroon

The dispute about the character of double unilineal descent was spearheaded by Jack Goody, and R. Harris rejected some of his conclusions. The argument died down many years ago, but here I shall re-examine the issues raised by both Goody and Harris in the light of the Kpe ethnographic material, because the Kpe have a variant of double unilineal descent which has not been considered and because Goody and Harris were both putting forward general characteristics of double unilineal system.

Goody started with definitions: descent could be defined as eligibility for membership in kin groups, and the term 'corporate' could describe those unilineal descent groups within which property is inherited. By descent group he meant a unilineal group of kin identifiable by a relevant technical name or term in the native language. (If such a name or term did not exist, he asserted that either an error in ethnographic recording had been made or that such a group had never existed, in which case the ethnographer had created something which was non-existent. This view should not be taken seriously, because we all know that not everything that exists has a name and not everything that has a name really exists. For instance, atomic energy has always existed but it has only recently been named, and it is doubtful whether flying saucers and witches do exist.)

When membership in two sets of corporate unilineal groups is derived from a person's parents, then a case of double descent emerges, which is typical of the Yakö system. But if one of these two descent groups lacks corporate status then it is a case of a unilineal system combined with a complementary descent group. Goody distinguishes between a descent group and a corporate descent group by maintaining that the latter is a property-holding unit while the former is not. To him property-holding is what makes a group corporate.

Goody classifies descent systems as follows:

1. Unilineal systems with complementary descent groups.
   (a) Patrilineal unilineal descent groups with:
      i Unnamed complementary uterine groups (technical term only), for instance, the Tallensi.
      ii Named complementary uterine groups, for instance, the Lowiili.
   (b) Matrilineal unilineal descent groups with :
      i Unnamed complementary agnatic groups.
      ii Named complementary agnatic groups.
2. Double descent systems, where both groups are property-holding corporations.

According to this classification (which Edmund Leach might brand as butterfly collecting) the difference between the Tallensi and Lowiili is that the Lowiili have a named uterine unilineal descent group while the Tallensi have an unnamed one referred to only by the use of the technical term. This is not a correct impression. The ethnographic records of these two peoples show without ambiguity that a Lowiili acts and thinks in terms of being a member of two unilineal descent groups, while a Tallensi thinks and acts in terms of being a member of a unilineal descent group with due consideration for his mother's patrilineage. This is the basic ideological and structural difference, not the fact that one is named and the other unnamed. A classification should reflect all possible characters, and no single one should be used prejudicially. I think this is the chief weakness of Goody's classification.

Goody also compared the Lowiili and the Lodagaba. The differences he described do not warrant the classification of the Lowiili as patrilineal and the Lodagaba as having double descent. Both are variants of double descent systems. The differences are in fact valid, but they only demonstrate that even in a double descent system variations exist, just as they do in patrilineal descent groups. Thus, compared with Igbo patrilineal descent group, the Fulani patrilineal descent group is not a property-owning and inheriting group. In spite of this difference in inheritance no one classifies the Fulani system as different from the Igbo. Both have adopted the patrilineal system, but they apply it in different ways; for example, they differ in their methods of inheritance. If Goody's criteria were accepted, the Fulani and the Igbo would be classified differently, which Goody might be reluctant to accept.

R. Harris defined 'corporate' in the same way as Radcliffe-Brown, thus giving it a wider range of meaning. She examined various societies with double unilineal descent of the Yakö type, and arrived at six major conclusions, as follows. In societies with double unilineal descent there is a lack of a high degree of lineage segmentation, which results in the sharing of political roles between two cross-cutting descent systems. The matrilineal ties bind together either large settlements or a number of settlements, and since the small dispersed matrilineages are held responsible for its members' delicts it is easy to apply penal sanctions to individuals. The principal of matrilineal responsibility leads to the dispersed group being recognized as the blood compensation group; this reduces the possibilities of conflict in the society. Problems of order are raised since two or more blood compensation groups exist within the same community. Hence, peace-priest institutions are essential features. The matrilineal inheritance of movable property combines with the sense of solidarity within the residential groups and encourages village endogamy, which raises serious problems for peaceful relationships between settlements unless it is counterbalanced by other factors. Double unilineal descent leads to a political system which appears to be remarkably effective in controlling disputes over a narrow social range, but carries the seeds of conflict in wider spheres.

Harris decried the narrowness of Goody's definition of corporate and suggested that classification according to the roles played by the complementary kin groups in societies would be more useful than classification based on patterns of inheritance and on whether or not the complementary groups were named or unnamed.

Before examining Goody's and Harris's conclusions in the light of Kpe material, I shall first proceed to describe briefly the nature of the economy, descent, inheritance, political and social organizations of Kpe (Bakweri).

The Kpe are one of the coastal Bantu peoples of Southern Cameroon. They live in small dispersed villages varying in size from about fifteen people in some to about a thousand in others. They are agriculturalists growing coco-yams, cassava, maize and yam, which is a secondary crop.

A village consists of several small patrilineages claiming descent from a common ancestor who founded the village. However, members of the patrilineages do not live in a compact settlement, but are dispersed all over their territory. Village land is divided among the patrilineages, and so each patrilineage is a land-owning unit whose members – for fear of witchcraft which is supposed to operate within the kin group – prefer to live away from one another. Some villages are large enough to have quarters or wards, and each ward is based on a founding patrilineal kin group with other persons such as sister's children or mother's sister's children.

Ardener classifies the Kpe kinship system as one of double descent. Marriage is virilocal, so that the patrilineages are localized and named, while members of the matrilineages are dispersed and unnamed. Individuals who claim to have a common ancestress belong to the same matrilineage. The matrilineages are unnamed and their composition depends upon the memories of their oldest members. An old man knows the names of the living members of his matrilineage and in some cases the shallow genealogy that links them up. Since all have accepted the principle of matrilineage, what the old man has to do is to send for them. (Why he does this will be explained later.)

The Kpe matrilineage is also an inheritance group but of a very limited type. Its real function and significance to a Kpe is not its political function but its ritual function, that of the fertility ritual, which concerns only members of the matrilineages. While every man or woman belongs to a patrilineage and a matrilineage, it is also felt that a woman belongs more closely to her matrilineage and a man more to his patrilineage. This is another type of variation in a double unilineal descent group based on sex dichotomy.

Kpe inheritance notion and practices state that the most acceptable heirs are the oldest son, a son, a brother, a sister's son, a daughter. The matrilineal relatives receive what is called *Intingo* which is a share of the goods of the deceased according to the individual's contributions at the burial feasts. It follows that *Intingo* is not given to those who do not contribute. There is no notion of movable or immovable property among the Kpe, so that a sister's son may be given a piece of land as part of his *Intingo* if he lives in the territory of the patrilineage of the deceased mother's brother.

The responsibility of holding the fertility rite lies with the matrilineage. The rite is held in the house of a senior male member where a collection to meet the expenses of the rite is made. This rite is performed if many children of the matrilineages die. The people are summoned by a diviner who states that a woman of the matrilineage has seen a shining bangle in her farm and has said nothing about it. Once the rite has been carried out, the bangle remains in the matrilineage indefinitely in the custody of a senior man of the lineage or a woman who is expected to be a peaceful person. When deaths of children again occur, people congregate again to perform the rite of the bangle. This rite is the major joint activity of the matrilineage, and without it the matrilineage would have no significance for the Kpe.

This is where Goody's theory crumbles. The people call themselves Kpe, and they believe that they have double unilineal descent. They refer to their patrilineage by name and their matrilineage without a name. They speak of the *Litumba* of their mother and the *Litumba* of their father. *Litumba* means lineage. The residential and land-owning units are the patrilineages. Inheritance is within the patrilineage and by contributing something to the burial feasts of members one can inherit something matrilineally also (*Intingo*). The matrilineage members are never keen about *Intingo* for various social reasons and because it involves duties and obligations. One may inherit land matrilineally provided one lives in the territory of the patrilineage concerned. The matrilineage members never fail to come together to perform the fertility ritual because of course everybody wants their child to live and everybody wants more children.

Among the Yakö (Goody's classical example of a double unilineal descent system) the property-inheriting group is only limited to the matrilineage. The matriclans do not have any property that is inheritable but their priests play a very significant role in Yakö political and social organization. A Yakö identifies himself equally with his clan and his lineage. Thus membership of a clan in one village is a passport to other villages, for matriclans in one village are held to correspond with matriclans in others. Furthermore, the importance of property inheritance in the matrilineage is of the same significance as the performance of joint activities during rituals, funerals, homicide and marriage. In short, property inheritance is only a facet of the total activity ascribed to the matrilineage. Goody emphasized inheritance in order to show that a part is greater than a whole. However it can be seen that even his classical example of the 'corporate' among the Yakö does not hold, and when applied to the Kpe it completely falls apart.

The political unit among the Kpe is the village which has a chief called 'father of the village' decended from the founder of the village through the most senior branch in the patrilineal line. In bigger villages with quarters, each quarter has its own head descended from the most senior paternal line from its own founder.

The village chief who is the leader of the village elders of the age-set called *Vambaki* makes laws and decides cases. This age-set enforces the laws made through the junior age-set. Murder is punished by hanging and other offences by fines. Where the author of a crime is in doubt or the crime unwitnessed, oath or ordeal is administered to suspects. The village chief has no power but that given to him by public opinion and the mandate given to him by the elders and other responsible men of the upper age-set of the village.

Each village is autonomous but alliances do occur between neighbouring villages. Villages do fight one another and peace is negotiated. Information about inter-village politics is meagre.

As Harris said in her analysis about double descent, there is a lack of high degree lineage segmentation among Kpe. The lineages are shallow with a depth of between only four and six generations, but this does not result in sharing of political roles between two cross-cutting descent systems. Instead we have the development of chiefship.

The binding effects of the matrilineal ties may contribute to the keeping of peace, since members are dispersed. Hence the chief, although without much authority, is able to command support from his matrikin men and women who are dispersed all over the village. This is not based on any notion of matrilineal responsibility, as suggested by Harris. All crimes and offences are treated by the 'central authority', so to speak. Here the principle of individual responsibility supersedes the principle of lineage collective responsibility in the political sphere. That is, lineages are no longer responsible as a group for law and order, but instead the individual has to render account for any misdemeanour to the chief and his council of age-sets. This, however, does not imply that lineage members do not help one another in time of crisis.

In Kpe village endogamy is not encouraged by inheritance and group solidarity, as argued by Harris. There seems to be some intermarriage between neighbouring villages, while some others are endogamous. The degree of village exogamy depends on its friendliness and its descent relationship with other villages.

Even though the Kpe material seems scanty it reveals some important facts. Double descent and chiefship coexist. A lack of a high degree of lineage segmentation does not necessarily result in sharing of political roles between two cross-cutting descent systems, but it may be compensated for by a type of centralization as shown in the Kpe chiefship. Lineages can function separately on a different basis, one that is not political. Thus the Kpe matrilineages operate purely on a ritual basis ensuring the fertility of their members. This is in no way tied up with Kpe politics. Descent groups should be assessed not according to one or two criteria but using the sum total of their roles as shown by the people's ideology and behaviour.

Here the evolutionary history of double descent has not been examined. I am only interested in analysing how double unilineal descent groups operate *pari passu* with chiefship, and also in examining Goody's and Harris's views of double unilineal descent in the light of material from the Kpe. By so doing it is possible to clarify the nature of the variations in double unilineal descent. My observation is that there are many variants of double unilineal descent groups, just as there are many variants of matrilineal and patrilineal descent groups.

II *Difficulties Confronted in Attempts to Assess the Strength of Patrilineality or Matrilineality: the Tiv, Somali, Bedouin of Cyrenaica, Tallensi, Nuer*

The major difficulty in trying to assess the strengths of patrilineality or matrilineality is the absence of criteria with which to mark out and weigh the strengths we attribute to them. Radcliffe-Brown was the first to sense this difficulty, and he warned that there are many varieties of ways in which the unilineal principle may be used. It is therefore misleading to talk about matrilineal and patrilineal societies, *per se*, as was formerly the custom among anthropologists. This custom was a result of looking at kinship as an irreducible factor. This was postulated by Fortes, who said that every sociological problem presented by the Tallensi hinges on the lineage system which is the skeleton of their social structure, their politics, economy, ritual ideas and values.

Gluckman based his main argument about the stability of marriage on the hypothesis that father-right is weak in matrilineal societies and strong in patrilineal societies. Yet in these societies marked differences do exist in the degrees of the strength of patrilineality or matrilineality. Gluckman and Fortes, have, indeed, been criticized by anthropologists, for example, Leach, Worsley, M. G. Smith, Lewis and Goody, who have pointed out that kinship is not an irreducible factor, and other factors come into play in the ordering of human beings living in a society. Leach in particular has demonstrated how father-right can be shown to exist in both matrilineal and patrilineal societies.

Seven criteria are commonly used when referring to a society as patrilineal. These criteria will be applied below to five classic patrilineal societies – the Nuer, the Tiv, the Tallensi, the Somali pastoral nomads and the Bedouin of Cyrenaica – in order to see how useful they are.

The first criterion is the range of genealogy and the number of generations involved. The Tiv, Somali and Bedouin of Cyrenaica have each one single total pedigree embracing the whole society, while the Nuer and Tallensi do not. The

Tiv record about fifteen generations, the Somali about thirty, the Bedouin about twelve. Does this mean that the Somali are more patrilineal than the others? This cannot be decided until other criteria have been examined.

The second is the nature and level of segmentation. The Tiv are segmented into four major levels of which the most significant is the minimal *Tar* of between three and four generations deep. The Bedouin and Somali recognize three levels of segmentation. The Tallensi are divided up into two important segments, the major and maximal, of which the latter seems more important. The Nuer are split into minor, major and maximal; in some cases the maximal segment forms a clan, in other cases groups of maximal lineages form a clan. Several clans with one dominant one make up a tribe.

The third is the constancy of lineality. The Nuer adopt outsiders, like the Dinka, into their lineage. Also females are grafted on to what is supposed to be a patrilineal system. The Tiv and Tallensi similarly adopt strangers. Among the Bedouin assimilation of client lineages is not uncommon. The telescoping, fusion and fission of lineage, the adoption and grafting techniques all make lineal descent very inconsistent with the defined principle of patrilineality.

Fourth comes the extent and range of the corporate group. Among the Tiv the effective corporate group is the minimal *Tar*, three generations deep. Among the Nuer the village with a dominant lineage is the most effective corporate group. The Somali and Bedouin have the same segments, primary, secondary and tertiary, of which the tertiary is the most significant corporate group. The composition of these groups differs according to the cultures.

Fifthly, uniqueness of descent as a principle : in all these societies the main principle of recruitment and organization of the agnatic group is by birth and through males of the lineage. But this principle is not always used. Among the Tiv, adoption, residence, age-sets, market and territory are all taken into account in the social and political organization. Among the Nuer, territorial as well as clan and lineage principles are used in defining membership of a group. Among the Bedouin, common residence, association and clientage defined in kinship terms feature significantly. The Somali pasturalists cooperate on the basis of kinship and alliance; territory has little significance. Among the Tallensi territorial, ritual and lineage ties are essential in their political and social activities. In not one of these societies is patrilineality unique and exclusively used.

Political, ritual, economic and jural functions comprise another category. The Tiv minimal *Tar* is the largest political unit and the compound is the largest economic unit. Only members of the same *Tar* can use *Tsav* on one another. The Tiv do not have ancestor worship binding the whole *Tar*.

Among the Tallensi the largest political unit is the maximal lineage. Clans of different maximal lineages are ritually connected; similarly, maximal lineages that are not connected through kinship are connected ritually. Thus in some cases ritual transcends kinship relationships. Certain moral obligations also transcend kinship among the Tallensi; for instance, a father will drive away a child who has stolen from anyone, whether a stranger or not.

The Somali, Tiv and Bedouin do not have ancestor worship, but the Tallensi do. The Somali and Bedouin are Muslims and venerate ancestors in a form of a cult of Muslim saints. The Nuer believe in deities and sub-spirits almost corresponding to the levels of their segmentary lineage system.

Patrilineal principles are thus interwoven with political, ritual, economic and jural activities in varying degrees in these societies. It is difficult to judge on this basis which society is more patrilineal than the other.

6 *Wooden figure* (*Tiv, Mid-Benue, Nigeria*)

The degree of the unilineal bond in terms of rights and obligation is the final category. Among the Nuer the ties between siblings of opposite sex are not strong; hence women are grafted on to the lineage. Among the Tiv the ties are strong and are expressed in exchange marriage; women are rarely grafted on to the lineage. Even though women are not accorded full lineage status in terms of rights they have full recognition as members of the patrilineage. Among the Somali the jural rights binding a woman and her lineage even after marriage are strong.

Patrilineality and father-right may not even coincide as Gluckman suggests. If father-right or the strength of the sibling relationship is used as a measure of the strength of patrilineality, then some matrilineally organized societies might be termed patrilineal.

An examination of the Nri (Igbo), Yoruba, Benin and Ashanti centralized states shows that the principle of lineality can be manipulated in various ways in the distribution of political roles and status. Each society differs from the other in the application of the rules of lineality.

It seems futile to try to find criteria by which to assess patrilineality and matrilineality and thus to measure which society is more patrilineal or matrilineal than another. Each society should be studied in its own context, because the application of the principles of agnation and cognation differs in each society. The terms patrilineality and matrilineality should be used as shorthand to mean simply that the principles and ideology of each are effectively adhered to in specific major contexts.

III *The Scope and Limitations of Kinship and Non-Kinship Factors Operative in an African Society: the Hausa-Fulani of Zaria, Northern Nigeria*

Among the Hausa-Fulani of Zaria (studied by M. G. Smith), the general criteria for assuming political, ritual, social and economic identities have a very wide basis. It is difficult to group them into the classes 'ascribed' and 'achieved' because such a division ignores intermediate and overlapping cases. (For more information about class among the Hausa-Fulani, see Chapter 13.) But it is possible to isolate the classifications that are based on kinship and non-kinship factors, and those based on both factors, thus:

1. Classifications based on kinship factors:
   i. Ethnic group.
   ii. Descent and affinity.
2. Classifications based on both kinship and non-kinship factors:
   iii. Free man.
   iv. Slave.
   v. Eunuch.
   vi. Ex-slave.
3. Classifications based on non-kinship factors:
   vii. Sex.
   viii. Socio-political maturity.
   ix. Skill and ability.
   x. Clientage or vassalage.
   xi. Friendship or partnership.

The above classifications need to be explained in order to clarify how they became active in Hausa society.

i. Ethnic Group

Before the Jihad of 1804 three ethnic groups were important in Habe society. These groups were the Habe, the Fulanin-gida and non-Habe peoples who were grouped together as one although they were of heterogeneous composition. Habe as well as slaves and eunuchs who were non-Habe held political offices; of course slaves and eunuchs were socially downgraded. The Fulanin-gida were politically inactive at this period.

After the Jihad of 1804 the main ethnic groups involved in the politics of Hausa society were the Fulanin-gida who were the conquerors and rulers; the semi-settled Fulani and the cattle Fulani; and the conquered subjects, who were in the majority, represented by the Habe and the non-Habe slaves.

At the beginning of this century, the British established their rule over what is now called Nigeria. 'Pax Britannica' made communication easier and safer. The Igbo and Yoruba began to filter gently into northern Nigeria. Fifty years later these two ethnic groups were fully established in various parts of Hausa land including Zaria. The ethnic groups who became involved directly or indirectly in Hausa political, social, economic and ritual life were the Fulani, of whom the Fulanin-gida represented the minority, the aristocratic ruling class; the commoners who were Habe, descendants of ex-slaves; and groups from other parts of Nigeria such as the Igbo, Yoruba and Kanuri.

During the rule of the Fulani and the Anglo-Fulani, the ethnic group became an important criterion for assuming political office. Only those who were Fulani descendants and who were of the ruling class held top political offices. This was consistent with the Hausa-Fulani concept of *Sarauta*, office-holding, according to which political power and economic wealth went hand in hand. Power could only be maintained by controlling the machinery of appointments, promotions and dismissals from office. By controlling this machinery a ruler was able to eliminate from the political arena all his opponents and appoint only his kith and kin and his trusted allies.

ii. Descent and Affinity

These two principles are used in Hausa society in the appointment of political offices. Certain political, ritual and economic offices are hereditary in certain lineages. In Zaria three lineages of three Fulani clans have for the past 150 years produced the kings of Zaria. Some (former) vassal chiefships and some political offices are hereditary or quasi-hereditary in one or more lineages.

Some members of the Fulani ruling group marry Habe women and even have non-Muslim concubines, but the myth of Fulani 'blood purity' protects this group from what might be called 'social pollution', by obscuring or masking the social mobility resulting from these marriages.

Ruling lineages were allied to one another through marriage. Mallam Musa, who ruled 1804–21, gave his daughter to the Waziri of Sokoto. The grandchildren of this marriage later on settled in Zaria and vied for political offices. Musa also gave his daughters to the Limamin Juma'a of Zaria; and to his own *Galadima*, a Fulani from Kano; and to Abdulkerim, the leader of the Katsinawa dynasty. By negotiating these marriage alliances Musa not only brought into existence relations of solidarity between him and other powerful Fulani lineages but also introduced new elements into Zaria politics.

Since top political titles are reserved for those who can establish their descent from a ruling lineage or an aristocratic lineage, and since the Hausa can evoke the bilateral principles to establish their origin, an individual who has even the faintest relation with a ruling lineage will never fail to exploit the situation in order to gain political influence. It is here that the qualities of skill and ability are assets.

iii. Free man; Slave; Eunuch; Ex-Slave

In both the Habe and Habe-Fulani periods a person would be either a free man or a slave. One's descent determined one's social status. A man might be free by birth or by redemption from slavery.

Among slaves a distinction was made between native-born slaves and captives. Native-born slaves of the first generation were called *matankarai*. Traditionally, the slaves lived in a separate quarter called *Rinji* established by the owner, called *Iyayengiji*. The slaves shared in their master's ceremonial exchanges and worked on their master's farm. In turn their masters arranged marriages for them, protected them and fed them. After the abolition of slavery by Lugard, the relationship between ex-masters and ex-slaves continued in a form similar to that of the patron–client relationship. This was possible because the former relationship had been based on economic interdependence whereby the master supplied the land while the slaves supplied the labour.

Formerly slaves were given certain state offices, as were eunuchs. Thus one of the conditions of being eligible for a political identity was being a free man or a slave or a eunuch. Free men would only compete for offices allocated to free men, slaves for those allocated to slaves, and eunuchs for those allocated to eunuchs.

The bases of being a free man, a slave, a eunuch, or an ex-slave were not kinship or non-kinship factors, but both. Thus a man might be born a free person and later be captured into slavery. The children of such a slave would *ipso facto* be slaves by birth and kinship. Any children could through their own efforts ransom themselves and so be free men, or they could be adopted as sons or daughters by their master and by this process become free persons. Eunuchs were made from free persons or slaves.

iv. Sex

Before the Jihad, women held important offices in Habe political organization, for example, Amina was one of the queens of Zaria. Certain political offices, also, were set aside for royal women only. During the Fulani rule only two titles were allowed to exist. According to Islamic doctrine, women are regarded as legal minors and the institution of purdah marriage limits their activities to the confine of the compound, the *gida*, where they perform important social and economic functions. Hausa men dominate the political and ritual scene, and their women share certain economic activities almost equally with them, but in different settings.

The sexual dichotomy of roles in Hausa society is based mainly on Islamic teaching, but the deviations in the application of the doctrines are caused by historical and cultural factors.

v. Socio-Political Maturity

In Hausa society only adult males are recognized as legally responsible. This is in accordance with Muslim law. A full-grown man whose relationship to the state is mediated through other persons is a political minor however physically mature he may be. A compound head, *Mai-gida*, is politically and socially mature since he deals directly with the local ward head or the village chief. Only persons who are socio-politically mature may hold important political, economic and ritual offices or titles.

Minors are attached to mature persons through kinship and non-kinship linkages. Thus sons are attached to their fathers, while strangers are attached to other persons through friendship or clientage.

vi. Friendship and Partnership

There are several non-kinship institutions used by the Hausa for widening the social, political, economic and ritual circle of the individual, of which friendship and partnership are examples. The friendship relationship is more developed among the Hausa women who are totally or partially secluded inside the compound, *cikin-gida*.

Here are some of the different sorts of friendships and partnerships.

1. Between females:
    (i) Bond friends, *Kawaye*.
    (ii) Elder sister/younger sister of the day, *Yaya/Kanwar Rana*.
    (iii) Mother/daughter of fortune, *Uwar/Yar Arziki*.
2. Between males and females:
    (iv) Mother/son of fortune, *Uwar/Yan Arziki*.
    (v) Younger brother of the day, *Kanen Rana*.
    (vi) Bond friend of opposite sex, *Baba Kawa*.
    (vii) Father of the day, *Uban Rana* or *Uban Daki*.
3. Between males:
    (viii) Bond friend, *Baban Aboki*.
    (ix) Father/son of fortune, *Uban Daki/Dan Arziki*, excluding the economic type.

In categories (iii), (iv), (vii) and (ix) the relationship between the parties is asymmetrical and is mostly employed in economic and political situations. In the remaining categories the relationship between the parties is symmetrical and is used mainly in social situations. I regard the asymmetrical types as partnership, and the symmetrical types as friendship.

vii. Clientage

One important feature of Hausa economic and political organization is clientage, *Barorinci*. Smith defines clientage as 'an exclusive relation of mutual benefit which holds between two persons defined as socially and politically unequal, and which stresses their solidarity'. Here I shall use clientage in a more restricted sense. Thus while Smith sees friendship as a kind of clientage, I see friendship and clientage as mutually exclusive. Clientage has an element of quasi-legality in its character once it is formed, and the relationship thus generated may be semi-impersonal. Clientage may be classified as follows:

1. Political clientage:
    i. Senior office holders who are clients to the king.
    ii. Clients of superior and inferior officers.
2. Economic clientage:
    i. Owner of the hut/son of fortune, *Uban Daki/Dan Arziki*.
    This refers to the purely economic type and takes various forms.
    ii. Master/ex-slave, *Iyayengiji/Dimajai*.

3. Social clientage:
    i. Concubinage, *Kwarakwaranci.*
    ii. Courtesan/client, *Karuwanci.*
    iii. Informant, *Yan-Labari.*

The divisions are not watertight, since, for example, a political client may be employed for economic purposes and vice versa.

Not all types of relationships between courtesan and client may be classified as clientage, but certainly the relationship of a wealthy man or a notable with a woman prostitute conforms to the type. Wealthy men vie with each other to win the favours of an influential and beautiful prostitute, spending large sums publicly in giving gifts and making payments to singers. The greatest spender wins not only the favour of the woman but also the applause of the public. The relationship of the man and the woman may not be sexual at all, even though it is semi-permanent.

A concubine in Hausa society is not a wife overtly or covertly. She dwells in her master's home, attached to one of her master's wives. The children she bears for her master legally belong to her master. The children inherit through the wife to which the concubine is attached. Before the British arrived, concubines were usually slaves who got their freedom after bearing children for their masters.

Let us now examine how clientage operates in the political context. In Hausa society a man's sons live with him in the same compound, *gida*, of which he is the *Mai-gida*. He remains responsible for them to the local officials. He pays their taxes to the ward head or to the village chief. He controls the external affairs of the *gida* *vis-à-vis* the community. All other occupants of his *gida* are regarded as political minors. If the *Mai-gida* is a chief he may also have other clients living in or near his *gida*. Even if his clients are politically active, they are political minors because they are dependants of their master. A political minor, in this case, is a person whose affairs and relations with the state are mediated through other superior persons on whom he depends.

The *Mai-gida* may be politically mature since he deals directly with his local chief or head, but he is a client of a more powerful person, his patron, through whom he also deals indirectly with the local chief. The *Mai-gida*'s patron may also be a client of another more powerful person through whom he deals with others of higher status.

Because of the structural, functional and quasi-legal relationship that exists between a patron and his client, especially when the patron is a state official or the Emir, clients are the first to be considered for promotion. How long a client remains in office depends on how loyal and efficient he is. Clientage plays a very important part in the economic, ritual, social and political life of the Hausa people.

viii. Vassalage

Vassalage has a hereditary character and is characterized by the use of force which sets it aside from clientage. Vassals often transmit their role to their descendants. The relationship between the suzerain and the vassal is defined in terms of force, after it has been established by a formal act of homage.

Zaria was a vassal state of Sokoto while Zaria had other vassal states under her. Sokoto would use force, or rather threaten to use force, if Zaria defaulted in the performance of her vassal duties. Similarly Zaria would threaten to use force if any of her vassal states defaulted.

The possibility of the use of force by the superior lord in maintaining the vassal relationship makes it different from clientage. However, in the absence of fault the relationship between a suzerain and a vassal is phrased in terms of clientage. This may be why Smith used the two words interchangeably.

ix. Skill and Ability

Smith's approach to the study of the political history of Zaria is based on the conception that the history of a semi-literate state can be studied by listing all the state offices and titles, finding the relationships between them, and stating how the struggle to attain these offices was conducted during the reigns of various rulers. It is therefore not surprising that Smith views politics as a struggle for power between segments at various levels of the political system. The logic of his approach is that since politics is a struggle for power and since power can only be achieved by the control and manipulation of state offices and titles for political ends, it may look as if the Fulani rulers only think of how to consolidate power within their lineages without consideration for efficiency or individual skill and ability.

My aim is to point out that Smith's approach forced him to this conclusion, and however splendid and productive it is, it obscures many historical facts. One of these is the extent to which individual skill and ability have played their role in moulding Hausa society, especially in the realm of politics. From my personal experience of Hausa society, and from the autobiography of Baba of Karo, and the works of D. Dry and R. Yeld, it seems that Smith overstated his case when he writes: 'Appointment in the Native Administration is not governed by merit or technical qualifications, but by ties of loyalty in a situation of political rivalry where the stakes are considerable', and 'it is clear that in 1945 familiarity with Roman script was neither a necessary nor a sufficient condition for appointment'.

The records used by Smith tell us only of the end-product of a long process; they do not inform us of why such and such a person was appointed, but only that such and such a person was a Fulani or Habe. Fortunately general statements about how individuals achieved offices are made here and there in Smith's work. These generalizations do sometimes illustrate occasions in which skill and ability were also considered. This seems to happen more in the economic and ritual spheres than in politics.

KINSHIP AND NON-KINSHIP FACTORS
IN POLITICAL AND RITUAL ORGANIZATION

In political development four periods may be distinguished: the Habe period, before 1804; the Hausa-Fulani period, 1805–1900; the Anglo-Fulani period, 1901–60; post independent period since 1961.

The Habe Period, before 1804

Not very much is known of this period. Zazzau was one of the Hausa Bokwai, the seven original Hausa states. The Zaria chronicle lists sixty rulers of Habe Zazzau before the Fulani conquest of 1804. As early as the middle of the fifteenth century the rulers of Zaria were Muslims. The first ruler of Zaria was Gunguma and the sixteenth was Mohamman Makau, who was driven out of Zaria in 1804 by the Fulani invaders under Mallam Musa. Zaria was once ruled by queens of which Amina was one of the most illustrious.

Makau fled from Zaria and established himself at Abuja, one of his former vassal states. He set up a political organization similar to that of Zaria. From what is known of the government of Abuja, and that of Fulani-Zaria which did not depart significantly from the Habe system, as well as from appropriate documents, it has been possible to reconstruct the government of Habe Zaria before the Jihad.

A close study of the political identities reveals that kinship factors dominated in the appointment of royal officials and the Sarki. However, both kinship and non-kinship factors were equally considered in the appointments of Mallams and vassal chiefs. Non-kinship factors dominated in the appointment of senior and junior public officials; chamber officials; officials of the royal household; and slave officials.

The Hausa-Fulani Period, 1805–1900

In 1804 Dan Fodio gave Musa a flag of leadership and authority to invade and conquer Zaria. Before 1804 there had been several Fulani lineages settling in or around Zaria. Mallam Musa lived in Zaria before the Jihad and was familiar with Habe politics. The Bornawa and Suleibawa Fulani lived near the present site of Kaduna and they were led by Yamusa and Audusallami respectively. Another Suleibawa Fulani under Jaye lived between Zaria and Kaduna. From the beginning of the Jihad each of these Fulani lineages began to vie for leadership in Zaria politics. But the Shehu Dan Fodio had already recognized Mallam Musa. The head of the other Fulani lineages compromised and helped Musa in capturing and driving away Makau, the Habe king of Zaria.

Musa set up a system of political organization similar to the type formerly in Zaria. Thus the Fulani system of government departed very little from the Habe system.

Musa ruled Zaria not as a Sarki, for he was never crowned king, but as a Mallam. During his lifetime the rivalry amongst the different Fulani lineages was intensified. Musa tried to stabilize his reign and rule by marriage alliances and by appointing his allies and his kin to top political offices.

Musa was succeeded by Yamusa (who reigned 1821–34), the leader of the Bornawa lineage. He abolished all the female titles by dismissing Musa's daughters who were holding these offices and by replacing them with his own sons. By this act Yamusa started the political game by which holders of state offices could dismiss junior officers suspected of being against their interests and appoint those who were supposed to support them.

Yamusa's death was followed by another wave of dynastic struggles. Sai Abdul-kerim of the Katsinawa succeeded Yamusa and ruled from 1834 to 1846. The appointment of Abdulkerim was mainly Sokoto's decision, because of the protracted struggle amongst the ruling Fulani lineages in Zaria. The autonomy of Zaria was considerably reduced by this intervention from Sokoto, and from then until the British took over in 1900, Zaria affairs were controlled to a considerable extent from Sokoto. It seems therefore that by 1834 three dynasties, the Mallawa, the Bornuawa and the Katsinawa, had been actively involved in Zaria politics.

In 1890 there was another deadlock; agreement could not be reached amongst the three dynasties as to which of them should provide the Sarki. Sokoto stepped in and appointed Audusallami of the Suliebawa Fulani clan which took part in the Jihad. This appointment created the fourth dynasty, although later on it collapsed because it failed to achieve the internal cohesion which was necessary to compete favourably with the other dynasties.

During Audusallami's reign the basic outlines of the Fulani system of government were fully established, but inter-dynastic rivalry made it unstable. Thus the foundations of kingship were built on fear and suspicion. The instability was made more acute by Sokoto exploiting the situation, although successive Zaria kings had attempted to maintain internal independence by eliminating or minimizing Sokoto's interference.

Kwassau (who reigned 1897–1903), the thirteenth king of Zaria since Mallam

Musa, invited the British into Zaria in one of his diplomatic moves to reduce Sokoto influence. In 1903 his British guests deposed him, accusing him of duplicity.

Up to the time of Ja'afaru (who reigned 1934–50), the chief characteristics of Fulani rule can be summed up as follows. The old Habe system was modified consciously or unconsciously, but the general framework remained Habe. The Habe were gradually eliminated from high offices. They were relegated to lower offices and more especially to the newly created occupational offices.

Dynastic competition was tense and led to political considerations being employed in the appointment and dismissal of political officers. Thus a new king's first political move would be to dismiss from office all those he considered to be political opponents and appoint his kin and allies. This was indeed a means of maintaining some stability. However, the system lacked an established promotional structure due to the frequent turnover of offices among supporters of the different dynasties.

More offices were created and all female offices were changed into male offices. This was to cope with the increase of personnel of the ruling class due to the proliferation of the ruling lineages. The tables below, complied from the lists of office-holders in the reigns of three Zaria kings as recorded by M. G. Smith, supports the view that Habe participation in Zaria politics gradually decreased.

TABLE 4
Total appointments of Mallam Musa, 1804–21 (Mallawa dynasty)

No. of state titles	Total appointments	No. held by Musa Kin	No. held by Fulani descendant	No. held by Habe
37	37	5	23	10

TABLE 5
Total appointments of Yero, 1890 (Bornuawa dynasty)

No. of state titles	Total appointments	No. held by Yero Kin	No. held by Fulani descendant	No. held by Habe
38	43	14	22	7

TABLE 6
Total appointments of Ja'afaru, 1934–50 (Bornuawa dynasty)

No. of state titles	Total appointments	No. held by Ja'afaru kin	No. held by Fulani descendant	No. held by Habe
37	31	9	15	6

A more critical analysis of the appointments of the period shows that kinship considerations predominated in the appointments of royal officials, whose number had increased. Kinship and non-kinship factors were equally considered in the appointments of the Sarki, the vassal chiefs, the order of Mallams, the order of occupational offices and the quasi-hereditary client offices. Non-kinship factors dominated in the appointments of client offices of the freely appointed type; free household officials and slave officials.

The tables show that M. G. Smith is only partially correct when he says: 'The rule was for a new king to dismiss his predecessor's kin and supporter from important office, and appoint people of his own.' It seems that the king considered other factors as well.

c. The Anglo-Fulani Period, 1901–60

After the deposition of Kwassau in 1903, Aliyi was installed Sarki of Zaria. The condition of his appointment emphasized his subordination to the British. Between this period and up to 1950 the indirect rule introduced by Lugard between 1903 and 1914 was fully established.

Several changes took place with the establishment of British rule. By 1907 Zaria was divided into thirty-two districts, although by 1950 they had been reduced to seventeen. The former fiefs were changed into territorial districts and fief-holders were converted into resident district chiefs. The district chiefs and the village heads and ward heads were paid monthly salaries in lieu of shares from tax as had been the case in the past. A new system of taxation was introduced and with it the former traditional occupational offices established during Fulani rule gradually dwindled in importance. This also meant that fewer Habe took part in government. The new judicial system that was introduced strengthened the position of the chief judge and made him and his subordinates new and independent forces in Zaria politics. Schools were established and the economy was geared towards the production of cash and subsistence crops. Laws for the liberation of slaves were enforced, the former slaves became theoretically free, and their relationship with their former masters took a new twist. Lastly, technical departments of the Native Administration were established. By 1950 every district had its district chief, village heads, its *alkali* (Muslim judge), a forestry officer, an agricultural officer, a veterinary officer, a number of teachers, a warder, scribes, police and treasury officials.

The expansion of the Native Administration increased the number of offices at the king's disposal, and this made up for the offices made redundant by the advent of British rule.

The appointment and dismissal of officers of the judiciary and of the new departments followed closely the traditional pattern developed during the Fulani rule, although it was limited to some extent by the application of the British concept of 'fair play and justice' as promulgated by the British administrators at Kaduna.

During this period a critical study of political identities shows that kinship factors were still predominant in the appointment of royal officials, although the numbers were decreased. Kinship and non-kinship factors were equally employed in the appointment of the Sarki, hereditary clients, the order of Mallams and senior departmental officers. Non-kinship factors predominated in the appointment of non-hereditary clients and the king's servants.

This supports Smith's view that all top state offices were allocated to Fulani; but it also reveals that Smith's view that only political considerations determined appointments and dismissals needs to be modified. It seems clear to me that kinship, when applied, only delimits the number of eligibles, and that after this delimitation other factors are considered.

KINSHIP AND NON-KINSHIP FACTORS IN ECONOMIC ORGANIZATION

There are many economic identities among the Hausa. All the identities associated with each economic category are attained by fulfilling conditions which are not connected with kinship. However, there is a tendency for sons to follow their father's occupation; this of course does not exclude others who can fulfil the conditions from entry. Certain occupational groups intermarry frequently, such as barber-doctors and blacksmiths, and Koranic scholars and hunters.

Since occupational classes are ranked in a certain order of prestige, there is a tendency for descent to determine occupation. A close system does therefore tend to arise, in the long run, but occupational mobility is still possible by means of the application of other criteria such as friendship, individual acumen, etc.

My conclusions are that in the economic sphere kinship factors like descent and affinity help to maintain the occupational categories which are nevertheless open to individual mobility. However, since the categories are graded according to prestige the tendency will be to move upwards rather than downwards. To achieve this upward mobility an individual has to employ other means such as skill, clientage, friendship, partnership, all of which are based on non-kinship principles.

KINSHIP AND NON-KINSHIP FACTORS
IN SOCIAL ORGANIZATION

Apart from identities based mainly on kinship relations such as father, mother, etc., other social identities are based on non-kinship factors. Of all the spheres of activities discussed, sex is only irrelevant in the social sphere.

General Conclusion

My general conclusion differs from that reached by M. G. Smith who writes: 'Despite clientage, marriage, occupational mobility, fortune and meritorious religious action, the Hausa system of status distribution remains primarily ascriptive.' If by 'ascribed' Smith means what Linton means: 'The bulk of the ascribed statuses in all social systems are parcelled out to individuals on the basis of sex, age and family relationships', then it is difficult to understand how Smith arrived at his conclusion.

I would argue that in describing Hausa society it is sociologically unsatisfactory to establish a dichotomy between 'ascribed' and 'achieved'. On the basis of sex, Hausa society is divided into two exclusive but interdependent worlds: that of the male, and that of the female. The females are excluded from political activities and from Muslim rituals, but play important roles in certain economic, social and non-Muslim ritual activities. The age factor as a means of differentiation does no more than help to understand Hausa domestic organization, where it plays an important role in ordering kinship behaviour. Similarly, family relationships are operative only at the domestic level and in aristocratic and occupational lineages, and in a few other lineages with hereditary or quasi-hereditary titles. It is therefore evident that the criteria of sex, age and family relations tell us only part of the story of Hausa society. This is because the bulk of statuses are not parcelled out to individuals only or primarily on the bases of sex, age and family relationships, but also on other bases such as clientage, socio-political maturity, skill and ability, and friendship.

The position seems to be that at one level kinship factors dominate, at another level both kinship and non-kinship factors are combined; and at yet another level non-kinship factors dominate. I should add that the extent to and the intensity with which these factors are activated vary according to the sphere of activity, political, economic, social, or ritual. A very broad generalization of Hausa society, like that made by M. G. Smith, is unacceptable, for it is only applicable to certain spheres or levels of activities.

BIBLIOGRAPHY

SECTION I
Works consulted
ARDENER, E. W. *The Coastal Bantu of the Cameroons*, Ethnographic Survey of Africa, West Africa Part II (section on Kpe), D. Forde (ed.) (London: International African Institute, 1956)
GOODY, J. R. 'The Classification of Double Descent Systems', *Current Anthropology* (Feb. 1961)
HARRIS, R. 'The Political Significance of Double Unilineal Descent', *J.R.A.I.* (1962), 92

Suggestions for further reading
FORDE, D. *Yako Studies* (London: Oxford University Press, 1964)
GOODY, J. R. *The Social Organization of the Lowiili* (London: HMSO, 1956)
LEACH, E. R. *Rethinking Anthropology* (London: Athlone Press, 1961)
NADEL, S. F. 'Dual Descent in the Nuba Hills', in *African Systems of Kinship and Marriage*, A. R. Radcliffe-Brown and D. Forde (eds.) (London: Oxford University Press, 1950)

SECTION II
Works consulted
BOHANNAN, L. and P. *The Tiv of Central Nigeria*, Ethnographic Survey of Africa, West Africa, vol. 3, Part 8, D. Forde (ed.) (London: International African Institute, 1953)
EVANS-PRITCHARD, E. E. *The Nuer* (Oxford: Clarendon Press, 1940)
FORTES, M. *The Dynamics of Clanship among the Tallensi* (London: Oxford University Press, 1945)
—— 'Kinship and Marriage among the Ashanti', in *African Systems of Kinship and Marriage*, A. R. Radcliffe-Brown and D. Forde (eds.) (London: Oxford University Press, 1950)
—— 'The Structure of Unilineal Descent Groups', *American Anthropologist* (1953), b, 55
GLUCKMAN, M. 'Kinship and Marriage among the Lozi of Northern Rhodesia and the Zulu of Natal', in *African Systems of Kinship and Marriage*, A. R. Radcliffe-Brown and D. Forde (eds.) (London: Oxford University Press, 1950)
GOODY, J. R. 'The Classification of Double Descent Systems', *Current Anthropology* (Feb. 1961)
LEACH, E. R. 'Aspects of Bride-wealth and Marriage Stability among the Kachin and Lakhar', in *Rethinking Anthropology* (London: Athlone Press, 1961)
LEWIS, I. M. *A Pastoral Democracy: Study of Pastoralism and Politics among the Northern Somali* (London: Oxford University Press, 1961)
—— 'Problems in the Comparative Study of Unilineal Descent', in *The Relevance of Models for Social Anthropology*, ASA Monographs, no. 1 (London: Tavistock Publications, 1965)
PETERS, E. 'The Proliferation of Segments in the Lineage: the Bedouin of Cyrenaica, *J.R.A.I.* (1960), 90
RADCLIFFE-BROWN, A. R. 'Patrilineal and Matrilineal Succession', *Iowa Law Review* (1935), 20
——*Structure and Function in Primitive Society* (London: Cohen & West, 1952)
—— 'The Study of Kinship Systems', *J.R.A.I.* (1964), 70
SCHWAB, W. B. 'Kinship and Lineage among the Yoruba', *Africa* (1955), 25, 4
SMITH, M. G. 'On Segmentary Lineage Systems', *J.R.A.I.* (1956), 86
WORSLEY, P. M. 'The Kinship System of the Tallensi: a Revaluation', *J.R.A.I.* (1956), 86

SECTION III
Works consulted
COLEMAN, J. S. and ROSEBERG, C. G. (eds.) *Political Parties and Natural Integration in Tropical Africa* (Berkeley and Los Angeles: University of California Press, 1964)
DRY, D. P. L. *The Place of Islam in Hausa Society*, unpublished D.Phil. thesis (Oxford University, 1952)

DUDLEY, B. J. 'Parties and Politics in Northern Nigeria', Ph.D. thesis (London University, 1965)

GREENBERG, J. 'Islam and Clan Organization among the Hausa. Some Aspects of Negro-Mohammedan Culture-Contact among the Hausa', *American Anthropology* (1941), 42

HOGBEN, S. J. and KIRK-GREEN, A. H. M. *The Emirates of Northern Nigeria* (London: Oxford University Press, 1966)

KUPER, L. and SMITH, M. G. (eds.) *Pluralism in Africa* (Berkeley and Los Angeles: University of California Press, 1969)

ONWUEJEOGWU, M. 'The Cult of Bori Spirits among the Hausa', in *Man in Africa*, M. Douglas and P. M. Kaberry (eds.) (London: Tavistock Publications, 1969)

SMITH, M. G. *The Economy of Hausa Communities of Zaria* (London: HMSO, 1955)

—— 'Hausa Status Systems', *Africa* (1959), 29, 3

—— *The Government of Zazzau, 1800–1950* (London: Oxford University Press, 1960)

YELD, E. R. 'Islam and Social Stratification', *British Journal of Sociology* (1960), 11

Part Three
POLITICS, LAW & ORDER

CHAPTER 10

Societies Without States

I *An Introduction to Politics and Law*

The political crises that occurred in Africa immediately after many countries became independent have made many African intellectuals reassess their political thinking, which had been based on models mirroring the American, British and French systems, with a bi-cameral or uni-cameral parliament, a president, a prime minister, political parties, government and opposition, the judiciary, constitution, etc.

It is becoming clear to Africans that the operation of these systems is affected both directly by the traditional politics and behaviour of those who run the government, and indirectly by the traditional political systems which are still alive in the non-urban and rural areas where over 90 per cent of the populations live. The need to understand African traditional politics cannot be over-emphasized, especially nowadays when various political ideologies are brandished in the name of aid throughout the length and breadth of the continent.

The traditional political systems in Africa are different from those of the people of the first and second worlds because the systems have developed in areas with different cultural and historical settings. Even then, the differences are not functional but structural. Thus, Europe has developed not more than three distinctive forms of political organization, while Africa has developed about a dozen. The concepts of individualism, communalism, socialism, freedom, liberty, democracy, adult suffrage, concensus, the common will, social welfare, despotism, tyranny, occur in both European and traditional African political thought and practice. However, because they occur in different political structures, they take different forms. Africans have not studied the operation of these concepts in their traditional forms and how they affect newly acquired concepts.

When anthropologists began to study the political systems of Africa they came up with fascinating ideas which rocked the early ideas about political organization put forward by Maine and Morgan, both of whom had defined political organization as a government claiming authority over a definite territory. Territoriality, in fact, need not be critical in defining political organization. The Australian aborigines, or the peoples of Namibia of south-western Africa, who move about in very small bands, each politically distinct, may not occupy definite territory in the real sense of the word, yet they have political organization.

Schapera has shown that a political community is 'a group of people organized into a single unit managing its affairs independently of external control'. This definition was intended to demolish Radcliffe-Brown's definition of a political system as 'that part of the total organization which is concerned with the maintenance or establishment of social order, within a territorial framework, by the organized exercise of coercive authority through the use, or the possibility of the use of physical force', and also Fortes and Evans-Pritchard's myopic typology of African political systems.

Politics, like kinship, is a kind of human relationship at another level of inter-action which can also be interwoven with other levels of interaction such as kinship, rituals and economics. This is exactly what one finds in traditional African political systems.

Law belongs to a wider field which social scientists call social control, although it is an aspect of government. African law remains largely untouched. Some anthro-pologists have written about African law, but until African legal specialists begin to study it seriously, nothing much will be known. The scanty data available have made it impossible for the African judiciary to reflect the people's concepts of justice. Up till now many Africans have regarded the police as 'cheats' and lawyers as 'liars'. The public image of the law is still ugly because it is a foreign one that does not take serious account of society. European-acquired legal systems seem to be invading the countries from the outside and not growing from the inside.

It is hoped that the following chapters will enable the reader to appreciate the effects of the acquired European political and legal models on the traditional models.

II *The Principle of Political Organization Based on Lineage Principles: the Tiv of Northern Nigeria*

The Tiv (studied by Bohannan) are semi-Bantu agriculturalists inhabiting the mid-valley of the River Benue in Northern Nigeria. (The population was about 800 000 in 1955, with a variable density of 150–300 people per square mile in the south and 5–50 in the north. This imbalance may be one of the causes of the Tiv migratory habits.)

The Tiv believe that they are descended from a single male ancestor who lived between fourteen and seventeen generations ago. This ancestor had two sons who in turn had sons. The process of lineage segmentation continues down the generations; lineages segment at each generation up to three or four generations from the present living elders, at which point segmentation is supposed to 'stop'. No further segmentation is recognized, though it has a name: the 'segment-within-the-hut'. (For more information, see Chapter 9, Section II.)

Each ancestor at the apex of a minimal lineage segment formed three to four generations ago is associated with a territory called '*Tar*'. Such a lineage segment is named after an ancestor, for example, *Mba-Duku, Mba-Gor*. Below the segments are components called compounds, *Ya*, whose members are agnatically related, although some are strangers, and cognates and sister's sons. Ideally, the territory called *Tar* which harbours a minimal lineage segment adjoins the territory of other sibling minimal segments. These lineage segments merge upwards, in each genera-tion, until the whole of Tiv land forms one indivisible territory. (For more informa-tion about Tiv land-holding and social structure, see Chapter 17, Section I.)

The Tiv political system is based on what is termed a segmentary lineage system which is organized from top to bottom in a single, embracing genealogical scheme. This scheme provides the dominant principle of social organization which is characterized by a correspondence between genealogical, spatial and social distance.

The minimal segment associated with a *Tar* is the largest politically important unit in Tiv and through it a Tiv gains the right of citizenship. In time of external aggression a person fights with his *Tar*. A *Tar* cooperates or competes with other equivalent *Tars*. Thus by the principles of opposability and sociability of equivalent segments, related *Tars* can cooperate and attack other equivalent *Tars*.

This process of segmentary opposition and sociability can best be illustrated by reference to Figure 3 below.

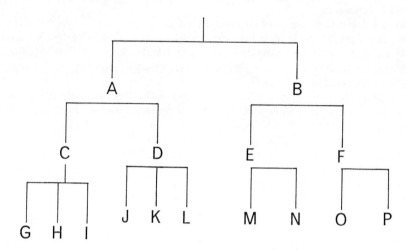

FIGURE 3   *Segmentary opposition: a model*

Each minimal segment (G,H,I; J,K,L; M, N; O,P,) is regarded as an autonomous unit. G,H,I will compete and cooperate mutually because they have a common ancestor C. But if someone from J attacks a member of I; and parts G, H, I will combine and fight J and will call K and L to help. Similarly C and D will combine to fight E and F if E attacks D. When fighting ends, the larger groups will rapidly disband and the effective political grouping will be minimal segments. The Tiv system does not necessarily work like this, because other factors influence it, which Bohannan failed to mention.

Tiv leadership is founded on knowledge, prestige, personality and the ability to manipulate the *Akombo* and *Swem*. A person possessing these qualities emerges as a leader of his segment and arbitrates in disputes. But leadership is punctuated by the relativity of political grouping and the equality of segments, for a leader wields greatest influence within his lineage segment, especially when he is leading it against another segment.

The only institutionalized group that can use force in the internal politics of Tiv is the age-group. Age-groups protect their members from the *Tsav* of their elders by using physical force to curb the indiscriminate application of non-physical force.

Four cosmological ideas play important roles in Tiv social, political, and economic life: '*Akombo*', '*Tsav*', '*Swem*' and '*Tor*'.

Akombo are 'forces' which interfere with the natural functioning of things, but they can only be ritually manipulated by one who has *Tsav*, which is a 'force', witchcraft substance, which grows in the heart and endows its possessor with certain powers, talent and ability. Thus *Tsav* is conceived as a mystical ability to tap and internalize the potency existing outside the individual by the mystical consumption of the flesh and soul of a victim.

Men with *Tsav*, all of whom belong to a society of *Mbatsav*, are feared and respected by their agnates. They meet to repair the great *Akombo* for the good of the community or to repair the small *Akombo* for an individual.

Economic prosperity, health, and fertility are indications that the *Mbatsav* of an agnate have transformed the deaths that have occurred in the group for the benefit of the *Tar*. If, on the contrary, the *Mbatsav* is accused of spoiling the *Tar*, it must be checked.

The Tiv have two means of controlling the illegitimate actions of the *Mbatsav*: *Swem* and *Tor*. *Swem* is used for taking oaths and making treaties. Violators of *Swem* are doomed to die unless they confess and make expiation. *Tor* is a dose used to determine guilt by oral administration. The guilty is expected to die while the innocent vomits it out.

Tsav and *Akombo* are ritual forces that define the locus of authority in the Tiv political system, while *Swem* and *Tor* are forces that provide checks and balance for it.

The Tiv traditional political system is based on the principle of patrilineages which are territorially and genealogically defined. Their political organization is not based on hierarchies of officialdom in which the maintenance of law and order is achieved by the application of physical force. Rather it is based on a lineage system with several checks and balances which are buttressed by the concept of mystical forces whence ritual sanctions are derived and applied.

III *The Principle of Political Organization Based on Membership of Various Associations: the Yakö of Southern Nigeria*

In *African Political Systems* Fortes and Evans-Pritchard formulated three types of system: a small autonomous band characteristic of the Bushmen, Hottentots and Congo pygmies; a segmentary lineage system, such as that of the Tiv, Tallensi and Nuer; and a centralized authority with kingship and chiefship, characteristic of the Akan states, the Hausa, the Benin, the Lozi and the Bantu.

Daryll Forde in his study of the Yakö revealed a system not discussed by Fortes and Evans-Pritchard. This system does not lay stress on segmentary lineages and has no centralized authority, but is able to achieve internal and external cohesion and peaceful government by means of membership of several inter- and intra-woven associations. This system based on association has also been reported in the political systems of the Mende, the Yoruba and the Igbo. The Yakö have a double unilineal descent system (for more information about this, see Chapter 6, Section III). For purposes of analysis of the Yakö political organization, a detailed study of one of the five villages in which they live will be made, since all five have basically the same pattern (for a general description, see Chapter 6, Section III).

Umor village (the largest) has four wards. At the ward level are several associations. One of these is the 'Men of the Ward', *Yakamben*, which holds general authority over ritual and secular affairs. The group has a head, *Ogbolia*, a deputy and an announcer. The membership comprises the head of the patriclans, the priests of the major village cults and about 35 per cent of the adult males of the patriclans.

Other associations independent of the ward group are the associations of fighters, hunters, and recreation, called *Ebiabu*. The head of all the ward groups, by virtue of his office, has moral authority over all other men's associations. In this way he is able to coordinate the policies and activities of other associations to fall in line with those of the ward groups without jeopardizing the independence of each association. When it is necessary to apply force to curb any unyielding offender or quell intra- or inter-ward disturbances, he appeals to the middle grade of the *Ebiabu* through the upper grade of which he is a member.

The *Nkpe* is another independent association which offers supernatural protection to its members. The leaders of the ward look on them with suspicion and never admit them as members of their associations, but on the whole they are accepted. They help to protect their members against theft and seduction and the abuse of power either by the Men of the Ward or by the village cult group.

There is another association called the 'Village Leopard' cult group, *Okengka*. Membership is made up of leaders of wards, *Ogbolia*, with their deputies, and some members of the Men of the Ward. Membership gives prestige and it is strictly selective; members of a patriclan vie to gain entry. The headship of this cult passes in turns between men of one of the oldest patriclans. Contravention of any judgment of this cult, as decided by the secret conclave, entails misfortune for the offender and his kin. Ward heads and leaders use the sanction of this cult spirit in settling disputes between wards as well as between persons and groups.

At the apex of the governmental machinery of a Yakö village is the council of village priests, *Yabot*. It is made up of the head of *Okengka*, ten priests of the fertility spirits associated with the matriclan, and thirteen other priests of the patriclan village shrines. The leading public figure in this council is the speaker, who is the custodian of the village drums and the emblems of the villages which symbolize its unity and continuity. One of the ten fertility spirits is regarded as supreme ritually. Its shrine is located in the centre of the village and its priest lives near the place, adjacent to the village market. The *Yabot* is the ritual authority of the village and the jury for ritual offences and major disputes. It controls all the external affairs connected with other villages. Any individual or ward or clan that flouts the council's decision is ritually excommunicated. Their judgment also implies the use of punitive action by other associations, whose intervention may be employed effectively since membership overlaps.

Two other independent associations at the village level are the *Okundom* and the *Ikpungkara*. The *Okundom* protects its members from theft, etc. Forty members, including priests, from various parts of the village form the *Ikpungkara*. On admission they are pledged by the supernatural sanction of their spirit cult. The members are concerned, among other things, with the settlement of land disputes. These two associations are backed by the priests' council who are members too.

In the system described above, it is obvious that government in Umor is achieved through independent coordinating 'legislative', 'judicial' and 'executive' machinery based on cult spirit associations whose ritual power and moral authority are strengthened by the physical coercion of recalcitrants. Neither in the village nor in the ward is there a hierarchy of centralized authority. Government is achieved through the overlapping of membership of various associations. (For land-holding among the Yakö, see Chapter 17, Section I.)

IV *The Principle of Political Organization Based on Age-Grades: the Nandi of East Africa*

The Nandi (studied by Huntingford) are one of the East African peoples of western Kenya with a population formerly estimated at 50 000 (the 1948 census made it 116 681). They are primarily pastoralists who also practise some agriculture.

Nandi country is divided into six territories, called *Emet*. This is a geographical division of the different parts of the country; the term is used in referring to the part where one comes from. The country is subdivided into sixteen *Pororosiek* which are made up of *Koret*. Each *Koret*, which is the smallest territorial unit, is made up of 20–100 scattered homesteads. A homestead consists of a simple or compound family, a cattle-fold, a granary and a living hut. The *Pororosiek* and *Koret* are both territorial and political units. The Nandi do not live in villages nor are they territorially organized on a clan basis, so that a *Koret* is made up of people of various clans.

The smallest political unit to coincide with the territorial division is the *Koret* which has a council called the *Kokwet,* made up of old men of the *Koret*. An old man is defined as any person who has passed the warrior grade. The leader of the council is not elected by any formal method, but the most influential, respectable and wealthy man will be accepted as a leader. Thus one can say that leaders emerge by a social process of 'natural selection'. By the time a leader dies, other potential leaders will have emerged, and out of those few the influence of one will be so overwhelming that his succession as leader will be indisputable.

The council meets almost daily under a suitable tree, preferably a fig. The leader sits under it with the other old men sitting around him. The young men who are observers and the litigants squat at the periphery. Women may be present only when called upon to give evidence. The council deals with all matters concerning the *Koret*, such as disputes about cattle, compensation cases, crimes against the tribe, drought and cattle diseases. The leader, on behalf of the *Kokwet*, pronounces the decisions taken, which are binding because they are backed by public opinion, ritual sanctions and force where necessary – by authorizing the warrior age-grade to act.

The *Pororiet* is the largest political unit and it coincides with the territorial division called the *Pororosiek*. The *Pororosiek* is made up of between four and thirty *Koret*. A *Pororiet* council comprises the leaders of its component *Kokwet,* two senior military commanders of the *Pororiet* and two representatives of the *Orkoiyot*. The council is presided over by two active old men called councillors. This council is made up of representatives whose duties are purely civil, military and ritual; each has his own speciality. The council discusses matters affecting the *Pororosiek* as a whole, such as going to war or raids, circumcision, agriculture and ritual. The *Pororiet* is not a higher authority than the *Kokwet* nor a court of appeal, although it can settle disputes between *Kokwets*. A distinction is made between the internal affairs of the *Koret* which are managed by the *Kokwet* council without interference from the *Pororiet,* and the external affairs of the *Koret* which are managed by the *Pororiet* council which is an amalgam of personnel from its component *Koret*.

The next council organized at the level of the *Pororosiek* is the military council. The warriors build themselves huts in the bush, where they take decisions about raiding; these are placed before the *Pororiet* council by the two senior commanders. If the council accepts the decision, the two representatives of the *Orkoiyot* inform the *Orkoiyot* who gives his assent, ritual blessing and war medicine to the warriors. The commanders at times override the elders, but their power is checked by the *Orkoiyot* whose assent is essential for any military expedition. The *Pororosiek* army is made up of fighting units which contain a varying number of warriors drawn from several *Koret*. These fighting units are not based on territorial division; for instance, one *Pororosiek* of twenty-seven *Koret* may have eight fighting units under eight section commanders. Many questions are raised by Huntingford's account, such as how the military council is formed, how and why the *Koret's* army is divided into fighting units, and how the section and senior commanders are appointed. Also he does not analyse the homestead organization, so that one must assume that all petty quarrels are sent to the *Koret*. This seems unlikely because of the dispersed nature of the homesteads. There may be a quick method of settling petty disputes among and between homesteads.

The *Pororosiek* cooperate in war and initiation ceremonies, although how much is a matter of conjecture, since no account is given in Huntingford's book.

The *Orkoiyot*, who has two representatives in every *Pororiet* council in Nandi land, is an intermediary between the God, Asis, and man. His person is sacred and several taboo and avoidances are associated with his person. All decisions of the *Pororiet* council are referred to him for supernatural sanction. He has the authority to sanction war, circumcisions and planting, and in this way he coordinates several activities of the Nandi nation. To gainsay him is to challenge the will of Asis. The military are all-powerful in the *Pororiet* council, but the *Orkoiyot* acts as check to their power, since no military expedition can be undertaken without his assent, which is given only as he hands over to the military the medicine club which is carried by a section commander in a raid or war. The office of *Orkoiyot* seems to be centred around a particular lineage, but the nature of the appointment is not recorded, save that it is of Masai origin.

Every male in the tribe belongs from birth to an age-grade called the *Ipinda*, of which there are seven. One grade consists of the warriors in power, two others are those of the small boys and initiates, and the other four are of old men. The chief difficulty is that circumcision for boys begins between the ages of ten and twenty, and lasts for four years, so that the age range in a grade will be fourteen to twenty-four. After that another eight years has to elapse before the initiated sets are officially recognized as warriors in a handover ceremony; this brings the age range to between twenty-two and thirty-two. Since men have to serve for fifteen years, it follows that by the end of their tenure the range will be between thirty-nine and forty-seven years of age. The Nandi fully realize that the best period for military service is between twenty and thirty-two, so they have adopted an arrangement whereby the older ones among the newly initiated take over active military service from the older existing warriors, who unofficially retire. Thus during the eight years between the closing of the circumcision and the handing over of the country to the new warriors, there is an overlap, for there are actually two warrior sets.

The warriors are expected to look after the country for fifteen years. After the official handover the old warriors become the first 'old men'; this process continues until they become the fourth and last 'old men', by which time, the official age is about 105 years. After the deaths of the last 'old men', the small boys take their name and a new cycle begins. The Nandi age-grade system is cyclic; each grade has a definite name which it retains till death, and which is then passed on to new grades at the bottom.

The age-grade is subdivided into four groups called 'Fire'. Each of these four groups is named, and each grade contains members from each of the other groups. Nothing has been said anywhere about the significance of this subdivision, but it seems to me to be one of those cross-ties necessary to maintain a balance and therefore common in such societies, since by this method the four sections of the warrior's grade have ties with others grades.

The age-grade system, apart from its military function, provides a recognized and institutionalized behaviour pattern. The initiation period is used for training and schooling boys in all aspects of Nandi life. The warrior grade is allowed free access to girls, but once warriors retire and marry they are expected to give up all interest in young girls. Age-sets regard themselves as equals and are expected to be kind to one another, even to the extent of allowing each other access to their wives. Junior sets are expected to obey and respect senior ones, and it is on this behaviour pattern – the fear of the aged – that the whole political and social organization is founded. Only old men belonging to the four old men's grades can be members of the *Kokwet*, and *ipso facto*, members of the *Pororiet*.

A man's first son should be in the next age-grade but one below his, and his youngest should belong to the grade next but two below his. Thus it becomes vividly clear that the age-grade organization cuts across the kinship system.

The principles of Nandi political organization may be summed up thus. It is based on an age-grade organization which is cyclic and transcends lineage or clan. The political organization is compatible with the territorial organization as represented by the *Pororosiek* and *Koret*, each of which have councils dealing with specific matters as indicated above.

They have a system of centralized authority based on a civil administration centred on the *Kokwet* and *Pororiet* councils and a military administration controlled by the military council. Some activities of the *Pororiet* and the military council have to be sanctioned by the *Orkoiyot*, whose position though ritual has significant political implications.

Nandi has a minimal unifying supreme government, and there is a consciousness of the unity of Nandi land. This is achieved by dispersal of the clans and an age-grade organization, which cuts across the territorial frontiers marked out by the *Pororosiek* and thus welds the whole of Nandi into one cultural entity. Another important unifying factor is the acceptance of one ritual head in the person of the *Orkoiyot*, who coordinates certain Nandi activities and keeps the warriors in check.

V *Factors that Encouraged the Development and Persistence of Stateless Societies Organized on the Segmentary Unilineal Principle: Examples from West Africa*

It is important first to define what I mean by stateless society and the segmentary unilineal principle, because these terms have given rise to much controversy in the past.

By a stateless society I mean a society which lacks a centralized system of political organization. (Centralization may or may not involve the existence of kingship.) By the segmentary unilineal principle I mean the continual segmentation of genealogically based lineages. Complementary opposition and segmentary sociability are characteristics of certain types of segmentary lineages. Thus the Nuer, the Tiv, the Yoruba, the Tallensi and some Igbo lineage systems are all species of the same genera.

West Africa can be broadly divided into three main ethno-geographical areas. The first is the coastal forest region which owing to heavy rainfall all the year round has thick and luxuriant vegetation. Owing to the prevalence of the tse-tse fly and the absence of pasture land, cattle and sheep rearing are unknown. Goats and a few short-horned cows are kept for social, ritual and domestic purposes.

The best-known peoples of this region are the Mende, Dahomeans, Yoruba, Benin, Igbo, Yakö and Ijo. Except for the Ijo, they are chiefly agriculturalists who grow yam, cassava and maize and exploit the natural resources of the forest, such as palm oil. The thick and swampy forest of this region is a great barrier to cross-cultural activity, although it has not totally barred the flow of culture.

Only a few centralized states with kingship have flourished in this region. Of these the Mende, Nri, Benin, Agbor, Ife and some Ijo seem to be of considerable antiquity. Dahomey and some of the Ijo states are of more recent origin, and they seem to have been formed in reaction to the development of coastal trade with European nations. However, recent research seems to indicate that some of the Ijo states pre-date European contact.

The second area is the deciduous forest region, which is intermediate between the forest zone and the savannah. It is more open country although it has the same vegetation as the forest zone.

Some of the inhabitants of this zone are the Yoruba states like Ilorin and Oyo, the Nupe, the Jukuns, the Tiv and the Nsaws. They are all agriculturalists exploiting the forest resources as do their forest neighbours. Communication is easier in this region. It is not therefore surprising to find numerically more centralized states here than in the forest region. The Ashanti, Bonni, Jukun, Nupe, some of the Yoruba states and the Nsaws are among the best known.

The next and the largest area of all is the Sudan savannah-scrubland zone. The people of this region mostly practise mixed farming, irrigation and manuring. Economic activity seems more diversified in this area. The whole savannah and scrubland is a vast open plain with two seasons in the year, the rainy and the dry. This annual seasonal variation encourages the growth of grass and cereals. As one moves northwards desert conditions become more prevalent. Animals such as cattle, goats and horses, and in the more northerly areas camels, are kept in great numbers.

The states and kingdoms which existed before the arrival of the Europeans such as Malle, Ghana, Songhai, Kanem, Zaria, Kano, Daura, Kebbi, Dogomba, Mossi and Mamprusi, were all located in this region. The open nature of the country; the easy means of communication due to the use of horses, donkeys and camels; climatic variation resulting in economic diversification; the intermediate position of the area between the forest zone and the Sahara and North Africa, which led to the early development of trade and early contact with the Mediterranean world; all these may have encouraged the development of state systems from very early times.

It seems that as one moves from the centres of these states to their peripheries, societies organized on lineage systems begin to increase. Thus on the Bauchi Plateau there is a concentration of societies organized on very shallow lineage principles. The Tallensi are hemmed between the Mossi on the north and the Dogomba and Mamprusi on the south, while the Lodagaba remain intact north of Ghana.

All over this region are to be found the nomadic Fulani who are organized in agnatic lineages. In the eighteenth and nineteenth centuries the Fulani who settled in the existing states took up arms against them and created new regimes in Senegal and northern Nigeria.

One might deduce that the conditions making for the creation of states are more favourable in open country. It is also a fact that state and stateless societies coexist; most of the states, especially those in the south, are still based on lineage principles. This is true of the Ashanti, Yoruba, Benin, Nri (Igbo), Agbor (Igbo), Nsaw and to a lesser extent the Habe and the Hausa-Fulani kingdoms. It is therefore safe to postulate that the segmentary lineage system was used by these societies before they acquired a state system. Ashanti, Dahomey and Benin are documented cases to support this view. Nri and Agbor oral traditions point to this fact also.

There are some interrelated factors which encouraged the development and persistence of stateless societies organized on the segmentary unilineal principle in West Africa. These are the historical and cultural trends of development, and ecological adaptation, combined with the ideologies of lineage perpetuity and continuity expressed in mystical and mythical idioms. Other important factors are the implications of using the lineage segmentary system as a system of land tenure and property distribution, as well as the lineage having some ritual attachment to land or property. Finally, it is significant that the inherent character of segmentation and the nature of the residence pattern both inhibit the emergence of an overall powerful leader internally and/or the imposition of an external foreign leadership.

Archaeological and anthropological evidence show that West Africa has been populated by various ethnic groups: Negroes, Semites, Hamites and Bantu. There is also sufficient evidence to prove that most West African cultures are of great antiquity, for instance the Nok Valley Acheulian culture dated at 37000 BC and the Iwo Eleru skeleton dated at 9250 BC.

The heterogeneous population seems to form a cultural unit, particularly in its traditional religious beliefs. There is therefore no reason to believe that the segmentary lineage principle is not as old as other traditional cultural complexes. If that is so, it is not surprising that this principle is widespread all over West Africa. The existence of so many variations of this principle points to the fact that they are not of recent origin, but have each for a long time pursued divergent courses of development. The concept might have spread by the process of diffusion, and each community might have evolved its own variants as a result of what Sahlin calls specific cultural evolution. If this view is accepted, then one can conclude that the West African stereotype of lineage segmentation and statelessness developed and persisted both in time and space by a historical and a cultural process.

The segmentary lineage systems seem to be at least partially a result of ecological adaptation. West Africa with its vast land and forest resources gives room for people to expand without encountering serious resistance. Where resistance occurs and the population continues to grow, but a segment is unable to break away totally from the parent nucleus, the Tiv-Nuer type of system characterized by segmentary opposition develops. Where the segment can totally break away from the parent nucleus and establish itself in a new habitat, the marked development of segmentary opposition and segmentary sociability is highly unlikely; such is the case with some of the Igbo and Yoruba.

The Tiv in response to their rapid population increase have expanded in all directions. One whole minimal segment shifts at once but related minimal segments remain in close sociability for defence purposes. During peace they are in opposition to one another.

Among the Tallensi the position is different. They expand very little compared with the Tiv. This is partly because population growth is relatively slower, but chiefly because they are ritually more attached to the land than the Tiv and their neighbouring societies are state-organized. In order to survive amidst the pressure of state societies they have contrived a means of attachment to ritual chiefships called *Namoos* who claim a relationship with the state of Mamprusi. It may be postulated that the Tallensi ritual attachment to land is a device adopted to check expansion and inhibit spatial segmentation of the Tiv type, which would be disastrous to a society without a state system but almost hemmed around by societies with one. The Tiv would probably not have developed in the way they did if they had been ritually attached to the land and surrounded by state societies.

Almost all West African societies have the history of their origin told in the idiom of myth. This is true of the Tiv, the Hausa states, the Tallensi, the Yoruba, the Benin and the Nri. The myths play an important part in the training and development of the personality of the children, since they are framed to validate the social order, give meaning and reality to the social system, strengthen and reinforce the people's beliefs and values, and also perpetuate the ideology that the society and the component lineages have an unbroken continuity which every member must try to maintain.

The ancestor cult is a common feature of many West African religions. Through it also the doctrine of lineage continuity is expressed and upheld. It has become a means by which social control is maintained by the older over the younger generation, and it is manipulated to perpetuate and sustain the social order in time and space.

Once a society begins to distribute its wealth and titles on the basis of a lineage principle, the result should be that the lineage principle tends to validate ownership and vice versa. Thus in England we still find the hereditary lords of feudal England surviving structurally although not functionally in the democratic England of today. This same cultural rigidity, or fixation, is also found in West Africa.

Land is usually divided on the basis of lineage segments. Thus as the lineages segment the land is subdivided. Each lineage, minimal, major or maximal as the case may be, claims exclusive rights over a portion of land. In due course ownership of the land validates the existence of the lineage and the existence of the lineage validates the ownership of the land. Land and lineage become inseparable. The land is passed down from generation to generation and with it all its land rituals and sentiments. This system of land ownership is one of the problems modern administrators have to cope with in the process of industrialization.

The Tallensi are a typical example of a people who have a highly developed ritual attachment to land. A quotation from Fortes will help to illustrate this point.

> The connexion between community and locality has three aspects found in all Tale social institution. It is utilitarian – for men build their homes on the land and gather livelihood from it, it is also morphological, particular units of the social structure being tied to defined localities so that the social unit and its locality form a single entity; and it has a moral and ritual coefficient. . . . The bounds between a community and a locality, or between an individual or a lineage and land, are summed up in the idea of ownership. . . . Thus in the case of land, exercising or acquiring 'ownership' for productive purposes is regulated by clanship and kinship ties and limited by the moral and ritual values of the ancestor cult and the Earth cult.

Once a concept is ritualized its development and perpetuity are ensured. Just as the concept of human brotherhood is ritualized in Christian belief and has been transformed into one of the tenets of Western democratic philosophy, so also the concept of lineage continuity with its implications is ritualized through the symbolism of land and ancestors among the Tallensi, most Igbo, Lodagaba, Kokomba and Yakö, which are stateless, and among the Nri, Benin and Ashanti which are state societies. Among the Fulani the emphasis is on cattle not land.

Thus lineages are backed by the holding of property or title. This in its turn strengthens the lineage as a corporate group in time and space.

Examination of the residence pattern reveals two major types of community: compact and dispersed. The dispersed communities seem to be of various types, such as the Owerri-Igbo type, the Yakö, the Tiv, the Tallensi and the Fulani. The societies here are mostly stateless. The state societies also vary in their settlement patterns even though they have a common feature of compactness. The variations in the settlement patterns of the state and (especially) the stateless societies are the result of the direct interplay of the inherent character of the forces of lineage segmentation on the one hand and ecological and environmental forces on the other.

To recapitulate, the dispersal of population and the segmentation of lineages inhibit internally the emergence of an overall leader and encourage resistance against the imposition of an external authority. The capacity to resist external authority is greater in the forest zones where communication is difficult. This is really why there are more state societies farther north.

Among the Tiv a leader emerges only within the minimal lineage, beyond which his influence dwindles because of the segmentary nature of the lineages. This is also true among some Igbo and Tallensi, although the character of leadership varies from society to society.

The segmentary unilineal principle *per se*, therefore, inhibits the emergence of a leader and thus the emergence of a state system. The inhibition also makes the segmentary lineage self-perpetuating.

It does happen that a state system is superimposed on a segmentary lineage system, as for example among the Ashanti, the Nri (Igbo) and some Yoruba. In this case the segmentary system is checked, but it becomes a means itself of checking the abuse of power by the state. Lloyd writes about the Yoruba: 'The political system does not render the lineage insignificant but rather enhances its importance . . . the genealogies are short and shallow.' In fact the importance of the lineage system is not enhanced. What seems to happen is that an uneasy balance is maintained between the state system and the lineage system, for while the state system has a centripetal effect, the segmentary lineage system has a centrifugal effect. It would be of great interest to examine how the segmentary lineage principle persists and functions in the modern states of West Africa.

One might ask why states exist at all in West Africa if the segmentary lineage system has an inherent character which is averse to the development of centralization. Two striking features of all the states are revealed. The first is that very few of the states attained statehood by the process of conquest. The second is that those which did attain statehood by conquest were bedevilled with the problems of unification, which even colonial governments found very difficult to cope with, in spite of their strong military backing, and which they have passed on to the African administrators of the present West African independent states.

Attempts to solve the problem of unifying the gamuts of dispersed lineages were made by various states. The Nri hegemony developed a concept based on the 'Children of Eze Nri'. The Ashanti adopted the federation system after Osei Tutu had claimed to be the ritual custodian of the 'golden stool'. The Benin and some of the Yoruba voluntarily invited their kings from Ife, thus giving the state a divine origin and sanction. The Benin developed a radial system which made the king the centre of all important activities, with all the citizens having vested interests in the administration of Benin. The Benin even attempted to conquer stateless societies and went to the extent of making these conquered stateless societies to adopt their system of government. The Yoruba tried for a compromise by rotating chiefship and various titles among lineages as a means of pinning down their interests in state administration. They also formed associations and societies whose membership was not lineage-based. These became agents of the state administration.

BIBLIOGRAPHY

SECTION II
Works consulted
BOHANNAN, L. and P. *The Tiv of Central Nigeria*, Ethnographic Survey of Africa, West Africa, Vol. 3, Part 8, D. Forde (ed.) (London: International African Institute, 1953)
BOHANNAN, P. 'A Genealogical Charter', *Africa* (1952), 22, 4
—— *Tiv Farm and Settlement* (London: HMSO, 1954)
—— 'The Migration and Expansion of the Tiv', *Africa* (1954), 22
—— 'Political Aspects of Tiv Social Organization' in *Tribes without Rulers*, J. Middleton and D. Tait (eds.) (London: Routledge & Kegan Paul, 1959)

Suggestions for further reading
EVANS-PRITCHARD, E. E. 'The Nuer of the Southern Sudan' in *African Political Systems*, M. Fortes and E. E. Evans-Pritchard (eds.) (London: Oxford University Press, 1940)
—— *The Nuer* (Oxford: Clarendon Press, 1940)
FORTES, M. 'The Political System of the Tallensi' in *African Political Systems*, M. Fortes and E. E. Evans-Pritchard (eds.) (London: Oxford University Press, 1940)
—— *The Dynamics of Clanship among the Tallensi* (London: Oxford University Press, 1945)
ONWUEJEOGWU, M. A. *The Traditional Political System of Ibusa* (occasional publication of Odinani Museum, Nri) (Onitsha: Tabansi Press, 1973)
—— 'The Political Organization of Nri', unpublished M.Phil. thesis (London University, 1974)

SECTION III
Works consulted
FORDE, D. C. 'Government in Umor,' *Africa* (1939), 12
—— 'Double Descent among the Yakö' in *African Systems of Kinship and Marriage*, A. R. Radcliffe-Brown and D. Forde (eds.) (London: Oxford University Press, 1950)
—— 'The Government Roles of Association among the Yakö', *Africa* (1961), 31
EVANS-PRITCHARD, E. E. and FORTES, M. *African Political Systems* (London: Oxford University Press, 1940)

Suggestions for further reading
GOODY, J. R. *The Social Organization of the Lowiili* (London: HMSO, 1956)
NADEL, S. F. 'Dual Descent in the Nuba Hills', in *African Systems of Kinship and Marriage*, A. R. Radcliffe-Brown and D. Forde (eds.) (London: Oxford University Press, 1950)

SECTION IV
Works consulted
EVANS-PRITCHARD, E. E. 'The Political Structure of the Nandi-Speaking Peoples', *Africa* (1940), 13
HUNTINGFORD, G. W. B. *The Nandi of Kenya: Tribal Control in a Pastoral Society* (London: Routledge & Kegan Paul, 1953)

Suggestions for further reading

EISENSTADT, S. N. *From Generation to Generation* (London: Routledge & Kegan Paul, 1956)
LAMBERT, H. E. *Kikuyu Social and Political Organisation* (London: Oxford University Press, 1956)
PERISTIANY, J. G. *The Social Institutions of the Kipsigis* (London: Routledge & Kegan Paul, 1939)
WILSON, M. *Good Company: a Study of Nyakyusa Age-Villages* (London: Oxford University Press, 1951)

SECTION V

Works consulted

ALAGOA, E. J. 'Long-Distance Trade and the States in the Niger Delta' in *Journal of African History* (1970), 11, 3
ARDENER, E. W. 'Lineage and Locality among the Mba-Ise Ibo', *Africa* (1959), 29, 2
BOHANNAN, L. 'Political Aspects of Tiv Social Organisation', in *Tribes without Rulers* J. Middleton and D. Tait (eds.) (London: Routledge & Kegan Paul, 1959)
BRADBURY, R. E. *The Benin Kingdom and the Edo-Speaking Peoples of S. W. Nigeria*, Ethnographic Survey of Africa, West Africa, Part 13, (London: International African Institute, 1957)
BUSIA, K. A. *The Position of the Chief in the Modern Political System of Ashanti* (London: Oxford University Press, 1951)
DIKE, K. O. *Trade and Politics in the Niger Delta* (London: Oxford University Press, 1956)
FORTES, M. 'The Political System of the Tallensi', in *African Political Systems*, M. Fortes and E. E. Evans-Pritchard (eds.) (London: Oxford University Press, 1940)
—— *The Dynamics of Clanship among the Tallensi* (London: Oxford University Press, 1945)
HERSKOVITS, M. J. *Dahomey: an Ancient West African Kingdom* (New York: J. J. Augustin, 1938)
HERSKOVITS, M. J. and F. S. *Dahomean Narrative: A Cross-Cultural Analysis* (Evanston: Northwestern University Press, 1959)
LITTLE, K. L. *The Mende of Sierra Leone* (London: Routledge & Kegan Paul, 1951)
LLOYD, P. C. 'The Traditional Political System of the Yoruba', *S.W.J. of Anthropology* (1954), 10
NADEL, S. F. *A Black Byzantium* (London: Oxford University Press, 1942)
ONWUEJEOGWU, M. A. 'The Typology of the Settlement Pattern in the Igbo Culture Area' in *African Notes* (1970), 6, 1
RATTRAY, R. S. *Ashanti* (Oxford: Clarendon Press, 1923)
SCHWAB, W. B. 'Kinship and Lineage among the Yoruba', *Africa* (1955), 25
SHAW, T. 'Radio Carbon dating in Nigeria' in *Journal of the Historical Society of Nigeria* (Dec. 1968), 4, 3
STENNING, D. *Savannah Nomads* (London: Oxford University Press, 1959)
TRAIT, D. 'The Political System of Konkomba', *Africa* (1953), 23
—— *The Konkomba of Northern Ghana* (London: Oxford University Press, 1961)

CHAPTER 11

Law and Order in Small-Scale Political Systems

I *The Existence of Law in Small-Scale Societies:*
the Comanche of North America

Before deciding whether people have law or not, it is imperative to define what law means. Radcliffe-Brown approached the study of law by examining and classifying types of sanctions:

1. Primary social sanctions:
   - (i) Positive: (a) diffuse, e.g. encouragements.
     - (b) organized, e.g. titles, honours.
   - (ii) Negative: (a) diffuse, e.g. satire.
     - (b) religious.
     - (c) organized, with definite procedure, not legal; imposed by authority, legal.
2. Secondary sanctions: procedures carried out by a community through its representative or by individuals.

It is clear that Radcliffe-Brown considered that law means organized negative sanctions which are imposed by a constituted authority. He says that 'the field of law will be coterminous with that of organised legal sanctions', and that other 'obligations imposed on individuals in societies where there are no legal sanctions will be regarded as matters of custom and convention but not of law'. Thus some 'primitive' societies have no law, but they may have customs supported by sanctions. Radcliffe-Brown, adopting the definition of Pound, who was a scholar of jurisprudence, says that law is: 'Social control through the systematic application of the force of politically organised society'. This definition is similar to his definition of political organization, and somewhat paradoxically, he also holds the view that all societies have political organization, although some have no law.

If we use the phrase 'organized physical force' to distinguish law from custom, then it will be difficult to distinguish law and custom in Igbo communities. The Igbo have a name for 'custom', *Odinani,* and a name for 'law', *Iwu.* Certain 'customs' are enforced by the use of 'organized force'. The distinction between custom and law lies in their origins. 'Law' is made by the council of elders, while custom is established by usage and handed down from generation to generation. Thus Igbo society maintains a distinction between 'law' and 'custom', and may use 'organized force' to enforce either. In this case Radcliffe-Brown's definition cannot be accepted, although his classification of sanction is very useful, because it helps to bring the definition of law within the compass of the use of physical force.

Some, such as Hartland and Driberg, have defined law by identifying it with custom; others, for example, Cardozo, Shapera, Gluckman and MacIver, have defined it as rules of conduct likely to be enforced by the courts. The difficulty is to establish what constitutes a court. Can we accept the 'bar of public opinion' as a type of court? It is also clear that even in advanced societies laws are made by a legislative body and rarely by courts. The aim of some traditional African courts, such as those of the Lozi and Igbo, is rather to mend the broken relations between two parties.

Radcliffe-Brown, Thurnwald and Hoebel define law in terms of the application of force. Hoebel, however, omits the word 'organized', since he considers that force is necessary, but not necessarily organized in the way suggested by Radcliffe-Brown. Hoebel's definition is: 'A social norm is legal if its neglect or infraction is regularly met, in threat or in fact, by the application of physical force by an individual or group possessing the socially recognized privilege of so acting.' In this definition he emphasizes regularity, the use of legitimate force and the prosecutor, who ought to be socially recognized. According to this definition it is possible to say that some of the Igbo customs could be called laws or 'customary laws', if law proper refers to rules which are enacted.

Malinowski's definition of law as 'a body of binding obligations, regarded as a right by one party and acknowledged as a duty by the other' may not be very useful in the study of law, although his insistence that law is an aspect of society and culture and that caution should be taken to locate the gap between the idea and the norm of law should be borne in mind.

In this chapter I shall use the Comanche for my analysis. In deciding whether the Comanche have law, the ideas of Radcliffe-Brown, Malinowski and Hoebel will be combined. Hoebel's definition may be accepted as a reasonably valid yardstick, as well as Radcliffe-Brown's classification of sanctions and Malinowski's warnings. Hoebel follows Malinowski in insisting that the whole culture of a people whose ways of law are to be studied should be fully grasped. The next step should be to search for instances of hitches and disputes and find out how they are settled. Then these disputes may be classified according to what sanctions are used to enforce them. If the sanctions are supported by the use of legitimate force they may be called laws. Here lies the difficulty. How can one distinguish legitimate from illegitimate force? Proper observation and correct questioning may reveal which is which; the key may be the regularity of use and the reaction of the society to the use.

I shall give two examples to show that the Comanche have laws of adultery and homicide. The Comanche ideal is that women are sexually and economically desirable, but are subordinate to men. Sexual rights over a wife are limited to the husband and his brother.

A medicine man has three wives of which one is his favourite. He returns from the Smoke Lodge and finds the favourite in bed with a young warrior. The father of the youth pays heavy damages to the medicine man and that settles that part of the case. However, if the damages are not paid, the youth can be killed; then no damages can be claimed. The father of the favourite wife, afraid that his son-in-law may mutilate or even kill her, since such punishments of an erring wife are accepted, comes to plead for her. He offers his son-in-law gifts and begs him not to hurt his child. He suggests that since she is guilty, it will be proper to make her the 'slave' of the other wives. The medicine man refuses the gifts but agrees to keep the woman safe, though she will no longer be his favourite wife. In this case adultery had been committed. The punishment might have been death for both parties, and the recognized executor would have been the husband or his kin. This threat to use force is recognized by the society. The society, acting automatically as the 'court', has condemned them, although they can pay fines or damages if the offended

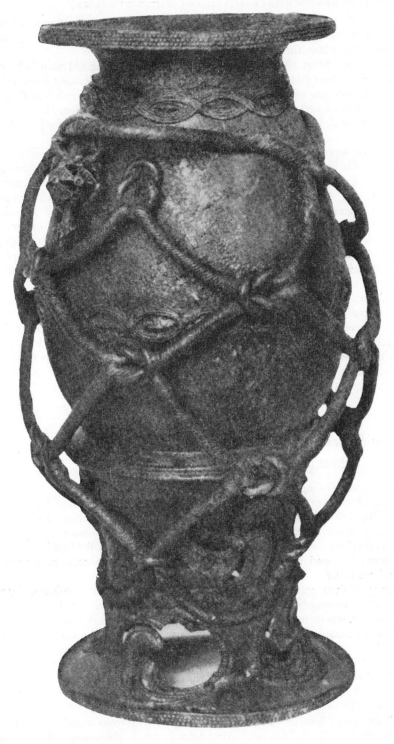

7 *Bronze roped pot (Igbo-Ukwu, Nigeria)*

party is ready to accept. This is done in this case and the matter closes. Other cases support the regularity of the above procedure. Therefore one can say that the Comanche have laws for adultery.

Cooks Dried Meat kills an old man. The kinsman of the old man kill Tongue, Cooks Dried Meat's father. By the end of it all, two people have been killed on each side; later one of the injured persons amongst the old man's kin dies. Cooks Dried Meat is chased out of the camp by the old man's grandson. He never comes back to the land. Here homicide is an individual matter. The law for killing is a life for a life.

Excessive sorcery is regarded by the Comanche as a crime against the whole society, and it is generally decided to kill the sorcerer. Wrongs which are regarded as purely against individuals and therefore to be settled according to traditional procedure are adultery, absconding with a wife, violation of levirate, sorcery, killing a favourite horse, homicide. Each has a sanction of force whereby the offended individual or his kin is socially recognized as 'prosecutor' or 'executor'. If A is too weak to demand the necessary damages from B, a warrior-chief may come to his aid. He goes between A and B and by the threat of the use of force, makes B pay the recognized damages. In Comanche justice such procedures are recognized as proper.

The Comanche do not have developed mechanisms or organs of law as known in 'advanced' societies. They have values which they accept as the ideal, but deviation occurs very often. Frequently recurring patterns become the norms which are enforced by sanctions. Those norms which are enforced by the sanction of 'force' might be considered to be Comanche law, if the person who threatens to apply the 'physical force' is a socially recognized agent. (For a general description of the Comanche, see Chapter 14, Section I.)

II *The Settlement of Disputes in Small-Scale Societies: the Cheyenne of North America*

The Cheyenne Indians, studied by Hoebel, were one of the most famous tribes of the Great American Plains. They originally inhabited the woodland lake country of the Upper Mississippi Valley; after adopting the horse culture and a buffalo-hunting economy, they lived on the Plains. They were nomads, about 4 000 in number, dwelling in bands of up to 100 persons. In summer the bands congregated for ceremonials and in winter they separated in order to cope better with the seasonal scarcities.

In spite of their nomadic life, they developed the concept of cultural, linguistic and political national unity. They were governed by a civil council of forty-four chiefs, out of whom five were priestly chiefs and two were doormen. The priestly chiefs, who outranked the others in ritual status, conducted the tribal rituals which included that of the chief-renewal, which was performed every year when the group assembled. One of the five priestly chiefs presided at the meetings of the council of forty-four and manipulated the sacred medicines. The doormen were sometimes called upon to sum up the gist of the discussion and to give a decision to the group when matters reached an impasse. When one of the five priestly chiefs retired, he chose his successor from the remaining thirty-nine members of the group, or if he died suddenly, the four living priestly chiefs chose one from the group. On retirement a priestly chief stepped down to the rank of the thirty-seven chiefs.

If any among the thirty-seven chiefs died without choosing a successor, the entire council chose one. Each ordinary chief could serve only ten years, and he could not choose his son as successor. New chiefs were chosen on the basis of merit, and it was considered bad taste for a man to choose his son. The personal qualities which made a chief were self-control, good temper, generosity and tribal integrity.

The forty-four chiefs never used or applied force to convey the will of the council. Force was applied by the members of one of the soldier societies. The council selected them on occasions of the camp moving, during the tribal buffalo hunt or during investigations. There was a close liaison between the council of forty-four chiefs and the soldier societies. The soldier societies were under the council of chiefs. Each band of 100 persons contained only four societies, but one of the societies, Dog soldiers, were members of one band. Two headmen and two doormen out of each of the men's societies formed a council of twenty-four war chiefs. A man could not be both a civil chief and a war chief. If a war chief was chosen as a civil chief he had to resign his position as war chief. Thus they were able to avoid clashes of interest.

In winter the Cheyenne were scattered, but when an incident occurred in which the chiefs were needed, riders were dispatched to notify each of the chiefs to assemble. Thus, even though the tribe was not in one locality, the governing machinery could be assembled without much difficulty.

If A killed B, the chiefs present and those near by would meet to decide whether the killing was justifiable. If they found A guilty, they passed a decree of banishment on him for five or ten years, and the ritual renewal of the arrows was performed. Banishment involved permanent prohibition from attending the ritual ceremony of the renewal of arrows, and from eating or smoking from a Cheyenne utensil without ritually polluting it. During the period of banishment the culprit might not acquire military or civil honours or officiate as chief. Non-murderers who banded up with A during the banishment incurred his disqualification with regard to acquiring honour. The chiefs in a band or tribal division might at any time after two years readmit the repentant culprit into the fold, provided the military societies and the kin of the victim gave their consent. Remission of banishment involved readmission to the performance of tribal functions, except for the permanent prohibitions named above.

Homicide within the tribe was a crime and a sin. It was a sin against the sacred arrows and endangered the very existence of the people. The kin of the victim was restrained from seeking redress by the society. It was the duty of every citizen, and especially the military societies, to intervene in disputes before they reached the point of murder. Self-defence, killing to remove a murderer, killing by 'military police' in the execution of an important duty, accidental killing, provocation and drunkenness resulting in killing, were not regarded as homicide.

C wanted to seduce his daughter, and she killed him in self-defence. The council decided that the girl was not guilty, because it was the only way to escape her incestuous father's approaches. A girl who deserted her husband was beaten by her mother. The girl committed suicide. The mother was charged with murder. The council found her guilty and she was banished. The wife of P refused to give her sister-in-law a buffalo hide and told her to get her own husband. The sister-in-law committed suicide. The chiefs decided that she had no reason to commit suicide, and so a verdict of 'not guilty' was passed.

A foetus was found in the camp, and the chiefs ordered the soldier society to investigate. All the young ladies and women were assembled and their breasts examined. The culprit was soon found. The council passed a verdict of murder and she was banished and the arrows were renewed.

The examples given above illustrate the roles of the chiefs and the military societies in the administration of law.

X removed Y's horse and did not return it although he left certain signs to indicate what he had done. A year passed and he did not bring it back. The litigant, Y, appealed to the soldier society who brought X before the council. X was discharged but a new law was passed ordering people to obtain the consent of owners before removing things.

The military society in charge of a hunt ordered that no hunting operations were to be undertaken by individuals. A group of men were determined to go out and hunt but the military society lashed them back. On another occasion Y went hunting, disregarding the society's order. The military society noticed him, and when he returned he was beaten and his tent was destroyed. One man refused to obey the laws of the band. The tribal chiefs and soldiers met and decided to ostracize him and banned anyone from helping him. Anyone who did help him would give a Sun dance. After some years he was readmitted after his brother-in-law gave a Sun dance.

From the above examples it can be seen that the council made and unmade laws; the military used force when necessary; and the principle of evidence was taken into consideration in the administration of justice.

Let us examine another aspect of Cheyenne law. Z accused P and Y of intimacy with his wife. He seized P's and Y's horses. P gave up his horse without resistance, knowing that he was guilty, but Y refused and swore on the holy hat in the hat-keeper's place, so Z gave him back his horse. Later, in a fight against the Crow, Y was killed and P was wounded. P confessed that Y had sworn falsely and he (P) had concealed it.

S ran off with T's wife. After some days he sent a horse through a chief to T. T smoked a pipe offered by the chief and accepted the horse and the matter was settled. S retained his new wife.

It is evident that the Cheyenne left all intra-family and inter-personal quarrels and disputes to be settled by self-help and the sanction of public opinion. But when an offender became a public menace society stepped in. For example, Pawnee was a thief and had little respect for people's property. He became worse, so one day after he had stolen two horses, the bow-string soldiers rounded him up and gave him a good beating, leaving him half-dead. A chief picked him up and by advice gradually rehabilitated him, so that he became an honest citizen.

The Cheyenne fully recognized private and public offences as well as those offences that fall between the two. They had machinery to deal with all public offences, but left private offences to be dealt with by self-help, oaths, or public opinion. The Cheyenne never left matters of public interest to be dictated by ritual instrument; instead they used the ritual to help and direct their efforts.

If law may be defined as a social control through the systematic application of force by politically organized societies, then the Cheyenne had law. They had an organ that could sit as a legislature in one instance and as judiciary in another. They had also another organ that acted as the police and executors of the legislature.

It seems that Hoebel holds the view that the Cheyenne had informal courts. There is also reason to think that they had formal courts. In spite of the fact that Cheyenne society was simple, with courts to serve only 4 000 persons in bands of 100 persons, in which everyone knew 'who was who', the judicial organ had a definite procedure, set codes, formalities and means of enforcing its decisions by the application of force. It also had specific and graded officers trained by experience in the law and rituals of the land. These men were picked for their tribal qualities, for specific purposes, of which one was the administration of justice. All these are to be found in our modern courts, which are formal and complex. Thus the Cheyenne's courts were equally formal, although simple. The difference is in the degree of complexity not of formality.

BIBLIOGRAPHY

SECTION I
Works consulted
LLEWELLYN, K. N. and HOEBEL, E. A. 'The Political Organization and Law-Ways of the Comanche Indians', *Memoirs American Anthropological Association* (1940), 54
RADCLIFFE-BROWN, A. R. 'Social Sanctions and Primitive Law' in *Structure and Function in Primitive Society* (London: Cohen & West, 1952)

Suggestions for further reading
BARTON, R. F. *Ifugao Law* (Berkeley and Los Angeles: University of California Press, 1919)
BIRKET-SMITH, K. *The Eskimos* (London: Methuen, 1936)
MALINOWSKI, B. *Crime and Custom in Savage Society* (London: Routledge & Kegan Paul, 1926)
SCHAPERA, I. 'Malinowski's Theories of Law' in *Man and Culture*, R. Firth (ed.) (London: Routledge & Kegan Paul, 1957)

SECTION II
Works consulted
HOEBEL, E. A. *The Cheyennes, Indians of the Great Plains* (New York: Holt, 1960)
LLEWELLYN, K. N. and HOEBEL, E. A. *The Cheyenne Way: Conflict and Case Law in Primitive Jurisprudence* (Norman: University of Oklahoma Press, 1941)

Suggestions for further reading
GLUCKMAN, M. *The Judicial Process among the Barotse of Northern Rhodesia* (Manchester: Manchester University Press, 1955)
—— *Politics, Law and Ritual in Tribal Society* (Oxford: Blackwell, 1971)
HOEBEL, E. A. *The Law of Primitive Man: A Study in Comparative Legal Dynamics* (Cambridge, Mass.: Harvard University Press, 1954)
LLEWELLYN, K. N. and HOEBEL, E. A. 'The Political Organization and Law-Ways of the Comanche Indians', *Memoirs American Anthropological Association*, 54, 1940
MAINE, H. *Ancient Law* (London: Murray, 1861)

CHAPTER 12

Societies with States

I *People Organized in Descent Groups with a Simple State Structure: the Birom of Northern Nigeria*

The minimal definition of a state is a society that is governed by a central single authority. This type of political system ranges from simple to most complex forms. Here it will be shown how a people organized in descent groups have a simple state system.

The Birom are one of the indigenous peoples inhabiting the Bauchi Plateau of northern Nigeria. (There were about 80 000 in 1952 when L. M. Baker studied them.)

They live in small compounds. Each compound is composed of a man, the compound head called *Dalo,* his wife or wives, his children, his mother and younger brothers. Larger compounds containing up to twenty people are rare and belong only to village chiefs, ward heads, or priests.

The Birom are mostly farmers who cultivate various grains such as acha, guinea-corn and millet. They used to trade in horses, pots, baskets, and slaves, etc. Things were valued in acha bags, goats, horses, and slaves. Blacksmiths used to be the only specialized craftsmen in the society.

The Birom live in about eighty villages, each of which is a compact settlement, one separated from the other by stretches of farm land and bush. A village may contain less than 100 souls; large ones have between 1 000 and 5 000 inhabitants.

The Birom claim a common origin framed in a legendary idiom, a common language and a common culture, but each village is ritually and politically autonomous. People from different villages do intermarry and exchange goods, but the relationship between villages is one of latent or open hostility. Ties of friendship and alliance tend to pull together neighbouring villages while traditions of hostility tend also to divide them. The origin of each village is expressed in myth and is traceable directly or indirectly to an ancient settlement called Riyom. But in some villages non-Riyom lineages have been incorporated.

There are two ways of becoming a member of a village: being born into a patri-lineage of the village; or obtaining permission from the village chief to settle in the village territory and finally becoming adopted into one of the village lineages.

Within the village the Birom live in localized agnatic kin groups. Small patri-lineages are localized while big ones are dispersed. Several patrilineages, each com-posed of up to 100 persons, make up a clan. Since each village is made up of several wards, and patrilineages are dispersed, members of any one ward are usually members of different clans.

Baker refers to each village as a 'rudimentary state'. What does this mean? The political structure of the village is that of a state. Each village has its own territory and its own chief called *Gwom.* The chief controls the political activities of the village. In his court he may condemn people to death and has the right to deal with various crimes including homicide. He also enjoys several prerogatives; in the past he would lead his village warriors into battle.

Succession to the throne of the chief is patrilineal; selections are made from brothers or sons. Some villages have chief-makers who perform the ritual of installation.

In spite of the chief's courts, the lineage settles certain kinds of domestic disputes between its members. Thus the chief's authority is limited.

The wards of each village are under a ward head whose appointment is sanctioned by the village head or chief, *Gwom*. Generally, ward heads are members of the chief's lineage. The chief's lineage is dominant both in number and in authority in the wards of the village.

Apart from the chief, *Gwom*, the village has two other officials: the *Gwom Ci* and the *Gwom Kwi*. There may be other minor *Gwom Kwi*. The *Gwom Ci* is the custodian of the *Ci* spirits and groves. He performs the rites of sacrifice of goats to the *Ci* spirits for the well-being of the society. The *Gwom Kwi* begins the rites of crop planting and the rites of the end of the year. These ritual offices are hereditary: either sons or brothers succeed.

The duties of the village chief *Gwom*, the *Gwom Ci* and the *Gwom Kwi* are to protect the crops and the ritual life and health of the villages. The sole duty of the *Gwom* is to protect the physical well-being of the village by seeing that law and order are maintained.

Through the complicated network of the lineage system and the territorial, social and ritual organization, each Birom village maintains its political cohesion and autonomy. Most of the affairs of the individual fall within the scope of kinship ties, but anything beyond falls within the scope of the 'state' – the village. The freedom of the individual is thus maintained by the checks and balances inherent in the structural and functional relationships between the lineages and the village mini-states.

There is no common authority above the village level. The hostile relationships between villages are minimized by alliances. Groups of villages federate from time to time, and there are fifteen of these federated villages, called village areas. One of the chiefs of the largest village is regarded as the senior chief in the federation, although it must be emphasized that he is the senior among equals. By these alliances states cooperate in war and trade, and intermarry.

According to Baker, the new local government system mirrors the traditional system. But the power of the village chiefs and the autonomy of the villages were reduced and placed under the Birom Native Authority during the period of her studies.

II *Factors that Affect the Development and Nature of the State: the Iroquois of North America*

ECOLOGY

According to Noon, the area of New York was the home of the Iroquois, before and a short time after European colonists arrived. The Iroquois believe that their League or Confederacy was created by Hiawatha who unified the various peoples into one nation called the Iroquois.

The Mohawks dwelled in the valley of the River Mohawk, the Oneida occupied the region of Lake Oneida, the Onondagas lived in the valley of the River Onondagas, the Cayugas lived on the shore of Cayuga and the Senecas lived near

Ontoria and Monroe. These five tribes, together with four other adopted tribes, comprised the League of the Iroquois.

The country was well forested. Rivers and lakes were the landmarks of each tribal territory. With the Atlantic on the east and a range of mountains on the north and south they occupied a strategic position which made them not only free from sudden attacks from outsiders but also enabled them to hold the gateways leading to other Indian territories.

The forest land and the rivers provided them with plenty of food and raw materials. The women cultivated grain and vegetables, while men provided meat and fish and did the heavy job of clearing new fields for planting. They practised a ten-year shifting cultivation system. With women as cultivators, and plenty of food, the men were free for military expeditions into neighbouring territories.

BACKGROUND HISTORY
With the arrival of the Europeans the Iroquois became acquainted with their culture. Joseph Brant, an Englishman, was adopted into Iroquoian society and was made a chief. In 1775 the American Revolution started, which marked the end of an era and the beginning of a new one in the history of the Iroquois.

Led by Brant, the Iroquois League took sides with the British. In reply to this the American colonists plundered and devastated the Iroquoian territory. Their economy and food supplies were paralysed and they were forced to depend on hunting alone. The war ended in victory for the colonists. A defeat for England was also a defeat for the Iroquois. The United States Congress created, from the former territories of the Iroquois, reserves for each member of the League. But many of them deemed it wise to abandon their traditional homes to live in Canada.

Haldimand granted them a tract of land bordering the bank of the Grand River. But Brant strongly argued that as the grant in Canada was to compensate the Iroquois for lands over which they had exercised sovereignty, the ownership of the Grand River territory should be vested in them. This suggestion was turned down and the title of the Canadian reservation was vested in the Crown.

SOCIAL STRUCTURE, PRE-REVOLUTION
The basic kin group among the Iroquoians was the matrilineage, which was a group headed by a 'matron' (the term suggested by Noon). Several matrilineages comprised the clan which had an animal eponym. The lineages of the clan were ranked, with the one possessing a chiefly title at the top of the hierarchy.

The local group which interacted daily was the extended family which dwelt in a long-house 50–150 ft long and 60 ft wide. The central portion was dotted with hearths at intervals of 10 ft. and both sides contained apartments which were the dwellings of simple families. The extended family under the matron was the smallest unit that controlled the economic, social and ritual activities of the long-house.

A number (20–120) of long-houses formed a village which was fortified by a moat and a stockade. Each village contained up to three clans. Groups of three or four villages formed a tribe. Five major tribes and four adopted ones made up the League. These tribes were divided into two moieties: the 'Elder' brothers and the 'Younger' brothers. Tribes of the same moiety called one another brother and members of the opposite moiety called one another cousin.

The clan government was dominated by women because it was centred around economic pursuits. The head of the clan was a woman called *Go Yani* who derived

8   *Bronze pendant (Igbo-Ukwu, Nigeria)*

her position from the fact that she was the eldest in a chiefly lineage. Her duty was to elect clan officers, to coordinate the economic activities of the female clan members, to decide adoption into the lineages, to check and even depose chiefs. The titular male head of the clan was the *Ho Yani* who was chosen by the head woman acting alone or in consultation with other women of the clan. Each titular chief had a sub-chief or messenger called the 'Ear' or the 'Cane'. The other officers of the clan were the 'great warrior' and two religious officials, one male and the other a female cook.

The function of the clan government was to allocate land to members, supervise the field work, keep the treasury and settle disputes between clan members. The chiefs were charged with the task of ordering and regulating all feasts and public games. They were also the welfare officers of the clan, caring for the poor and the helpless.

The tribal government was composed of the clan chiefs, the matriarchs of each clan, the Pine Tree chiefs who represented the warriors, and a council of elders. Since each tribe had corresponding clans in other tribes, the cross-cutting ties contributed to the fostering of inter-tribal interaction. The process of arriving at a decision was as follows. The matter was discussed by a meeting of the women of the clan, then by the chiefs and matriarchs together, then by a secret session of elders, and it was finally brought to a mass public meeting in which the decision of the elders was confirmed. The function of the tribal government was to regulate all internal matters of the villages and clan, to deal with other matters related to other tribes, and to declare war or make peace.

The tribes had functions. Thus, the Seneca occupied the western boundary and its duty was to drive off any enemy of the League from that quarter. It was honoured by being allowed to have two hereditary war chiefs in the League. The Mohawk tribe was called the 'Shield' and had the prerogative to collect tribute from subject tribes. The Onondaga were called the 'Fire-keepers' of the Confederacy and one of their chiefs was the custodian of the Council *wampum*, the Confederacy's emblem of peace and power. The Oneida tribe was called 'Great Tree' and the Cayaga was called the 'Great Pipe'.

The government of the Confederacy was vested in the Council of the Confederacy, which was composed of fifty hereditary chiefs ceremonially installed, and some Pine Tree chiefs elected to the tribal councils for their ability in public affairs. The method by which a decision was reached was called 'passing the matter through the fire'. The process was as follows. The Mohawk chiefs began the discussion and their decision was passed to the Seneca chiefs by Mohawk speakers. The Seneca's decision was similarly passed to the Oneida chiefs and to the Cayaga chiefs and finally to the Onondaga chiefs. The decision was final unless it was decided to send the matter back to the chiefs. The Council dealt with inter-tribal matters and those intra-tribal matters which could not be settled by the tribes concerned. All matters of affairs such as wars, peace and expansion of territory were the responsibility of the Council.

THE CONFEDERATE COUNCIL (GRAND COUNCIL): POST-REVOLUTION

It has already been stated that the Iroquois moved to a new abode after the wars of the American Revolution. The effects of this transfer and the intervention of extraneous forces left their marks on the economic, political, religious and social systems.

They adopted an entirely new type of economy and techniques. The old shifting cultivation was abandoned and villages became permanent. Women were replaced in farm work by men, and with this their authority dwindled. New systems of production, distribution and consumption gradually emerged, and each situation resulted in the creation of new officers to cope with the innovations. A new concept of land ownership was developed and with it new laws were made.

The former social pattern was altered. The clan was reorganized and soon lost its function in the Grand Council. The long-houses continued in a modified form.

The old religion competed with the new Christian religion. This split not only the members of the long-houses into two opposing camps but also the chiefs of the Grand Council. Thus religion, which had in the past helped to coordinate, became a disintegrating factor. The values of the society took a new shape.

The Grand Council lost its power and authority to deal with external affairs. Internally, however, it was supreme, for it had absorbed all the functions of the clan, the extended family and the tribal government. It even assumed new functions of legislating, adjudicating and appointing all officers of the state. Later on, the hereditary chiefs were replaced by an elected body. This was a result of the opposition organized by the old warrior groups.

The old concept of citizenship based on matrilineage membership was replaced by a wider concept of birth and residence. Thus with the loss of sovereignty the pattern of government became elaborate and complex as a result of acculturation. The question of the state's sovereignty dominated the relationship between the Grand Council and the British government, and later on the Canadian government.

FACTORS AFFECTING THE DEVELOPMENT AND NATURE OF THE IROQUOIAN STATE

According to history, Hiawatha's valour and political aptitudes led to the foundation of the Iroquois Confederacy, which was primarily formed so that the Iroquois might liberate themselves from the Adirondacks. How Hiawatha did it has passed into legend, but the inequalities of the lineages and the absorption of four other tribes suggest that it was partly by conquest and partly by 'lineage dominance'.

The individualist and separatist tendencies of the Iroquois have already been demonstrated above. There was extreme atomization of power from the clan level to the tribal level. Thus, during the American Revolution, the tribes of the Confederacy were divided about which party to help, the English or the colonists. The tribes were autonomous and could declare war on other non-member tribes. Each tribe was really a small 'sovereign state' within a bigger sovereign state. (The question of why it developed in this way might be answered by reading the material.) It is true that the League Council was dominant to a certain extent, but its power was limited by the prevailing ideology that each tribe had the sacred prerogative of autonomy. This was intensified by the spatial distance and ecological distribution of the villages. Each village was fortified and each tribe occupied a natural fortified valley. Without good means of transportation and communication it was difficult to bring these tribes under a ruler or group of rulers. The United States government realized this and offered to create reserves in areas which would make each tribe accessible, but the offer was turned down.

The means by which the Iroquois coordinated the activities of the widely separated tribes and villages was by having related clans represented in each village. Thus tribal relations were strengthened in the absence of effective centralization and the villages were weakened. The system also inhibited the rise to power in a village of anyone who might want to subjugate the other villages. It was not even possible for a man to keep a following by using surplus wealth. Women were dominant in the economic field and the family and clan government were in their hands.

It is not surprising that the Iroquois state developed as it did in spite of Hiawatha, the emergence of some powerful chiefs in the Council, and the threat from neighbouring tribes.

The principle of moiety organization adopted by the Iroquois fostered cohesion and increased the integration of the tribes. Thus the ideology of citizenship based on territoriality was expressed in the fiction of kinship. This principle allowed the absorption of new tribes as members of the state.

The concept of chiefship was not based on the exercise of force. Chiefs only took decisions; they left the warrior associations to execute them. Each clan within a village had its own warrior association. Each warrior was subservient to the matron of the clan and the long-house. The religion of the long-house demanded complete obedience and valour, but only when demanded by the clan. Among the Iroquois, therefore, the existing social organization was a very important factor in the moulding of the state.

Today, within a limited territory, the Council has acquired legislative, judicial and administrative powers in the government of the Iroquois reserves. Every aspect of Iroquois government is a microcosm of the state machinery found in any modern state. The Iroquois of 1770 constituted a state in their own right, but at present they have a form of local government within the state of Canada.

In Africa the development of some of the states, such as the Zulu, was similar to the Iroquois, for instance, in the spheres of leadership and unification. Chaka unified the Zulu into a strong military state; however, neither Brant, a stranger, nor Hiawatha, the founder of the League, was able to unify the Iroquois. (A comparative analysis of the Zulu and Iroquoian state system in terms of the nature of their development might be rewarding, but it cannot be attempted here.)

III *The Ideology of Kingship and Royal Descent: the Perak and Selangor of Malaya*

THE ORIGIN OF THE MALAYAN KINGSHIP AND POLITICAL SYSTEM

The history of the Malay states forms an important and significant element of their culture. According to Gullick, the earliest written Malay history was written around 1540, but there are copious accounts of earlier periods. The social significance of this history and literature is that they serve to transmit the traditions and values of the community, especially of its ruling class.

Up to AD 1400 Malaya lay on the periphery of various political units centred around the Indonesian Archipelago. Earlier in the Christian era there were outposts of Hindu kingdoms in north Malaya, and in the seventh century the Malay Peninsula was within the sphere of the Sumatran Buddhist kingdom of Sri Vijaya. In the fourteenth century the Javanese kingdom of Majapahit overshadowed the Sri Vijaya. About AD 1400 a Malay prince established a dynasty at Malacca on the west coast. This event marked the beginning of an indigenous system of major political units in the Malay Peninsula.

The Malacca Sultanate formed the heroic period in the historical traditions of Malay Sultanates which succeeded it. It lasted just over a century, 1400–1511, but its influence was great and lasting. The later Malay states inherited from Malacca a tradition in which some of their major values were expressed and also a form of political organization which they strived to preserve.

The rulers of Malacca reproduced on a smaller scale the political system of the earlier kingdoms of western Indonesia. The Sultanate was a compact and centralized political system. The head and centre of the system was a ruler drawn from a royal patrilineage and his authority was supported by the attribute of divine kingship of the Hindu dynasties. Under the ruler and other princes of the royal house the government was managed by ministers from aristocratic and non-royal lineages. There were also outlying districts and political officers; the administrators of these districts were the appointees of the Sultan of Malacca. Thus the foundation of the royal dynasty of Perak was allocated to an elder son of a Sultan of Malacca.

After the collapse of Malay, the Sultan of Malacca and the nobles as a result of Portuguese aggression in 1511, the semi-independent states took full advantage of the situation and completed their independence. Thus the sultans of Perak became a fully independent dynasty.

At the end of the eighteenth century Bugis adventurers from Celebes obtained control of what remained of the moribund Malacca Sultanate. A branch of this Bugis dynasty established itself in Selangor state, a dependency of Malacca. During the eighteenth century the Bugis rulers of Selangor obtained general recognition as a royal dynasty after much fighting with the Sumatran dynasty.

On the whole, the history of these kingdoms was one of conquest after conquest. The establishment of each dynasty meant a rewriting of the history of conquest that supported its claim, validating the claim of the ruling class as a whole and the sultanate in particular. This history, for effect, was recorded in the most romantic style.

THE POLITICAL ORGANIZATION OF MALAY STATES

The new Malay states of Negri Perak, Negri Selangor, Negri Simbilan and others, copied heavily from the Malacca system. In Perak and Selangor the state was the largest political unit and was called Negri. Such a state was a territory under an independent ruler. Since Malay states tended to congregate on the banks of rivers, a state territory was typically the basin of a large river or group of adjacent rivers, forming a continuous area of land extending from the coast inland to the interior watershed system. The state as a political unit was under a ruler. He was chosen from a royal patrilineage and was invested with attributes of supernatural power and dignity. He was called 'he who is made lord', or Sultan. His functions were to exercise the limited powers of central government, to conduct external relations, to provide the leadership in foreign wars, and to embody and symbolize the unity and welfare of the state. He was assisted and supported by his kinsmen in the royal lineage and by a number of executive assistants. The lineages of chiefs formed the ruling class of the states. The existence of a ruling class and a subject class was a dominant element of the Malay political and social system.

The next unit was the district. Like the state, the district was a territory accessible by using rivers as a means of communication. The ruler of a district was drawn from a lineage which usually had long-established connections with the district.

The functions of a chief in his district were local administration, justice, defence, revenue collection and general leadership, as well as a few ritual functions. He was assisted by a number of helpers and deputies who were generally close kinsmen.

The relationship between the Sultan and chief, in political terms, was that the

Sultan, who also controlled a royal district, which he governed after the fashion of a district chief, was the fountain of the political authority of all chiefs. Each chief received a sword of authority and a sealed written document validating his authority. However, the Sultan had no effective political power of control over the chiefs. The chiefs of the state were the electors of Sultans. The chiefs acknowledged the Sultan as the formal head of the state. They could fight and intrigue to put one claimant on the throne instead of another, but they would never destroy or usurp the Sultanate itself.

The smallest unit in the political system was the village. This was a unit of common residence and to some extent of kinship and economic cooperation. The head of the village was the head man who was responsible to the chief and who was generally a member of the subject class. The head man was not a ruler but a caretaker. (For another discussion of the political organization, see Chapter 18, Section III.)

THE IDEOLOGY OF THE SULTANATE AND ROYAL DESCENT, AND ITS IMPLICATIONS

We have seen that the Sultan was the head of the state and was called 'he who is made lord'. The meaning of these words should enable one to make a full analysis of their ideology of kingship and royal descent. To do this we should be able to provide answers to the following questions:

1. Who made him lord?
2. How and when was he made lord?
3. How was it shown that he was lord?
4. Was lordship reserved for him and for him alone?

In answering these questions we should try to reason like the average Malayan of that period; and we should also bear in mind that we should not expect logicality or rationality in the answers. Our concern is to find out whether the ideology serves as an effective medium for the transmission of power from generation to generation.

Who made him lord? According to Gullick, in Perak and Selangor, government was the state of having a ruler, and this ruler was sacred, with divine powers. The ruler derived his supernatural power from the accumulated beliefs of the past. The Sultan therefore derived his political authority from the belief that he was divine. His person was sacred and touching it was forbidden. It was said that white blood ran in his veins. This was part of the mnemonic or idiom used to express the whole concept of his divinity and dignity. His people accepted him as lord, because he was derived from a supernatural being; he was therefore not like an ordinary man.

How and when was he made lord? The 'when' is shown in the 'history', in a period of what Nadel calls 'ideological history'. Malaya was a literate society only in the sense that the court had secretaries who recorded state decisions and state history; few of the aristocrats were literate. The subject class was illiterate and it was the romantic ideological history that appealed to it. The romantic period was the timeless past when the Sultans became lords. This written history was the 'charter' of the state kept by the royal dynasty. The 'how' was also contained in the charter.

How was it shown by the people and the royals that he was lord? This question is of great sociological importance, because it deals with the evidence of the divine 'origin' and the sacredness of the ruler. Visual evidence was the most effective vehicle of transmitting and transferring political rights in both literate and pre-literate societies. At ceremonies of succession, burials, and so on, several forms of symbolism were used to convey the impression of divine kingship. The Sultan sat impassive and immobile on a raised platform. This was a sign of divinity. Yellow clothing and state umbrellas were a royal monopoly. The installation of a Sultan was marked by the most elaborate ritual, in which the royal person became a Sultan, more king than the rest. There was ceremonial washing to mark the making of a new man.

The king's sacredness was believed to be transferable to objects. Thus his regalia – musical instruments, sceptre, a secret spoken formula, weapons such as swords – were looked upon as sacred. Many forms of clothing, weapons and domestic household adornments were reserved for the exclusive use of the Sultan. There was a special vocabulary used in referring to the various activities of the Sultan. Certain animals, fruits, and even people, were reserved for the Sultan. For example, tame elephants were the mounts of royalty, and ivory was the royal property. Albino buffaloes and illegitimate children born contrary to natural and social rules belonged to the Sultan who was vested with supernatural power to own and handle them.

The major public occasions of his reign were his installation and his funeral. The chiefs of the state took their customary part in the ritual of these occasions. There was usually a large gathering of the subject and ruling classes to witness his greatness and divinity. On the major festivals of the Muslim year the Sultan held a levee at which some of his chiefs made obeisance to him. The formal submission of the chiefs to the Sultan was symbolic, for it also meant the submission of the subject class to the Sultan as a person, to his lineage and to the ruling class as a whole.

Was lordship reserved for him and him alone? This question is important because it probes the complex question of royal descent. It is not as simple as it seems and needs patient analysis.

Eligibility for succession to the office of sultan was confined to a single royal patrilineage distinct from the chiefly lineages. There was no automatic right of succession. The choice of a successor from among the members of the royal lineage rested with the chiefs. An aspirant to the throne had first to conform to the charter by being from the royal 'inner ring', and then he had to win the support of the chiefs, for from the start of his reign he had to be accepted by the majority of the chiefs. His mother must be of royal descent: the daughter of a Sultan was especially suitable. It may be mentioned that these principles were often disregarded, because of feud and intrigue among dominant personalities in the ruling class.

The tradition of Malay monarchy, upon which the values of the society depended, required that royalty should be based on descent. The limited freedom of choice permitted by this rule gave rise to its own problems. A lineage within which office was held was segmented in each generation; some lineages might become extinct. In the absence of any strict rule, such as male primogeniture, there would be more claimants to office than could ever hold it. This difficulty was lessened in the Perak royal dynasty by instituting a system of rotation of office among branches of the lineage. Another problem was that members of the lineage who actually were in office had a natural preference for transmitting their rights to their children, in defiance of the principle laid down. This tendency was counterbalanced, to a limited extent, by marriages between office-holding members. This gave rise to the creation of an 'inner' and 'outer' circle of royalty. Those in the inner circle were more closely related to the ruler than those in the outer. The monarch was thus the centre of the royal kinship system. The inner circle tried to exclude from office the collateral branches of each generation. In Perak this inner group was called *Waris Negris*. They had well-known tests for membership and carried the right to fill the lesser offices as well as the Sultanate.

The office of *Raja Muda*, Junior Ruler, who deputized for the Sultan, came next to that of the Sultan. In Selangor the office was normally held by the son of a Sultan. Although a *Raja Muda* stood a better chance of succeeding, the final decision remained with the electors, the chiefs. In Perak, with its system of rotation of the Sultanate among the branches of the royal house, the *Raja Muda* was usually a son of a past Sultan rather than the reigning one. The next junior 'office' was that of *Raja Bendahara*. In Perak the system worked in this way: if the reigning Sultan came from branch 'A', his successor *Raja Muda* would come from branch 'B', while 'C' would provide the *Raja Bendahara*. When Sultan 'A' died, branch 'B' supplied the Sultan, while 'C' supplied the *Raja Muda* and 'A' supplied the *Raja Bendahara*. Irregularities did occur but the proper system was always remembered and serious attempts were made to follow it, for by doing so the charter on which kingship was based was upheld.

Every person of either sex descended in the male line from a sultan bore a title showing royal status as a personal prefix to his or her name. In Perak and Selangor this title was *Raja*. If a woman of royal descent married a man of non-royal descent her children did not inherit the royal status. Nevertheless the children had a special status distinct from that of ordinary commoner. A male member of the royal lineage could transmit his descent status to his children through a non-royal wife. A male member of course preferred to take a member of the royal lineage as principal wife; a *Raja* in the inner circle secured the position of his children by so doing. A *Raja* on the outer circle might have little hope of holding the Sultanate, but he would prefer to take a marriage partner from the royal class. Thus, he still looked to the Sultanate as the origin of his own exalted status and to the inner circle and the throne as the model of his conduct.

The royal lineage accepted one group of outsiders as equal in status to themselves. These were the supposed descendents of the Prophet Mahomet. They did intermarry with royal persons, especially those of the 'outer circle'.

In Selangor the royal lineage took over all the district chieftainships and replaced all the non-royal lineages completely. In Perak members of the royal lineages lived around the Sultan, occupying various court offices and leaving the districts to non-royal lineages of the ruling class.

The relationship between the Sultan and his close kinsmen was not usually cordial. There was a great deal of jealousy about the right to fill royal offices and the sharing of royal revenues. But all had one common aim: to preserve the royalty on which their own exalted position was based.

To sum up, Malay was a society where the ideology of kingship and royal descent permeated every aspect of political, legal, military, and to some extent, economic and ritual life. This ideology gave the Malays a feeling of belonging to a total political unit under the Sultan. This ideology was deeply embedded in their past history, validated by a written document, and transferred from generation to generation by various mechanisms. Similar ideologies of kingship and royal descent are common features of African kingdoms; Audrey Richards has done excellent work on this aspect of African kingdoms (see suggestions for further reading, Section III).

IV The Criteria of Eligibility for Political Office among the Yoruba and Nupe of Nigeria

In 1970 there were between eight and nine million Yoruba people of similar culture and language occupying the western part of Nigeria. They live in large settlements many of which used to be the capitals of chiefdoms. They are agriculturalists in the rain and deciduous forest zones, growing yam, maize, cassava and beans. At present cocoa farming dominates their farming activities.

According to Lloyd, the Oke Ewi are Ado Ekiti, who are Yoruba. Oke Ewi consists of three adjacent settlements, each with its own chief acknowledging a common ruler, the *Ewi*. Oke Ewi, the seat of the chiefdom, has a population of 16 000. It is made up of five quarters, each having compounds of one or two large lineages and two or three smaller ones. There are compounds of segments of the royal lineage in each quarter. The royal lineage traces its descent patrilineally from a royal prince in Ile Ife and is eleven or twelve generations deep some with more than 1000 persons. Other lineages are shallow in depth, between five and six generations; this is characteristic of Yoruba commoner lineages which have 'fused generations' as a result of factors such as migration and segmentation. Members of a lineage generally live in a single compound or in adjacent compounds under a lineage head who is normally the oldest male member. Such a lineage is a corporate land and title owning group whose welfare and harmonious organization lie in the hand of the oldest male member. This lineage head has little more than moral authority and ritual sanction over his members.

Every man in Oke Ewi belongs to an age-set. Age-sets are informally constituted every two or three years when some boys reach the age of nine or ten. Each set receives a name from the Ewi and a leader emerges as a result of personality and ability. At weekly meetings, members discuss the town's affairs and personal problems and leaders are able to muster moral pressure against offenders.

Age-grade also plays a very important role in political organization. A man passes through five grades, each of a span of nine years, from childhood to adulthood. Each grade marks his economic status and allocates to his specific state duties such as road-making and warfare. Promotion in the grades is a purely personal matter, one of achievement. There is no admission ceremony for the first two lower grades, but for the subsequent higher ones admission entails providing a feast to the members. The *Elegbe* chiefs organize and supervise the age-grades.

The chieftaincy titles of Oke Ewi may be grouped into four categories according to their rank. The first is the *Ewi*, which is the title of the *Oba*, who is a divine ruler and the personification of the whole town. The *Ewi* title is hereditary in two segments of the ruling lineage founded by the first *Ewi*. Members of segments tracing descent from the earlier *Ewi* are not eligible. The present lineage was founded by the sixteenth *Ewi* about the beginning of the eighteenth century. The *Ewi* is selected alternatively from the two royal segments, and he must be a son born to an *Oba* while on the throne, but not the first of such sons; he must have been born to a free woman and also physically fit. The candidate is presented by the lineage to the *Ihare* chiefs whose responsibility is to make the final selection by the use of *Ife* oracle. The *Ewi* chief holds office for life, but he can be removed by being asked by those who appointed him to take poison and die. Members of the royal lineage have no extra authority nor right to take over other titles save that of the lowest grade chief, the *Elegbe*.

Next in order of status are the *Ihare* chiefs, who are divided into five higher and five lower chiefs. The higher ones are hereditary in the four oldest and largest quarters, of which one has two *Ihare* chiefs; the fifth quarter has no *Ihare* chief since it is a new creation. The *Ewi* has the right to appoint three of the hereditary chiefs, who by tradition have free access to his private apartments in the palace. Some of the lower *Ihare* titles are hereditary in certain lineages and others are bestowed by the *Ewi* in council to persons of influence and ability.

The *Ijoye* title is next in rank. There are over twenty-two titles associated with this rank and only the most senior is hereditary within one lineage; others are bestowed by the *Ewi* and chiefs to men of ability and popularity.

The *Elegbe* chiefs come next in status and rank, and are distributed partly on a lineage basis and partly on ability and influence. These are the lowest grade of chieftaincy titles and their duty is to organize the age-grade of their lineages. The first nine *Elegbe* chiefs are selected from any lineage by the *Ewi* and chiefs, and of these, two are reserved for the royal lineage. Each lineage has one or two *Elegbe* chiefs whose titles are hereditary within the lineage.

When the title of a chief is hereditary within a lineage, it is usually the right of the lineage members to elect the holder, but if they fail to agree, the *Ewi* and chiefs may appoint anyone from the legal lineage. No *Ihare* or *Ijoye* chief may lay down a title in order to take up a higher one; *Elegbe* chiefs, on the other hand, may do so. Royal lineages cannot take *Ihare* titles, but they can take *Elegbe* titles. After the candidate for a title has been presented to the *Ewi* and chiefs for approval, he begins to make a series of payments to them. The installation ceremonies of all *Ihare* chiefs are carried out by the *Ewi*.

On the whole, because of the dominance of lineages in Yoruba political organization, more status is based on kinship than achieved, although the age-grade and age-set systems are exceptions.

Bida, the capital of Beni district and later the Nupe kingdom, is one of the walled towns in the Nupe kingdom. (In 1934 the population density in Bida Division was about thirty-five persons per square mile.) The Nupe are agriculturalists, in what may be called the Niger–Kaduna River basin. They are also organized in a guild system for the domestic manufacture of metal and non-metal goods.

According to Nadel, the Bida political system is highly hierarchical and its history is chequered. The Nupe kingdom was founded in the fifteenth century by Tsoede; then came the Fulani conquest, followed by the establishment of the Mallam Dendo dynasties, by 1833; then the intervention of the Royal Niger Company; and finally, the establishment of British rule. This account refers to the post-Fulani period, before the arrival of the British.

The Nupe live in domestic family groups which form a larger social unit called the 'house' which is both a kinship and a territorial group. The group consists of a body of patrikin to which wives and others are attached. Its head is known as 'owner of the house', a position which falls to the senior male member of the group, who is succeeded by the next in order of seniority of the same generation, and so on. The size of the house differs; smaller ones may contain between six and eight individuals, and bigger ones among the nobility up to sixty. Groups of 'houses' merge to form wards, and wards form villages or towns, which are usually walled and have an independent internal organization.

Bida town is governed by *Etsu Nupe*, the ruler of the nineteenth century Nupe kingdom. The *Etsu* is the highest title-holder, and only three dynasties stemming from *Mallam Dendo* succeed to the throne, in strict rotation. The next in rank is the *Shaba* who is heir presumptive, followed by the *Kpotun*, the head of the third dynasty. Bida town is divided into three sections, each bearing the name of one of the royal dynasties, and each having its own royal palace. Any physically fit man of senior age, of loyalty and ability, and a member of the lineage, is eligible to the above titles.

The next title-holders come from the office-holding nobility, which is made up of three groups, each of which is a sharply defined social order. First is the group of civil and military nobility made up of town elders and war leaders. The 'father of the town' is the highest in this group, since he is in charge of the affairs of Bida. The second in order of rank comprises the Mallams and judicial officers (*Alkali*), learned in the Koran. The lowest in rank are the court slaves, who nevertheless possess great influence.

A few titles of the first group are hereditary in certain families, but most of them are granted to those who win the favour of the *Etsu*, though wealth and financial influence are also important. The order of Mallams and *Alkali* is a specialized class based on ability and knowledge of the Koran, some of whom tend to be hereditary, reflecting the tradition of learning in certain families. Otherwise any clever person can become an *Alkali* or *Liman*, an officiating Muslim priest, depending on his loyalty and influence.

Below these groups come the minor office-holders which are political and economic offices. These are the heads of Bida craft guilds, who receive their titles and the customary gift of the turban from the *Etsu*. The lowest titled class in Nupe society is that of the court slaves. They can rise in the service of the king as bodyguards, police, messengers, etc. Below the orders of title-holders are the commoners, who are grouped in houses.

From the above account we can draw some valid generalizations. The Yoruba and Nupe political systems are both pyramidal in structure, but while the Nupe system is not based mainly on either lineage or kinship, that of the Yoruba is based on lineage. The result of this is that achieved status is dominant in Nupe society, while status derived from kinship is more common among the Yoruba.

The kingship title is hereditary in both cases, but the number of other titles for the royal lineage is limited among the Yoruba, and even more so in Nupe society. The tendency to despotism and nepotism seems greater among the Nupe.

The Nupe *Etsu* with its three dynasties associated with military origin gives room for many candidates and so is very competitive, while the Yoruba *Ewi* with its divine kingship superimposed on a lineage system is restrictive, for only sons 'born on the throne' by an *Ewi* (except the first sons) can compete for the title.

Other titles among the Nupe are mostly acquired by personal ability and qualities, while the other Yoruba titles are mostly bestowed by lineage inheritance. We may therefore expect keener competition among the Nupe society than among the Yoruba society, although the Yoruba age-grade system gives room for competition within a small group. The Nupe system lends itself to more diversification and specialization.

Titles among the Nupe carry types of state duties which need special ability and training. Thus the criteria of eligibility are based more on ability than the chance of birth. We see that promotions are gradual and systematic, and many, among the Nupe. However, they are few and restrictive among the Yoruba, for example, *Ihare* chiefs cannot give up their titles for higher ones.

At the domestic level, the Nupe 'house' head is appointed by adopting the principle of the oldest in the senior generation, while the Yoruba lineage head is appointed according to the principle of the oldest male.

Finally the Nupe *Etsu* can create and unmake titles, while the Yoruba *Ewi* cannot create or unmake. This is because title-holders are more predetermined in Yoruba society than among the Nupe. A title is also more a matter of lineage entitlement among the Yoruba than among the Nupe.

BIBLIOGRAPHY

SECTION I
Works consulted

BAKER, L. M. 'The Biroms', unpublished thesis London University, 1952

HAROLD, D. G. **Pagan Peoples of the Central Area of Northern Nigeria*, Ethnographic Survey of Africa, West Africa, Part 12, D. Forde (ed.) (London: International African Institute, 1956)

ONWUEJEOGWU, M. A. *The Traditional Political System of Ibusa*, an occasional publication of Odinani Museum, Nri, Institute of African Studies Project, University of Ibadan (Onitsha: Tabansi Press, 1973)

SECTION II
Works consulted

MORGAN, L. H. *League of the Iroquois* (reprint of 1851 edition) (New York: Corinth Books, 1952)

NOON, J. A. 'Law and Government of the Grand Iroquois', New York: Viking Fund Publication in Anthropology (1949), 12

Suggestions for further reading

FORTES, M. and EVANS-PRITCHARD, E. E. (eds.) *African Political Systems* (London: Oxford University Press, 1940)

LOWIE, R. H. *The Origin of the State* (New York: Russell & Russell, 1962)

—— 'Some Aspects of Political Organisation among the American Aborigines', *J.R.A.I.* (1948), 78

SCHAPERA, I. *Government and Politics in Tribal Societies* (London: Watts, 1956)

SECTION III
Work consulted

GULLICK, J. M. *Indigenous Political Systems of Western Malaya* (London: Athlone Press, 1958)

Suggestions for further reading

BEATTIE, J. H. M. 'Checks on the Abuse of Political Power in Some African States', *Sociologus* (1959), 9, 2

EVANS-PRITCHARD, E. E. *The Divine Kingship of the Shilluk of the Nilotic Sudan* (Cambridge: Cambridge University Press, 1948)

FORDE, D. and KABERRY, P. M. (eds.) *West African Kingdoms in the Nineteenth Century* (London: Oxford University Press, 1967)

GOODY, J. R. (ed.) *Succession to High Office*, Cambridge Papers in Social Anthropology, no. 4 (Cambridge: Cambridge University Press, 1966)

* 'Pagan' here means non-Muslim and non-Christian, that is those who still follow the traditional religions. It is a term wrongly applied to traditional religions.

RICHARDS, A. I. 'Social Mechanisms for the Transfer of Political Rights in some African Tribes'
J.R.A.I. (July–Dec. 1960), 90 (2)
—— 'African Kings and Their Royal Relatives', *J.R.A.I.* (1961), 91
—— 'Keeping the King Divine' (Myers Lecture), *Proceedings of the Royal Anthropological Institute*, 1968

SECTION IV
Works consulted

LLOYD, P. D. 'The Traditional Political System of the Yoruba', *South-Western Journal of Anthropology* (1954)
—— 'The Yoruba Lineage', *Africa* (1955), 25
—— 'Sacred Kingship and Government among the Yoruba,' *Africa* (1960), 30
NADEL, S. F. *A Black Byzantium: the Kingdom of Nupe in Nigeria* (London: Oxford University Press, 1942)
SCHWAB, W. B. 'Kinship and Lineage among the Yoruba', *Africa* (1955), 25, 4

Suggestions for further reading
SMITH, R. S. *Kingdoms of the Yoruba* (London: Methuen, 1969)

CHAPTER 13

Role Differentiation
and Social Inequality

*Caste and Class as Systems of Political and Economic Differentiation:
Tanjore (India) and the Hausa-Fulani of Nigeria*

TANJORE

Ecology
Tanjore village, studied by Gough, is in the Tanjore district, which is situated on
the delta of the Kaveri River. The alluvial soils are excellent for wet paddy rice
cultivation which occupies about three-quarters of the arable land. Dry millets are
alternated with two wet paddy crops; also coconuts and garden vegetables are
grown. Irrigation works improve the yield per acre and also increase the acreage of
wet paddy land.

The population in 1951 was nearly three million in an area of 3 250 square miles,
having a density of about 900 persons per square mile. The district had six muni-
cipalities and a number of small market towns and ports, but the bulk of the population was supported by agriculture, petty trade and handicrafts. There was very
little mechanized industry. Railways and bus services linked the larger towns, and
roads linked the larger villages.

Historical Background
By the beginning of the first century AD the Tamil Chola kingdom was established
on the delta. The structure of government, the settlement patterns of multi-caste
villages and towns, the land tax and systems of irrigation, the Brahmans' ritual
supremacy and their role as counsellors of the king had been established much as
they were to be later. After many troubles, the Chola dynasty finally disappeared
by 1534. The kingdom, reduced to the limits of the present district, came under the
rule of the Nayaks. In 1674 Tanjore was conquered by Maratha invaders. The
Maratha dynasty held Tanjore, in spite of several Muslim invasions, until its
annexation by the British in 1799. The royal family was pensioned off, and died
out in 1855. Tanjore became a district of Madras Province in 1947.

Caste Structure
The Hindu are divided into three main castes: Brahman, non-Brahman and Adi
Dravida. Each of the larger caste communities is traditionally a localized unit with
kinship, social, economic, religious and administrative functions. Furthermore, each
caste community belongs to an endogamous group distributed in many villages. The
endogamous group is merely a clearly defined group within which marriage,
visiting and free commensality take place. Its existence gives a certain unity to an
area wider than the village. Affinal and cognatic ties, cross-cutting villages, help to

counteract the tendency towards collective disputes between neighbouring villages. Among landlords, that is the higher caste, movement from one village to another is confined to adoption; for lineages and extended families remain permanent and stable on their sites over many generations. But among the lower castes, a serf or specialist may, with the consent of landlords, move from his village to another where more work is available. The kinship system of lower castes, which emphasizes matrilateral and affinal ties as strongly as patrilineal descent, permits a high proportion of both matrilocal and uxorilocal residence. It contrasts with the deep patrilineages and the weak and narrow range of matrilateral and affinal ties among Brahmans. Among the lower castes, inter-village kinship ties provide a means of keeping the supply of labour steady.

The Brahmans form a single caste with five or more subdivisions. The Tamil Brahmans are the most numerous of all and are indigenous. They receive grants of land from the Chola kings and settle in Brahman villages near the main branch of the sacred Kayeri, worshipping Siva and Visna. Each subdivision is divided into small regional endogamous sub-castes each comprising the local communities of some ten to twenty villages. Each specializes in one religious function in temples or in non-Brahmans' households.

Brahmans, although they comprise only one-fifteenth of Tanjore's population, own the bulk of land in 900 out of 2 400 villages. They are also wealthier and more numerous than in any other South Indian district.

They occupy a special area in Tanjore village and form a corporate community of six households with a total of 290 persons, of which only 56 remain permanently in the village and dominate its social life.

The Brahman community comprises four dominant exogamous patrilineal lineages with a few related households of recent arrivals. They are all related to each other by patrilineal, affinal, or cognatic ties. They show a high degree of internal interaction and external exclusiveness. They have common residence, a common cremation ground, and common social and cultural activities to the exclusion of others. Children are socialized within their street, and until the age of five do not mingle with those of other castes. Their women only know the roads of the village outside their own street and never visit the streets of non-Brahmans and the low castes. Social distance between Brahmans and other castes is phrased in terms of rules of ritual pollution. They have a different kinship system and terminological structure, a different culture, and they hold the monopoly of rituals and knowledge of Sanskrit religion and culture.

The heads of the four Brahman lineages form a group responsible to the government for the village's administration and revenue collection. Their duties are as follows: allocation of lands and servants to separate households, the common control of the village specialist castes, and the organization of Adi Dravidas for such joint tasks as the digging out of irrigation channels and the administration of justice among the Brahmans and within the village as a whole. They also administer the village temple dedicated to the Dravidian goddess. The temple is a kind of nerve centre of the village. All castes owe allegiance to the deity and participate in her festival in May. And it is at the temple that low-caste offenders are tried and punished by the Brahmans. This deity controls the harsh forces of nature which can bring blessings or curses on all villagers irrespective of caste; this is controlled by the Brahmans.

The non-Brahmans form three major classes. The first are aristocratic castes of traditional land managers and village administrators, who in their separate 'non-Brahman villages' occupy a position of authority comparable to that of Brahmans in 'Brahman villages'. On the whole they include the descendants of royals and aristocratic castes, that is, former soldiers of various rulers and conquerors of Tanjore who have received land and estates in the past. The second category consists of tenant farmers and specialized village labourers who serve the dominant Brahman and non-Brahman aristocratic castes. Specialist village workers, mostly of indigenous origin such as artisans, carpenters, fishermen, washermen, oil-mongers, barbers, musicians, potters and low-caste temple priests come into this category. The third non-Brahman class is that of craftsman and traders in the towns. They include highly skilled wood-carvers, stone-carvers, goldsmiths, etc.

It seems that the non-Brahmans of the village Kumbapettai now invite each other and eat freely together at marriages and funerals, with the exception of the lower-ranking barbers, washermen and basket-makers. A kind of fictional kinship has also grown up between these castes. The present trend is that the former caste community is no longer a localized, administrative or communal unit, and has ceased to perform exclusive ritual rites. These trends appear to be determined by modern economics and political expediency.

The Adi Dravidas comprise the three lowest castes of the district and they form about one-third of the total population. The Pallans before 1840 were agricultural serfs of landlords of the dominant castes, but are now landless labourers. The Paraiyans, who are also agricultural serfs, in addition beat tom-toms for non-Brahman funerals, guard cremation grounds and remove dead cattle from the streets of landlords. The Devendra Pallans and the Tekkatti Pallans each form a single community with exogamous patrilineal groups distributed in various house-holds. The two sub-castes dispute for ritual precedence, have a separate social life and separate cremation grounds and never eat together. Like other castes each has its head man. The Devendra Pallans own collectively a shrine dedicated to the god-dess Kaliamman who is responsible for smallpox and female barrenness.

The Economic Aspect of Caste

A typical village, Kumbapettai, which is a 'Brahman village' (population of 962 in 1952), consists of 483 acres of wet paddy land and 144 acres of dry garden and waste.

The spatial distribution of castes corresponds to a very great extent to their occupational specializations and relative ritual rank. The Brahmans live secluded in their street of large brick-and-tile houses. The Pallans, the lowest caste of landless labourers, live in small mud-and-thatch shacks in two isolated hamlets across paddy fields outside the village proper. The non-Brahman castes, mostly tenant farmers and specialist workers, occupy a middle position in their streets of larger thatched houses, separated from the Brahmans but within the main village site. Nowadays, however, on the whole the non-Brahman communities are no longer strictly segregated, although some degree of caste concentration remains.

Two types of villages are common: the 'uni-caste' village in which Brahmans are predominantly owners of the lands which are granted to them by the *Raja*, and the multi-caste villages in which the management is centred around the Brahmans and high-caste-Brahmans. The first type of village is partly or wholly exempted from revenue payment, while the second type is jointly assessed for revenue twice annually by the government. Revenue is sometimes paid in cash and sometimes in kind.

The fundamental characteristic of the traditional economy is that castes are, by law, associated with specialized occupations and with differential rights to maintenance from the produce of the village land. The major productive organ is the village land which is controlled either entirely by the Brahmans or jointly by the Brahmans and high-caste non-Brahmans.

The Brahmans administer their lands. The lower castes perform rites within their homes, conduct agricultural and temple festivals, and perform public sacrifices for the welfare of the kingdom.

The cow-herders are distributed among and controlled by the Brahman four lineages. This right is inherited patrilineally. Konan men do garden work and tend the Brahmans' cattle. Konan women clean the houses of their husbands' masters but are forbidden to enter the kitchen. In return for their services, each family of cow-herders receives materials for house-building, the right to fish in village pools, gifts, clothing, etc. They further eke out their livelihood by keeping goats, chickens and cows.

The landless labourers, whose ancestors have served the Brahmans, are strictly serf by law. Their work is more arduous, for both men and women work in the field. They receive daily payments in grain and gifts and their total remuneration is less than that received by the herders.

Barbers, carpenters, potters and village temple priests serve the village as a whole. Barbers are required to shave the body hair and a portion of the head and to trim the fingernails of Brahman and non-Brahman men twice a month, and to shave the heads of Brahman widows. They are also herbalists and dentists. Their women are midwives for all the castes above Adi Dravida. Carpenters work for all castes. Other groups of workers also serve the whole village. Each of these groups receives shares from the total grain harvest of the village in February and September; for example, priests and carpenters receive six measures for each Brahman and non-Brahman house.

One important point to note is that the range of a village servant's clientele is in part determined by the nature and ritual quality of his task. Hair-cutting, midwifery and laundry work, having to do with the refuse of the body, are polluting tasks and ritually lower, so that all groups engaged in them are ritually lower than all whom they serve. It follows that non-Brahman barbers and washermen may not serve the Adi Dravidas, who rank below them. So herders have their own barbers' and laundrymen's sub-castes, one family of which serves a group of villages and is paid in grain. These sub-castes rank below the majority groups of their castes and are endogamous. Two households of the lowest Adi Dravida castes serve all castes by hereditary right. Their jobs are to provide wood and cow dung for cremations, and guard bodies and burning in the cremation grounds. They are paid separately in grain by each household.

The economy of the village therefore functions through the medium of hereditary caste-determined occupations and economic relationships. Economically this rigid system is not always workable, especially with regard to the operation of the law of supply and demand both for labour and crops. However, there is room for flexibility, because considerable movement of labour between villages is allowed. Also, members of a whole caste can change their occupation to meet local demand. It must be noted too that for the non-Brahman specialist castes, agriculture provides a secondary source of livelihood.

The characteristics of the economic relationships of the castes are as follows. Each caste group is homogeneous in occupation and wealth; the Brahmans are considerably wealthier than their non-Brahman servants, and non-Brahmans slightly wealthier than Adi Dravidas. Except for a few cases like making ploughs or bullock-carts, specialization within the caste, except on the basis of sex and age, is almost unknown. All economic relationships consist of the provision of goods and services in direct exchange for paddy. Within the village there is no middleman trader, no market, and very little economic competition. The village has non-hereditary economic transactions (with unfixed prices) with castes from outside the village, and also a variety of cash transactions, under marketing conditions, through con-tractual relationships with castes of traders and town craftsmen.

With the advent of British rule the old economic edifice started to crumble down. This was chiefly due to the new political system, the expansion of trade and opport-unity, the mobility of labour, the even distribution of wealth, and finally the acquisition of land by purchase by other sectors of the community.

Caste and Village Politics

The administrators of the villages are generally Brahmans. They are traditionally the judges of five types of cases: disputes between persons of the same lower castes which have failed to be settled by the caste community's assembly; disputes between persons of different lower castes; offences by a lower-caste person against a person of another village; attacks by lower-caste persons upon the rights and dignity of the Brahmans, and general breaking of the moral law of the village. The rule of law is the rule of caste; for a lower caste may not obtain full redress from a higher caste. The lower caste suffers the severest punishment. The Brahmans decide and main-tain peace within their group through the heads of their patrilineages. Nowadays, with the partial loss of their lands and dwindling of economic control over the village, the Brahmans have lost the power to judge cases.

THE HAUSA-FULANI OF NIGERIA

Political Organization

The Hausa of northern Nigeria are organized in states. Each state has a walled capital called *Birni* surrounded by other satellite walled towns and villages. The territorial and political organization is not only structurally hierarchical, but also pyramidal. Thus, in descending order of importance, and increasing order of size and number the arrangement is as follows: the state capital (Birni), the districts (*gundumomi*), communities (*jama'u*), villages (*kauyka*), wards (*unguwoyi*), com-pounds (*gidajai*). The state officials are also hierarchically and pyramidally arranged: the king (*Emir*), the district heads (*hakimai*), the chiefs or village heads (*dagatai* or *sarkunan kauyka*), the ward heads (*masu unguwa*). Other subordinate officials within the state capital, districts, etc., are also hierarchically arranged according to rank, seniority and prestige.

The Hausa population is also pyramidal and hierarchical in the arrangement of personnel. At the top of each state is an Emir or Sarki, and descending the structure through the various interconnected stages of office-holders, the personnel of each hierarachy increases in number until at the base are the village chiefs and ward heads who directly control the commoners, called *Talakawa*.

According to M. G. Smith, the minimal political unit in Zaria is the community (*jama'a*) which may be defined as a group of villages having a common chief (*sarkin ungwa*), a common prayer-ground (*masallacin Idi*), a common priest (*limam*) and probably a common market (*kasuwa*).

Status Differentiation in Hausa Society

Anyone staying in Hausa land cannot fail to observe the operation of status differentiation in the various aspects of their culture and society.

Amongst women, age and marriage order in the husband's compound, as well as descent, fertility, difference of wealth and position, and the prospect of offspring, are some of the criteria used to identify status.

Amongst men, apart from age, which is generally applied in immediate situations, two important criteria are commonly combined to define status and class. These are the political and occupational (economic) roles.

There are three clear political statuses: holders of hereditary offices (*Masu Sarauta Na Asali*); holders of offices of allegiance (*Masu Sarauta Na Cafka*); commoners without offices (*Talakawa*).

There are four economic statuses. First, the higher aristocrats, state officials without economic roles except for their political position, Emirs, chiefs and higher state officials. Second the lower aristocrats, Mallams, wealthier merchants and those (modern) politicians who are not high aristocrats. Thirdly, the commoners, farmers, traders, craftsmen, miscellaneous government workers. Last, the lowly commoners, musicians, butchers, porters, ex-slaves and serfs, beggars, etc.

If the two criteria are combined, a rough picture of Hausa social stratification emerges. The *Masu Sarauta Na Asali* are the 'upper' class: Emirs and members of the ruling class. The *Masu Sarauta Na Cafka* are the 'lower upper' class, the top state officials, some merchants and some politicians from the ruling class. The *Talakawa* are divided into a 'middle class', moderately rich merchants, some Mallams, government officials, some politicians; a 'lower class', farmers, craftsmen; and a 'classless' category of ex-slaves and serfs who are still poor, beggars, porters, strangers.

Social mobilitiy has always been possible and is enhanced by marriage, migration, personal achievement, Western education and adoption.

The upper class is becoming narrower in range and is now limited to specific lineages. Marriage does not enable a woman to claim membership of a class she does not belong to. However, a child can claim the status and class of either parent, whichever is more advantageous. He can validate this claim by going to live with whichever nearest kin enjoy the chosen class or status. Many members of the upper class who do not hold office are economically relegated to the middle or lower classes, but they may still enjoy the honour of the upper class.

Many of the 'classless' are ex-slaves or descendants of ex-slaves and serfs. They can change their status and class by moving to another part of Hausa land to live and achieving wealth and prestige there. Although this process is not very easy, it is possible.

It is interesting to note that in Hausa land before 1967 the majority of those who received higher education of the Western type came from the upper and middle classes. The social stratification of Hausa society needs a much more comprehensive and intensive study, and our present knowledge is still very tentative and sketchy. (For more information, see Chapter 9, Section III.)

CONCLUSIONS

I suggest that in order to understand caste and class in non-Western societies their historical, structural, religious and economic systems must be examined. Class and caste may be characterized by endogamy, hierarchy and occupational specialization, but they differ in the intensity of these elements. It is clear that the ideology of caste is different from the ideology of class, for while the former stresses a rigid and almost watertight structural hierarchical arrangement of people, the latter is much more flexible both in structural arrangement and in occupational assignments.

BIBLIOGRAPHY

Works consulted

BETEILLE, A. (ed.) *Social Inequality* (Harmondsworth: Penguin, 1969). Especially Parts 1, 2, 6, 7

COHEN, A. 'The Social Organization of Credit in a West African Cattle Market', *Africa* (Jan. 1965)

DRY, D. P. L. *The Place of Islam in Hausa Society*, unpublished D.Phil. thesis (Oxford University, 1952)

DUDLEY, B. J. *Parties and Politics in Northern Nigeria*, Ph.D. thesis (London University, 1965)

FORDE, D. 'The Cultural Map of West Africa', in *Cultures and Societies of Africa*, S. and P. Ottenberg (eds.) (New York: Random House, 1960)

GOUGH, E. K. 'Caste in a Tanjore Village', in *Aspects of Caste in South India, Ceylon and North-West Pakistan*, E. R. Leach (ed.), Cambridge Papers in Social Anthropology, no. 2 (Cambridge: Cambridge University Press, 1960)

GREENBERG, J. H. 'The Influence of Islam in a Sudanese Religion', American Ethnographic Society Monograph no. 10 (1946)

—— 'Islam and Clan Organization among the Hausa', *South-Western Journal of Anthropology* (1947), 3

—— 'Some Aspects of Negro-Mohammedan Culture-Contact among the Hausa', *American Anthropology* (1941), 43

LEACH, E. R. (ed.) *Aspects of Caste in South India, Ceylon and North-West Pakistan*, Cambridge Papers in Social Anthropology, no. 2 (Cambridge: Cambridge University Press, 1960)

MAHIR, J. M. (ed.) *The Untouchables in Contemporary India* (Tucson: University of Arizona Press, 1972).

ONWUEJEOGWU, M. 'The Cult of the Bori Spirits among the Hausa', in *Man in Africa*, M. Douglas and P. M. Kaberry (eds.) (London: Tavistock Publications, 1969)

SMITH, M. *Baba of Karo* (London: Faber, 1954)

SMITH, M. G. *The Economy of Hausa Communities of Zaria* (London: HMSO, 1955)

—— 'Exchange and Marketing among Hausa', in *Markets in Africa*, P. Bohannan and G. Dalton (eds.) (Evanston, Ill.: Northwestern University Press, 1962)

—— *The Government of Zazzau, 1800–1950* (London: Oxford University Press, 1960)

—— 'Kebbi and Hausa Stratification', *British Journal of Sociology* (1961), 12

—— 'The Social Functions and Meaning of Hausa Praise-Singing', *Africa* (1957), 27, 1

—— 'A Study of Hausa Domestic Economy in Northern Zaria', *Africa* (1952), 22

—— 'Pre-Industrial Stratification Systems', in *Social Structure and Mobility in Economic Development*, by N. J. Smelser and M. L. Symour (eds.) (Chicago: Aldine Publishing 1966), pp. 141–76

TREMEARNE, A. J. N. 'Marital Relations of Hausa as Shown in Their Folklore', *Man* (1914), 14

YELD, E. R. 'Islam and Social Stratification', *British Journal of Sociology* (1960), 11

CHAPTER 14

The Uses and Abuses of some Concepts
Derived from Western Political
Thoughts

I *The Validity of Using Terms such as Democracy,
Egalitarianism and Individualism in Describing
Other Non-Western Societies: the Comanche of North America*

It is important first to make clear definitions of the concepts of democracy,
egalitarianism and individualism.

Harold Laski, in the *Encyclopaedia of Social Sciences,* points out that no
definition of democracy can be considered as adequate, because the concept varies
with different eras of human history. From Greek to modern times the following
concepts have been considered to be the cornerstones of democratic principles:
government of the people by the people for the people, equality before the law,
economic equality, social equality for women, extension of the suffrage, the referen-
dum, majority rule, one man one vote, etc. The modern concept is basically equality
of political, economical and social opportunity.

The criteria by which a society may be accepted as democratic should be that
there are mechanisms for universal equality of opportunity in all spheres of human
endeavour, and that the decision-making group, formal or informal, represents the
people's legitimate wishes.

Lindsay, writing on individualism in the same encyclopaedia, says that it is a
modern word. He defines it in De Tocqueville's words: ' A mature and calm feeling,
which disposes each member of the community to sever himself from the mass of
his fellow creatures, and to draw apart with his family and friends, so that, after
he has thus formed a little circle of his own, he willingly leaves society at large to
itself.' He maintains that individualism is of democratic origin, and that in any
society in which individualism is practised there is little respect paid to tradition or
authority, for individuality: 'is as far removed as possible from that primitive type
of social organisation where the overpowering dominance of tribal custom and
tradition leaves little scope for individual initiative and concern, and the members
of the tribe are so absorbed in the group that it forms what anthropologists have
called a tribal self.' However, it can be demonstrated that individualism can exist
in 'primitive' types of social organizations where authority and tradition are
respected.

Lindsay also says that an individualistic society is one where people 'think for
themselves and are regarded as being the best judges of their own interests'. He
concludes by pointing out that individualism as a philosophy of social life is bound

to break down at a certain point, since the individual and society interact and depend on one another.

According to Sahlin, an egalitarian society should be one in which every individual is of equal status, so that no one outranks anyone. Such a society does not exist. But one in which the only principles of allocation of rank are based on age and sex is bound to have minimal stratification or organization; in this way every individual should have an equal opportunity to succeed to whatever statuses are available.

The social, political, economic and religious organization of the Comanche must be examined before deciding whether terms such as democracy, egalitarianism and individualism may be applied.

The Comanche are an offshoot of the Northern Shoshonean tribes. They are hunters of buffalo. They raid their neighbours in parties or individually. (By the eighteenth century they had acquired horses which gave them greater mobility and improved hunting and raiding techniques.) Their values are oriented towards warfare in which individual achievement and prestige are almost over-emphasized.

The Comanche are made up of groups of bands which maintain peace by the bonds of common language, culture and marriage. They have no machinery for institutionalized political action on a large scale. (Indeed, the first all-Comanche council was held to discuss peace with the United States government.)

The most effective group is the band, which occupies an ill-defined territory. The unit of camping is usually a single or extended family. A band might number a few persons, or, in the largest ones, several hundred. The kinship principle is weak even within the smallest extended family. Linkage is chiefly by association and residence. A change of residence to another band is very easy and no permission is necessary before leaving or joining a band. Marriage within the band is common, although inter-band marriage does occur and to some extent inter-tribal marriage is practised. Residence is usually virilocal (patrilocal) and children belong to the band of their father. The mobility of the band, coupled with the mobility in space due to the use of the horse, makes the social organization of the Comanche a fertile ground for the development of individualism. During the summer season, groups of related bands camp together and operate as a unit in the communal dance and buffalo hunt.

The band, which is the largest and most effective social unit, is also the smallest political unit. The band has a permanent leader who is a person of ability and is called the 'peace-chief'. He is usually an old man in whom people have confidence. His advice is listened to, but he has no power and no powers of enforcement. His duty is to decide the time and place of camping and moving. For this he relies on a consensus of opinion among the old men and his own personal experiences. He gains his office through the personal and warlike achievements of his youth. His chief concern is to advise on internal and civil matters; he might be better called an 'assessor of public opinion'. He is not appointed or even elected; it is simply a process of social selection based on his past record. He is expected to be kind, generous and well-informed about Comanche custom and tradition. The band members call him 'father' and he calls them 'sons'. He has no special privileges of office. If he is a big peace-chief he has an announcer and usually two bodyguards.

Each band has an 'old men's society' called a 'smoke-lodge'. Only old men of the band, who have retired from military and active service, are allowed into the lodge, which is informally organized. It has a leader who conducts the rituals of the smoke-lodge proceedings. In the lodge the day's activities are discussed and past adventures retold. It is neither a legislative nor an executive body, but seems to be the place where public opinion crystallizes; for views put forward by members are generally accepted as the standard social norms, and these influence the peace-chief who is also a member.

Each band has a number of war-chiefs of various categories. They are men who have done great deeds in wars and raids, and they are the hub and focus of wars and raiding activities. Warriors usually rally themselves around a war-chief whose duty it is to organize wars and raids and control those under him. Warriors only follow leaders in whom they have confidence, and withdraw their allegiance if they lose confidence. So it is very easy both to join a group under a war-chief and also to withdraw.

Groups of bands usually gather together during the summer for the communal hunt and the annual Sun dance. During this period a temporary council of peace-chiefs is set up to look after the internal and civil matters of the amalgamated bands. Also a temporary council of war-chiefs is formed to decide questions of peace, war and the hunt. Each council has a leader appointed by each group. How the two councils coordinate their activities has not been indicated.

The band leader is regarded as a peace-maker and is never expected to use force. This is the parodox of Comanche social and political life. As a young man an individual is free to be turbulent and to undertake dangerous adventures, but in old age he is expected to be a peace-maker.

'War' can be undertaken by an individual alone or by a group. Any Comanche is eligible to lead a war party or to go alone, for in either case the honour belongs to him only. A man can have a dream and on waking up mount his horse and attack an enemy's camp all alone. If he is brave and lucky enough to return alive with a scalp, all the honours and glories go to him.

However, individuals, aware of the hazard of war, find it better to rally round an older warrior who has a war 'bonnet'. These leaders are absolute dictators, for the activity of war demands immediate obedience. Although this collective action tends to negate the principle of individualism, there exists the escape of being able to withdraw allegiance to a group very easily. The desire to team together is not contradictory to their spirit of individualism, because within the group individual achievement is emphasized. Thus this group activity serves only as a mechanism to protect the individual in the face of great danger in order that he may achieve his individual objectives.

The first and most important honour which a Comanche wants to gain is to become a wearer of the 'full-feathered war bonnet'. This is achieved by accumulating sufficient coups, or by recovering a 'bonnet' discarded by its owner in flight. Thus, for example, one youth, the brother of That's It, was so successful in coup-taking and raids at sixteen that he was made a war-chief at nineteen. This was an exceptional case of very rapid success. It portrays how individual achievement can lead to the highest social prestige irrespective of age or inheritance.

The 'Crow Tassel' wearers are another set of warriors. There are never more than four such groups in a given generation, and each group never exceeds four in number. A group forms an intimate association with its own emblem under the leadership of a man who possesses an emblem. The men dedicate themselves to perpetual warfare and may never spend more than one night at any camp with their people. They have rejected society and live apart, exposing themselves to the jeopardy and hazards of war. Men from two distinct backgrounds wear the Crow Tassel hat: those who have a family tradition of wearing the hat and those who have no surviving family members, to whom the way of life serves as a road to death. This shows that no matter how individualist a society may be, the family still has an important role to play in the life of men. This also helps to explain why Crow Tassel wearers can be persuaded by their kinsmen to re-dedicate themselves to the society. They usually return to the band in middle age. They are allowed to take off their hats and put on the war bonnet and become war-chiefs, and after marriage become peace-chiefs. This is because they have accumulated scalps during their days of adventure out of society.

The 'Crazy Dogs' and 'Big Horse Owners' are also small and limited groups among the Comanche. Persons rated as good-for-nothing take up these insignia. They are known to be acting contrary to orders. They continue their anti-social activities until they have performed what is generally considered to be a brave act, when they take off the insignia and become men of importance and prestige in the society. This seems to be a technique for correcting abnormal personalities.

There exist three other ways of achieving military honours. They may be transferred but never sold or even inherited. They may be given as a gift: thus A, a warrior of 'full-feathered bonnet' rank, can in a special ceremony transfer his honour to B, and this is socially recognized as equal in status, and in no way inferior, to an honour acquired by personal bravery. Hence a peace-chief without war honours can gain one by such a gift which will enhance his prestige as a peace-chief. The transfer is a matter between the individuals concerned, but it has to be validated by a public ceremony.

There is a lower order, that of the 'Buffalo Scalp' hat. The hat can be taken by anyone who thinks himself brave enough to wear it. Such a person is watched and in the next raid he is expected to do a brave deed; otherwise he will have to return to the camp to be ridiculed as an 'elder sister', a term a Comanche warrior would rather die than be called.

Women among the Comanche are also privileged to bestow a war bonnet upon fighters. They can grant a bonnet publicly to any man who is talkative or who boasts very much. He is expected to live up to the obligations of the war hat thus bestowed on him, or he will lose it and be called an 'elder sister'. This seems to be a mechanism for keeping troublesome youths quiet.

The Comanche society thus has several ways in which an individual could achieve social, political and economic status. He is also free to select his leader. The social and political organization permits freedom for the individual, and often he is the best judge of his own interests. Then there are the extreme cases where individuals reject society, through an established institution, and later on after they have achieved satisfaction they can be re-integrated into society as men of prestige.

Comanche society values military prowess. Equal opportunities exist for people to achieve the society's goals, and the spirit of individualism is encouraged within a social context, although politically it is most apparent for those between the ages of fifteen and thirty-five. After this age a Comanche man is obliged to retire and become a camp dweller, a frequent attendant of the smoke-lodge, where every one is regarded as almost equal. This is the phase of egalitarianism.

Throughout life the principles of democracy are available, but the age between thirty and thirty-five is a period of great tension, when sorcery accusations are most often made; it is a transitional period, when a young man's power has begun to dwindle. He is doomed to retire and this he does very reluctantly. The clash that exists is in fact between individualism and egalitarianism. To appreciate this, Comanche religious and economic institutions must be examined.

The Comanche are hunters of buffalo and keepers of horses. Horses are owned individually by both men and women. To own a large herd of horses is the ambition of an average Comanche. Thus all military expeditions have as a primary motive the taking of horses, which represent wealth and capital. A herd can be increased by careful breeding. Mexican captives are employed as herdsmen.

To be a man of prestige a man has not only to be a brave warrior but also a successful 'capitalist'. He should have a large herd of horses, plenty of ceremonial clothes, plenty of pounded dried meat, bows and arrows, etc.

9   *Clay pot of valour (Igbo-Ukwu, Nigeria)*

The chief means of obtaining buffalo meat is by the communal hunt during the summer months or by sporadic and uncontrolled individual hunts. The decision to hunt is taken in a council of warriors where leaders discuss the matter and anybody can come to listen. The communal hunt retains traits of individualism, for each buffalo killed belongs to the man who has his arrow-head buried in the beast. The arrowheads are marked, and the leader's decision on such matters is accepted as final.

Thus Comanche economy permits the accumulation of wealth by individuals who are able and powerful. It is not therefore surprising that retirement from active service is a blow both politically and economically. It connotes the beginning of a political and an economic 'death'. People resist retirement and use their magical powers to keep themselves in office in the face of opposition from the lively warriors.

To understand these magical powers, it is necessary to describe briefly Comanche religion. It is based on the concept of the guardian spirit. Religious practice consists of obtaining supernatural favours, so that one has constantly to be in contact with one's guardian spirits. These relationships are matters of individual concern. Power comes in the form of 'vision visitations', or 'hallucinatory experiences'. A quest for a vision means a solitary visit to a mountain, or to the grave of a dead medicine man. Fasting and certain rituals are involved. As religion is an individual matter, the taboos which it enjoins are, with some exceptions, also limited in the same way; it is the individual who suffers if the avoidance associated with a taboo is broken. The breaking of a taboo never endangers the community and the idea that 'sin' and punishment must emanate from taboo is unknown to them.

Men who have developed their magical power and have great successes in war, as well as accumulating much wealth, will naturally be jealous of their power and achievements and will try to remain in office as war-chiefs. The young warriors accuse them of sorcery. It is believed that any major crisis in the life of youthful warriors is due to the sorcery of the older ones who are trying to eliminate their successors.

The Comanche concept of law is based on individual responsibility. The individual, and rarely his kinsmen, is held responsible for his misdeeds. He has to admit his guilt to protect his honour, and make restitution. These procedures are laid down by social usage. (For Comanche law, see also Chapter 11, Section I.)

One might almost apply Harold Macmillan's concept of political and economic advancement to the Comanche: 'Individual merit, and individual merit alone, is the criterion for a man's advancement, whether political or economic.' However we must not fail to appreciate that the Comanche also makes allowance for its weaker members to share in the 'cake' of the society's social, economic and political prestige by the institution of the transfer of honour. To sum up, the Comanche are democratic and individualist before the age of thirty-five, and democratic and egalitarian after. To use one descriptive term to describe them would simply blur these facts. Most African societies have a mixed system of elements of democracy, egalitarianism, individualism and communalism. Hence to describe such societies by using one item seems inadequate, improper and unsatisfactory.

II *The Aptness of Using the Term 'Feudal' in Certain Types of African Polity: the Bunyoro of Uganda*

There is still a division of opinion about how the word 'feudalism' should be defined, and its sociological implications are still disputed. It has been looked at as a political system which occurs after a period of chaos, as an economic system, or as a combination of both. Students of law are more concerned with the person-to-person relationships of feudo-vassalage which are inherent in the system. For example, E. M. Chilver suggests that feudalism should be defined in terms of the feudo-vassalage associated with the 'multiple states' resulting from the dispersal of the function of government.

It has been often remarked that some aspects of the African polity exhibit feudal features. Nadel describes the Nupe as feudal, Maquet describes the Ruanda as feudal, and Beattie did the same with the Bunyoro. Smith used feudal terms like 'fief' and 'client' in describing some types of relationship in Zaria state, without

describing the Hausa state as feudal. L. Mair considers that the general characteristics of African kingdoms which are considered similar to those of medieval Europe
may be phases in the development of African centralized institutions. Goody says
that comparative work on African centralized states should be completed before
attempting to include European society in the analysis. However, here I shall
compare the Bunyoro system with the European.

The Bunyoro, who were studied by Beattie, are Bantu-speaking people living in
a fertile country of hillocks and swampy valleys in western Uganda, in the east
part of Central Africa. (The Bunyoro numbered 188 000 in 1959.) Bunyoro has an
area of 4745 square miles and (in 1959) a population density of about 32 per square
mile.

The society is stratified into the Bito clan from which the Mukama is chosen
from the appropriate lineage, the Huma overlords, mostly pastoralists, and the Iru
who are cultivators. It is possible for Nyoro commoners to rise to positions of high
authority, for these social strata do not constitute a rigid class system.

The king, called the Mukama, is the head of the political system and ruler of
the kingdom. He is the symbol of Nyoro nationhood, the source and focus of the
society's ideas about political authority, and the centre of social relations. According to myths and belief he is of a divine origin; his physical health is a matter of
great concern since on it depends the health of the nation. He lives in his capital
and rules from there on the advice of his formal and informal counsellors.

He appoints all territorial chiefs to office, down to the lowest level. He can also
remove them at any time, even though the office is hereditary. There are two
classes of chiefs but the distinction is not very marked. The great chiefs rule the
counties and the lesser chiefs rule the sub-counties and districts. The head men
manage the affairs of the villages. The lesser chiefs can hold their areas of jurisdiction directly from the king just as the larger chiefs do, or they may be assistants or
dependants of the major chiefs to whom they are responsible. But the Mukama is
informed about all political appointments, which he formally validates in the milk-
drinking rite, a swearing of allegiance.

The system of appointing territorial chiefs is one of the delegation of power. The
king assigns territories to distinguished persons who have served the nation or to his
own personal friends who have been loyal to him, but they can be withdrawn if
there is any reason to question their loyalty.

Each great chief has to maintain residence at the king's capital and attend the
king's council constantly. When he is away from the capital he has to leave behind
him a deputy. The chiefs are therefore both councillors and administrators. A great
chief considers his territory personal property whose jurisdiction is within a greater
political unit owned by the king. The people of a district supply services and
tributes to their chief who in turn passes on a share and so on up the hierarchy of
authority until the king gets his share. This is probably one of the points which
impressed Beattie and tempts him to conclude that Bunyoro is feudalist.

In order to find out whether Bunyoro is feudalist, answers to the following
questions are needed. What is the relationship between the Mukama and the chiefs
on the one hand, and the chiefs and the ruled, on the other hand? Are the hierarchical divisions within the state independent or dependent, and to what degree?
How is justice administered? What is the system of production and distribution?
How are political officials and administrative personnel rewarded?

The chiefs are appointees of the king. Chiefship means having a territory to
administer. Beattie calls it a gift, but the territory is not a gift. It is a technique of
rewarding loyal citizens by giving them distinguished posts in the administrative

machine. This is why the chiefs have to reside permanently in the capital and are also members of the king's council. This system has not only the effect of inhibiting rebellion but also symbolizes the fact that the chiefs are only deputies of the king in their territory. It prevents the fragmentation of power and authority and the formation of multiple states. Each county is dependent on the central government. Bunyoro kingdom is a centralized state with a system of local government, that is, the system is one of indirect rule based on the delegation of authority without total decentralization.

This was not the case in Europe under feudalism, where each state under a lord was autonomous politically and economically. The European king could not enforce his authority, neither had he the power to do so, for the lords, with their fortified castles and professional fighting men, had usurped the authority of the central government. Thus, one of the causes of the collapse of European feudalism was the obtaining of gunpowder from the East, after the Crusades, with which kings and their followers blew up the castles of the lords and re-established their authority and a new order.

Beattie says that the membership of a group of patrilaterally related kinsmen or agnates is still very important in connection with personal loyalties. We can safely assume that this was even more important in the past. This sort of relationship, real or fictitious, would not be able to survive side by side with the sort of relationships characteristic of feudalism in Europe. The question is whether feudal relationships of the European type could coexist with kinship relationships of the African type. Marc Bloch says that the immediate cause of feudalism in Europe was the collapse of monarchy and the absence of an alternative wider kinship system such as the clan or tribe which would have been able to give minimum security to the individual family units. Since Bunyoro society is not sufficiently stratified to create rigid horizontal strata which would block the vertical flow of kinship relationships, and since it is recorded as well that commoners are also made chiefs, it is difficult to imagine how feudo-vassalage of the European type could develop.

The administration of justice follows the same hierarchical system. The *Mukama*'s court deals with special types of cases. The chiefs' courts are regarded as lower courts, and one can, if one wishes, appeal to the next higher court. Feudalism in Europe with its pyramidal structure had courts to deal with each stratum of the society and appeals to a high court were impossible. In practice the lords' courts, not the kings', were considered supreme. In Bunyoro, the king reigns and rules, whereas in feudal Europe he only reigned.

The kingdom of Bunyoro has no standing army, so the smaller units do not have them either. The king and his counsellors sanction the decision to invade. The chiefs pass down the decision and action is taken further down the hierarchy. Each chief is the head of the armed men collected. After the war the booty is distributed accordingly and the army disperses. This is nothing like the military organization characteristic of feudal Europe, where the lords had specialized fighting men called knights who were also vassals to the lords; their relationship was that of service, for the holding of fief. The *Mukama* does not enter into contracts of this sort with the chiefs. He simply rewards loyal citizens with high offices of the state. These offices of chiefship are territorially defined, and politically under the *Mukama*. The relationship between *Mukama* and chief is that of king and subject.

On comparing the economic aspects of Bunyoro and a typical European feudal state, one finds that they differ greatly structurally. The distribution of lands in Europe was mainly of two kinds: either individual farmers handed over their land to lords who protected them in return, or the lords got land from the king as a reward for military service, and later became powerful enough to establish a mini-state within the kingdom. No such thing is reported to have happened in Bunyoro. Land 'belongs' to the king and every citizen has the right to use land in the territory he lives in. The *Mukama* does allocate territories to his chiefs and favourites, but they are not 'gifts', as suggested by Beattie, because he can withdraw them and the chiefs can be reappointed to other territories. In a non-monetary society it is easy to confuse devices for rewarding work with feudo-vassal relationships. The people of the districts contribute their annual payments of tribute to the chief. These payments should not suggest a service-protection relationship, since they are the duty of citizens as members of a political unit. The chief passes on part of the tribute to the next higher chief, and so on until some reaches the king, who uses part of it to maintain his household and feed the poor. Much of it is saved in the king's store for redistribution to the people during ceremonials and other occasions. Thus it is really a mechanism for distributing the surplus products and a method of paying officers.

We can deduce from the above that using such terms as 'feudal' or 'vassal' in the study of some African systems may be unnecessary and dangerous if not fully defined, because they mask their actual sociological character. A comparative study, as suggested by Goody, would help to clarify the typology of African systems. Then, perhaps, a comparative study with European systems would help to demonstrate how certain structural or institutional similarities, such as fiefs and vassals, could occur in dissimilar systems.

BIBLIOGRAPHY

SECTION I
Works consulted
LASKI, J. H. 'Democracy', *Encyclopaedia of Social Sciences* (1931), Vol. 5
LINDSAY, A. D. 'Individualism', *Encyclopaedia of Social Sciences* (1932), Vol. 6
LLEWELLYN, K. N. and HOEBEL, A. E. 'The Political Organization and Law-Ways of the Comanche Indians', *Memoirs American Anthropological Association* (1940), 54
SAHLIN, M. D. *Social Stratification in Polynesia* (Seattle: University of Washington Press, 1958)

Suggestions for further reading
FALLERS, L. A. *Bantu Bureaucracy* (Cambridge: Heffer, 1955)
KUPER, H. *African Aristocracy: Rank among the Swazi* (London: Oxford University Press, 1947)
LEWIS, I. M. *A Pastoral Democracy: A Study of Pastoralism and Politics among the Northern Somali* (London: Oxford University Press, 1961)
TAX, S. *Penny Capitalism: a Guatemalan Indian Economy* (Washington, DC: United States Government Printing Office, 1953)

SECTION II
Work consulted
BEATTIE, J. H. M. *Bunyoro, an African Kingdom* (New York: Holt, 1960)

Suggestions for further reading
BLOCH, M. *Feudal Society* (English translation by L. A. Manyon 1961) (London: Routledge & Kegan Paul 1961)
CHILVER, E. M. 'Feudalism in the Interlacustrine Kingdoms', in *East African Chiefs*, A. I. Richards (ed.) (London: Faber; New York: Praeger, 1960)

GOODY, J. 'Feudalism in Africa', in *Journal of African History* (1963)

HOYT, R. S. *Feudal Institutions: Cause or Consequence of Decentralization* (New York: Holt, Rinehart & Winston 1961)

LOEB, E. M. *In Feudal Africa* (Bloomington, Ind.: 1962)

MAIR, L. P. 'Clientship in East Africa', *Cah d'études afr.* (1961), 2

MAQUET, J. J. *The Premise of Inequality in Ruanda* (London: Oxford University Press, 1961)

POCOCK, J. G. A. *The Ancient Constitution and the Feudal Law: a Study of English Historical Thought in the Seventeenth Century* (Cambridge: Cambridge University Press, 1957)

POTEKHIN, I. I. 'On the Feudalism of the Ashanti', paper read to International Congress of Orientalists, Moscow, 1960

SMITH, M. G. *Government in Zazzau, 1800–1950* (London: Oxford University Press, 1960)

STRAYER, J. R. 'Feudalism in Western Europe', in *Feudalism in History*, R. Coulborn (ed.) (London: Oxford University Press, 1956)

Part Four
ECONOMIC ACTIVITIES

CHAPTER 15

Socio-Economic Order

I *An Introduction to Traditional Economic Activities in Africa*

The Economic Commission for Africa, headed by an Executive Secretary, was established on 29 April 1958. The task of the Commission was to accelerate the economic and social development of the regions in Africa on the one hand and to promote cooperation among its member states and with the rest of the world on the other. The Secretariat at Addis Ababa engages in various activities such as statistics, planning natural resources, agriculture and industry, transport and communications, housing, human resources and trade. Its primary task is to help Africa know herself. It therefore engages in surveys and research work.

In 1971, the Commission became more daring in its economic ventures, as was indicated by the programme of work adopted for 1971–6 in the first conference of Ministers in Tunis 8–13 February. The programme emphasized the need for research, technical assistance and economic cooperation among African states. To achieve an overall rate of growth of 6 per cent the programme stressed planning to mobilize national and external resources, and integrating the traditional sector of the economies, by bringing about structural changes that would increase the participation of all sectors of the populations in economic and social development.

Indeed any development programme or project in Africa that does not take account of the traditional sector must be considered unbalanced. Economic behaviour is a type of relationship and is determined by other types of relationships operative in a given society. In Africa kinship, ritual and symbolism, politics and economics, are types of relationships operating at various levels but closely interwoven with one another.

New economic programmes can probably be introduced with the minimum of friction and the maximum of cooperation if only the traditional systems are encouraged to respond to the new ideas. All traditional systems may not be inimical to progress. Projects and programmes fail not necessarily because traditional systems kill them, but probably because their planners are incapable of harmonizing the new ideas with the existing ones.

What is the traditional system and what is the traditional sector? How do they operate? How can they be harmonized with new ideas? How can they be integrated in new development programmes? Answers to these questions cannot be obtained by armchair theorists. They are field research problems.

I do not intend to provide answers to any of these problems, but I will attempt to highlight some of the major issues in traditional economic systems which still dominate the economic activities of African countries.

II *The General Trend in the Development of Economic Anthropology*

Economic anthropology is defined as that branch of social anthropology that deals with the economic problems of 'primitive' systems. It is not regarded as an autonomous branch of anthropology, like the study of kinship. It is dependent on economic science, as political anthropology is.

'Non-industrial' in this context refers to simplicity and primitivity of technology. A 'primitive' or non-industrial economic system has certain characteristics which mark it out from the economies of advanced technological systems. These are as follows:

1. The technology is simple, and is incorporated into the total system.
2. There are no innovations based on purposeful technological research, and so it is basically static.
3. The productive units are small.
4. The agents of production are not sharply separated, that is, the roles of labour, capital, land, entrepreneurism are not differentiated.
5. Production may be organized in terms of kinship and a producer performs many roles.
6. There is no direct calculation in regard to production and reward.
7. The system of control of capital is limited and there are many social mechanisms to disperse wealth in order to level down inequalities.
8. The concept of the market is narrow. There are no markets to create new wants as in 'advanced' systems. There is no general medium of exchange and no price system. In some cases prices may be fixed by custom, in which case there is no free market.
9. Economic ties are looked at in terms of social roles, for example, labour is regarded as a social matter. Economic activities and the relations thereby generated are highly personalized.

All these criteria may not occur in all 'primitive' economies, and, of course, they may occur in 'advanced' economies too. The gradation between 'primitive' and 'advanced' economic systems is a continuum that does not imply an evolutionary process, for there have been 'primitive' economies with complex monetary systems, for instance, the Igbo, the Yoruba and the Kapaukus.

In the study of primitive economic systems three anthropological approaches have emerged. First, the classical approach, in which it is argued that the general framework of economic theories will fit both the 'advanced' and the 'primitive' systems. Malinowski, Einzig, Mauss, Thurnwald and Armstrong, for example, used this framework in examining primitive economies but recognized the need for further analysis and a new approach to some basic problems.

The second approach, that of economic separation, is followed chiefly by Polanyi, Arensberg and Dalton. The idea is that primitive economics needs a completely new approach. Polanyi defines market not in economic terms, but substantively, that it is where people meet to buy and sell; this is distinct from its conceptual definition. He rejects the common notions of demand, supply and scarcity held by economists, and defines them in terms of their material aspects. To Polanyi the 'primitive' economic world is unique and distinct, and this I find difficult to accept. However his success has been that his ideas have encouraged anthropologists to examine primitive economic systems more critically than before.

Some of his colleagues put forward new concepts, which Polanyi had previously supported, such as the reciprocative system, the redistributive system and the market system. All these are stimulating but present great difficulties in application, as they cannot be isolated. The ideas of reciprocity and redistributivity were first formulated by Malinowski.

The third approach is called neo-classical. Scholars like Firth advocate combining economic theories and applying new terminology to fill in the gaps. Thus Firth examined the economies of Malay fishermen and New Zealand Maori and Tikopia and illustrated how the notions of capital, trade and market, prices and values, exchange and money, credit and loan, property rights, land and labour, reward, savings, distribution, etc., are applicable and operate in these societies.

The neo-classical approach has probably built up a stronger armoury than the others. It might be profitable here to examine in some detail how Firth treated one of these notions, capital.

THE DEFINITION OF CAPITAL

Firth says that capital is the stock of goods and services not used for immediate consumption but employed to increase the future consumption either directly or indirectly, through production. To him the primary criterion of capital is 'its capacity to assist future consumption', and it is directed towards the future, not merely stored or hoarded.

He also maintains that 'the stock of capital at any moment of time is the sum of the existing assets, that is, resources capable of yielding goods and services in a future period.'

Firth says that capital exists in primitive and peasant economies. Thus the anthropologists seeking to find out how capital operates in these societies has to unearth the answers to some basic questions, such as why goods are withheld from consumption; what kinds of reasons induce people to save now and consume later; what types of goods are withheld from present consumption; what kinds of selection are involved; what kinds of estimate are made. These questions suggest that there are social factors involved here.

THREE ASPECTS OF CAPITAL

Firth distinguishes three aspects of capital. It may consist of productive assets; it may afford control over purchasing power, and it may consist of a fund for investment. Anthropological studies have shown that even in the simplest economic systems these three aspects are identifiable.

For example, among the Tikopia, the productive assets involve a capital of canoes, paddles, digging sticks, nets, etc., which in use yield crops and fish. They also have some fixed capital of land improved by generations of labour. The control over purchasing power is provided by food, wooden bowls, barkcloth, pandanus mats, etc., used as 'gifts' to secure or repay various kinds of goods and services. Such goods are also used as a fund for investment by accumulating them over a period and then disbursing them. They may be used to pay for the building of a new canoe, or distributed at a ceremony. The recipient is under an obligation to reciprocate with goods and services at a later period. The question of economic interest is not significant in this type of activity. A considerable quantity of the food, barkcloth, etc., is produced and accumulated with the aim of using it in the future.

In a non-monetary economy where no general medium of exchange exists a direct comparison of all types of goods and services is impossible, and so it is difficult to value assets. Firth argues that in primitive economies assets have a low liquidity or ease of conversion into goods or services of another kind. But it is important to understand that liquidity or ease of conversion into goods or services of another kind is not confined to a monetary economy, or to the monetary sectors of an economy.

The Tikopia do not have to express 'capital' or 'income', but the idea is subsumed in notions of 'valuable goods', 'reciprocity', etc. Among the Igbo, Yoruba, words exist for interest, capital, investment, credit, etc., and yet the traditional economics of these people may be considered as relatively less complex.

THE FORMATION AND USE OF CAPITAL

In primitive economies capital and income are low, so the conditions for saving and capital formation are unfavourable. Some of the problems, according to Firth, are associated with finding out what social and economic conditions are associated with a low income level and small capital assets. What may be the effects on social relationships of capital improvement, for individuals and for the community as a whole?

Some observers hold that people of primitive economies are not careful about the maintenance of their traditional equipment. This is a misconception. They are very careful. In recent times failure to maintain new types of equipment is due to lack of proper technical training, lack of money to pay for running costs and repairs, and the competing claims of other interests.

In primitive economies the incentive to accumulate capital takes various forms in the social norms and taboos, and through competition. Among the Igbo and Ijebu the traditional norm is for a man to save hard for a rainy day. Among the Mbaise Owerri a communal taboo is placed on harvesting palm produce for about three months, and then at the end of the period the fruits are harvested and sold communally. The lump sum is deposited in the bank. At the end of three years the money saved is used to build a community college or a big church. This is a traditional method of accumulating capital, but used in modern times for a modern purpose.

Even in *potlatch*, some goods are destroyed, that is, converted to social prestige, but this has the general effect of increasing indebtedness and creating scarcity. Other goods are distributed for social prestige. These processes of social destruction and distribution constitute a complicated mechanism 'of credit transactions by which at some future time other materials and goods may have to be returned, perhaps with increment'. (Firth.) These transfers usually stimulate further production. *Potlatch* should not be regarded as a destructive activity. Firth regards *potlatch* as 'a type of exchange, a powerful element in the incentive pattern of capital accumulation, an equilibrating mechanism which allows goods to flow where there is temporary scarcity'.

It has always been argued that the extended family system inhibits capital formation. Polly Hill's study, 'The Migrant Cocoa Farmers of Southern Ghana', shows that migrant peasants with extended family systems produce the cocoa that has made Ghana the largest cocoa-producer in the world. According to Meyer Fortes, 'in the society where sale, mortgage and credit are institutions long ante-dating the advent of the modern economy, corporate land-owning can serve as a spur to expansionary enterprise and as a form of "banking" resources, and often promotes rather than impedes individual economic achievement.'

In Nigeria, rehabilitation after the civil war has been accelerated by 'self-help' within the extended families. The African élite talk glibly about the pressure the extended family exerts on their income and salary. They do not realize that this system is a mechanism for levelling out the great disparity in the various income groups in a developing society; without it most of them would not become élite. After all, the education of most Africans is paid for by savings accumulated by a member or members of the extended family. This method will continue to be a sure method of capital formation and investment in African economies, and a symbolic way of expressing kinship solidarity in a new economic context.

Firth's neo-classical approach to the study of pre-industrial non-technological or 'primitive' economies might be rewarding if it were more impartial. It is possible that this approach might not be able to cope with the problem of establishing economic analysis right in the heart of anthropological study. On the other hand, if the advocates of neo-classicism put more emphasis than Firth on how the patterns of relationships are moulded, how social categories are defined symbolically and physically in the process of production, distribution and consumption, they might open up new concepts in the study of economic anthropology.

BIBLIOGRAPHY

SECTION II
Works consulted

ARDENER, E. W. 'Lineage and Locality among the Mba-Ise Ibo', *Africa* (1959), 29, 2

ARMSTRONG, W. E. *Rossel Island* (Cambridge: Cambridge University Press, 1928)

BASOM, W. 'The *Esusu*, a Credit Institution of the Yoruba', *J.R.A.I.* (1952), 82

BOHANNAN, P. and DANTON, G. (eds.) *Markets in Africa* (Evanston, Ill.: Northwestern University Press, 1962)

CODERE, H. *Fighting with Property: a Study of Kwakiutl Potlatching and Warfare* (New York: J. J. Augustin, 1950)

FIRTH, R. W. *Primitive Economics of the New Zealand Maori* (London: Routledge, 1929)

—— *Human Types* (London: Nelson, 1938)

—— *Primitive Polynesian Economy* (London: Routledge, 1939)

——*Malay Fisherman: Their Peasant Economy* (London: Routledge, 1946)

FIRTH, R. W. and YAMEY, B. S. (eds.) *Capital, Saving and Credit in Peasant Societies* (London: Allen & Unwin, 1964)

HARRIS, J. 'The Economic Aspect of Life among the Ozuitem Ibo, *Africa* (1943). 14

HERSKOVITS, M. J. *Economic Anthropology* (New York: W. W. Norton, 1965)

HILL, P. The Migrant Cocoa Farmers of Southern Ghana, *Africa* (1961), 31, 3

MAUSS, M. *The Gift*, translated by I. Cunnison (London: Cohen & West, 1954)

POLANYI, K. and ARENSBERG, C. M. (Eds.) *Trade and Markets in the Early Empires* (New York: Free Press, Falcon's Wing Press, 1957)

POSPISIL, L. *Kapauku Papuan Economy* (New Haven: Yale University Press, 1963)

THURNWALD, R. C. *Economics of Primitive Communities* (London: Oxford University Press, 1965)

Suggestion for further reading

FIRTH, R. W. (ed.) *Themes in Economic Anthropology*, A.S.A. Monographs, no. 6 (London: Tavistock Publications, 1967)

CHAPTER 16

Enviroment, Technology,
Demography and Social Organization

I The Interrelation Between Environment, Technology, Demography and Social Organization: the Fulani of Northern Nigeria

The Fulani, originally of non-Negro stock, are spread over the vast West African savannah belt. (For their origin, see Chapter 3, Section I.) The Wodaabe Fulani inhabit the western part of the Bornu Emirate in north-east Nigeria. In the past the Wodaabe experienced great political events such as the invasion of Kano by Bornu, the rise of the great Fulani leader Usuman-Dan-Fodio, the invasion of Bornu by Hausa-Fulani Emirates, the rise of Rabeh, and finally the British occupation. These political incidents have had a very profound influence on their social organization.

During the long sojourn in the savannah, the Fulani have become formed into groups: the ruling Fulani aristocrats, the settled Fulani, the semi-settled Fulani and the pastoral Fulani, who depend completely on their herds of zebu cattle for subsistence.

The pastoral Fulani inhabit this savannah zone, an area with about sixty inches of rainfall on the southern limit and twenty inches in the north. There are only two seasons: the dry and the wet. The wet runs from May to October; November to April is the dry period. The southern part, which is wetter than the northern, is infested with tse-tse fly, the carrier of trypanosomiasis. These ecological limitations have necessitated the constant movement of the Fulani. Three major types of movement are distinguished: transhumance, migratory drift and migration.

The basic residential and economic unit of social grouping among the pastoral Fulani is the simple or compound family moving its few belongings on pack animals with a herd of between ten and twenty-five cattle. According to Stenning who studied them, this family may be regarded as a herd-owning and milk-selling enterprise, since the men are herdsmen and the women are milkmaids. Each household is an independent economic unit which relies on the herd for subsistence, while on the other hand, of course, the herd relies on human management as well as ecology for its survival.

Stenning argues that the balance between the family and the herd is greatly disturbed by three factors: the regular seasonal variation; the irregular natural hazards; and the properties of the simple or compound family in relation to its means of subsistence.

The regular seasonal variation affecting the family and the herd is the alternation of the dry and rainy seasons. In the rainy season the family and herd move northwards away from the south, the area infested by the tse-tse fly. The cattle have plenty of water and pasture and so give a high milk yield. At this period lineage groups congregate and social activities such as marriages are organized. In the dry season the family drifts southwards again in search of pasture and water; the lineage groups scatter, the milk yield is low, and hardship prevails. This is the period of a high divorce rate.

The balance of the family and herd is also disturbed by the irregular natural hazards of accidents or diseases resulting in the death of cattle and humans. Bovine diseases such as trypanosomiasis, rinderpest and pleuropneumonia are prevalent. However, there is a marked absence of skin diseases, sores and ulcers among the Fulani, unlike their sedentary neighbours, because their diet is helpful towards resistance against disease. Their daily lives, though, are jeopardized by injuries, snake-bites, and waterborne disease. Their rudimentary dwellings and the exposure to cold, heat and wet predispose them to respiratory and muscular disorders. It has been observed statistically that infantile mortality and calf mortality are high and almost at par. It follows, therefore, that in the event of a high herd mortality with a corresponding human mortality, the subsistence level will be lowered and the family become non-viable. There must be a constant ratio of labour and cattle. The Fulani recognize this, and to safeguard against an imbalance they have evolved a non-technological system of readjustment and assurance based on the cooperation of the lineage groups.

The third factor which affects the equilibrium and viability of the family and the herd is the nature of the family itself. (For the structure of the family and its close interrelation with the supply of cattle, see Chapter 8, Section III.)

The unit of cooperation is the agnatic lineage group. This group consists of between five and twenty households containing between twenty-five and one hundred persons. It is also the unit of defence. Households arrange the marriages of their daughters; the lineage group is endogamous. The lineage group also controls the inheritance of cattle and widows under the supervision of a leader who is their representative *vis-à-vis* other groups.

A cluster of agnatic lineage groups, supposed to have a common ancestor, forms a clan. The clan is also endogamous and is the unit that formerly congregated in the wet season. Various political changes have caused the clan to degenerate into a loose association devoid of its former social and ritual functions.

The settlement pattern of the pastoral Fulani is very closely related to their habitat and mode of life and it also symbolizes the relationship between the family and the lineage, and also between the family and its herd. There are about three settlements to a square mile. Movement is determined by the settlement pattern and the population of other sedentary neighbours, the political situation, the condition of pasture and water, and bovine disease.

The household lives in a circular homestead which faces west and is divided into two sections, the male and the female, by a calf rope. The male section is regarded as the front and contains the cattle corral. Household equipment is limited to the amount which may be carried on the head or pack animal. Shelters are made of tree foliage collected around the camping vicinity. When agnatic lineage groups camp together they arrange their homesteads in southerly and westerly positions corresponding to genealogical seniority and age respectively. This arrangement has been modified with the passage of time, reflecting recent political and economic change.

The Fulani have contributed little to improve their domestic technological culture. In the past they employed slaves to dig wells during the dry season, but since the abolition of slavery they have taken no steps to tap the natural resources of water around. They are satisfied with what the enviroment offers, and because of this they live a pastoral life without any state or any complex political organization. However they are renowned for their negotiations with both 'acephalous' and 'non-acephalous' societies around them.

Their main problem is to maintain a balance between the family and the herd which is disturbed by biological and ecological conditions. To achieve this with their primitive technology they operate their social organization so as to obtain an uneasy equilibrium. Evidence from the past shows that they do have a flexible society adaptive to changes. The careful introduction of Western technology in animal husbandry might convert them to a 'semi-settled' or 'settled-pastoralist' state. It is interesting to note that up to 1970 the Fulani nomads supplied Nigeria with over 80 per cent of her beef and other bovine by-products.

II *Settlement Patterns and Demographic Circulation: the Igbo of South-Eastern Nigeria*

INTRODUCTION

The Igbo of south-eastern Nigeria number about 8·5 million (1970 figures) of which 7·5 million live in the East Central State. The rest live in the north of the Rivers State and the east of the Mid-West State. Their population is the most dense in West Africa, ranging from 300 to 1000 persons per square mile.

The Igbo are traditionally predominantly farmers and traders. They exploit the palm produce in the equatorial forest and cultivate yams, coco-yams, maize and cassava. Domestic technology in bronze-casting, ironwork and pottery dates back to the ninth century AD, as indicated by the Igbo–Ukwu archaeological finds. Excellent craftsmanship still exists in wood and ivory carving, ironwork and pottery.

The area traditionally occupied by the Igbo has been defined as the Igbo culture area, where they live in groups of patrilineages (*Umunna*) which are hierarchically arranged. Patrilineages of various levels and origin form villages, and groups of villages form towns (*Obodo*). Recent studies show that these towns have been peopled by nine major migrations, beginning before AD 900 and continuing into the beginning of this century.

The Igbo are grouped into five sub-cultures. The southern Igbo centred around Owerri-Ngwa have the distinctive cultural features of the absence of elaborate title and *mmuo* societies and the presence of Mbari temples.

The northern Igbo are centred around Nnewi-Nri-Awka-Nsukka. Their distinctive features are the *Ozo* title and an elaborate ancestor temple system, *Obu*. This area is the heart of Nri hegemony. A recent study shows that the kings of Nri, Eze Nri, built a political and ritual hegemony around AD 1000 which was probably at its peak between the twelfth and seventeenth centuries and was liquidated by 1911 as a result of British and missionary intervention. (See also Chapter 4, The Nri Study.)

The distinctive features of the eastern Igbo comprise an elaborate age-grade system and inheritance through the male and female lines. Among them are the Aro who are patrilineally organized. They developed one of the greatest monopolies in Atlantic trade with Europeans in the eighteenth and nineteenth centuries. The north-eastern Igbo have a distinctive horse title system and an ancestor cult associated with graves.

The west Igbo are characterized by having either a centralized kingship authority superimposed on hierarchies of patrilineages as in Agbor, Aboh, Oguta, Ogwashi-Ukwu, or a gerontocratic centralized system as in Ibusa and Okpanam.

In spite of these cultural diversities, the Igbo share a common basic culture in their language which has a cluster of dialects that are mutually intelligible. They share a common political system based on decentralization of power and delegation of authority exercised by the holder of the staff of authority, *Ofo*. This system is

10   *Bronze snail-shell (Igbo-Ukwu, Nigeria)*

epitomized in the hierarchy of lineages called *Umunna*. Their economic system is based on yam culture ritualized in the yam cult, *Ifejioku*. They also have common cosmological beliefs based on the interrelationships between the World, *Uwa*, the dead ancestors, *mmuo*, the supernatural forces, *Alusi*, and the Great Creator, *Chukwu Okike*. There are also personality cults, such as the *Ikenga* (see Chapter 21, Section II), the cult of the right hand which symbolizes individual achievement. Finally, certain distinctive cultural traits bind the Igbo into a cultural unit. These are the kola-nut custom, the vigour in their music and dance movements, their arts of wall and body painting, their folklores and oral literature, their *mmuo* drama and their traditional games and pastimes such as wrestling, acrobatics, archery and fencing.

THE TYPOLOGY
This typology arises from the fifty-six settlements which I visited during a pilot survey of the Igbo culture area. In building this typology nine factors have been considered, as follows:

1. The degree of homogeneity or heterogeneity of the population and the nature of the population.
2. The degree of the presence or absence of Igbo traditional social structure and organization in the settlement.
3. The degree of the presence or absence of kinship and non-kinship relationships between individuals as shown by the informal behaviour of neighbours.
4. The degree to which Igbo or the English language, pidgin English, is used as a medium of communication in both formal and, especially, informal relationships.
5. The degree to which strangers are integrated into the existing social structure.
6. The nature of the settlement pattern in terms of its compactness and dispersion. Thus if the houses or compounds are consistently 60 ft apart the settlement is described as dispersed. If they are less than 60 ft apart, the settlement is described as compact. If a settlement has both in equal proportions, it is described as mixed. These measurements are not arbitrarily taken. In typical urban situations, houses are usually 1 ft apart, that is, the thickness of the wall separating them if they are adjacent, and about 60 ft apart if they are on the opposite sides of a street. So 1–60 ft is a constant measure for compactness characteristic of urban towns.
7. The history of the settlement, especially its cultural, political and economic development.
8. The degree and nature of external influences on the political, social, ritual and especially the economic life of the inhabitants.
9. The focus of political loyalty as ascertained and observed.

Applying these criteria in describing each of the fifty-six settlements, three main categories each with subdivisions are found:

> Villages, subdivided into simple, compound, complex.
> Village towns, subdivided into amalgamated, federated, confederated.
> Urban towns, subdivided into traditional, dual and hybrid.

Villages
Villages have the following major characteristics. The population is homogeneous in the sense that there exists a concept of oneness, based on kinship ideology binding the inhabitants into one social and cultural unit. Because of this, membership is mostly by birth, by marriage, or occasionally by naturalization. Naturalization may be ritual adoption of a stranger into one of the lineages or units, or by gradual assimilation due to long residence with the lineage usually buttressed by marriage, blood-brotherhood, or personal achievement such as wealth.

The social structure and the organization of the village are basically traditional: lineages, title-taking, age-groups, associations, etc.

The population is relatively small, usually under 2000 and possibly less than 100.

The males and females still cling to the traditional economy: agriculture, local trading, domestic industries.

Villages are politically independent and autonomous in many respects. Even in villages that have become complex or have evolved into village-towns, traces of the original independence can still be found on close observation.

Villages may have a modern school, maternity clinic and several modern institutions, but in the main they still remain traditional. Igbo villages of today are the relics of Igbo traditional society and culture.

Villages may be of various types. I have distinguished three types: simple, complex and compound.

Simple villages are single units that claim single origin and are independent in many respects. Most of these villages are today components of larger units. It is rare to find a typical simple village that is not a component of a larger unit. Achalla village, near Ibusa, on the west of the Niger, is a typical simple village.

Complex villages are made up of several semi-autonomous units which claim various origins. On a closer examination one finds out that some of the component units are results of the fission of its former major component units. Akamkpisi in Nri is typical. On the surface, a village may claim to have a common origin but it may be found that the component units have various origins.

Compound villages are made up of several semi-autonomous units which claim one origin. Ogboli village in Ibusa is typical of this class.

These three types of villages may be dispersed, compact, or mixed. There are several factors, environmental (especially topographical), cultural, historical, economical, and demographical, which explain the nature of the settlement pattern of the villages. These factors differ from settlement to settlement.

Village-towns

The simple, complex or compound villages discussed above may become more heterogeneous in composition, and more populous and more complex in character, because of the amalgamation, federation, or confederation of several villages of various types. When this fusion of villages occurs, the first stage in the development of a village-town has begun. As time goes on, given the necessary conditions, a typical village-town emerges. The main features of a typical village-town are as follows.

The population is less homogeneous than that of the village in the sense that the concept of oneness is not only based on the ideology of kinship but on the ideology of the interdependence and the long period of association. On the other hand it is heterogeneous – of course less heterogeneous than towns – in that strangers are easily accommodated into certain levels of the social structure. For example, I live in Obeagu village. Obeagu is a compound village (as defined above) which has amalgamated with other villages to form Nri village-town. At the village level, I am not regarded as a member since I do not belong to any of the village lineages that make up Obeagu, but at the town level, I am referred to as an Obeagu man, a general term showing that I live there.

Membership is chiefly by birth and adoption, marriage or naturalization, and to some extent by residence.

The social and political structure and organization are also based on systems other than the Igbo traditional ones, that is, kinship, lineages, a council of elders (*Ndi Ichie*), a council of title-men (*Ndi Nze*), associations (*Otu*) and age-grades or groups (*Ogbo*).

New systems such as government institutions like local councils, the town union, various religious bodies, such as the Roman Catholic Mission, the Church Missionary Society, the Apostolic Church, trade unions, political parties, are becoming effective in varying degrees in the internal organization of village-towns.

The population is considerably higher than those of the villages. For instance, Nri village-town has a population of about 12 000 (1972).

The traditional economy is still practised but men and women have acquired new techniques. In these settlements there are scattered signs of modernity: pipe-borne water supplies, hospitals, tarred roads, churches, schools and colleges, post offices, police stations, government offices, etc.

The English language is occasionally spoken, and there is a real effort to speak it well. Any educated person is called 'white-man' (*Onye-Ocha*). In this context it means a modern literate man who has taken to the white man's fashions.

All 'white men' are expected to be nominal Christians. There is a sharp dichotomy between the Christians and the traditionalists, referred to as 'pagans' by the Christians. This is a theoretical dichotomy, for in practice all Christians at the lineage level participate in the 'great traditional culture'. The traditional moral values are held high. The various traditional ritual concepts, *Alu, Ana, Ajana, Nso, Alusi, Iyi*, etc., are regarded by both Christians and traditionalists as still valid and no one infringes them with impunity. Also the traditional superstitions are still upheld, like sorcery, witchcraft, the power of charms, omens and dreams.

There are three main ways in which villages become village-towns. These three ways give rise to the three main types of village-towns. In the evolutionary process each type is to be considered as a stage.

Amalgamated village-towns are villages fused together into one town, and it is difficult to distinguish their origins. They have also lost their former identities and political autonomy except in very exceptional cases. The component villages are so fused together that it is difficult to perceive how a major fission can take place. Nri village-town falls into this class.

Federated village-towns are villages of different origins, which continue to retain their original identity and some of their former political autonomy in spite of the fact that the name of a dominant component village may represent the name of the village-town. In some cases a completely different name is given to the town. Some towns have changed their names several times between 1920 and 1950 primarily to incorporate and unify their component villages, for example, Ovolo became Mba Ukwu, Osunagidi became Enugu-Agidi. Typical examples of federated villages are Ibusa, Mba-Ukwu, Igbo-Ukwu.

The component villages of a federated village-town may not break away because of the strong kinship, economic, political and sentimental ties. But there still exist cleavages which are potential lines of weakness through which fission may occur. The important safety-valve built into the unwritten constitution of federated villages is that each village is autonomous at certain levels and can assert this autonomy on certain occasions without endangering the existence of the village-town.

Confederated village-towns are the loosest type of village-town. Two types may be distinguished: those formed before the arrival of Western European culture and those formed afterwards.

A confederation is based on the principle that association should not endanger the political and ritual autonomy of the component villages. It is therefore based on the theory of self-determination: by this, villages only combine to satisfy some political or economic urgency, apart from which they remain separate.

Before the introduction of the Western system of government, villages confederated and 'separated' as occasion demanded. British administrators stepped in and were exceedingly successful in making some of these loose confederations into stronger confederations. In some cases they failed hopelessly and the by-product of their failures was political and social unrest amongst the frustrated settlements. Orlu, Mbaise and Mbitolu are examples of confederated villages which are successful, while Nibo and Nise and the Umunri clan are the unsuccessful ones.

The British aim of championing the federation or confederation of villages was for administrative convenience arising from shortage of funds and personnel. These considerations overrode the people's demands. It would be interesting to find out why the British were successful with some village groups and unsuccessful with others. It might help us to understand the nature and implications of federation and confederation as political techniques for achieving some kind of political association.

Amalgamated, federated and confederated village-towns may be dispersed, compact or mixed, but on the whole the amalgamated village-towns have a more compact settlement, and federated village-towns less so. The confederated village-towns are mostly dispersed.

Towns

Towns are characterized as follows. They have a heterogeneous population in the sense that persons from different villages of the Igbo culture area and from other non-Igbo culture areas dwell together in the same territory and in the same 'yard', as urban compounds are generally called. In other words there is no concept or ideology of oneness based on common origin.

In a heterogeneous population of this type it is difficult to delimit the unifying factor. In such a segmented population, the segments strongly reflect the federal political structure, and political loyalty is focused towards the person's region of origin. Thus the Igbo is Enugu-oriented, the Edo is Benin-oriented, the Hausa or Nupe is Kaduna-oriented, and the Yoruba is Ibadan-oriented. The Western Ibo attitude is ambivalent and shifts between Enugu and Benin.

People in 1966 had very nebulous notions about the Nigerian Federal Government as a unifying factor. Not everyone saw the political connection between the Federal and Regional Governments. Some more politically sophisticated referred to the Lagos Government as 'Hausa Government', while the Hausa called it 'our Government'.

It is interesting to note that in the towns under discussion there is a general tendency for people from the same villages or village-towns in the Igbo culture area and people from the same culture area outside the Igbo culture area to live either in the same 'yards' or streets or to occupy a definite area. Such groups have been referred to as 'sub-cultures'. The sociological interest of such 'urban islands' is that they serve the individual and the group as an effective economic, political, ritual and psychological 'defence–offence mechanism' in the uncertain conditions of urban life.

These people speak not only different Igbo dialects but also other Nigerian languages. Since it is a sign of literacy to speak some English, two people in a 'yard' will address each other in mixed English–Igbo sentences if they are Igbo, or in a dialect of pidgin English if one or both speakers are non-Igbo. English is used in big shops and offices, but Igbo predominates in the markets.

The settlement pattern is of a compact or mixed nature, and the population per square mile is denser than in the village or village-towns.

The Igbo traditional system is absent at some levels, although a modified Igbo traditional system is present. Village-town unions are very strong and effective in the urban areas. These unions act as another type of 'defence–offence mechanism'.

The inhabitants of the towns operate two different systems of moral values. They go back to their villages frequently and share in the village values which they highly respect. But in the towns village morality is brushed aside, and a new urban morality dominates. This partly explains why towns are dirtier than villages, and why crimes committed in the towns may not be committed in the villages with impunity.

Things regarded as evidence of modernity are in abundance in the towns: schools, colleges, government institutions, cooperative societies, missionaries, trading firms, foreign enterprises, hospitals, electricity, water supply, television in some bars, hotels, night-clubs, cinemas, factories, banks, political parties, trade unions, intellectual groups, criminal gangs.

Igbo towns are not all at the same level of development for several political, economic and historical reasons. Three main types, each with two main sub-types, may be distinguished: hybrid urban towns, traditional urban towns and dual urban towns.

Hybrid urban towns have developed to the fullest extent the conditions listed above. One of their main characteristics is that they are almost devoid of Igbo traditional systems, although new patterns based on the traditional systems have been developed. The various so-called tribal unions which are really village-town unions are typical examples. The culture that emerges is of a hybrid nature, which is why they may be described as hybrid urban towns. These towns are where one must put off 'village values' and put on new 'town values'.

Most of the hybrid urban towns have grown because of European influence in the past seventy years. Typical among these are Enugu and Port Harcourt, which are isolated hybrid urban towns because they have no satellite villages or village-towns surrounding them on which the inhabitants of the towns depend for certain important economic services and to which workers in the town can return. By 'satellite' is not only meant the physical existence of settlements around urban towns but also the functional relationship between the settlements and the urban towns. It may be argued that Port Harcourt has satellite settlements, but it seems to me that the percentage of people who commute from them to the city is very low. A characteristic feature of Port Harcourt is its continuing expansion through which it dwarfs and absorbs other surrounding settlements.

Some of the hybrid urban towns have satellite villages and village-towns. These urban towns may be called clusters of hybrid urban towns. Owerri and Aba are typical examples. It has not been possible to investigate the nature of the interdependence between these urban towns and their satellite villages and village-towns.

Dual urban towns arose because of the growth of twin towns, of which one sector is typically hybrid urban while the other is a typical village-town. Onitsha and Asaba are examples. In Onitsha there are two separate sectors developing along parallel or converging lines: the area traditionally occupied by Onitsha indigenes and the area occupied by strangers who are mostly from other parts of Nigeria, especially Eastern Nigeria. The former is still a village-town in the sense described above, while the latter is urban. Administratively these two sectors have a chequered history. At one time the two sectors were considered as one unit, at another as separate units. One thing is clear, and that is that the two sectors have different patterns of development, and their political and economic history is that of conflict and unrest. Territorially, the two areas used to be separate but were linked by a network of roads and paths. Recently, the two territories have been coalescing gradually, and this coalescence presents its own special social and political problems. The dual nature of Onitsha and Asaba urban towns, in spite of their modern cultural development, places them sociologically in this category. The nature of their growth, history and sociology are yet to be ascertained. Dual urban towns may also be with or without satellites. Thus Asaba has no satellite, whilst Onitsha has satellites.

Traditional urban towns are known for their traditional outlook, that is, they are traditional village-towns that have acquired some urban characteristics even before the advent of modern urbanization. Two types can be distinguished: uni-nucleated and multi-nucleated.

Uni-nucleated traditional urban towns are interesting because many Eastern towns, especially in the Igbo culture area, are developing in this direction. Here the original village-town is undergoing a radical change. Certain of the village-towns where government and other modern institutions are located are gradually becoming thickly populated with strangers and the overall picture is a village-town with a nucleated urban centre. This type is different from the dual type in many significant ways, one of which is the absence of dual development and social conflict generated by dualism. Awka is an example in which traditional village patterns operate at certain levels and sectors while modern patterns operate at others. Modernity is infused into traditionality. How both accommodate one another is a matter to be studied.

A multi-nucleated traditional urban town consists of several modern urban nuclei which have sprung up at different localities; between them are village-town conditions which are basically traditional. Nsukka and Agbor may be classified in this group. It will be interesting to watch the growth of towns of this category.

DEMOGRAPHIC CIRCULATION

Close observation of the general movement of people in these settlements shows that the overall effect is of a circulatory nature. It may be summed us as follows:

Village to village;
Village to village-town;
Village to traditional urban town;
Village to hybrid or dual urban town;
Village-town to village;
Village-town to village town;
Village-town to traditional urban town;
Village-town to hybrid or dual urban town;
Traditional urban town to village;
Traditional urban town to village-town;
Traditional urban town to traditional urban town;
Traditional urban town to hybrid or dual urban town;
Hybrid or dual urban town to village;
Hybrid or dual urban town to village-town;
Hybrid or dual urban town to traditional urban town;
Hybrid or dual urban town to hybrid or dual urban town;
General movement from these settlements to outside the Igbo culture area.

This pattern of demographic circulation within the Igbo culture area is not only structurally significant but also important in its content. The movement from village to village is motivated by different factors from those which motivate the movement from village to village-town or to urban towns. These factors have yet to be studied. The analysis tabulated below is only an attempt to spell out some of the important factors.

Movement	*Main Factors*
Village to village:	Kinship, friendship, ceremonies, traditional entertainments, farming.
Village to village-towns:	Kinship, trading, ceremonies, traditional entertainments
Village to traditional urban-town:	Kinship, ceremonies, traditional entertainments .
Village to hybrid or dual urban town:	Trading, business
Village-town to village:	Farming, kinship, traditional entertainments, ceremonies
Village-town to village-town:	Farming, kinship, ceremonies, trading, business
Village-town to traditional urban-town:	Kinship, ceremonies, business
Village-town to hybrid or dual urban-town:	Trading, foreign entertainments
Traditional urban town to village:	Farming, traditional entertainments, ceremonies, kinship
Traditional urban town to village-town:	Farming, kinship, ceremonies, trading, meetings
Traditional urban town to traditional urban town:	Trading, business, kinship, ceremonies
Traditional urban town to hybrid urban town:	Business, trading, foreign entertainments
Hybrid or dual urban town to village:	Farming, meetings, kinship, traditional entertainments
Hybrid or dual urban town to village-town:	Farming, kinship, ceremonies, meetings
Hybrid or dual urban town to traditional urban town:	Trading, traditional entertainments, kinship, ceremonies
Hybrid or dual urban town to hybrid or dual urban town:	Business, foreign entertainments
Igbo settlements to outside the Igbo culture area:	Farming, business, leading to partial settlement

Internal movements are made easy and possible by various factors such as the existence of many daily markets, a complicated network of roads and paths, cultural dynamics, and adequate transport facilities, that is lorries, cars and bicycles.

The phrase 'demographic circulation' has been used here to describe a process of a constant flow of people from one settlement to another. When this pattern of circulation is altered qualitatively or quantitatively by season or economic factors, or a political crisis, then one can validly talk of movements and migrations. Movements and migrations may be regarded as critical in the demographic circulation in the Igbo culture area.

The character of Igbo migration in the past and present remains a challenge to sociology students interested in West African studies. Interdisciplinary studies in the fields of anthropology and linguistics, such as Igbo dialectology and traditional literature, would help to throw more light on this.

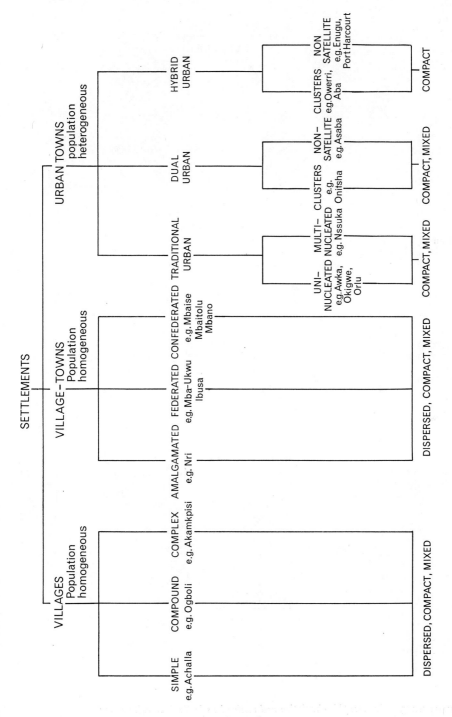

FIGURE 4   *The typology of settlements in the Igbo culture area*

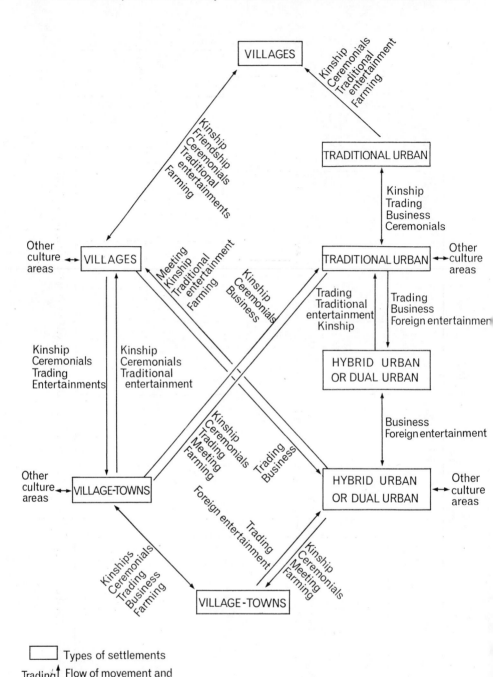

FIGURE 5 *Demographic circulation and motivations in the Igbo culture area*

CONCLUSION

The above typology is only an attempt to make some systematic generalizations. One cannot understand a village or a village-town or an urban town by staying there for a short period, asking a few questions and observing a few activities. But by doing so in various settlements within a given area a general picture may emerge. This picture will then be a general guide for further detailed studies.

This typology should not be regarded as watertight and static. It is dynamic in the sense that villages are evolving at various rates to village-towns, and village-towns to urban towns. Similarly urban towns are evolving.

The socio-cultural evolution I am referring to may take various forms, some lineal, some multi-lineal, some circular, some multifarious. It is interesting to note that some village-towns have recently started to evolve into compound villages.

The determinants of the socio-cultural evolution of settlements in the Igbo culture area are ecological, economical, political, cultural, historical and demographic. It means that the evolutionary direction of a settlement depends on the nature and character of the above determinants.

Villages and towns in the Igbo culture area afford rich laboratories for students of social change. It is indeed unfortunate that such unique opportunities are not made use of, because of our preoccupation with politics and our total ignorance of, and apathy towards, the need to understand African cultures and societies. It is indeed alarming how much money is wasted in projects directed blindly towards developing our villages and towns which we only pretend to understand.

If the nature and character of villages, village-towns and towns are known, if their demographic composition, their manpower potentialities, their economic, social and cultural resources are statistically assessed, we shall have sufficient data on which to plan development projects.

BIBLIOGRAPHY

SECTION I
Work consulted
STENNING, D. J. 'Household Viability among the Pastoral Fulani', in *The Developmental Cycle in Domestic Groups*, J. R. Goody (ed.) (Cambridge: Cambridge University Press, 1958)
—— *Savannah Nomads* (London: Oxford University Press, 1959)
—— 'Transhumance, migratory drift, migration', *J.R.A.I.* (1957), 87

Suggestions for further reading
FOSTER, G. M. *Traditional Cultures and the Impact of Technological Change* (New York: Harper 1962)
SPICER, E. H. *Human Problems in Technological Change: A Casebook* (New York: Russel Sage Foundation 1952)

SECTION II
Works consulted
ONWUEJEOGWU, M. A. 'The Typology of the Settlement Pattern in the Igbo Culture Area', *African Notes* (1970), 6, 1
—— 'An Outline Account of the Dawn of Igbo Civilisation in the Igbo Culture Area', in *Odinani Journal* (March 1972), 1, 1

CHAPTER 17

Some Patterns of Production and Consumption

I *Patterns of Land-Holding and Social Structure: the Ifugaoans, Tiv, Yakö, Benin, Egba, Lozi, Ashanti*

J. W. Salmond has said: 'Ownership in its most complete significance, denotes the relation between a person and any right that is vested in him. That which a man owns is in all cases a right. To own a piece of land means to own a particular kind of right in the land.'

Gluckman, following Salmond, maintains that in describing the systems of property ownership in Africa and other non-Western communities, it is necessary to set out clearly the specific right owned by each individual and group over each kind of property.

In the introduction to his book *African Agrarian Systems,* Biebuyek emphasizes that

> in the analysis of clusters of rights and claims, privileges and liabilities which are related to the ways in which Africans hold and work the land, live on it and use its products, is complex, on the one hand, because of difficulties in evaluating the exact nature of rights and claims, and on the other hand because of the imbrication of economic and social, political and religious factors.

To complete the list it is also essential to add cultural, historical, ecological and demographic factors.

It is obvious that the task of an anthropologist in the study of land-holding systems is not simply to set out clearly the specific rights and duties which individuals or groups have in respect to land, but also to analyse them and show their relations to other factors.

Three non-centralized societies of special interest will be examined here: the Ifugaoans, the Tiv and the Yakö; and one centralized society, the Benin. Mention will also be made of the Lozi, Ashanti and Egba.

THE IFUGAOANS

The Ifugaoans live on Luzon Island, one of the Philippines. They occupy the valleys and slopes of the eastern range of the Cordellera central range. Rain falls almost all the year round, but there is a marked drought between March and June when it is fairly dry with high temperatures which encourage the ripening of rice. When studied by Barton at the beginning of this century, the population was 120 000 in an area of about 750 square miles of usable land with a density of 160 per square mile.

Agriculture is the most important occupation. The soil is very fertile and the Ifugaoans are skilled in terracing and irrigation. Rice does well between the altitudes of 2500 ft and 5000 ft. They also grow maize and sweet potatoes, each of which is grown in separate fields. After the rice harvest the straws are pulled up and piled into mounds, on which are planted tobacco, cotton and other minor crops. After the beginning of the rainy season fish are placed in the rice field ponds where they are cultivated. So the rice field serves both as a garden and a fishing ground, and it is therefore the most valuable asset of a family.

Forest lands are of importance too, because the Ifugaoans obtain from it timber for house-building and firewood, as well as bush animals and wild food. Also in case of necessity forest land may be converted into rice fields. Other valuable land assets are coconut, coffee and areca.

The water supply plays a very important part in agriculture. Springs are owned and there are laws governing the use of streams and flowing water.

Barton wrongly says that the Ifugoans do not have political government or law based on judicial decisions, but correctly says that they have developed a corpus of laws concerning contract, property, inheritance, water rights and the family.

They live in eight districts which are the largest territorial units within which members can acquire land and dwell in comparative safety from the hostility of other districts. They have a bilateral system whereby a child inherits from both father and mother. The law of primogeniture is always maintained without sex distinction. They distinguish between family property consisting of rice lands, forest lands and heirlooms, and personal property consisting of houses, valuable trees and sweet potatoes.

A piece of rice land consists of all the contiguous fields in one area, or scattered, that are the property of one man. It is never divided for sale or inheritance. The rice land and forest lands are only sold in cases of great need and after due consultation with one's kin. Rice and forest tenures are regarded as perpetual. However, if an owner leaves a rice field for any period, another person may farm it without the owner's permission, unless the owner protests at the beginning. The owner can get back his land after harvest and he has to pay something for the labour used in clearing the field.

Pawning of land is common. In its most elaborate form A can borrow 50 pesos from B, leaving his field to B's charge; B gives it to C for the same amount or a lesser amount (never more), and C gives it to D and so on. When A is able to pay the debt, he goes to B and pays the sum plus the agent's fee, and B meets C, and so on until the land is recovered. These arrangements are modified by the field being in crop, or the harvest being near.

If it is decided in the council of kin to sell a field, a go-between negotiates between the buyer and seller, and the sale is completed when the two parties eat together at the ritual feast of *Ibuy*. If after a sale a rice field is subject to unusual sliding in the terrace wall, the buyer may at any time within the year of purchase return the field and demand the return of his money on the grounds that the seller had not relinquished its welfare and fertility.

Rice fields and forests are transferred within the family or to relations by two processes. The first is by assignment. As children get married, they are assigned fields and the last child receives the remainder; the parents then retire and are cared for by their children. The second method is by inheritance. In the case of the death of the parents or the owner, the law of primogeniture is applied. There is a clear distinction between a husband's kin's land and a wife's kin's land. If spouses die childless, the respective land goes back to the respective spouse's kin. The family lands of the spouses coalesce and are identical for their children and children's descendants.

Water is also a part of the land tenure system. Anyone is free to use water, subject to the following laws. Water which is flowing to an area of irrigated lands may under no circumstances be diverted to irrigate a different area. A spring belongs to the person in whose land it is situated. The owner may sell surplus water to whom he pleases; the sale is outright. A person can sell the land without selling the spring which is on the land, that is, he can go on using the water from it. There is a distinction between streams and rivulets which are for the use of the public, and springs which are regarded as personal property.

Clearings are made for sweet potato fields on the mountain sides around the villages. They are always on steep slopes and so lose their fertility quickly and are usually abandoned by the owners. However, the owners still have rights over these fields as long as weeds do not grow on them. The first person to clear them again becomes the possessor for a period of years. Sweet potato fields are sometimes sold, but it is not the land that is sold, but the crop with the temporary possession of the land.

Land which is not rice field or forest and which is not owned by someone in the district becomes the property of whoever makes it into a rice field. The land on which a house stands is of no value as houses are wooden and movable and can be dismantled and set up somewhere else at any time the owner wishes to do so.

Crop-producing trees such as coconuts, coffee, areca palms, are sold without the land on which they grow being sold or transferred, as a rule.

The Ifugaoan kindred, consisting of up to the second cousin or more, depending on the person's influence, is the unit ego can rely upon for help in time of crisis, and it is also the unit in which kinship obligations are morally and legally important.

The Ifugaoan community is stratified into three classes: the rich, the middle and the poor. The stratification reflects the distribution of wealth, which means rice fields. Big landowners have become land 'leasers' and so are influential because they have large followings and dependants of kinsmen and non-kinsmen. Although the big landowners have no specific political power within the village or district, they still influence the maintenance of law and order therein. Inter-district trade and contracts are made possible through some of them who make contacts with their equals in other districts.

The Ifugaoans are an example of a people who through ecological adaptation have developed a system of land tenure and body of laws guiding the rights of every individual in the ownership of land, water and their products. The unequal distribution of land is reflected in their social stratification. Their territorial organization and their political system are based on contracts arising from land ownership. Land is sold, leased and pawned. Land is valued. The statement that in a simple society land is never sold is therefore not applicable to the Ifugaoans. The statement that in a simple society land has no value is equally not applicable to the Ifugaoans, and Maine's contention that primitive societies do not enter into contracts is refuted by what happens there. Similarly, the idea that in a non-monetary society land has no market value and that when land has a value it is a result of Western economic influences, is found to be not at all true for the Ifugaoans.

They were first studied around 1913, and at that period they never exported their rice beyond neighbouring districts. Real estate was valued in pigs and carabus, and the rice produced was used as a medium of exchange.

THE TIV

The vegetation of the area in which the Tiv live, in the mid-valley of the Benue River, is deciduous. Rain falls seven months in the year between April and October with a dry period between November and March. The southern area has more rainfall than the north. This variation is reflected in the vegetation and types of crops grown. In both areas agriculture is the main occupation, but while the southern Tiv specialize in yam production and grow very little grain, the northern Tiv grow more grain and less yam. Cassava, millet, maize, guinea corn are grown, usually in separate fields from yam. The Tiv used to be almost entirely subsistence farmers, but now they grow some cash crops and sell their yams and grain to local traders who export them to other parts of Nigeria. Other crops are soya beans and benniseed which are newly introduced cash crops sold overseas.

11　*The* Eshu (*Oyo, Nigeria*)

Some three or four generations above the living elders are the apical ancestors of each segment of a minimal lineage, each of which is associated with a territory (which is named after him). (For the political and lineage structure of the Tiv, see Chapter 10, Section II.) Below this level are components of the minimal lineage, called compounds, which are composed of groups of between two and forty huts, with between 15–150 people altogether. The members of a compound are related agnatically. A minimal lineage is associated with a territory called *Tar* and is the largest land-holding unit in Tiv land.

According to Bohannan, Akwar begot Nyam and Ika Nyam begot Gor and

SOME PATTERNS OF PRODUCTION AND CONSUMPTION

Wandia. Gor, Wandia and Ika occupy territories, each of which is called a *Tar*. Gor's territory is called *Mba-Gor*, Wandia's is called *Mba-Wandia* and *Ika*'s is called *Mba-Akwar*.

Let us examine *Mba-Gor*'s minimal *Tar* which is the largest land-holding unit in *Mba-Akwar*. Here there are 22 compound heads of 477 persons occupying 1200 acres. Each compound head is entitled to farm a piece of land which is subdivided into smaller units. Each unit is farmed by a man and his wife or wives. Each wife is entitled to farm a piece of land in her husband's share.

A man's grownup sons usually farm with their father, and as each one marries the compound head gives him land. On the father's death the crop is inherited, not the land.

On the average, particularly in southern Tiv, a minimal *Tar* is 200–1000 in population in an area of 2–20 square miles. A minimal *Tar* is made up of 83 per cent males agnatically related, 15 per cent non-agnates, usually sisters' sons, and 2 per cent strangers. There may be anything between five and fifty-five compounds in a *Tar*.

When the Tiv discuss their land-holding system they mean two things: the specific rights in cultivated land, and sufficient land to cultivate. Every compound head has a right to sufficient land to feed himself and all the members of his compound. This also includes the rights to sufficient fallow land. A compound head who fails to provide members of his compound with sufficient land will find his compound abandoned, for his dependants will leave him and either establish their own compounds or go to their collateral kinsmen or their *Igba* to ask for land. The compound head's right is a 'right against the world'. There is no higher authority to give him land or take land from him. If he is short of land, he takes it at the expense of the genealogically most distant man whose land bounds his own. To do this he has to gain the support of his minimal *Tar*. This process of land seizure and the resultant activation of one segment against another is one of the chief features of Tiv politics.

On the whole, the size of farmland depends on need. Every adult male who lives in the compound has a right to farm sufficient land to feed himself and his dependants. Every wife or widow of a compound member has a right to a farm from which to feed herself and her dependants.

To grant a stranger residence implies the granting of farmland which is validated by residence in the compound. Every member of the *Tar*, resident or non-resident, has perpetual rights to use the land of the *Tar*, but the notion of heritable fields does not exist. A person only has the right to sufficient land to meet his basic needs of subsistence. The territorial aspect of the lineage system acts as a regulator of the relative spatial positions in which people can exercise this right. The right to land is protected by ritual and mystical sanctions and by erecting on the land the magical emblems of *Akombo* against intruders. A person has the right to the portion of his father's land farmed by his mother, but he does not inherit it. Land cannot be sold or exchanged. When it is given it is simply the transfer of a temporary right of use. Rents on land are considered immoral.

Land shortage activates two types of migration: expansion and disjunction. The territory of the *Tar* is constantly enlarging through expansionary activities. This may lead eventually to a change in the geographical location of the lineage territory. Disjunction means groups or individuals leaving the *Tar* for another territory.

Each compound has its water-well or pond and any stranger wishing to use it must obtain permission from the compound head. Clay can be taken from anywhere without permission. Hunting is allowed in any part of the bush, but hunters are obliged to give some of their booty to those who 'own' the area. Women may only gather mushrooms, etc., in their cultivated farms or on fallow land. Caterpillars and termites may be gathered from anywhere. Trees such as the locust bean, the shea, etc., are exploited by the people who cultivate the land they stand on.

Both men and women work in groups. Men do the hard work of hoeing and ridging and preparing land for planting, while women do the lighter work of planting and weeding. Both sexes participate in weeding. Intercropping, two- or three-year rotation of crops and fallowing are practised. The Tiv living in the Benue River system have not shown much initiative in the exploitation of these resources. This points to the fact that they have quite recently acquired this habitat and have not fully adapted to the new life.

THE YAKÖ

Among the Yakö a man with his wife or wives constitutes a single farming unit and each wife has her own rights and duties in the exploitation of the land. The yams of both the husband and wife or wives are planted and harvested separately by the same unit of labour. (For a description of the vegetation and crops, see Chapter 6, Section III.)

Men collect palm produce and the women extract the oil which the men sell with their yams to get money. Women retain the kernel and about a gallon of the oil produced out of the quantity extracted for their own use.

Each family dwells in a large group of patrilineal relatives and their wives, and the patrilineages in their turn form larger groups or patriclans which are also territorially compact. (For a more detailed description of the kinship system, see Chapter 6, Section III.)

Each ward of the village owns its own territory which it defends jealously. The ward land is divided up among patrilineal kin groups. On each farm road used by the patriclan there is a farm path elder who is expected to know the established rights of all the individuals of his clan on that road. A man may migrate from his patriclan area in the village and go to live in the area of another patriclan where he may be given farming sites. Also a man can obtain temporary rights to make a farm on the land of another kin group by the traditional offer of a gourd of palm wine to a path elder of that patriclan.

If serious pressure develops on the farmland new and permanent farm paths are opened. This is possible because there is plenty of spare land. Only 4 square miles out of the 18 are really used; also there is still the residue of about 5 square miles of unfarmed forest to the east of Yakö land.

A man is entitled to a piece of farmland when he marries and has an independent household. In the first few years he receives a part of his father's farmland. In later years the father, not the young man, goes to the farm path elder of his patriclan to ask for and establish his claim to a new piece of unoccupied farmland. It is not stated when this process is discontinued, but it is safe to assume that it goes on until the father retires from farming or dies.

The patrilineages of a clan dwell together in a given territory. Each family head has a right over a certain portion of land on which to build, and this with the trees on it is inherited from father to son. Daughters do not inherit land but have the right to use their father's portion. Owners of trees or land may allow others to use them after the customary consultations. In almost every patriclan there is a communal square, a shrine, and a common house which are owned in common and are inherited by the next generation in common.

Oil palms, coconuts and other trees are acquired by patrilineal kin groups, each of which collectively claims the trees in their home territory. Any member who clears the path leading to the palm tree can claim its use. A distinction is made between palms tapped for wine and those from which fruits are collected. Trees on farmland that are being tapped are claimed by the person who has done the preliminary necessary treatment. There is another distinction, between the palm trees on the farmland and those in the residential area. Those in the residential area are owned and inherited patrilineally, while those on the farmland are not, and are only used by members of the patriclan. Timber trees are owned by the patriclan.

As shown above, the individual's claims to land and economic resources are established within the patrilineal kin group. The matrilineal kin groups claim all movable property. But there are two exceptional cases when they can claim immovable property. At the funeral rites of an elder, the dead man's matrilineal kinsmen can enter the elder's matrilineal tract of land and take palm wine from any part irrespective of who owns it. They also have rights over the valuable raffia palms which either grow in swamps or are planted. These palms are transmitted matrilineally.

The Priest of *Odjokoba* lives in the centre of the village on land which does not belong to any patriclan. Although it has not been stated how this piece of land is inherited or managed, it may be safe to assume that it is inherited matrilineally.

Although matrilineal kin have no farming rights, the general activities are controlled by the priests of the matriclan who are in charge of the fertility cults. Thus the new farm rite held in January, the new yam rite held in early July, and the harvest rites held in November are initiated and directed by the matrilineal priests who are leaders of the Council of Priests, *Yabot*. In this way ritual values are correlated with the means of production. Land is controlled by the patrilineal group while the mysteries of land are controlled by the matrilineal group.

The Yakö distinguish between those villages in which the original migrants settled and the remaining villages which are held to have been founded a generation or two later. This points to the fact that changes did occur in the past, which is corroborated by the present fission or accretion of the patriclan, and by the fact that when dwelling areas in the village become fully occupied, the pressure is reduced by moving away from the main village and settling some half a mile away on the land belonging to the patrilineage or patriclan. (See also Chapter 6, Section III, and Chapter 10, Section III.)

Among the Tiv and the Yakö changes have and still are taking place. With the coming of British rule, the Tiv migratory habit was checked, and they were pinned down to an area. For both peoples the increase in population, the new value on land as a result of the introduction of cash crops, the intrusion of a centralized policy, the pace of industrialization and urbanization, and the new generations with their different cultural outlook, may mean new problems and a reorientation of the land tenure system.

Both the Tiv and Yakö illustrate how social, ritual, and political organization is related to land and its usage. Land is one of the ways by which jural and political authorities are channelled.

Before the arrival of the British, the Tiv migrated very often and were not sentimentally or ritually attached to the soil, as some anthropologists hold to be true of small-scale societies. An attachment does exist, but there are mechanisms for breaking it. Even the Yakö, who were ritually tied to the soil, migrated quite often. Before each migration a ritual was performed which loosed them from the bonds of the earth.

THE BENIN

We shall now examine a centralized state (studied by R. E. Bradbury). Benin city is the capital of Benin kingdom and it had a population of 54 000 in 1952. The people of Benin kingdom live in several hundred compact village settlements ranging in size from 20 to more than 6000 inhabitants. The ruler of the kingdom is called the *Oba*. The kingdom is ruled by the *Oba*-in-council. The *Uzama* chiefs, the town chiefs and the title-holders of the palace association are the chief political and administrative bodies of the kingdom.

All the land of Benin kingdom is said to belong to the *Oba*. This statement refers primarily to his position as the political ruler of the territory rather than to his actual control over the ownership of land. The land is vested in him as trustee for the whole people. The 'ownership' in this sense is symbolized at the installation of each new *Oba* when after a mock battle to capture the city, the chief *Ogiave* puts oil into his palm. As far as the Benin are concerned, his actual control of particular blocks of territory only refers to the allocation of building sites in Benin city and the permission to found new settlements in unclaimed forest.

Outside Benin city the village is the typical land-holding unit, though boundaries are vaguely recognized. Within the village no smaller group is recognized as having permanent rights over any tract of land, even though the wards of villages are groups of patrilineages of three or four generations deep. A villager may farm anywhere on village land without seeking permission from anyone as long as the piece of land he chooses is not occupied by another's crops, or a person had not previously intimated his intention to clear the land progressively in a given direction, in which case he may not be obstructed. If disputes arise they are settled by the village council. Disputed land rights refer to the rights over permanent crops such as rubber and cocoa, which are cash crops, rather than the land itself.

There is recognition of rights over fallow land. Once a man has cleared land and planted it over two or three years and then let it go fallow, it reverts to the community.

An Edo who wishes to farm on the land of a village other than his own must seek the permission of the village head. He presents gifts to the villagers in kind or cash, which they share with the elders, and he must continue to do so each year unless he settles in the village permanently.

The freemen of Benin city appear to have established rights to village land in two ways: by arranging with the head man of an existing village to station their farm workers there and to farm on the village land; and by clearing virgin forest outside the control of any village and establishing a camp there to house their dependants. This eventually develops into a village.

Yam is the basic crop and it is mainly cultivated by men, although women usually assist in weeding and planting and the whole labour supply is mobilized for the harvest. If there is a large crop the farmer may set aside some yams to be sold by his wives on his behalf. The rest he divides among his wives to feed himself and his children. He sells any surplus. Corn and other crops are usually inter-cropped with yams and these are generally owned by women and used for family consumption. Cassava, coco-yams and rice are grown on separate plots by both men and women. Young men who still depend on their parents can earn some income by making their own cassava plots and selling the produce.

The most important tree crops are kola, coconut and palm. Kola trees and coconut are planted, owned and inherited by individuals. All men and some women have kola trees of their own. Oil palms are held collectively by the village community and any member of the village may reap their fruits or tap them for wine. The only exception to this rule is when a tree is growing on land under cultivation, in which case the farmer's permission is necessary for its exploitation. Close periods are declared at intervals to allow the trees to recuperate, which are usually followed by a general assault on the fruits.

Farming units are on a family basis, although a man can call his age-mates and friends to help him or employ paid labour.

The cultivation of permanent crops has brought about some changes in the traditional pattern of land rights, theoretically, but it has not resulted in individual ownership of the land. Once planted, permanent crops can be alienated by the owner by sale, pledge or mortgage, though in theory the land on which they are grown is not involved in the transaction.

The influx of non-Edo people has resulted in various regulations controlling their rights in land use, forest and river resources, and house sites. Fixed annual charges are made for each type of land use.

Traditionally, the allocation of house sites in Benin city was in the hands of the *Oba* who usually consulted the chiefs and elders of the ward concerned. He seems to have given up this job to the local administrative officials. The state government has adopted a new policy for the allocation of land, for sale of land is now common.

Benin is interesting for several reasons. It illustrates how a diversified centrally organized state that has been in contact with Western ideas and the Western economy for the past four hundred years, and increasingly for the past one hundred and fifty years, did not develop individual ownership or the alienation of land until quite recently. It can not be said that land is not valued, since the value of forest products such as timber and the rubber tree is fully appreciated and exploited. Formerly, however, land itself was never sold; instead, the product of the land was negotiated on the open market.

Lord Hailey, in his introduction to C. K. Meek's book, *Land, Law and Custom in the Colonies,* suggests that over most of colonial Africa the primary factor making for the individualization of land-holdings was the introduction of export agricultural crops, particularly tree crops. While this statement can hardly be denied it seems to have no significance among the Benin.

In the Egba Division of Western Nigeria, the upheavals and tribal wars of the nineteenth century created a situation similar to what one would expect in newly settled areas. Each adult carved out for himself individual holdings over which he had freehold rights. The missionaries and the Sierra Leone immigrants who arrived soon after the settlement of Egba introduced new concepts of land alienation into an already fluid situation. In this case individual freeholding and the right to sell had become established long before the impetus was accelerated by the introduction of cocoa as a crop.

The Benin case also illustrates the situation in which the king, although called the owner of the land, has no control over it as the Lozi king has. Among the Lozi, although politically not territorially organized, the king derives his political control from the fact that he is the hub and centre of land distribution. Without these rights over land allocation, it is doubtful if the Lozi king would be of any political significance. Lozi political authority and power are based on land, which is controlled by the king. (For a more detailed description, see Chapter 5, Section II.)

Why is it that among the Benin the lineage is not a land-holding unit, while among the Ashanti it is? This may be related to the degree of opportunity, differentiation and security which the state offers to her citizens. It seems that the Benin state offers more economic and political opportunities to the individual than the Ashanti state. Thus the Benin lineages have, so to speak, given up their landowning rights for other more rewarding opportunities offered by the state.

In conclusion, some of the facts which Biebuyek's generalizations tend to obscure might be clarified here. There are variable relationships between land-holding and the political structure in some societies; in others there are no such relationships. The sale of land is not uncommon in small-scale societies, and neither is individual ownership. Both may be conditioned by factors such as religious ecology, economy and politics, and may not be related at all to the introduction of cash crops or Western influences, as, for instance, the Ifugaoans. Some small-scale societies, like the Tiv, are not at all ritually or sentimentally attached to the land. Even among those peoples who are ritually tied to the land, some mechanisms to untie the ritual bonds always exists and are frequently used. The Yakö are examples of this. The introduction of cash crops may even not lead to the sale and individualization of land, as among the Benin. The symbolic aspect of land has not been fully analysed by anthropologists.

II *The Principles of the Division of Labour: the Tiwi of Australia and the Nsaw of Cameroon*

To the economist concerned with industrialized societies the term division of labour means the technique of production whereby every worker directs his labour effort towards the production of a very small part of a particular commodity. This refers more to specialization. But in small-scale societies, that are not industrialized, where each person's status and roles are determined by sex, age and other cultural factors, such a rigid definition may not be too useful. In such small-scale societies, the term division of labour does have its orthodox reference. But it also refers to the division of jobs among the whole population, determined by sex, age, clan affiliation, heredity, caste, guilds and associations. The principles of the division of labour in the societies of the Tiwi and the Nsaw will be compared from this angle which stresses differentiation more than specialization.

The Tiwi are Australian aborigines who have long inhabited the islands of Melville and Bathurst in the north-west of the Australian continent. The long isolation from both the mainland and the ouside world has made the Tiwi culture unique in certain respects. The ecology of these islands differs from that of the mainland. Vegetable food supplies, game and fish are comparatively abundant. Much of the country is a mixture of dense shrub and open savannah rich in kangaroo, other marsupials, lizards, fruits and wild yams. The availability of manpower to tap these wild food resources is the preoccupation of the Tiwi.

They have a complex social structure with very ineffective technology. They speak the same language and identify themselves as Tiwi when speaking to a stranger but among themselves they identify themselves with their bands. The Tiwi are not a corporate group in the sense that they never come together for any purpose.

The band is the territorial group which a man closely identifies himself with. There are nine bands in Tiwi, each comprising 100–300 people spread over an area of 200–300 square miles of band territory whose boundaries are well known.

The composition of the band is rather fluid, as people change their membership frequently. A band never lives together in one place except during initiation and funeral ceremonies.

The smallest domestic unit in Tiwi is the household which consists of a man, his wife or wives, their children and/or stepchildren, and cousins. The Tiwi household does not include any grownup women over fourteen years old, for the culture insists that all women must be married, and to achieve this, pre-natal betrothal and remarriage of all widows is the rule. Thus the Tiwi fathers control the marriages of their infant daughters who are betrothed and married to old men of their own age-set. Widow remarriage supplies young men of thirty-five with old wives of fifty. With this as a start the 'politics' of acquiring more older and younger wives occupies all the lives of the men.

In every household the young married wives and the old wives do the gathering and collecting of food in the bushes, from morning to evening. They return in the evening to prepare supper. In all these activities the older wives of aged between forty and sixty years old supervise and direct the younger wives who are aged between fourteen and thirty. The older wives also act as spies, watching the moral uprightness of the younger ones who tend to be easy prey to the young bachelors around. The women look after the children and satisfy all their needs.

The young men between eighteen and thirty-five who are agile and keen-sighted do the hunting, while those between thirty-five and forty-five direct and advise them. Older men, who are usually the head of households, with plenty of experience but a decline in stamina and sight, do little hunting. They become the wood carvers, painters and artists of the society. They make hunting and ceremonial spears which are their monopoly, and carved utensils, throwing sticks and funeral boards. They make baskets and decorate them with paint. Women also make baskets but pass them to their husbands to be painted since paint is taboo to women. The old men officiate during funeral ceremonies, while men under forty-five are charged with the initiation ceremonies. The songs for all occasions are composed by the old men who are also the chief priests of the household. Thus in Tiwi society the symbols of prestige and power, such as the carved ceremonial spears carried by old men, paint, wives and ceremonial songs, are all concentrated under the control of the old men. This is echoed in the division of labour.

Group activities, such as the kangaroo hunt, funeral ceremonies and initiation, are periods of production and distribution of food; and here the division of labour features markedly. At a kangaroo hunt, the hunters surround the area, the older men supervise and direct the hunt, while the women and children act as beaters. The grass is set on fire and as the women retreat the hunters advance.

A male between the age of one and twenty-seven is a nonentity until after his initiation has finished; it begins at the age of fourteen and lasts until the age of twenty-seven. He is considered a boy until he has completed the final stage of initiation. After twenty-seven, he begins to look for a wife and he may have his first old widow wife of forty-five when he is between twenty-eight and thirty-five. The old widow is experienced in food gathering and will be available to train and direct a young wife who joins the household at fourteen; by this time the husband will be between forty and fifty. Gradually by acquiring new wives both young and old, and widows, the man will build a big household and with his ceremonial spears he will become a man of prestige and high status.

Thus in Tiwi society the status differentiation based on the success of old men is controlled by the principle of the division of labour based on age and sex.

. . . . .

The Nsaw (studied by P. Kaberry) are one of the peoples of Bamenda in the Cameroon. (The population in 1953 was about 50 000 of which 5000 live in Kumba, the capital.) They occupy an area of 700 square miles and the density is about forty persons to the square mile. Its characteristic geographical feature is a high grassy plateau, and there is about 65 inches of rainfall per year. The people are subsistence agriculturalists growing cereals, tubers, plantain, pulses, gourds, greens and sugar-cane. Maize, coco-yam and yam are staple foods. Raffia palm is valued for tapping wine and building poles. The men derive cash income from sales of kola, livestock, honey, tobacco, various tools and utensils. Oil is obtained from the people living in the forested zone. They have a more diversified economy and technology than the Tiwi.

The Nsaw are ruled by a paramount chief whose office is hereditary within the patrilineage. He is called the *Fon*. Nsaw includes a number of villages that have become tributary to the *Fon*. The villages are ruled by *fon* whose succession to office has been ratified by the *Fon*. He hears cases and discusses public affairs. His messengers, police and attendants are recruited from a special society. The 'Fathers of the Palace' guard and control the stores and wives of the *Fon*. The high priests and priestesses and the queen mother help in the government of the Nsaw.

Villages are made up of various patriclans that are made up of lineages. Each lineage is made up of 20–70 members. Several lineages are under a *Fai*. The clans and lineages express solidarity in the ownership of offices, rituals and deaths, and the lineages in communal labour. The lineage head *Fai* is appointed by the *Fon* and he is vested with the power to call on all his dependants for assistance in clearing and cultivating his garden and in bridge and house construction. He is also the chief priest and arbitrator in minor disputes within the lineages. Matrilineal ties are also recognized and expressed in joint participation in various ceremonies and activities.

The elementary family is the clearly defined residential, social and economic unit. The male members and unmarried females are related to the compound head by patrilineal ties.

Women are in charge of agriculture. The men do the heavy clearing while women do the hoeing. Both men and women do the planting but women alone do the weeding. Men help the women in harvesting and transporting the baskets to the compound. Men tend the tobacco, raffia palm and kola-nut tree plantations, and from the sales provide money for the family's use. Men and women make pottery, but men sell the pottery outside the villages. Women do the general cooking and feeding of the families. Men do other types of job such a smithing, trading and tailoring, etc. Women do the internal petty trading while men do the external trading that involves travelling. From time to time men sweep the compound, clear paths, wash clothes, set small traps, weave baskets, graze goats, superintend the poultry, build houses, make pipes, etc. Small children look after the small babies and stronger ones fetch water for domestic use. When the children are big enough they help their parents, according to their sex. The women organize work groups to help to lessen farm work,

Among the Nsaw there is no rigid division of labour based on sex and age. In accordance with their concept of fertility, they have laid the farm work on the shoulders of the women, but the men never fail to do the heavy jobs of clearing and harvesting. Certain roles are achieved and some are ascribed in Nsaw society.

Having sketched briefly the ecology, social organization and the principles of division of labour in the Tiwi and Nsaw societies, what remains is to compare the two. The value of this comparison is to show how two different societies, one hunting and gathering, the other agriculturalist, in two different types of ecological environments, have solved their various problems by adopting different principles of the division of labour.

The Nsaw notion of fertility involves the concentration of agricultural pursuits in the hands of women. The men always help the women when the work is heavy. This emphasis on sex fertility is symbolic. The Tiwi notion of prestige which is male-centred makes it impossible for women to play any part in politics. The Nsaw women, however, do take part in politics. The old men of Tiwi monopolize carving and painting, since these pursuits are symbols of prestige. Young men are assigned to hunting. The long initiation ceremony is an example of how youth is suppressed. The old women are used as spies to check on the young men and they also direct the young inexperienced wives. Division of labour among the Tiwi is based on sex, age, culture and environment. The Nsaw women do little trade; the men do all the external trade. This is in line with their cultural concept that women should be in charge of the home. Nsaw men, depending on their lineage, can climb up the social ladder. This does not happen among the Tiwi where men achieve their status after long initiation ceremonies. Nsaw society tends more towards specialization and diversification, while the Tiwi economy is undiversified.

How can we explain the principles involved in this type of division of labour? It has been argued that the division of labour contributes to the preservation of the individual and the perpetuation of the race. Surely the subjection of Tiwi youth to a long period of celibacy cannot be explained in this way? Buxton considers that the basis is the concept of man as 'primarily the breadwinner'. However, the dominance of the Nsaw female in agriculture cannot be explained in this light. D. Forde refers to the biological differences between the sexes, to the environmental settings of different cultures, and to the different historical and cultural experiences.

One point is clear and that is that the division of labour in these societies is encapsulated in their ritual and kinship activities whence they derive their rationale and sanction. Thus economic interdependence, which is also an aspect of some kind of social solidarity, operates within the context of kinship and ritual. Such interdependence is symbolically expressed in the sexual dichotomy of labour found in all societies.

It is not surprising that Emile Durkheim in discussing how a multiplicity of individuals make up a society or how individuals achieve consensus, does it by describing the concept of the division of labour. But the phenomenon Durkheim is trying to explain, that is the division of labour, differs from what the economists understand by the same concept. Durkheim's division of labour refers to a structure of the society as a whole, of which the economic division of labour is an expression and an aspect. Hence he distinguishes two types of solidarity, mechanical and organic.

Mechanical solidarity is based on resemblance. The main characteristic of a society in which mechanical solidarity prevails is that the individuals resemble one another and are not sufficiently differentiated and so the society is coherent. Organic solidarity is one in which consensus or unity is expressed by differentiation.

In Durkheim's mind, the two forms of solidarity correspond to two forms of social organization. To him 'primitive' societies are characterized by mechanical solidarity, while 'advanced' societies are characterized by organic solidarity.

It seems that Durkheim may have failed to realize that all societies are differentiated and the difference is a matter of degree. Differentiation as an expression and an aspect of solidarity is the greatest sociological legacy Durkheim bequeathed to the theory of division of labour as a social phenomenon.

III *The Relation Between Production and Consumption and the Achievement of Status in Primitive Economic Systems: the Tolowa Tututni of California, the Ponapeans of the Pacific, the Tiv of Nigeria, the Lele of Central Africa*

Cora Dubois, W. Bascom, L. P. Bohannan and M. Douglas have adopted similar approaches in analysing the relation between production and consumption and the achievement of status in primitive economic systems.

Cora Dubois divides the economy of the Tolowa Tututni into two parts: that of subsistence and that of prestige. She defines a subsistence economy as 'the exploitation of plentiful natural resources available to any industrious individual' and prestige economy as 'a series of social prerogative and status values, ranging from wives to owning supernatural formulae'.

She lists dentalia and buckskin dress as media of exchange, among several other things in the Tolowa economy, and calls them money. She considers that their money serves as a medium of exchange primarily in the sphere of prestige economy, whereas in the realm of subsistence barter is used. She modifies this statement by adding that the two parts of the economy overlap at times. Her famous equation is that in Euro–American society subsistence→money→prestige, while in Tolowa society subsistence →money← prestige.

Her analysis has two main weaknesses. In the first place the definitions of subsistence and prestige are questionable. Also the relationship between subsistence, money and prestige is not 'linear' but 'cyclic'.

Secondly, the things Dubois lists as Tolowan money are prestige-loaded goods quite different from American dollars. Both of them may be media of exchange, but they differ in their functional value, and so may not be comparable.

W. Bascom, following Dubois, distinguishes three main economic categories among the Ponapeans: subsistence, commerce and prestige. By a subsistence economy Bascom means that which is concerned with food, clothing and other commodities which are consumed by the household which produces them. By a commercial economy he means those goods such as copra which are produced for export and sold to obtain money with which to purchase clothing, hardware, etc. By a prestige economy he means those goods such as big yams, pit breadfruit, kava and pigs, with which social approval and social status are gained. As with subsistence goods, prestige goods are produced and consumed locally, but they are also shared with other households. In short, a prestige economy is associated with feasting. Bascom agrees with Dubois that overlaps are common. However, most goods do fall clearly within one or other of the above categories. The foodstuffs which are essential for their diet are not classified as belonging to the traditional prestige economy, apart from small yams. The goods used for prestige feasting are sent back home to be used as food.

Dubois' definitions of prestige and subsistence differ from Bascom's. While Dubois is using activities as references for her classification, Bascom uses goods. Thus for Bascom it is the goods that matter, not how they are produced; while, on the contrary, for Dubois it is how the goods are produced that matters, not the goods themselves. In any economy the goods and activities associated with production cannot be considered separate entities. If they were separated, the result would be distortion of the basic principles of production. In dealing with the nature of production and distribution in any society we should devote our attention not only to the goods but also to the activities associated with their production, and the type of relationship generated.

Achievement of prestige is one of the primary motives in Ponapean production. To produce big yams an adequate labour force and food supply are necessary. A man of prestige is therefore the entrepreneur who organizes and mobilizes labour and its reward. He produces big yams and by displaying them he converts his achievement into prestige. The result is that by his efforts he increases the production level and the food supply. By redistributing his economic achievement while still retaining his social prestige which has increased considerably, he strengthens his future entrepreneurial role. Here, as can be seen, it is not very useful to talk of subsistence and prestige economies. He is also able to mobilize labour and to obtain more copra, which is exported. In return more imported goods are pumped into the Ponapean economy. There is no justification in calling this a separate type of economy, as Bascom does. The processes are within one economic milieu and not within different parts of the economy.

Bohannan, in his discussion of exchange and investment among the Tiv, says that the Tiv economy is a subsistence agriculture supplemented by an effective network of markets. He delineates spheres or categories of exchange. The following are his three categories of exchangeable commodities:

1. Foodstuffs including locust beans, pepper, chickens, etc.
2. Slaves (formerly), 'Big White' cloth, brass rods.
3. Rights in human beings, particularly women.

Bohannan says that these categories represent the fundamental Tiv notions about exchange and investment. However, perhaps because he is dealing with notions rather than facts, he seems to have omitted many important points that would have helped to analyse the Tiv economy fully.

For example, he does not say how the Tiv get their 'Big White' cloth, cows and brass rods. But in his *Ethnographic Survey of the Tiv*, Bohannan says that the Tiv get their brass rods from the Igbo, their cows from the Fulani, and some of their 'Big White' cloth from Jukun traders. They acquire all these things by barter with the so-called 'subsistence' goods. Thus the Tiv have to pump out a lot of food from their economy (yams, maize, grain, etc.) in order to acquire brass rods, cows, cloth (and, in the past, even slaves) from their neighbours. If food is pumped out it must be replaced by more production. Thus the desire to acquire prestige goods activates the production of food, which involves the mobilization of man-power through the channels of kinship.

Bohannan says that since land is not exchangeable it does not enter into the sphere of prestige. In his ethnographic survey he says that a compound head who is not able to find sufficient land for his dependants will soon find himself alone. Men of prestige and influence are those who have *Tsav*, a magical power, and they are usually compond heads. In order to have a large compound a man must have sufficient land to give to his dependants. So the use of land is exchanged for loyalty and willingness to stay in a compound. But the compound head's ability to seize it from a genealogically distant *Tar*, which depends on his prestige and influence in his *Tar*. If he fails, his prestige flops and his compound decreases; if he succeeds, his prestige increases and he is feared as a man with powerful *Tsav*. Furthermore, to gain great prestige a man has to give out a lot of food and beer during marriages and hoeing periods, kill a cow for his wife, own a horse, acquire *Akombo* drums and titles which are bought from the Jukuns, and have his own *Swem*.

In discussing the categories of exchangeable commodities Bohannan does not mention all the types of important exchanges which he carefully recorded in his ethnographic work on the Tiv. However, he introduced two useful terms: 'conveyance' and 'conversion'. The former refers to exchanges of items within a single category, and the latter to exchanges of items from one category to another. These terms are useful only when the Tiv economy is looked upon as a whole and not as separate disjointed units of subsistence, prestige and 'super-prestige' economies, or as categories of exchangeable commodities. Thus, when a Tiv exchanges a chicken for a goat, a goat for a cow, and a cow for a foreign wife, he really has increased his labour force and his prestige as well; he has made a social and an economic profit. But when he exchanges his sister for a brass rod or a cow, or a cow for food, he looks on it as a material and social loss. Also, when he exchanges a cow for a brass rod or some 'Big White' cloth, he makes no profit or loss socially or economically. Thus, conveyance and conversion should refer to the nature of circulation of goods in a barter system rather than to categories of economic activities. These modes of circulation of goods, conversion, characterized by vertical movement (of the goods), and conveyance, characterized by circular movement, are the results of trade by barter. It is by barter that goods are given their economic and cultural values. Each level represents a level of imperfect competition in a barter economy which is characterized by an imperfect market.

Mary Douglas has described the methods of distribution among the Lele. (For the Lele descent system, see Chapter 6, Section II.) She has classified them into four categories: subsistence, prestation, barter and rights over persons. She feels that there is nothing mysterious about the existence of distinct economic categories, and that they are universal. Douglas's approach, although drawn from those of Dubois, Bascom and Bohannan, is less rigid. She bestows some dynamism upon the Lele economy. According to her the wealth of the Lele nation is distributed by the processes of reciprocity, barter, prestation and rights over women, but not all the goods are circulated. Recently she has introduced the idea of primitive rationing by coupon system.

An old Lele man has at least two wives, and probably more. These women are producers of children, some of whom will be future women, and food. Thus the old married Lele man controls women who are also the source of food production. Therefore he also wins the services of young men who work for him. They hoe his farm and help him to make raffia cloth. A young man needs a lot of raffia cloth to get a wife and to become a member of the various clubs. Sufficient raffia cloth can only be obtained through organized labour, which only old married men can organize effectively. Although the Lele old married men lack authority, they act as the bankers and entrepreneurs of their society. They regulate production and control the flow of wealth, that is, raffia cloth. The ability to have this stock of wealth and services under their control enhances their prestige. Lele young men are always on the move and old men are always competing for them. However, they have their preferences. They settle where they can easily get wives and raffia to pay debts, and there alone they give their services.

Putting the above situation in economic parlance, one might say that Lele women are like symbolic gold bullion, giving value to the raffia currency. Without them the raffia currency would be as valueless as our paper money would be without gold or credit backing. The desire to own women is thus the prime mover in the productive activities of the Lele economy.

Douglas holds that raffia cloth is not a medium of exchange because it does not help to pump the circulation of goods through the economy. But in fact the Lele youths require raffia for various purposes, and so they are willing to work, and because they work they increase production. They are not only given raffia as a reward, but they are fed and in some cases given a wife. So the young men exchange their services for various rewards, among which raffia cloth is at the top of the list. Douglas says that imported goods are bartered for raffia cloth. Iron bars and tools are imported from Njemba and Luba. All these goods are paid for with raffia cloth. Thus in fact raffia cloth pumps in goods and services into Lele society, and so it may be considered as a medium of exchange. Regarding raffia cloth as coupons seems to stress more on its restrictive value.

It is clear from the above description that the ability to mobilize and control the scarce resources of women and raffia gives prestige to the old men. When successful the production of food, raffia, and even females, is higher. Higher production means higher consumption and higher prestige. However, the departmentalization of Lele economy into categories blurs this process. Raffia is used for prestation, barter and acquiring rights over women. The tendency for goods of similar 'values' to circulate around one locus at different points of the distributive mechanism is simply a function of trade by barter, which always tends to create an imperfect market.

The work of Dubois, Bascom, Bohannan and Douglas is extremely illuminating, because it draws the attention to elements peculiar to all economic systems in which the concept of economic value is also based on prestige. They demonstrate the nature of the distribution of goods in a barter economy and the imperfect market competition that arises from such a method of distribution. However, although they show why people desire things, their division of economies into spheres obscures the dynamics of supply and demand which operate as one unit. Such abstractions blur the real situation by discarding many important facts about the economic activities of the peoples, which in fact they have themselves clearly set out in their ethnography.

There are recorded cases where subsistence goods once converted into prestige items are not readily convertible, and also where prestige items have a limited circulation. However this does not warrant the rigid classification of an economy into spheres of subsistence and prestige. Among the Trobrianders, for example, only one economic sphere exists. The Kula is not an economic activity as such, but a symbolic prestige 'gift-exchange' which operates within the framework of the Trobriand external politics and economy, and yet follows the principles of reciprocity built around the concept of partnership and mutual trust.

BIBLIOGRAPHY

SECTION I
Works consulted
BARTON, R. F. *Ifugao Law* (Berkeley: University of California Press, 1919)
—— *Ifugao Economics* (Berkeley: University of California Press, 1922)

BIEBUYEK, D. (ed.) *African Agrarian Systems* (London: Oxford University Press, 1960)

BIOBAKU, S. O. 'An Historical Sketch of the Egba Traditional Authorities', *Africa* (1952), 22, 1

BOHANNAN, P. *Tiv Farm and Settlement* (London: HMSO, 1955)

—— 'Tiv Political and Religious Ideas', *South-Western Journal of Anthropology* (1955), 11, 2

BRADBURY, R. E. and LLOYD, P. C. *The Benin Kingdom and the Edo-Speaking Peoples of South-West Nigeria*, Ethnographic Survey of Africa, West Africa, Part 13, 1957

BUSIA, K. A. *The Position of the Chief in the Modern Political System of Ashanti* (London: Oxford University Press, 1951)

FORDE, D. 'Land and Labour in a Cross River Village', *Yakö Studies* (London: Oxford University Press, 1964)

GLUCKMAN, M. 'Essays on Lozi Land and Royal Property', Rhodes-Livingstone Paper, no. 10 (1943)

MABOGUNJE, A. L. 'Some Comments on Land Tenure in Egba Division, Western Nigeria', *Africa* (July 1961), 31, 3

MAIR, L. P. 'Modern Developments in African Land Tenure', *Africa* (1948), 18, 3

MEEK, C. K. *Land Law and Custom in the Colonies* (London: Oxford University Press, 1946)

RATTRAY, R. S. *Ashanti* (Oxford: Clarendon Press, 1923)

—— *Ashanti Law and Constitution* (reprint of 1926) (Oxford: Clarendon Press, 1969)

SALMOND, J. W. *Jurisprudence* (London: Sweet & Maxwell 1966)

SECTION II

Works consulted

BUXTON, L. H. D. *Primitive Labour* (London: Methuen, 1924)

DURKHEIM, E. *The Division of Labour in Society*, translated by G. Simpson (New York: Free Press, 1947)

FORDE, D. *Habitat, Economy and Society* (London: Methuen, 1934)

HART, C. W. M. and PILLING, A. R. *The Tiwi of North Australia* (New York: Holt, 1960)

KABERRY, P. M. *Women of the Grassfields* (London: HMSO, 1952)

THURNWALD, R. C. *Economics in Primitive Communities* (London: Oxford University Press, 1966)

Suggestions for further reading

CHILVER, E. M. and KABERRY, P. M. *Traditional Bamenda* (Ministry of Primary Education and Social Welfare and West Cameroon Antiquities Commission, 1967), Vol. I

FIRTH, R. *Human Types* (2nd edn.) (London: Nelson, 1938)

—— *Primitive Polynesian Economy* (London: Routledge & Kegan Paul, 1939)

GOODALL, J. C. *Tiwi Wives* (Seattle: University of Washington Press, 1971)

SECTION III

Works consulted

BASCOM, W. 'Ponapean Prestige Economy', *South-Western Journal of Anthropology* (1948)

BOHANNAN, L. P. 'Some Principles of Exchange and Investment among the Tiv', *American Anthropologist* (1955), 57

DOUGLAS, M. *The Lele of the Kasai* (London: Oxford University Press, 1963)

—— 'Primitive Rationing: A Study in Controlled Exchange' in *Themes in Economic Anthropology* R. Firth (ed.) (London: Tavistock Publications, 1967)

DUBOIS, C. 'Wealth Concepts as an Integrative Factor of the Tolowa Tututni of California, North America', Essays in Anthropology Presented to A. L. Kroeber, 1936

VEBLEN, T. *The Theory of the Leisure Class* (London: Unwin, 1899)

Suggestions for further reading

BOHANNAN, P. and DALTON, G. (eds.) *Markets in Africa* (Evanston Ill.: Northwestern University Press, 1963)

POSPISIL, L. *Kapauku Papuan Economy* (New Haven: Yale University Press, 1963)

CHAPTER 18

Some Patterns of Distribution

I *The Principles of Gift-Exchange and Trade: the Trobriand Islanders*

The Kula district may be roughly described as all islands between the eastern coast of New Guinea and the Trobriand Islands on the north, studding the sea eastwards to between the islands of Missima and Laughlan in the Pacific. Some of these islands are of coral origin and others are volcanic. These differences in topography provide the inhabitants with suitable backgrounds for the development of the myths of the Kula.

The islands have an insular type of monsoon climate with the prevalent south-east wind blowing between April and October and the north-east wind blowing between November and March. These winds are important for the Kula expedition. A less dense monsoon type of vegetation dominates. Coconut trees, areca palm trees, fruit trees and timber-producing trees are common.

There are some degrees of specialization in arts and local industries in the islands. Trobriand Island is rich in agricultural products, quick-lime and basketry; Sinaketa and Vakuta in the red shell disc industry; Amphletts in pottery; Tube-Tube in canoes; Dobu in sorcery and agricultural products; Sanaroa in fishing and the spondylus shell; the Marshall Bennet Islands in greenstone, love magic and flying witchcraft; Kitava in yam and carving on black ebony; Misima in areca nut. All these islands, except Dobu, are culturally alike and the same language is spoken. The kinship systems are matrilineal and chieftainship has been developed to varying degrees. Only the Dobuans differ linguistically and have a different social organization and institutions.

Mauss maintains that the Trobrianders are typical examples of people to whom the exchange of goods is not a mechanical but a moral transaction bringing about and maintaining human and personal relationships between the individual and groups. To understand the full implications of Mauss's view it is necessary to examine the social organization of the Trobriands.

Trobriand Island is divided into seven territorially ill-defined districts which are distinct politically but not culturally. Each district acknowledges its own chief. The districts are made up of villages and the head chief lives in one important village. Other villages have head men or chiefs who in effect are subordinate to the head chief to whom tributes are paid in form of gifts. Other chiefs also receive gifts from their subjects. Each village specializes in one or two industries and this necessitates the exchange of goods between and within villages and districts.

The smallest unit of social organization is a man, his wife or wives, and children, that is, the family. Since the Trobrianders are matrilineal, the children are of the same clan as the mother. In matters of inheritance a man does as much as he can for the children considering his obligations to his sister's family. A man gives gifts to his wife and children but his matrilineal kinsmen may purchase from him during his lifetime, by instalments, the titles to garden plots and trees and the knowledge of magic which by rights ought to be inherited by his sister's children or mother's brother. The matrilineal kinsmen play prominent roles in ceremonies where all of them share in the responsibility of providing food. A man is also expected to fill his sister's husband's storehouse with yam annually, and to perform certain services; these are not reciprocated symmetrically by the in-law.

The four totemic clans, each having a series of linked totems with a bird as the principal one, cut right across these political and social divisions. The members of the four totemic clans are scattered over the whole tribe of Trobrianders and in each village members of all four clans are to be found. In every family there are at least two clans represented, since a husband must be in a different one from that of his wife and children. All the members of each clan express their solidarity during a mortuary rite. But the solidarity is better expressed between members of a sub-clan which is a local division of a clan; the members claim common descent from one ancestress and they each hold a specific rank. The highest sub-clan is that of Tabalu, to which the chief of Kiriwina belongs. The status of sub-clans determines the status of individuals in the society. The most influential chiefs come from the highest sub-clan.

According to Malinowski, chieftainship in the Trobriands is the combination of two institutions: that of headmanship and that of totemic clanship. The chief is a master of tribal ceremonies and the spokesman of the tribe within and without. Tributes and services are given to him by his villagers. If he is a high-ranking chief he receives tributes from low-ranking chiefs in other villages. His influence and power is maintained by marrying many wives, for all his wives' brothers are obliged to fill his store with yam annually. With all this accumulated wealth he is able to organize ceremonies, rituals and shows, give gifts and make payments.

The Kula communities form another group of social organization within which reciprocal gifts and obligations are practised. In the Trobriand Islands there are four of these groups that make the Kula expedition in a body, and they have the same limits within which they carry on their exchange of valuables.

The Trobrianders' movable wealth may be grouped as follows: land and sea products such as yam, toro, fish, shells; manufactured goods such as canoes, pottery; heirlooms such as shells and beads, ceremonial axes; magic arts; Kula valuables, that is the long necklaces, *Soulava*, and the shell armlets, *Mwali*. The Kula valuables are circulated with other valuable goods. The *Mwali* go with the circular boars' tusks and the *Soulava* go with red spondylus shell-belts and axe blades. To the natives the Kula valuables are more important than other goods.

Apart from the relationship ties which make giving and receiving obligatory, other factors encouraging the distribution of goods must be considered. The Trobriand Islanders (as well as others) have canoes fitted with outriggers for stability. The sails are made of pandanus mats. The wood for the canoes and the leaves for the mats are found locally. The labour for canoe construction is provided by communal labour organized by the chief. The specialist who builds the canoe is paid for his services. Thus the manufacturing of a canoe is made simple and the canoe solves the problem of transporting goods.

The north-east and south-east winds sail the canoe, and because these winds are regular, the hazards of sailing are reduced. The islands are near to one another so that a journey of one hundred miles with several halts can be made. Prominent landmarks act as a compass to the sailors. Confidence in sailing the sea with such a diminutive vessel is enhanced by the belief in magic which is employed in the building of canoes and during any voyage.

Another factor is linguistic. Two languages are popular: the Trobriand and Dobuan. The Trobriand language is spoken by all the inhabitants of the islands, save the Dobu, and almost every one living near to the Dobuans speaks Dobu. This has made communication between partners easy.

The last and most important factor in encouraging the distribution of goods is the Kula exchange. Kula is the exchange of the *Mwali* and *Soulava* valuables, but its operation has facilitated other trading business. The Kula concept encourages the ideal partnership between two unrelated persons, thus reducing hostility and fostering the confidence and security which are necessary for trade. The Kula expedition encourages production and distribution in economic terms, but the natives do not look at it from that angle.

The significance of Kula may be understood by describing it further. Kula is a form of intertribal exchange which is carried on by communities inhabiting a wide ring of islands. Along this route, articles of two kinds are constantly travelling in opposite directions. The *Soulava* move clockwise and the *Mwali* move anti-clockwise. In every island and in every village a limited number of men take part in the Kula. Each man receives periodically one or several shell armlets or necklaces which he then passes on to one of his partners, from whom he receives the opposite commodity in exchange. No man ever keeps any of the articles for any length of time in his possession. Each man has one partner or more (high-ranking chiefs may have many) with whom he does the Kula. The rule is: 'Once in the Kula, always in the Kula,' and it applies both to men and to the valuables. Kula is a prestige exchange. Ordinary trade is carried on side by side with the ritual exchange of shell armlets and necklaces. In one Kula expedition more than sixty canoes with a total crew of over 600 and about 650 valuables are involved. It is necessary to emphasize that the Kula is sociologically most important to the natives. However, economically, the quantity of other goods exchanged by gift and barter exceeds the Kula valuables in tonnage by over a hundred per cent. The Trobrianders and their neighbours look at the Kula in terms of prestige, and so it plays an important role in their society.

There is also an inland Kula which involves the exchange of valuables and ordinary goods within the inland communities. The overseas Kula is followed by the inland Kula, by which method the overseas goods are redistributed in the hinterland. Similarly, of course, the inland Kula precedes the overseas Kula so that a collection of valuables for the overseas voyage is got together. Not all villages practise Kula, but all villagers make voyages to other islands outside the Kula zone and carry on trade; the nature of the partnership is not known.

The various exchanges of goods among the Trobrianders may be symmetrical or asymmetrical. They fully know the distinction between gifts, customary payments, payments of services, exchange of material goods against privileges, titles, etc., ceremonial barter with deferred payment, gifts to be returned in economically equivalent form, and trade, which they call *Gimwali.*

A typical example of ceremonial barter with deferred payment may illustrate their idea of partnership. In the ceremony called *Wasi*, a village in which yam and taro are plentiful will bring a large quantity of these vegetables after the harvest to a fishing lagoon village. Each man puts his contribution before his partner's house and returns home. This is an invitation, which can never be rejected, to return the gift by its fixed equivalent in fish in the future.

From the foregoing one can deduce that the idea of wealth is tied up with the social organization which stresses relationships. It is through these lines of relationship that wealth flows, and where relationship by blood or marriage does not exist partnership is created. The principle of the distribution of movable wealth is based on relationships and partnerships. The family, the village, the clan, the chief provide the relationships. Partnership is created by initial gifts which once accepted seal a 'perpetual' contract. This contract is developed fully in the Kula. The concepts of relationship and partnership are crystallized in Trobriand's social organization in what Mauss calls the three obligations of giving, receiving and repaying. The Kula is a prestige-loaded type of gift-exchange based on the principles of reciprocity-giving, receiving and repaying, and it operates under certain economic conditions.

Each Kula voyage generates not only the production of capital goods such as canoes but also the distribution by barter of many tons of other goods. Thus prestige gift-exchange, which is not an economic activity but a symbolic one, is influenced by certain economic laws, and flourishes side by side with trade by barter, which is a pure economic activity.

II *General Conditions that have Favoured the Development of Trade: the Ijo of the Niger Delta of Nigeria*

The Niger Delta area is the coastal region of south-east Nigeria including the adjacent hinterland. It has heavy rainfall all the year round, and swamp and mangrove vegetation dominate the part nearest the sea. Northwards, there is equatorial forest; the land is firmer, and palm trees and hardwood comprise the principal vegetation. Because of the fan-like structure of the Delta and the coastal indentations, the area is connected with the hinterland by a network of water systems. Wherever the land on the coast was firm, towns sprang up, such as Forcadoes, Brass, Bonny and Duke. At first they were not thickly populated, but as time went on the towns became larger.

According to K. O. Dike, the history of the Delta may be broadly divided into three periods. The first period was between 1481 and 1640, when the city-states of Brass, Bonny, and several others, were founded by the Ijo and other migrants from the hinterland. Fishing and salt-making settlements sprang up. Recent work by E. J. Alagoa indicates that this first period might have happened centuries before.

The second period was 1640–1807. This was the period of the development of the slave trade, when the small coastal towns received a new influx of settlers from the hinterland. The Atlantic seaboard was transformed from a bleak, swampy zone into a frontier of trade and commerce.

The third period was 1807–85, the period of the palm-oil trade. The slave trade was abolished during this century, and thus the future of the coastal region was at stake. The Industrial Revolution, however, salvaged the situation by creating a new demand for palm-oil and cotton. The inhabitants of the coastal states became the middlemen. This period ended with the penetration of the English traders into the interior, which broke the long-established trade monopoly of the coastal states. The result was that the coastal states gradually dwindled in importance and population, until recently.

There have been two distinct types of trade in the Delta at all periods of its history: internal and external. The internal trade was purely localized. The Delta states exchanged with the hinterland people yam, palm produce and other articles of food, for salt and fish. Ecology and environment necessitated diversification of production which led to exchange. Local markets and comparative security and

12   *The Great Walls of Zimbabwe (Central Africa)*

peace were essential for such exchange or trade to flourish, and these were maintained by the chiefs and various organizations in the hinterland.

The most important and far-reaching trade, which may be considered to have altered the life, outlook and culture of the Delta peoples, was the external trade with Europe and America on the one hand, and with the Igbo of the hinterland on the other.

Some of the conditions which favoured the growth of this trade will be set out here. The discovery of America and the establishment of sugar-cane and tobacco plantations in the sixteenth and seventeenth centuries made European countries direct their attention to the usefulness of African labour. The Delta chiefs wanted arms to strengthen their position and also some of the European goods which they could use as status symbols. The hinterland was populous. The situation was ripe for trade if only the Europeans would make a move, and this they did.

By the time of the abolition of slavery, the Industrial Revolution was already in full swing. The Liverpool and Manchester industries wanted markets from which to buy raw materials such as palm-oil and cotton as well as places to sell the manufactured goods. The hinterland of the Delta satisfied all the conditions required, so in the early days the old trade partnerships continued with only a change in commodities.

Even though markets were established, trade could not grow without a minimum of peace and security. The city states of the Delta did all they could to create a congenial atmosphere for trade. These states were either monarchical or republican in form, and most of them had a house system. Each head of the house tried to coordinate the activities of the individual members, and so with the aid of centralized organization (where it existed) comparative peace was achieved. In some towns like Calabar associations were formed, the members of which were the chief traders of the town. They combined to deal with any trade infringement or any conduct likely to jeopardize the peace of the town.

In the hinterland two types of trading organization operated. The first centred upon the Aro. Their influence was based on the Aro Chukwu Oracle which was feared in some parts of Igbo land. The Aro opened up trading stations and settlements at strategic points, and soon controlled most of the hinterland slave trade. Many other oracles existed, but they merely supplemented the work of the Aro Oracle.

The Nri also helped to maintain peace in the interior, for the religious and political sway of the Nri was universally accepted by most of the Igbo peoples. Nri itinerant priests and political diplomats ministered to the people's religious and political needs, and above all helped to negotiate covenants which played the part of treaties among hostile states and communities.

On the British side peace was achieved by the combination of the masters of the super-cargoes in dealing with offenders. The British had invested huge amounts of capital, and for the sake of their profits they valued the existence of peace more perhaps than the Africans. After the abolition of the slave trade the British government posted warships in the coastal waters. The super-cargoes were always influencing the Navy to use force in places that challenged British authority. A court of equity was established through which both African and European traders could settle their disputes. With the growth of trade consuls were appointed. Some of them cajoled the chiefs to sign treaties in which they signed off their rights and sovereignty, and gradually 'peace-keeping' on the coast became a function of the British government.

The ease of transportation and communication also encouraged trade. The creeks afforded waterways into the interior and there were fairly good harbours at Calabar and Brass. Also it was the age of steam-boats; for by 1852, through the undaunted efforts of Laird, steam-mail services had started to run regularly between Europe and the West Coast.

Every commercial concern needs personnel and entrepreneurs. On the African side were chiefs like Jaja, Pepple and several others; on the English side were men such as Beecroft, Laird and Goldie. It was not surprising then that by 1850 the Delta trade was worth £1 million.

The last, but not least, encouraging factor was the development of a new monetary system. In the interior the system was purely barter, although cowrie shells and manillas were used (40 cowries = 1 string = $\frac{1}{4}$d). However cowries and manillas were too cumbersome to be used except domestically. One currency which gained wide circulation in the dealings between Africans and Europeans was the Spanish one of doubloons and dollars (1 doubloon = £3·20; 1 dollar = 20p). A credit system called 'trust' was also used. Goods were entrusted to the Delta middlemen by the British merchants for a year or so. African recipients were required to trade them for interior produce and pay back their European partners the equivalent in oil, ivory and timber. This shows what a high degree of confidence existed. The Delta community also had its methods for fixing prices on barter goods. The standard medium of exchange was a bar, worth about 25p. Every manufactured article was valued at so many bars. The bar was not a circulating currency but merely an accepted standard for valuing trade goods.

A word might be said about British government policy after the slave trade had been abolished. The British wanted to stop the slave trade, but they did not want to acquire the responsibility of governing the people, so between 1807 and 1860 the British policy was one of non-intervention in the politics of the Delta as long as they did not hamper trade. But after 1860, for various reasons, British government policy changed, and with it an inward thrust was made into the hinterland. The coastal middlemen resented this and conflicts resulted. Finally, the hinterland was gained, but this was a stab to the backbone of the Delta states, and they rapidly dilapidated.

The negative side of this story is gloomy. Even though trade flourished, there were many difficulties. On the European side, the coastal area was infested with malaria-carrying mosquitoes. This impeded the rapid expansion of trade. However, the use of quinine began to place malaria under control. The opposition of the Delta people, the political unrest in the city-states and the breakneck competition among the white traders were some of the obstacles that were surmounted during the development of trade in this area.

For the development of trade, there should be demand and supply for certain goods, entrepreneurs ready to take risks, means of communication, and minimum peace, trust and confidence under which trade can flourish. All these conditions were present in the Niger Delta.

III *The Control of Economic Resources in Relation to the Elaboration of State Institutions: Perak and Selangor, Malaya*

ECOLOGY, POPULATION, COMMUNICATION, RESOURCES

The main geographical feature of north and central Malay is a series of ranges of hills which run north-north-east to south-south-west across the Peninsula. The Malay states used to be centred on river valleys. The western states of Perak and Selangor lay between the central ranges and the west coast.

This area has a rainfall of 75–125 inches every year without any dry season. It is well supplied with rivers which afforded good means of communication and transportation in an area thickly covered with tropical rain forests which are impassable unless a path is laboriously hacked through it.

Agriculture and mining were the chief occupations in 1870. There was fertile alluvial soil in the river basins and valleys, which became centres of settlement. Alluvial deposits of tin ore were also found in gravels and sands in the river valleys.

The population in 1891, quoting Gullick, who studied them, was as follows:

State	Malays	Others	Total	Area (sq. miles)
Perak	106 393	107 861	214 254	7980
Selangor	26 578	55 014	81 592	3166

The population density was about ten persons per square mile. The non-Malayans were predominantly Chinese immigrants who had come to work in the mines.

POLITICAL ORGANIZATION AND STATE INSTITUTIONS

The political organization of these states may be considered under three divisions: the village, the district, the state. The Sultan, who was the head of the state, was the source of political authority, for the district chiefs derived their authority from him. The village heads derived their authority from the district heads. The Sultan had no power to control the chiefs, but the chiefs had power to control the village heads. In practice the Sultan had only the power to control the chiefs in his own district, and he had no power whatsoever to control the chiefs in other districts which were part of his state.

The authority of the Sultan was based on the concept of kingship and royal descent; his lack of political power lay in the economic domain. The authority of the district head was derived from the concept of the sultanate, but his political power was derived from his control of economic resources. The head man was an appointee of the district head and might be considered to be an economic and political agent. (For more details, see Chapter 12, Section III.)

THE ECONOMY

The smallest economic unit was a simple family of a man, his wife and children, living in a house in one of the clusters of houses forming a village. A small village might have up to five houses while a big one might have up to one hundred. Each village, small or big, had a head man, a mosque and a market place. A village might often contain the residence of a chief whose district included a number of other villages and hamlets with a total population of about a thousand people.

The village was usually on a river bank, which was the highway, the source of water supply, the bath and the drain. The size would be limited by the availability of suitable land for rice cultivation. Dry rice was grown on hillsides while wet rice, which was the staple food crop, was grown on level and well-watered land. Land was plentiful and free for the taking but the Malays congregated in villages instead of living in scattered settlements. This was because cooperative work such as the construction of ditches and banks, defensive earthworks, as well as administrative convenience, forced them to live compactly.

Land use was influenced by political factors. Flight was a recognized response to hostile invasion or undue oppression. The period round about 1870 was one of civil wars due to rivalry between chiefs and *Rajas*. When political pressure was intolerable a villager could pack off to another village or district where he would be welcomed. If it was possible to change residence with such ease, it obviously did not pay to invest personal labour in land. It was therefore done communally and to meet immediate necessities.

Apart from rice, other crops were coffee, tobacco, sago, banana and maize. Tree crops were grown on a small scale: sugar palm, areca, betel, coconut, durian, etc. Having a good surplus attracted the attention of the chief or *Raja* of the district, who confiscated it.

Mining came next in importance. This was done by Chinese, who not only had some technical and mechanical skill, but were less involved in the politics of Malaya.

Examples of other occupations were blacksmithing and carving. A few successful full-time craftsmen were in the retinue of the Sultan and great chiefs who could afford to provide steady employment for them.

Labour supply in Malaya could be classified as follows. There was free labour whereby an individual offered his labour freely when performing a kinship obligation. Communal labour was when people of a village congregated together for communal work. Forced labour was forcing people into the service of the Sultan or chief of any notable. There was also a debt-bondage, in which a person gave his services because he could not pay a loan at a given time; he could redeem himself at a future date when he had the means to do so. Lastly came slavery, by which the person lost his or her personal rights and freedom and was regarded as his or her master's property.

SYSTEMS OF PRODUCTION
AND DISTRIBUTION AND STATE INSTITUTIONS

The first type of productive unit was that of the individual family. The productive power of the family depended on several factors. An individual family, except one from the ruling class, never seemed to take the initiative to increase production. A commoner family could have all its surpluses confiscated by the district chief or *Raja*. Therefore, any little surplus was either consumed or sold to the Chinese mining communities living near by. The money realized from surpluses sold in the local market was used not only for future eventualities but also for paying taxes which were collected by the head man for the chief or the Sultan.

There was also communal production. The head man called the villagers together to build ditches, stockades, etc. These were basically improvements to the land to increase yield and improve security. By the system of forced labour, villagers could be made to build defensive stockades and work in the fields for the *Raja* or the Sultan. This type of production served a twofold function. The *Raja* owned everything produced, and this sort of production was geared to strengthening the security of the district which was always being threatened by other, similar, districts. The aim of this sort of production, therefore, was the maintenance of the *Raja* and the sustenance of the state's security. A part of the proceeds which resulted from state production was distributed among the villagers since they were usually fed and cared for by the lord who engaged them.

The chiefs relied more heavily on the tin mines. They invested whatever capital they obtained from European and Chinese financiers and expected the largest and most rapid returns. The financiers were usually reluctant to supply food and stores on credit direct to the Chinese head man of a small mining community for fear of default or cheating, or still more, robbery by the local Malay chief. They therefore preferred to go into partnership with the chiefs so that they would have an interest in supervising the mines and ensuring their success. They supplied the miners' requirements to the chiefs who passed them on to the miners.

Chiefs also provided the capital with which a village head man financed new settlements. By opening new settlements chiefs could attract more followers with which to boost their prestige and military strength.

In this system of production and distribution the chiefs were the focal points, and this was also evident in trading activities. Three types of trade could be distinguished. Local trade consisted of the buying and selling in each village. Every village had a market where goods were sold. Internal trade was that between districts and villages. Goods moving from one district to another were taxed at a 10 per cent *ad valorem* rate paid in kind as they passed the chief's riverside stockade.

The mining community paid royalties on the tin mined to the landowner, who also collected export duty on the tin exported, as well as import and excise duties on spirits, gambling booths, etc. This last category might be called the external trade.

The chiefs formed the basis of the economic system in all the areas of production, consumption and distribution.

THE ECONOMIC ASPECTS OF POLITICAL LEADERSHIP

Political power in the Malay states rested on the control of manpower. In order to attain and hold power a chief had to have a sufficient following of armed men. He therefore had to command the means to support a sufficient following. Revenues for this could be obtained from taxing a rich and populous district. So a chief always aimed at promoting the develoment of his district, maintaining justice and peace, and increasing its productive population so as to maximize the surplus which could be diverted into his own hands for use as the instrument of power.

If he failed to make his district prosperous he risked being ousted by an outside rival, since he lacked the means to support an adequate force with which to keep his military position. Alternatively the chieftainship might be lost to his lineage at his death and given to someone who would be able to use the opportunity.

The power of a chief was economic. The inability of the Sultan to obtain more than a small proportion of the total revenues of the state was the main cause of the dispersal of power from the central government of the state to the districts. Communication was difficult save by rivers, and the district heads built stockaded 'palaces' for themselves from which they could resist the Sultan. The Sultan's district was not prosperous enough to provide men and capital to deal with these distant chiefs.

Wealth denoted status. The chiefs and the Sultan had to maintain large followings of both men and women. To command those services they had to be able to feed those who render them. There was a constant inflow of goods and money to the chief in the exercise of the political function of taxation and an outflow of services essential to the maintenance of political power. A chief had to distribute the wealth which came into his hands by sharing his income with his followers; any surplus was laid out in loans to bind him yet more debt-bondsmen. Therefore even if a chief was relatively wealthy he had little surplus income in 'liquid' form available for other purposes. It seems that the few chiefs who were exceptionally successful were those who held part of their wealth in 'liquid assets'. This did not mean that other chiefs were poor, for they had minor sources of income. Besides their tax revenues, they had the profits of trading and tin-mining. The food which was consumed by their households was produced by the agricultural workers among their debt-bondsmen. But their situation was bad, and that of a Sultan even worse, because they were both expected to keep open house for the poor and the needy.

To sum up, the economic activity of Malay chiefs showed how power tended to absorb into itself the control of all spheres from which a rival power might grow. Chiefs controlled and directed the economy of their districts because they needed the surplus to sustain themselves and the armed following which was the basis of their power. Wealth was a means to achieve an end, which was political rather than economic. To do this all state institutions were orientated politically, so that it was very difficult to separate politics from economic pursuits. Thus the Sultan, the chiefs and head men were all political and economic agents. They controlled, at different levels, the economic resources directed towards the manipulation of political power and authority and the elaboration of state institutions in Malaya.

BIBLIOGRAPHY

SECTION I
Works consulted
MALINOWSKI, B. *Argonauts of the Western Pacific* (London: Routledge, 1922)
MAUSS, M. *The Gift*, translated by I. Cunnison (London: Cohen & West, 1953)
POWELL, H. A. 'Competitive Leadership in Trobriand Political Organisation', *J.R.A.I.* (1960), 90
UBEROI, J. P. S. *Politics of the Kula Ring* (Manchester: Manchester University Press, 1962)

Suggestions for further reading
BARTH, F. *Political Leadership among Swat Pathans* (London: Athlone Press, 1959)
BOHANNAN, P. and DALTON, G. (eds.) *Markets in Africa* (Evanston, Ill.: Northwestern University Press, 1962)
SAHLIN, M. D. 'On the Sociology of Primitive Exchange', in *The Relevance of Models for Social Anthropology*, ASA Monographs, 1 (1965)

SECTION II
Works consulted
ALAGOA, E. J. 'The Development of Institutions in the States of the Eastern Niger Delta', *Journal of African History* (1970), 11, 3
DIKE, K. O. *Trade and Politics in the Niger Delta* (London: Oxford University Press, 1956)
FORDE, D. and SCOTT, R. *The Native Economics of Nigeria* (London: Faber, 1946)
JONES, G. I. *The Trading States of the Oil Rivers, a Study of Political Development in Eastern Nigeria* (London: Oxford University Press, 1963)
ONWUEJEOGWU, M. A. 'The Political Organization of Nri, South-Eastern Nigeria', M.Phil thesis (London University, 1974)

Suggestions for further reading
BOHANNAN, P. and DALTON, G. (eds.) *Markets in Africa* (Evanston, Ill.: Northwestern University Press, 1962)
HORTON, R. 'From Fishing Village to City-state: a Social History of New Calabar', in *Man in Africa*, M. Douglas and P. M. Kaberry (eds.) (London: Tavistock Publications, 1969)
POLANYI, K., ARENSBERG, H. W. and PEARSON, H. W. (eds.) *Trade and Market in the Early Empires* (New York: Free Press, 1957)

SECTION III
Work consulted
GULLICK, J. M. *The Indigenous Political Systems of Western Malaya* (London: Athlone Press, 1958)

Suggestions for further reading
BALANDIER, G. *Political Anthropology*, translated by A. M. Sheridan Smith (London: Allen Lane, 1970)
FORDE, D. and KABERRY, P. M. *West African Kingdoms in the Nineteenth Century* (London: Oxford University Press, 1967)
SMITH, M. G. 'Political Organization', *International Encyclopedia of Social Science* (1968), 1, 12, pp. 193–201

Part Five

RELIGION, COSMOLOGY & ETHICS

CHAPTER 19

Men and Their Gods

I An Introduction: the Origin and Character of Religious and Scientific Systems of Thought

Some of the thoughts about the effect of religion on scientific and technological development in Africa are to be re-examined. It has been argued that Africans rely more on magic than on science, that science and magic are confused as identical and that the African physicist who believes in supernatural transmutation can make no headway in physical sciences. Two questions arise: to what extent are Africans more ritualistic than scientific? Is the ritual mode of thinking identical to the scientific and technological mode of thinking, and does one impede the development of the other?

I shall show that in the development of *Homo sapiens sapiens* technological thought probably manifested itself before ritual; that both develop along identical lines, each explaining the cosmos at different levels. In Africa technological development was inhibited in the past, as it is at present, by factors other than religious or magical beliefs.

There is probably archaeological evidence to support the view that technological thought may have emerged before ritual thought. Tool-making involves the ability to think conceptually with the attainment of a certain skeletal morphology which enhances bipedalism, and the ability to use the hands and fingers for gripping and picking.

Chimpanzees in captivity have been reported to have 'made' very simple tools; this is not a surprise, because apes have some powers of conceptualizing, limited to their circumstances. Also their feet and hands have the rudimentary qualities which make bipedalism and finger-gripping possible.

The earliest tools are associated with Australopithecines, one of the two genera into which hominids have been divided. These man-apes lived during the Lower Pleistocene period between half a million and a million years ago, in South Africa. *Australopithecus africanus*, as these ancestors of man are named, made use of selected animal bones for tools or weapons. But convincing evidence of the earliest making and using of tools comes from the chopper industry of Bed 1 at Olduvai in East Africa (Lower Pleistocene). This industry is associated with a man-ape creature named *Homo habilis* who had not only a larger brain than the Australopithecine but also had hands and fingers capable of being used to make tools.

Then came *Homo erectus*. He and his fellows inhabited parts of Africa, Java and Western Europe during the Middle Pleistocene period between 500 000 BC and 200 000 BC. They had better brains, better feet and better hands and fingers. The hand-axes they made and used were found in Morocco and Tanzania in Africa, Abbeville and St Acheul in France. They were indeed better stone technologists than the Australopithecines.

By the Upper Pleistocene period, between about 200 000 BC and 75 000 BC the creature called *Homo sapiens* had emerged on the southern and eastern shores of the Mediterranean, North and East Africa, Levant, Iraq, Iran, Western Asia and

Western Europe. These ancestors of men were associated with elaborate flake industries. They were more refined stone technologists than *Homo eructus.*

Men of a modern type may have emerged from the *sapiens* stock. These are named *Homo sapiens sapiens* and they appeared in the context of the Advanced Upper Pleistocene period about 40 000 years ago. They made composite and specialized tools: blades, burins and bone needles.

This was the period when man probably first manifested his ability for ritual thought. It is in the Upper Palaeolithic cultures of Europe, especially in France where the early sites were found and the cultures named after them – Perigordian, Aurignacian, Solutrean, Magdalenian – that the arts of carving, engraving and painting are known to have developed.

My argument is that technological thought is probably a more 'primitive' form in terms of the development of human thought. *Homo* learnt how to fashion stones and woods into crude tools in order to survive. Having achieved this, he gradually evolved into *homo sapiens* by developing his powers of abstract thought. Thus the tempo of technical and social evolution was accelerated.

Since then, thousands of years ago, it seems that *Homo sapiens sapiens* has not basically changed his mode of abstract thought. But he has made gigantic advances in technology or concrete thought. It might be helpful here to examine the thought behind religious systems and compare it with the thought behind scientific and technological systems.

European Roman Catholic Christians believe that the Blessed Virgin Mary was conceived by the power of the Holy Ghost, who is symbolized as a dove, and that Mary delivered a son named Jesus without sexual knowledge. Jesus is the son of God. (Catholics are aware of the natural process that leads to conception.) The thinking process involved, showing a leap of thought which is not to be proved but to be believed, is as follows.

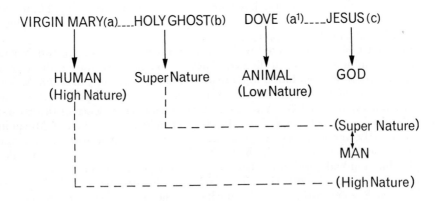

Man in the animal kingdom is considered to be higher than other animals, so man is 'high nature' and other animals are 'low nature'. Anything beyond natural existence is referred to as 'super nature'. The above model may be represented as a 'logical' formula:

a   represents 'high nature' (Virgin Mary).
b   represents 'super nature' (Holy Ghost).
a'   represents 'low nature' (dove).
c   represents combined 'super nature' and 'high nature' (Christ).

Below,

    +   means: combine mystically.
    →   means: transform mystically.
    $a + b(a') \rightarrow c$ ----- (1)
    But c is $a + b$
    ∴ $a + b(a') = a + b$

This cannot be tested. If one does not believe this, one has no faith. If a Roman Catholic opposes this belief, the Church condemns the person. The explanation is that when 'high nature' is combined mystically with 'super nature' in the form of 'low nature', it is transformed mystically into 'super nature' and 'high nature'.

The Murngins (Australian aborigines) believe that the wife conceives when the husband dreams of a fish, from the totem well, entering the wife's womb. The child belongs to a totem group when he is born and goes back to the totem when he dies. (The Murngins are aware of the natural process that leads to conception.) The thinking process involved, showing a leap of thought which is not to be proved but to be believed, is as follows.

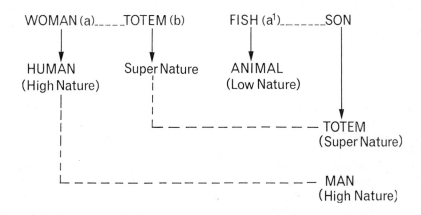

This may be represented as a 'logical' formula:

    $a + b(a') \rightarrow c$ ------ (1)
    But c is $a + b$
    ∴ $a + b(a') = a + b$

This is to be believed and not to be tested.
    The explanation of the formula is that when 'high nature' combines mystically with 'super nature' in the form of 'low nature', it is transformed mystically into 'super nature' and 'high nature'.

The structural similarity in the 'logic' of European theology and the Australian aborigines is thus basically the same. Both are either 'logical' in the ritual sense or 'illogical' in the ordinary sense. One thing common to both is the rapid leap of thought which psychologically prohibits the testing of the conclusion. The psychological prohibition is also reinforced by the social sanctions imposed by the ritual community, which believes in the conclusion, on those who question or challenge the conclusion. Those who challenge are branded heretics and ostracized. Scientific and technological propositions, formulae and conclusions, however, are subjected to empirical observations. Every step is queried and tested until a valid conclusion, which can be verified by another person, is reached.

Scientific and technological thought involves transforming 'supernatural forms' or 'abstract natural forms', symbols or formulae like H_2O, or engineering drawings, into 'concrete cultural forms', like water or engineering structures. Ritual thought involves transforming 'supernatural forms' or 'abstract natural forms', symbols or formulae, into other 'abstract forms' which cannot be verified empirically.

The two systems of thought – the religious, and the scientific and technological – are attempting to explain cosmic relationships at different levels. Both have common data based on abstract symbols, but they diverge in the way these symbols are transformed. What separates religion from science and technology is the difference in the symbolic transformation. Hence, African physicists, like the European ones, can operate both systems without much confusion.

The main factors that have impeded scientific and technological development in Africa may not be religious, but partly environmental and partly historical.

Homo sapiens sapiens who lived around the shores of the Mediterranean experienced ideal conditions for technological and scientific development, which once started, grew and expanded northwards. Its southward movement was impeded by the natural barriers of sea and mountains. Black Africa was thus shut off from the main centre of the early development of technological and scientific thought. Although black Africa, of course, developed her own distinctive technology and science, the development was hampered by the absence of written records which are essential for their transmission, in order to transform abstract forms into concrete forms. On the other hand religious thought can be developed and transmitted in a non-literate situation because the process involves the transformation of abstract forms into more abstract forms that need not be verified.

The science and technology which were developed in Africa south of the Sahara, a few examples of which are seen in the Igbo-Ukwu, Benin and Ife bronze objects, as well as the Zimbabwe objects, were lost to future generations partly because the processes were not recorded and partly because there was no further cultural impetus.

The arrival of Europeans with a higher technology in Black Africa tolled the knell not only of the final downfall of African technology as so far developed, but also threatened her religious systems. The slave trade, imperialism, colonization, apartheid and racial discrimination are the instruments used to degrade past African achievements.

Now that a large part of Africa has been decolonized, she has the opportunity, though inhibited by many socio-psychological factors, to progress in all fields of human endeavour. The rate at which Africa grows depends on her ability to acquire technological knowledge with regard to the making of modern machine tools which are the basis of industrialization.

The African challenge, today, is similar to that faced by Japan, China, or Russia at the beginning of this century. Only Africa can help herself. The raw materials are all there, and Africa has to search for her models in her own way.

At present, emphasis should be on technological and scientific thought but efforts should be made to keep the ritual processes alive because they are rich reservoirs from which other processes of thinking such as philosophy, ethics and even science are fed. The foundations of African science, art, technology, music, architecture, drama, poetry, etc., are in her cosmology, religions and ethics.

It is incorrect to argue that black Africa cannot be scientific until she sheds her religions and magical processes of thought or that these are responsible for her lack of development in science and technology.

II *The Relation Between Religion, Magic and the Moral Community*

Sociologists and anthropologists have adopted three main views concerning religion.

1. Religion is different from magic (Durkheim).
2. Religion is a continuum between manipulation and communion (Nadel and Horton).
3. Religion and magic are one, and indistinguishable in so far as every religious rite has some elements of magic in it.

Durkheim holds that in every society a twofold division of the world exists: the profane and the sacred. He defines religion as beliefs and practices related to the sacred which unite into one single moral community, called a church, all those who adhere to them.

Magic, he says, belongs to the profane and has no moral community. Although magic has its myths, dogmas, beliefs and rites like religion, they are all more elementary, because when magic seeks technical and utilitarian ends it does not waste time in pure speculation. In short, magic is practical and aims at 'compulsion' instead of 'supplication'.

Since religion refers to the sacred, Durkheim considers that society is sacred, symbolized in the notion of God. Thus society worships itself and religion, therefore, symbolizes the expression of the solidarity of the society.

Anthropologists have criticized Durkheim, on the grounds that the sacred and profane are not universal concepts, and that some religions are only magical in form. Religion, too, does not always bind a group of people, it may even be the cause of disintegration, as in the past in Europe and in modern African communities. Furthermore, magic does have a community. Let us examine some aspects of Judaism, Christianity and other religions with regard to the relationships between religion and magic.

When Moses was leading the Israelites from Egypt into the 'promised land' he performed several magical acts in the desert. On one occasion he struck a rock with a rod and water began to flow out of it, and in this way he supplied water to his people. This act was performed as part of the religious beliefs of the Israelites. Moses was a part of the community and the Israelites looked on him as the leader and an intermediary between them and God.

The Christian churches believe that by pouring water on the forehead of an initiate, a child (or adult), and by repeating certain formulae, original sin is cleansed from his soul. This ritual act is called baptism. In structure and function it is a magical rite incorporated into Christian belief. In fact it is the first initiation ceremony into Christian religion.

The Muslim religion has its own magical rites. Hausa Muslims believe that the power of vanishing can be acquired by wearing a specially prepared talisman of a verse of the Koran written on a special paper by a Mallam. The talisman urges certain spirits to give the wearer the power of invisibility.

Lloyd Warner in his book *A Black Civilization* shows how the Murngin belief in black magic is institutionalized. When a person is believed to have had his 'soul stolen' by a black magician, a state of affairs which is usually predicted by a white magician, the community does two things while the person is still sick. They first withdraw from the person and declare him socially dead, so that the sick person finds it difficult to readjust. This act involves a high degree of suggestibility. The withdrawal of the community is a signal to the sick person that he should 'dance' his totem dance and get ready to die.

The community after a while returns to him, this time to mourn him. They dance round him singing the Murngin mourning song, which is believed to usher the sick man into the land of the dead and back to his totem well. Warner holds, and he is correct, that the magicians are the leaders who crystallize this group attitude. They organize social opinion and attitudes through their rituals as effectively as a Murngin ceremonial leader does through the sacred totemic ritual. Both the magician and the totem leader depend upon the group's participation to make their power effective. It is therefore a group situation, not an individual one, that is operative in both circumstances. It is the power of the 'church' or community which binds together the whole group directed by a ceremonial or totem leader in his ceremonies. So also it is the power of the church, the clan group, which destroys a man under the leadership of its magicians.

From the above examples it is clear that even though religion and magic may be operatively distinct in a given situation, they usually belong to the same moral community. Every religious system has some elements of magic; in some cases the elements remain apart, one system working within the other. Examples have been cited from Christian and Muslim religions as well as from the Australian Murngin. It is puzzling that Durkheim (and his disciples), who refer to the Christian religion and who are also familiar with the Muslim religion, do not see that these religions have some elements of magic in them too. The Catholic doctrines of transubstantiation, miracles, baptism, for example, are magical to a great extent.

It was not till 1937 that anthropologists realized that magic and religion belong to the same system and are interdependent. The priest and the magician may be one and the same person or different persons operating within the same community. Some religions are predominantly magical; this has persuaded some anthropologists to consider magic as an instrument of religion. However, the indisputable fact is that magic and religion have a moral community. Religion does differ from magic in one important area, which is how a desired goal is achieved. Magic operates like a switchboard system, so to speak; once the proper rites, spells and ceremonies have been performed correctly, the desired effect is automatic. In religion, on the other hand, supplication and resignation, or reference to a higher being or beings, are necessary.

The extent of the moral community of magic and religion differs greatly amongst societies. Among the Murngin the two communities overlap, while among the Hausa Muslims the religious community is greater than the community practising Muslim magical rites. The same is probably true of the Christian religion.

III *How Religion Reflects
the Preoccupation of a People's Culture; and how it is Related
to the Moral Code: the Murngin of North-West Australia*

South of the Arafura Sea is Arnhem Land in the north-west of Australia. In the northern and eastern parts of this area live some people whom Lloyd Warner calls the Murngin. They use wooden and polished stone implements. They practise no cultivation; men are chiefly hunters while women are food gatherers.

The climate of this area is tropical monsoon with strong north-west winds which bring heavy rains between November and March, and south-east winds which are associated with a dry period between April and October. During the rainy season the country is flooded; communication becomes difficult and food becomes scarce. However in the dry season the water recedes to the water holes and ponds, food is abundant and social life attains its greatest heights.

The Murngin have patrilineal clans, moieties, phratries, tribes, hordes, age-grades and a sub-section system. The clan is the most effective group. It is exogamous and patrilineal, averaging 40–50 individuals who own a common territory of about 360 square miles. This group possesses one or more totemic water holes, formed by a creator totem, in which the whole of the clan life is focused. All members of the clan believe that they are derived from these water holes, and that they will go back to them at death. In the water holes the totemic spirits live with the mythological ancestors, the souls of the dead and the unborn children.

All Murngin clans, which include living beings and non-living things, are divided into two moieties named by the mythical ancestor as *Yiritja* and *Dua*. The moiety division is fundamental, because thus the mother's people are divided from the father's. Within the moiety the incest rule and exogamy are very rigidly upheld. Their myths repeat over and over again the evils of incest within the clan and within the moiety. Moieties are divided into eight sub-sections. According to these sub-sections A1 and A2 can marry from either B1 or B2; their children will belong to C1 and C2 respectively, that is their respective matriclans (fig. 6). There is much antagonism between the two sub-sections competing for wives in the other sub-sections.

The sub-section system is interwoven with a classificatory kinship system based on five generations including both maternal and paternal lineal and collateral relatives, to produce a complicated kinship pattern.

Groups of a clan within the moiety form loose groups called phratries. The feeling of belonging to a phratry is based on a mythological idea of a common association with a common creator totem and an alleged similarity of language. The phratry organization is very weak and may represent a feeble attempt to create new and larger groups than the clan in order to control intra-moiety interactions.

Murngin religious concepts and philosophy are based on two myths: the *Wawilak* and the *Djunkgoa*. Each has its sets of rituals. The *Wawilak* myth has four important rituals, dramatizing by the use of songs and symbols the incidents of the myth.

The relationship between the rituals and myth can be illustrated as follows. The four rituals, named 'A', 'B', 'C', 'D' here for simplicity, are used during specific periods. The A ritual is used during circumcision and the initiation of male children of the clan into the first age-grade. The B ritual is for the purification of the clan as well as initiation into the senior age-grade. The C ritual is for the promotion of

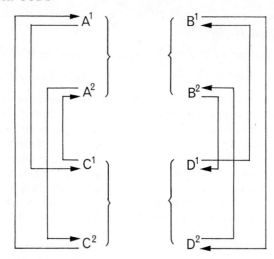

FIGURE 6   *Schematic arrangement of a Murngin moiety*

the lower age-grade into the senior age-grade, and the D ritual is used for emergency circumcision to stop boys growing too big for the next circumcision.

The *Wawilak* myth tells how, before the time of present-day man, two *Wawilak* sisters and their children marched out of the southern inland area after committing clan incest, and came to the Liaalaomir totemic hole. Here the elder sister profaned the pool of the divine Python because her menstrual blood fell accidentally into the water hole. The Python was angry, the food they gathered started to run away, and a great flood threatened. The two sisters tried to stop these calamities by singing the A, B, C and D rituals, but failed. Before they could circumcise their children, the divine Python swallowed them. After a while they were vomited out and finally swallowed up again. The flood abated when the Python went back into its hole. The spirit of the women appeared to *Wongar* men in a dream and taught them the secrets of the rituals. The Murngin dance these things now, because their Wongar ancestors learnt them from the two Wawilak sisters.

The *Djunkgoa* myth is concerned with the relationship of man to his totems, and the rituals are performed before the totem wells with the totemic symbols. In this myth two sisters came into Murngin country on a raft from the south and then started walking with two yam sticks. On their way they divided the countries, clans and animals into two groups and made the totem wells with their yam sticks. The younger sister was incestuously raped by an ancestor man in her own moiety. Their ritual power was lost when the men stole away their totems, and so they became ordinary women.

The following points from the myths should be emphasized.

1. The origin of the totem.
2. The two sisters: the first set came from the southern inland area, and the second set from the south, by sea.
3. The committing of incest: in the first myth, clan incest; in the second, moiety incest.
4. The consequences of the profane acts whereby the women lost their ritual powers.

5. The anger of the divine Python was followed by scarcity of food and disharmony in nature.
6. The fate of the uncircumcised children.
7. The dream of the *Wongar* men.
8. The origin and usefulness of the yam stick, one of the most valuable of tools.

The above points clarify the ritual and social significance of the life cycles of Murngin men and women. A Murngin baby comes from the totem well through a religious experience of the father. The father dreams of a fish entering the wife's womb, and then he knows that his wife has conceived. She cannot dream because women have lost their ritual powers, and all ritual information comes from dreams. The Murngin do in fact know about conception, but the mystical processes are paramount, because through them society can impose sanctions at the social level. The man's status is raised by the birth of a child, so that he is permitted to eat certain foods which were formerly taboo to him, and he can now be initiated into the senior age-grade where he may be allowed to see the higher totems of the clan.

At seven a boy is removed from the general camp to the men's camp. He is circumcised with other boys of his own clan, using the A ritual. He enters for the first time the sacred realm which is forever barred from his sisters. At the initiation he is shown the low totems and educated in Murngin norms. He is told by the ritual leader that incest and adultery result in childlessness; that quarrelling or fighting during rituals and ceremonies results in illness; and that revealing the totem's secrets to outsiders means death.

The male remains in the men's camp until he is ready to marry. After marriage he moves to the general camp and until the birth of his first child he abstains from certain foods. The birth of the child strengthens his ties with his relatives. He may now partake of the C ritual, during which more mysteries are shown to him. When he is aged between forty and forty-five, he is finally allowed to partake of the B ritual; he is now fully grounded in all the sacred knowledge. In order to go through these rituals the elders must be satisfied that he is a peaceful clan man, and ritually clean according to clan standards.

There is a mortuary ritual which starts when the man is dying. This is the final *rite de passage*. It is intended to purify him and to separate the good totem spirit which goes into the totem hole from the bad spirit called *Mokoi,* which goes into the bush. The body is buried and after several months it is exhumed and the flesh removed from the bones which are placed in a wooden coffin and left in the bush. Thus for the Murngin life is in stages; a person moves from a lower to a higher stage depending on the ability to socialize and adjust to the social order, and all this is mirrored in rituals.

The Murngin also believe in magic. The black magicians are the cause of all deaths in Murngin society – apart from death from old age. They derive their powers from the *Mokoi* spirits, the bad spirits of the dead. The evils of black magic may be checked by white magicians who act as doctors of the society.

The myths of the origin of the totems after the coming of the two sisters, provide the belief in one origin which gives the whole Murngin people a feeling of oneness. Nevertheless this concept of oneness is never expressed socially. Clan solidarity is centred around the totem hole when every member comes and whither every member goes after death. The age-grade system, by which initiates are allowed to see the totems at various points of their lives, gives the old men control of the social order. It is partly through the exercise of the sanction of refusing to allow a man to be initiated into certain ceremonies, or threatening to do so, that they maintain the effectiveness of the gerontocracy.

Social organization is divided into two, as reflected in the myths, and a stric dichotomy between the sexes is upheld. Women are ritually inferior and so socially lowly. They do not participate in ritual experiences. However, this does not mean that women are socially degraded; their superiority is recognized in domestic affairs, but not in politics and ritual. Women play a complementary part in ritual especially in the B ritual, when during the purification of the clan wives are expected to have ritual sexual experiences with men of other clans. Women also perform ritual dances in the general camp.

The B ritual period affords an opportunity for inter- and intra-clan settlement of disputes. Disputes are forbidden during this period, which lasts for a year or more.

The circumcision ceremony and other rituals are used as controls over their moral and social values. Initiates are taught that incest, adultery, the breaking of taboo, disrespest to elders, etc., are antisocial. Through the process of ritual indoctrination children are oriented towards the social order. The separation of boys from the general camp until their marriage reduces the opportunities for committing incest or adultery, or for competing with the old men for their young wives. A man who breaks taboo constantly or who commits antisocial acts may be refused further ritual experiences; he is then considered to be ritually dead, which means he cannot dream or have children.

Lloyd Warner overemphasized his view that there is a direct connection between the social organization of the Murngin and nature, that is, that the Murngin think that they are able to control nature with their rituals. This functionalist interpretation would mean an assumption that Murngin religion is magic pure and simple However, they do distinguish between magic and religion. It is clear from the myth that the ritual of the two sisters failed to prevent the flood, and that the Python was angry because of the profane condition of the sisters. The Murngin know that the rainy season is both inevitable and important (which Warner reports), and they also know that their society is ritually profane because of its various shortcomings. Thus the aim of some of the rituals is to purify the society so that the divine Python may be less angry and so give them a moderately rainy season and a dry season of plenty. By performing the rituals correctly, the community is absolved from profanity, and so the anger of the Python is appeased. Then nature will be in harmony with society.

Murngin religion is analogous with the Christian religion. Christians offer thanks to God during the harvest season for present and future harvests. However, no one suggests that there is a direct relation between Christian society and nature in terms of ritual control.

Elements of the Murngin myth story may be compared to the Bible: the fall of man due to the frailty of woman; the anger of God; the loss of Paradise; the coming of a Saviour; the beginnings of rites and ceremonies; death; hell and heaven. All of these are expressed in Murngin religion: the fall of the two sisters; the anger of the Python; the loss of the good seasons; the adoption of rituals; attempts to be ritually fit; death; the totem hole for good spirits, the bush for bad ones.

As in medieval Europe, rituals are incorporated into the social organization, and the ritual dramatization of an 'ideal state' reminds members that only the attainment of the ideal gives harmony to social life. In short, the Murngin have projected their concept of an ideal society into the realm of the ritual; the myths represent their 'Bible' and 'constitution'.

We may assume that religion is applied by the Murngin to strengthen their social organization by giving it unity, solidarity and a purpose. Through rituals, which dramatize the ideal society, members are socialized and gradually made part of the society's constitution, as well as being familiarized with its morals and values. The misfortunes of this world and disturbances in natural phenomena are caused by the Python's anger at man's imperfections and the profanity in the conduct of society. The performance of rituals which mimic the ideal gives society confidence that the 'divine' anger is appeased so that nature will be in harmony. Through religion they express their hopes and anxieties which they communicate to one another and to the supernaturals in the complex symbolic codes of totems and taboo.

Social anthropologists have long been interested in the relationship between animal symbolism and social organization as epitomized in the study of totemism and taboo by Durkheim and Mauss, Radcliffe-Brown, Turner, Evans-Pritchard, Lévi-Strauss and Fortes. They have constantly stressed the relationship between specific social segments and some animal species. They have demonstrated how animal symbols illuminate the meaning and significance of social structure and values. They have also shown how animal species are used symbolically for thinking, communicating and controlling. Some, like, Lévi-Strauss, Leach and Douglas have taken great pains to demonstrate the internal logic of conceptual systems, how social reality and the moral order are constructed and reconstructed, and how the natural order is reduced to the social order and vice-versa. They have also attempted to analyse the character of the various assumptions about the universal structure of human thought.

Here I have been content to show quite simply how the total religion of the Murngin reflects the preoccupations of their culture, because African traditional religions have similar functions.

BIBLIOGRAPHY

SECTION I
Works consulted

BREUIL, H. *Art of the Stone Age: Four Hundred centuries of Cave Art* (London: 1970)

CLARK, G. *World Prehistory: an Outline* (Cambridge: Cambridge University Press, 1969)

CLARK, W. E. le G. *The Antecedents of Man* (Edinburgh: Edinburgh University Press, 1959)

—— *The Fossil Evidence of Human Evolution* (Chicago: Chicago University Press, 1964)

DERRY, T. K. and TREVOR, I. W. *A Short History of Technology from Earliest Times to AD 1900* (London: Oxford University Press, 1960)

GARLAKE, P. S. *The Great Zimbabwe* (London: Thames & Hudson, 1973)

HODGES, H. *Technology in the Ancient World* (Harmondsworth: Penguin, 1970)

LEAKEY, L. S. B. *Stone Age Africa* (London: Oxford University Press, 1936)

—— *Olduvai George* (Cambridge: Cambridge University Press, 1951)

OAKLEY, K. P. *Man the Tool-maker* (London, 1961)

RODNEY, W. *How Europe Underdeveloped Africa* (London & Tanzania: Bogle – Louverture Publications, 1972)

SHAW, T. *Igbo-Ukwu* (London: Faber and Faber, 1970), Vols. 1 & 2

SINGER, C. and HOLMYARD, E. J. *A History of Technology* (Oxford: Clarendon Press, 1954) Vols. 1 & 2

TOMAS, A. *We Are Not the First* (London: Sphere Books, 1971)

UCKO, P. J. and ROSENFELD, A. *Palaeolithic Cave Art* (London: Weidenfeld & Nicolson, 1967)

SECTION II

Works consulted

DURKHEIM, E. *The Elementary Forms of the Religious Life*, translated by J. W. Swain (New York: Collier, 1961; London: Allen & Unwin, 1915)

FRAZER, J. G. *The Golden Bough* (London: Macmillan, 1911), Vol. 1

HORTON, R. 'A Definition of Religion and its Uses', *J.R.A.I.*, (1960), 90, 2

LAMMENS, H. *Islam, Beliefs and Institutions* (London: Methuen, 1929)

LEVY-BRUHL, L. *How Natives Think*, translated by L. A. Clore (London: G. Allen, 1926)

MALINOWSKI, B. *Magic, Science and Religion and Other Essays* (Glencoe, Ill.: Free Press; London: Allen & Unwin, 1948)

NADEL, S. F. *Nupe Religion* (London: Routledge & Kegan Paul, 1954)

TRIMMINGHAM, J. S. *Islam in West Africa* (Oxford: Clarendon Press, 1959)

WARNER, W. L. *A Black Civilization*: A Social Study of an Australian Tribe (New York: Harper & Row, 1958)

Suggestions for further reading

BEARDSLEY, R. K., HALL, I. W. and WARD, R. E. *Village Japan* (Chicago & London: University of Chicago Press, 1969), Chapter 14

DOUGLAS, M. 'Magic and Miracle', in *Purity and Danger* (London: Routledge & Kegan Paul, 1966)

GOODY, J. R. 'Religion and Ritual: the Definition Problem,' *British Journal of Sociology* (1961), 12

LÉVI-STRAUSS, C. M. *Totemism*, translated by R. Needham (Boston: Beacon Press 1963; London: Merlin Press, 1964)

LIENHARDT, G. *Divinity and Experience: the Religion of the Dinka* (Oxford: Clarendon Press, 1961)

SECTION III

Works consulted

WARNER, W. L. *A Black Civilization*, A Social Study of an Australian Tribe (New York: Harper & Row, 1958)

Suggestions for further reading

DOUGLAS, M. *Purity and Danger* (London: Routledge & Kegan Paul, 1966)

—— (Ed.) *Rules and Meanings* (Harmondsworth: Penguin Books Ltd, 1973)

DURKHEIM, E. *The Elementary Forms of the Religious Life* translated by J Swain (New York: Collier, 1961; London: Allen & Unwin, 1915)

DURKHEIM, E. and MAUSS, M. *Primitive Classification*, translated by R. Needham (Chicago: University of Chicago Press, 1963)

EVANS-PRITCHARD, E. E. *Nuer Religion* (London: Oxford University Press, 1956)

FIRTH, R. W. *Symbols: Public and Private* (Ithaca, New York: Cornell University Press, 1973)

FORDE, D. *African Worlds* (London: Oxford University Press, 1963)

FORTES, M. 'Totem and taboo', *Proc. Anthrop. Inst.* (1966), 5–22

HORTON, R. 'The Definition of Religion and its Uses, *J.R.A.I.* (1960), 90, 2

LEACH, E. R. 'Anthropological Aspects of Language: Animal Categories and Verbal Abuse', in *New Directions in the Study of Language*, E. J. Lennenberg (ed.) (Cambridge: Cambridge University Press, 1964)

LÉVI-STRAUSS, C. *Totemism*, translated by R. Needham (Boston: Beacon Press 1963; London: Merlin Press, 1964)

NADEL, S. F. 'Nupe Gunnu Ritual', *J.R.A.I.* (1937)

RADCLIFFE-BROWN, A. R. 'Murngin Social Organisation', in *American Anthropologist* (1951), 53, 37–55

—— 'The sociological theory of totemism', in *Structure and Function in Primitive Society* (London: Cohen & West, 1952)

TURNER, V. *The Forest of Symbols* (Ithaca: Cornell University Press, 1967)

YINGER, J. M. *Religion, Society and the Individual, an Introduction to the Sociology of Religion* (New York: Macmillan, 1957)

CHAPTER 20

Men and Morality

The Relationship between Morality and Social Structure: the Tallensi of Northern Ghana and the Tiv of Northern Nigeria

Before describing the relationship between morality and social structure, some of the ethical theories of relativism and absolutism must be discussed.

Ethical absolutists are usually branded as right-wing, old-fashioned and conservative. Their belief is that there is one eternally true and valid moral code that applies to all men. There is but one law, one standard, one morality for all men. What is right may be distinct from what people merely think is right. Absolutists consider it their duty to find out what is the true moral code for all men of all ages. They do not deny moral diversity, but they think it is a result of ignorance of the true morality.

Absolutism is a development from Christian monotheism, in which morality is conceived as issuing from God. With the decline of Christian beliefs and the development of religious scepticism, a new school of moral philosophers emerged. These philosophers are left-wing, modern, ethical relativists; they are represented by Westermarck, and in the field of modern anthropology by Raymond Firth, Ruth Benedict and E. B. Tylor, who may be called the father of cultural relativism.

Relativists argue that the moral judgments of men are completely derived from the customs of the society in which they live, so that moral terms such as 'right' and 'wrong' or 'good' and 'bad', for example, mean that which is approved or disapproved by a particular society. They have observed the very wide variability in the moral standards accepted by men in different societies and at different times; they cite sociological and anthropological evidence of cases in which the same type of action is considered 'right' in one culture and 'wrong' in another. They argue that there is no universal right and wrong which is binding on all men, and that there is no basis for any claim that one culture is morally superior to another.

Raymond Firth is not convinced that anthropologists should be concerned with ethics, which he says is: 'the problem of the existence of intrinsic good and evil, and their relation to human conduct and human society'. He feels that the anthropologist's task is to illustrate the existence of standards of right and wrong, and judgments passed in their terms. He says that such standards are in an obvious relationship to the structure of the societies where they are found.

Another school, whose position might be said to be between absolutism and relativism, is best represented by Morris Ginsberg. He decries the relativist concept of morality, defined by Tylor as 'man's conformity to the customs of the society he belongs to'. Ginsberg attacks the narrowness of this definition, and points to a wider one which would include the 'ideal' which is above the conventional, and a good greater than has so far been achieved or required. He says that morality is universal in the sense that 'everywhere we find rules of conduct prescribing what is to be done or not to be done, and some conception of a good going beyond what is desired at the moment'. However, behind this similarity of form, there is considerable diversity of content. This is due to much variation, for example:

1. In the range of persons to whom rules are held to be applicable.
2. Differences of opinion or knowledge regarding the non-moral qualities of acts or their consequences.
3. The different moral import of the 'same' acts in different social situations and institutional contexts.
4. Differences in the emphasis or balance of elements in the moral life.
5. The possibility of alternative ways of satisfying primary needs.
6. Differences of moral insight and the general level of mental and intellectual development.

The approaches advocated by the relativists and the absolutists raise several problems. For example, the concept of a 'moral system' which is related to the social structure, advocated by relativists, cannot stand the test of ethnographic scrutiny. It can be demonstrated that in a society some morals are related to the social structure and some are not. Similarly absolutists refer to a true morality and distinguish between what actually is right and what is thought right. How does one know what is actually right and how does one measure morality?

Perhaps the middle course, that followed by Ginsberg, is practicable. In the following analysis, using the Tallensi and Tiv ethnography, I shall demonstrate that morality is universal in the sense that it is recognized everywhere that there are certain basic modes of behaviour which are regulated according to certain principles. Moral systems vary greatly, mostly as a result of differences in the social structure. It is the social structure that validates the morals, and not the very fluid morals that validate the social structure – as the relativists would want us to believe. The relationship between morality and social structure is a matter of chance. Hence, the social structure may change whilst morality remains unchanged. Similarly morality may change and the social structure remain unchanged. Thus there is no one-to-one permanent relationship between morality and social structure, although the social structure is strengthened by the basic moral system of the society.

The Tallensi (studied by M. Fortes) are one of the peoples who occupy the basin of the Volta River in the northern territories of Ghana. They are sedentary farmers whose language, social organization and economy constitute a cultural homogeneity. The Tallensi have an agnatic system which is segmented into maximal lineages.

The Tallensi are internally divided into two clusters of clans: the Namoo and the Tale. These two groups are distinguished by differences in their myths of origin, their religious and political functions connected with the earth and ancestor cults, and to some extent by their local distribution. They have been traditional enemies who have cooperated or fought as occasion demanded.

The complementary roles played by these two groups are shown in their political functions. The office of chief, Na'am, is considered to be an attribute of the Namoo who are believed to be the descendants of immigrant Mamprusi. The chiefship is derived from that of the paramount chief of Mamprusi and therein lies the validity and sanction of the political and ritual status of the Namoo. The office of custodian of the earth, Tendaana, is an attribute of the Tale who claim to be the aboriginal inhabitants of the country; the ritual validity and sanction of their office is based on the cult of the earth. The political and ritual offices are vested in particular maximal lineages or clans which are the basic units of Tallensi social organization and also the units that perform corporate activities.

The unity and solidarity of all the Tallensi are demonstrated during the annual cycle of the 'Great Festival', which is celebrated with a series of rites and ceremonies in which the cooperation of both groups is ritually sanctioned and in which the common interests and values of the whole society are reaffirmed.

A clan, which is a localized unit, is made up of segments of a maximal lineage, or a whole maximal lineage. Maximal lineages and clans are exogamous, with few exceptions. Clans are internally unified by a common ritual connected with the worship of the ancestors and the earth, and by locality and genealogical linkage. A striking feature of Tallensi social organization is the system of inter-clan linkage which is one of the principal forces of cohesion. Thus, if two adjacent clans have maximal lineage segments, A, B, C, and D, E, F, G, respectively, A may have clan-ship ties with G and D, and B only with E, and C only with F. Each of these maximal lineages may also have clanship ties with other neighbouring clans. This cross-cutting device balances political and social differentiation and provides cohesion. Warfare may be checked because enemies are related directly or indirectly by clanship ties.

Each segment of a maximal lineage has its lineage 'Boyar', whose symbol is the shrine of the lineage ancestor, under the custodianship of the lineage head man who is the most senior male. But groups of maximal lineages belonging to different unrelated clans join in the cult of their collective ancestors known as the 'external' *Boyar*, which is a sacred grove or cave where the community meets for the ritual of the cult during the harvest festival. This cult unites segments of different clans in the 'worship' of their ancestors, and since it cuts across those of clanship, it is another factor making for social cohesion.

To summarize, each maximal lineage of a composite clan has three fields of operation: in clanship ties, in the 'external' *Boyar* cult, and in the earth cult. There is also the ritually regulated opposition of Tale and Namoo expressed in the re-lationship between chiefship and '*Tendaana*'.

The maximal lineage is divided into a number of major segments. A major segment embraces the agnatic descendants of one of the sons of the founder of the maximal lineage. Each major segment is divisible into other segments and this process recurs downwards to the smallest order of segmentation called the minimal segment or lineage. Fortes defines the minimal lineage as the group comprising only the children of one man, but it seems better to call this the elementary family and call what he calls the 'effective minimal lineage', the 'minimal lineage' which is two or three generations in depth.

The degree of ritual, economic, political and social autonomy which a segment of a particular order has, alters with each generation. Thus the minimal lineage is the basis of a domestic family which constitutes a single unit of food production and consumption. During the father's life, his sons have no ritual, political, economic or jural autonomy. Similarly a grandfather has jurisdiction over both his sons and his grandsons.

The head of each minimal lineage controls and regulates the internal *boyar*, that is, the ancestor shrine of the lineage. While A is alive (see Fig 7) he controls the ancestor shrine and thus the jural and political, and to a certain extent the economic and social, activities of his children and grandchildren, as well as those of his brothers to a certain extent, especially in ritual and politics. Thus A is morally, ritually and socially responsible for the actions of those under his jurisdiction, and those under him are responsible to him. They can only approach their ancestors, who are the source and fountain of authority and the final sanction of their conduct, through him.

The rule of succession is the senior man in the senior generation, that is A is succeeded by his senior son, A1. When A1 dies, A2 succeeds, and so on. He himself becomes an ancestor to be 'worshipped', not particularly because he is dead but principally because he has left sons to continue the lineage. Hence the continuity and perpetuity of the lineage are paramount. The ancestors are regarded as the mystical custodians of the living minimal lineage. The punishments and rewards of the living members are meted out through the lineage head.

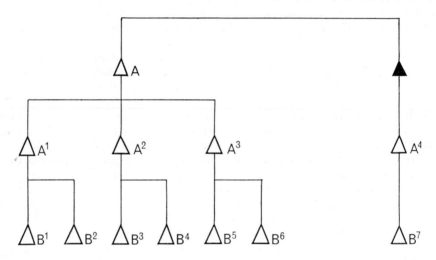

FIGURE 7   *The control of the ancestor shrine*

Thus the concept of ancestorhood, with the religious institutions in which it is ritually and socially moulded, serves as the medium that helps the individual to interact with his father, dead or alive. The very father who controlled his conduct during his lifetime turns into the ancestor who censors his conduct when he is dead.

The system of allocation of rights and duties encourages the latent antagonism between the outgoing and incoming generations. This antagonism is openly expressed in constant conflict between a man and his eldest son, not only ritually but also physically. Since the father is the head of the family he is morally and ritually bound to look after those under him. He loves his children and caters for them while his children love him and obey him. His first son will take his place and inherit all he has when he dies. However, during his father's lifetime, the eldest son is ritually bound to avoid his father in the physical sense: they must not eat together, he must not wear his father's garment or look into his father's barns. After his father's death he is morally bound to perform the mortuary and funeral rites of his father which validate, ritually, his succession. If he fails or delays, there is no sanction that can be used against him materially, but the ancestors will become offended and he will suffer for the negligence.

The son's duty to his father is what Fortes has called filial piety, or *pietas*. It is inherent in the relationship of living parents and children and between the dead parents and living children. It enforces obedience and respect towards parents, submission to their discipline, and economic service to them. The reward for keeping the rules is the praise and satisfaction of parents and kin and the approval of society as a whole. Also, because *pietas* towards the living is also *pietas* towards the ancestors, and since the ancestors reward and punish conduct with illness, misfortune or death, moral and ritual satisfaction is obtained for performing these obligatory acts.

Does the concept of the good man exist in Tallensi society? If it does, what is its nature? Is there 'absolute' goodness in their normal systems? (Here 'absolute' goodness means virtue for its own sake or reward.) To what extent is their concept universal or relative? On what basis do they justify their actions?

A 'good man' among the Tallensi is one who fulfils in its accepted forms all the duties and obligations enjoined by the virtue of *pietas*. Such a man is not only a success but is also a model, because *pietas* exemplifies all that is good in Tallensi social life. If he is the head of a lineage he will be a good family man, a good leader, and one who is obedient to the ancestors. The concept of *pietas* is a function of the minimal lineage and so is only a part of the social structure. Fortes has pointed out how the virtue of *pietas* is threatened by sons going to work in Kumasi as miners. Thus the minimal lineage remains unchanged, yet the morality which is applied to it is threatened.

The concept of filial piety is almost universal, but differs in various societies in its emphasis and application. It exists among the Tiv who have a social structure similar to that of the Tallensi, but it is not embedded in their ritual system. It exists among the Ashanti, the Trobriand Islanders, the English, the French and the Arabs. There is only one society in which it seems not to exist and that is the Nayar. This is because the father is 'non-existent' in the Nayar 'family'. One might draw the conclusion, therefore, that the family is the basic structural unit for the existence of filial piety. Among the Tallensi this principle has been exaggerated and extended within the maximal lineage. It is almost non-existent at the clan level. In this case it is not related to the total social structure, nor does it validate the social structure. Rather it adds more strength to the basic social structure.

There are some elements of absolute goodness in the Tallensi ethical system which are worth discussing, because they are neither based on the social structure nor on their legal or religious notions. They are genuinely 'absolute' and may be classified, following Ginsberg, as universal. Here are three examples.

The Tallensi look after their sick wives with great devotion and care. Those whose wives contact leprosy are reported to have taken care of them with extra care under great economic strain. They would simply justify their actions as 'their duty'. Since divorce is easy to obtain it would have been easy to do away with these sick wives who are strangers in their lineage and also burdens to them, at least economically. Their actions are based on the principle of what is 'good' or 'bad' to do. It is not related to their social organization. This challenges some of Firth's propositions and confirms Ginsberg's.

Another example is the Tallensi attitude towards theft. A father will drive away a son who steals, although they may be reconciled later. The act of driving the son away from the lineage contradicts the continuity and solidarity of the agnatic lineage principle which is the foundation of the social structure. Theft is regarded as 'not good', and some people would rather die than steal. This is the idea of a good going beyond social structure; Ginsberg would call this an example of universal morality.

Let us compare this attitude with the Tiv. Here a man must not steal within his minimal segment; to do so is magically dangerous and morally bad: In the past the elders would respond to repeated offences by selling the culprit as a slave or killing him by witchcraft. On the other hand, theft from those whom one may fight with bow and arrow is equated with warfare and might be called individual raiding – a laudable activity. This again is a case of the relationship between morality and social structure. But if this relationship really exists, why is an agnate who steals in his minimal segment killed? Is this not a case of breaking a morality to support another morality? If this relationship is really of any significance, why should a morality related to the social structure be broken by the sanction of another morality which is related to the same social structure? Thus it seems that any relationship between morality and social structure is one of chance.

The Tallensi regard killing as a crime against the earth, and the shedding of human blood, even in self-defence or in justifiable anger, as sinful. However, to kill a man in war is not homicide, and the heavy expiatory sacrifices to the earth are not necessary. Yet the blood taint cannot be got rid of. The most heinous sin of all is to instigate a war. It does not matter if the man has justice on his side. Why do the Tallensi have this type of moral code with reference to homicide? Relativists would say that it is because killing is related to the Tallensi social structure. Fortes says: 'considering their lack of a single, all-embracing government and their segmentary social structure, it was inevitable that conflicts should often arise that could only be settled by fighting.' And historically, fighting was frequent and wars were less frequent. In the past wars took place between the Tale clans or between some Tale clans and neighbouring non-Tale clans. Wars began between adjacent clans which were not united by direct or indirect ties of clanship and then spread by mobilizing the opposing forces along the lines of structural interconnection. Tale warfare in its corporate aspect was considered to be a mechanism for redressing wrongs that could not otherwise be put right.

The moral function of the lineage system is exemplified by the Tiv, among whom enmity is stated in genealogical terms. Thus people of two minimal segments with an immediate common ancestor may fight with stone and club. Between segments of a slightly greater depth, bows and arrows may be used. Between segments of some eight or ten generations in depth, the possibility of real war is admitted – with guns and poisoned arrows and permitted killing. Here structural distance due to segmental position is involved, that is, it is all right to fight with certain types of weapon depending on the structural relation between combatants. Similarly the moral attitude to homicide in peace or war is on a scale determined by the social distance in lineage terms between the people involved.

The Tiv notion of homicide is similar to that of the Tallensi, but differs in application. The variations are correlated with the social structure in the case of the Tiv, whereas among the Tallensi there seems to be no such correlation.

Another interesting example is the Tallensi notion of incest with a sister or daughter. They explain that a normal man does not even have sexual desire for a sister or a daughter. Such an act is taboo but it is neither a crime nor a sin. It is just an immoral act which one ought to be ashamed of. This type of incest is not sanctioned as other types are. It is left to the good sense of the individual to conform to the accepted standards of responsible persons. Not committing, it, therefore, is a virtue based on its own reward.

At this stage some conclusions may be attempted. In Tallensi society the concept of the good man exists and is manifested in the notion of *pietas*, using Fortes' terminology. The Tallensi justify the act of *pietas* by what Fortes has called the 'irreducible fact of procreation', and this is sanctioned by the belief in the ancestor cult.

Respect for people's property, care for a sick wife and avoidance of certain types of incest, are virtues having no reward but themselves. They are absolute and have no relation with the social structure, as *pietas* has. Therefore it seems that virtue for its own sake and the concept of the 'good man', are realities in Tallensi society.

Morality is both universal and individual. The moralities of homicide, honesty, and so on, exist in all societies, but differ in how they are applied in various societies, for a number of reasons. Also certain aspects of a people's morality may be related to the social structure, while others may not be. Others may even tend to negate the principles of the social structure. It is therefore difficult to accept the absolutist or relativist approach totally.

BIBLIOGRAPHY

Works consulted

BOHANNAN, P. *Justice and Judgment among the Tiv* (London: Oxford University Press, 1957)
—— *African Homicide and Suicide* (Princeton: Princeton University Press, 1960)
FIRTH, R. *Essays on Social Organization and Values* (London: Athlone Press, 1964)
FORTES, M. *Dynamics of Clanship among the Tallensi* (London: Oxford University Press, 1945)
—— *The Web of Kinship among the Tallensi* (London: Oxford University Press, 1949)
GINSBERG, M. 'On the diversity of morals', *J.R.A.I.* (1953), 83
MacBEATH, A. *Experiments in Living, a Study of the Nature and Foundation of Ethics or Morals in the Light of Recent Work in Social Anthropology* (London: Macmillan, 1952).
TYLOR, E. B. *Primitive Culture* (2nd edn.) (London: John Murray, 1871)
WESTERMARCK, E. *Ethical Relativity* (London: Kegan Paul, 1932)

Suggestions for further reading

EDEL, M. M. and A. *Anthropology and Ethics: the Quest for Moral Understanding* (Cleveland, Ohio: Press of Case Western Reserve University, 1968)
HOBHOUSE, L. T. *Morals in Evolution*: a Study in Comparative Ethics (London: Chapman & Hall, 1951)
MARETT, R. R. 'The Beginnings of Morals and Culture: an Introduction to Social Anthropology', in *An Outline of Modern Knowledge*, W. Rose (ed.) (London: Gollancz, 1932)
MBITI, J. S. *African Religion and Philosophy* (London: Heinemann, 1969)

CHAPTER 21

Men and their Cults

I *The Nature and Significance of Sacrifice in the Ancestor Cult: the LoDagaa of Northern Ghana*

LoDagaa is the ethnographic name given by Goody to two peoples, the Lowiili and the Lodagaba, who live on the banks of the Black Volta River in northern Ghana. Culturally they are more or less alike.

The Lowiili are agriculturalists who keep cattle and grow guinea corn, millet, maize and some yam. They also keep sheep, goats and poultry. The simplest dwelling group consists of an elementary monogamous family. A group of agnates dwells in a compound under a compound head who is the oldest man and custodian of the ancestor shrine. Some seven or more large compounds situated about a hundred yards apart from each other constitute a typical patrilineage. These lineages are shallow in depth but form a corporate group in that they own land jointly and have a lineage shrine under the head of a senior member. Dispersed patrilineages having one earth shrine and claiming a common descent form a clan sector. A few clan sectors amalgamate into clans which are not corporate groups. The unity of the clan arises from the concept of a common descent and prohibitions against endogamy and killing clan members, which is unpardonable sin. There are also matriclans.

The Lodagaba are the neighbours of the Lowiili and have an identical social organization and economy. They have a double unilineal descent system whereby movable property like livestock and grain is inherited matrilineally, while immovable property and wealth such as land are inherited patrilineally. They are organized in single or compound families. Groups of such families live in a compound under a compound head. A number of compounds form a patrilineage. These lineages are shallow in depth but form a corporate group owning land jointly; each has a lineage shrine under the custodianship of a senior member. Dispersed patrilineages having one earth shrine and claiming common descent form a clan sector. A few clan sectors combine into clans. These clans are not corporate groups, but the unity of the clan arises from the concept of a common descent and the prohibition against killing clan members, which is an unpardonable crime against the earth.

There are also matriclans whose members are dispersed in the patriclan territories. Members of a matrilineage come together to sacrifice to their ancestor. The matrilineages are the most important corporate group with regard to ancestor worship.

The Lodagaba and the Lowiili differ in one respect, although both have a double unilineal system. In the Lodagaba system the matrilineal and patrilineal groups are both units which hold and transmit property; in the Lowiili system inheritance is patrilineal and the matrilineal group serves a ritual purpose.

The double unilineal inheritance system adopted by the Lodagaba as against the Lowiili patrilineal inheritance system accounts for three major differences in certain relationships in the two societies: the mother's brother–sister's son relationship tends to be hostile among the Lodagaba but cordial among the Lowiili. The father–son relationship is cordial among the Lodagaba and tense among the Lowiili. The productive group is larger among the Lowiili than among the Lodagaba, where the fission of the elementary family occurs earlier to avoid inheritance conflict.

The ideas of the dichotomy between body and soul, and the concept of the soul, provide the basis for the transformation of human beings into ancestors and supply a link between the living and the dead. They fill the gap created by death in the readjustment of the network of relationships. They are the foundations on which the belief in afterlife is laid, and the validations for the beliefs in mysticism, ghosts, witchcrafts, sorcery and magic. The ideas of transmigration and transmutation, reincarnation and rebirth, purification and self-denial, all have their bedrock in the concept of the soul.

According to Goody, the body–soul dichotomy is the foundation of the religion of the LoDagaa. They believe that a human being is made up of a soul, breath and body, with skin. The soul and breath leave the body at death, although both differ in that the soul can leave the body, as in witchcraft, while the body continues to breathe. Also it is the soul that continues to exist after death.

The doctrine of the plurality of the soul as conceived by the LoDagaa is consistent with their beliefs. They believe that the soul consists of three elements : the one that leaves the body when a man dreams; the one that becomes first a ghost and then a spirit and finally journeys to the land of the dead where it is rewarded or punished; and the one that stays with the body wherever it goes and disappears at death. Thus it is easy to understand why they believe that the soul and body of a living person can be in a state of dissociation for three or four years before the person dies. This condition can be discovered by a diviner; by appropriate sacrifices to the ancestor the soul can be 'swept' back into the body. If this sacrifice is unavailing and the patient dies, the soul starts its journey to the land of the dead, which entails crossing a river where witches are tortured and debtors delayed. In the end all will meet God who rewards the good and punishes the evil.

Goody's interpretation is that death is a social separation, and also a separation of the soul from the body. This separation is seen in physical terms which takes the form of a symbolic journey to the west where the sun always sets. The river is the discontinuity between the world of the dead and that of the living, similar to the separation between areas by rivers in the physical world. Goody argues that the concept of reward and punishment after death appears to be an extension in the supernatural plane of the system of social control that operates on earth. This time the system is idealized as having been achieved by God.

The belief in a future life among the LoDagaa serves as a means of adjusting the differences between the ideal and the actual, of readjusting the new roles and statuses caused by deaths, and of reinforcing the system of social and moral control, thus placing them above human doubt and reducing the sense of loss in bereavement as well as supporting the belief in the ancestor cult.

The LoDagaa cult of the dead implies not only the idea of survival after death but also the active participation of the dead in social life. It is the notion of the constant intervention of the dead 'fathers' in the lives of their descendants that makes the LoDagaa propitiate the dead by offerings of goods, services, words and other gestures to win them over and obtain their favours.

First, the nature and significance of the sacrifices they offer and the roles ascribed to their ancestors must be understood. The ancestor cult has many facets. In order

MEN AND THEIR CULTS

to establish some correlation between the religious system and other aspects of the social and moral order, Goody examined five important factors.

1. The nature of shrine organization and management.
2. The occasion for which sacrifices are made.
3. The roles of and the relationships between the recipient-ancestor, the officiant-custodian, and the donor, the provider of the offering.
4. The types of congregation and their relationships with the recipient, officiant and donor.
5. The procedure of a sacrifice and the nature of distribution that takes place.

Firstly, shrine organization. During the last stage of the funeral of a man who has left children behind, a shrine is carved and put in his byre by his eldest son. This is kept beside the ritual figurines of earlier ancestors. Any man with a male child born to his name may have a shrine. A child is said to be born to a man's name when the bride-wealth for the mother has been given on his behalf. The bride-wealth is laid first at the foot of the ancestor shrines of the groom, for the dead ancestors watch over the rights of women's procreative powers. If a man has no son before he dies, his daughter will be helped by a 'father's brother' to put up a shrine. In this case the father's brother is supposed to inherit his brother's wife in levirate marriage, and beget a male child who will offer in the shrine.

Men who have died childless or who have suffered an evil death are denied a shrine. Also, men who have sinned against the earth such as those who have killed their 'fathers' or 'brothers', can never have a shrine. They are doomed to die and be forgotten by society.

A woman who has left children may have a shrine made in her name. At first it is left in her husband's house, but after the final funeral ceremony it is taken to her father's home and placed near the shrines of her patrilineal ancestors, which is where she socially belongs.

The duty of creating a man's shrine falls upon his eldest son by his senior wife. He provides the cock for the initial sacrifice, assisted by the eldest son of the second wife who supplies a hen. After a series of rites the shrine is placed in the dead man's byre. The senior son is regarded as the 'owner' of the shrine, but as long as his paternal uncle (the inheritor of the deceased's estate) lives he (the senior son) cannot remove the shrine to another house. He can, however, do so if there is no living paternal uncle. If the eldest son of the second wife wants to build a house he is allowed to take a provisional shrine of his dead father to put in it.

Goody points out that the logic of this concept of seniority derives from the fact that the group of siblings in patrilineage differ by maternal filiation and that the fission of domestic groups of an agnatic core first occurs along the matri-segment. (This does not explain why among the Benin custodianship of the shrine is ordered by the rule of primogeniture irrespective of the matri-segment.)

The custody of ancestor shrines is in the hands of the head of the compound. He addresses the ancestors in prayer before offerings are made to them. These compound shrines usually represent the dead members of a lineage segment. If there is more than one segment in a compound, each segment will have its own shrine. Residential fission also determines the custodianship of the shrines. Thus in Wakara's compound (Fig. 8) all descendants of B1 and B2 were living in one compound. Later C1 and D1 built themselves a house of their own and took with them the shrines of C2, B1 and B. Soon after D5 moved to a new house and took his father's (C4) shrine with him leaving the offspring of C3 in the original compound. If misfortune subsequently befalls C1, for example, in the new house, a diviner may advise the transfer of the shrine to the old house whether occupied or not.

Among some societies such as those of the Igbo, Tallensi and Benin, the custodian-ship of the shrine coincides with the distribution of authority within the lineage. There seems to be no such correspondence among the LoDagaa. The shrine of the senior member of a lineage may not contain the shrine of the founding ancestor, which may be left in its original site. However, the custodian addresses the shrine

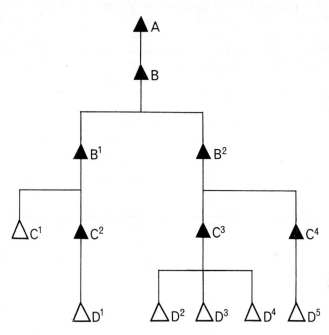

FIGURE 8   *Wakara's compound*

at any sacrifice made on behalf of the lineage. Below this level the senior member of each compound approaches their ancestors directly. The mechanism of 'tele-scoping' is used for limiting the number of shrine objects. Only important and more recent ancestors are remembered, others are forgotten and represented as unknown ancestors in one collective shrine in the senior man's byre. Also at the collective shrine ancestor-worship merges with the earth cult and is most difficult to dis-tinguish.

The occasions for sacrifice may be divided into two types: those that fall within the 'cosmic cycle', marked by the seasonal periods of production; and those that fall within the human 'life cycle', which correspond to the processes of socialization from cradle to grave.

The LoDagaa have no specific planting ritual, but they have two ceremonies after the harvest: the 'earth shrine festival' and the 'general thanksgiving festival'. In the former, each compound in the area contributes grain for a general sacrifice at the shrine. In the latter, descent groups make offerings together at the same time to their ancestors.

The life crises of an individual are always a matter of concern to the family unit and the lineage as a whole. The most important are birth, illness, misfortune or fortune and deaths. Sacrifices are made at every one of these moments, and 'quasi-sacrifices' are made on less notable occasions.

During labour a woman is taken to the byre to deliver the child in the presence of its ancestors. Immediately after the birth, a chicken called the 'fowl of the breasts' is sent to the mother's natal home for sacrifice to her patrilineal ancestor; this permits her milk to flow. Sacrifices are also made to the ancestors during initiation ceremonies to the *Bogre* society. When a man wishes to marry, bride-gift cowries are placed in the front of the ancestral shrines before they are taken to the bride's patrilineal kin. The new wife will provide a child for the lineage, so the ancestors must be informed, since they have an interest in the productive power of all the wives of the lineage. That is why adultery is an offence against the husband and a sin against his ancestors, and requires a sacrifice to the ancestors to expiate the sin and give compensation to the husband. A sexual offence with an unmarried female member of the group, that is, 'incest', does not require a sacrifice, although when committed with a married 'sister' it is a double sin, against her husband's ancestors and against her lineage ancestors. The culprit is excluded for ever from partaking of the flesh of the 'bull of child-bearing', which is a part of the bride-gift payment made to the lineage and sacrificed to the ancestors. He has contravened the law of reciprocity; for he cannot have his cake and eat it.

Every new acquisition of wealth and success need to be followed by a sacrifice of 'thanksgiving' to the ancestors. They must have their own share through sacrifice. Sacrifice does not imply a gift; it is giving a share to the dead of the jointly owned property. If neglected, misfortune will soon occur, which a diviner will never fail to point out.

To sum up, the LoDagaa distinguish two types of sacrifices: expiatory and rogatory, which may overlap in any one offering. Sacrifices can be initiated by the ancestors who speak through diviners and wield their influence through misfortune or fortune. The allocation of the custodianship of the shrines, its organization and the nature of sacrifices to the ancestors, reflect and sanction some aspects of their morality and closely correspond to the nature of their social groupings and differentiation.

There are five actors in the sacrifices: the donor, the officiant, the assistant, the recipient and the congregation. The roles of two or more of the actors may be played by one person.

The relationship between the actors is very interesting. The recipients are usually first indicated by the diviners, who locate which category of ancestors needs the sacrifice. Among the Lodagaba who have double unilineal descent, the sacrifice is usually directed to a mother's brother and ancestors of one's matriclan. Sacrifice is rarely made to one's father. This is consistent with the Lodagaba's maxim of 'I worship the dead man by whose death I benefit'. The officiant is the senior man of the segment within which the ancestor-recipient falls, but this also has to be determined by the nature of the offering, which in its turn is determined by the kind of domestic animal the diviner recommends.

There are two major types of offering: the 'black' and the 'white' animal sacrifice. The 'black' animal sacrifice involves the killing of a cow, a sheep, or a guinea-fowl. This sacrifice is regarded as 'dangerous'; it involves the whole lineage and is conducted by the eldest man in the lineage himself. Members of the lineage are allowed to attend and participate as it is a matter of concern to all. The 'white' animal sacrifice involves the use of a goat or fowl. It is not dangerous and may be conducted by the compound head at the ancestral shrine which comes under his custodianship. No outsider need be present. Most thanksgiving sacrifices fall under this category.

Among the Lowiili where the clan sector is organized into a definite number of patrilineages, unlike the Lodagaba, it is customary for the lineage offering a sacrifice to invite the heads of other lineages of the patriclan, especially when the sacrifice is expiation for adultery or killing the 'bull of child-bearing' for marriage. Sometimes a sister's son may be asked to be officiant at the ceremony; he is not a direct member of the lineage, but one by 'complementary affiliation'. On these occasions the ancestors are said to be very angry with all members of the agnates. This is consistent with the real-life situation where a mother's brother is expected to be loving and affectionate towards a sister's son while the father is expected to be strict and chastising.

When sacrifices are offered to expiate suicide or murder, the members of the lineage do not consume the meat, but it is given to members of a reciprocal lineage, or to the sister's son or the joking-partners, to whom the meat is not forbidden. This may be considered as a reward for the 'cathartic' services rendered.

The relationship between the recipient and the donor differs greatly among the Lowiili and the Lodagaba. The Lowiili inherit only patrilineally from father to son. Sacrifices are only made to one's father or father's father, etc., because fathers hand down to sons all reproductive and productive resources – the ability to pro-create, land, and tools. Among the Lodagaba, where the system of inheritance is double unilineal, and so the objects of sacrifice, that is movable goods, are inherited matrilineally, sacrifices are chiefly made to one's mother's brother and the ancestors of his matriclan, and rarely to fathers.

Ancestors do demand sacrifices, or they can be offered voluntarily by an indi-vidual. The ancestors' demands follow certain principles, for they may not demand from those to whom they have not given. Hence the major obligation to sacrifice exists between members of the same property-holding group.

Here is a typical example (see Fig. 9). Jerry inherited the movable property of his mother's brother and was entitled to all unpaid debts including the bride-wealth cattle owed by a head man marrying the deceased's daughter. The child of the head man became ill and a diviner was consulted who suggested that the child's maternal grandfather was angry because he had not yet received the share of the 'bull of child-bearing' due to him. Since the head man wanted his child to live he was forced to pay his long-outstanding debt by providing the cattle. Jerry, the rightful heir, was happy to receive his payment but he knew that it was his duty to sacrifice immediately, otherwise he would attract the attention of his maternal ancestor, and if the child died all the blame would fall on him. So he offered the sacrifice which was attended by his lineage members, each person receiving his own share. Thus in one sacrifice several conflicting interests were served: those of the male affines because of their different interests in the women and their children; those of the man and his wife; those of the deceased and his heir and his daughter; those of the inheritor and his lineage; and those of the two lineages concerned. Furthermore, when the sacrifice was offered Jerry stood aside because as he was a sister's son, he could not approach the ancestors directly.

This is also the case with women. The ability to approach the shrines directly reflects status differentiation within and between the lineages. Women can only offer indirectly to their patrilineal or matrilineal ancestors, but it is doubtful whether sacrifices are made to women ancestors, whose shrines are always merged with those of their patrilineal forebears.

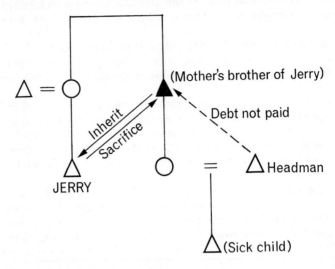

FIGURE 9 *A case history of Jerry's sacrifice*

The relationships between donor, officiant and recipient in any given type of sacrifice reflect the mode of status differentiation within the lineages and the domestic domain and also between lineages. The relationships between donor and recipient reflect the systems of inheritance in the two societies and stress the general principle of 'to whomsoever it is given so much is demanded'. Hence a Lowiili will not take seriously a diviner who tells him that his mother's brother's ancestors demand a sacrifice from him. Indeed, such a suggestion may be regarded as a 'heresy'. A Lodagaba, however, will not hesitate to offer to his mother's brother.

Each sacrifice entails addressing the earth and then the ancestor, after which the sacrifice is made and distribution takes place. The way meat is distributed is of great sociological importance. It depends on the nature of the sacrifice and it is different among the Lowiili and the Lodagaba.

When sacrifices are offered to expiate suicide or murder, the meat is not eaten, but given to members of reciprocally linked lineages or joking-partners. If the animal is a 'bull of child-bearing', those who have committed incest with a married sister and those who have committed patricide or fratricide are excluded. The left front leg is given to patriclan sisters of the bride since they are said to 'bear' the children. One leg goes to the 'fathers' and one to the 'brothers' of the groom's patrilineage. The fourth leg goes to the joking-partners of the lineage. The fillet goes to the mother and another part to the father's father, the ribs to the attendant and cook. The dried skin is made into a mat for the new baby.

The portion given to the shrine is a part of the liver. The liver is roasted on the spot and divided only among the elders except for a small part which is cut off and thrown to the shrine. Some of the blood is also poured over the ritual figurines; the rest is consumed on the spot. The rest of the flesh is taken home and redistributed.

The quantity given to the shrine is very small, but it is significant and symbolic. Blood represents the life of an animal and the liver is an important organ. By offering these they have offered the life of the animal to the ancestors. The idea of

MEN AND THEIR CULTS

sacrifice as a means of offering their own lives symbolically through a scapegoat seems to be absent among the LoDagaa.

The sharing of meat at the sacrifice, apart from serving a ritual purpose, is a means of expressing lineage solidarity, communality and reciprocity. Since certain types of sinners are excluded it serves also as a mechanism of social control. Lastly it is one of the very few means of achieving distribution of a scarce commodity in LoDagaa society.

The types of sacrifice described above have a congregation of membership limited to lineages in range and scope. The cult of the spirit-guardian, however, provides for a wider congregation. Each clan or linked clans have their spirit-guardian, whose altar may be situated near a rocky hill. Every senior house head of the lineage has in his byre a stone from the spirit-guardian's altar, which is kept at the front of the ancestor's shrine. All sacrifices to the ancestors are also sacrifices to the spirit-guardian and the earth cult.

Many theories have been put forward to explain the meaning of sacrifice. Durkheim's communion theory does not apply to the LoDagaa for they do not believe that they are eating with their dead fathers. Tylor's gift theory also does not apply to them. It is not a magical rite, as Alfred Loisy would want to brand all primitive sacrifice. Rather it has certain aspects of the 'confirmatory and peculiar' sacrifice, to use Evans-Pritchard's terms. It is expiatory and rogatory, and also symbolic in that it is a useful device for expressing and dramatizing their concern about life and their social structural relationships. In no case is it regarded as a symbolic offering of their own lives. It is regarded as a fulfilment of obligations to ancestors who expect and demand offerings, because the living are beneficiaries of those material goods they contributed during their lifetimes and which they continue to 'provide' after they are dead. The ancestor cult extends to a super-natural level Meyer Fortes' concept of *pietas*, which requires sons to obey and help fathers and fathers to cater and provide for their children. The father who while alive holds predictable physical control, now dead holds an unpredictable supernatural control, and can only be approached through the lineage elders. The elders derive their authority from mediating between the dead ancestors and the descendant generation.

The significance of LoDagaa sacrifice is that it reflects their social and moral systems, such as status differentiation within the domestic and lineage group, the centrifugal tendency of the lineages and the centripetal tendency of the clan, the system of inheritance, some of their morals and values, and their ideas of reciprocal relationships. The ancestor cult can be considered to be an extension of society beyond human bounds so that people are dependent on the ancestors.

The ancestor cult has four main characteristics which may be isolated. It is a ritual memorialism by which every son commemorates the death of his father by installing an altar in his honour. It is the cult of the immediate jural superior; through it elders have jural authority and political and social power over the activities of their dependants. This is because the ancestor cult has a hierarchical structure as defined by the lineage segments. It is the cult of the structurally signi-ficant ancestor. The cult is arranged to correspond to the genealogical and seg-mentary structure of the society. Thus the worship of more and more distant ancestors brings together wider and wider groups in cooperation. It is the cult of the property-owning group. This group is the most effective ritually, jurally and socially in ancestor worship. Above the level of patrilineages, ancestor worship fuses with the earth cult, and ceases to be of significance socially or jurally. At this level the earth cult predominates.

The roles ascribed to the ancestors are authoritarian. They sanction the concept of *pietas*, they validate all sanctions, making them beyond human challenge. The ancestor cult in this respect is a symbolic system of social and moral control.

II *The Ikenga: the Cult of Individual Achievement and Advancement among the Nri, Igbo of Southern Nigeria*

PSYCHIC POWER IN MAN

The hegemony which the Nri people established over certain areas of the Igbo culture area and the state system they operated were based on the premise that through the instrument of religious beliefs human beings were disciplined into obeying a higher supernatural authority who was believed to dwell physically in Nri town. This earthly supernatural authority is the Eze Nri who is regarded as a king and a spirit. (For the Nri, see Chapter 4.)

Nri cosmology and religious beliefs are shared in common with other Igbo peoples some of whom Nri ritually and, to some degree, politically controlled in the past. The traditional cosmology and religious beliefs of the Nri are interwoven and centred around five interdependent concepts. They are as follows:

Chukwu, the Great Creator of all things.
Alụsi, the invisible supernatural beings and/or forces.
Mmụọ, the invisible spirits of the dead.
Ụwa, the visible world.
Ike Mmadụ, the 'power' in the individual person that drives him into action.

Ike mmadụ is the psychic 'power' stored in every human being. This power can be developed and it is believed to be epitomized in five cults.

1. The *Ikenga* cult: this is the cult of the right hand, symbolically represented by the *Ikenga* image of a man with a ram's head. It represents the right hand with which a man works out his living.
2. The *Ụkụ-na-ije* cult: this is the cult of the feet, symbolized by a carved wooden figure of a foot. It represents the feet of successful adventure into foreign land.
3. The *iru* cult: this is the cult of the face symbolized by a wood-like chalice. It is the face that charms whoever that gazes on it.
4. The *uho* cult: this is the cult of the tongue, symbolized by a wooden object tongue-like in shape. It symbolizes the powerful tongue that can persuade and reduce into submission the heart of people.
5. The *ụmụ ọkụ*: this is the cult that conserves accumulated wealth. It is symbolized by a wooden saucer with flat handle.

Every traditional adult Nri man has these five cult objects. They are placed on the altar of the ancestor and sacrifices offered to them as occasion demanded. Here I shall deal primarily with the *Ikenga* cult.

THE MAKING OF THE IKENGA IMAGE

If a person is constantly successful in his undertakings, the traditional diviner, *Dibia afa*, will say to him: 'You need an *Ikenga*.' In this case the person's *Ikenga* is said to have ritually manifested itself, *Ikenga ai wa*. The person goes to the wood-carver, *onye na tụ nka*, to carve an *Ikenga* for him. The *Ikenga* image takes various forms. The most common is a figure of a man with two ram horn-like

13   *The* Ikenga (*Nri, Nigeria*)

projections in his head. His hair is plaited and dressed in the traditional fashion.
He is nude; his penis and fat navel are shown. His nose is straight and upright and
his eyes sharp. He is carved to look young, strong and healthy. He may be sitting or
standing and holding vertically a curved wooden sword, *Atata*, in his right hand
and a skull, *Isi*, in his left hand (see figure in Plate 13).

The two ram-horns mean that the person must go ahead in his business with the
stubbornness of a ram. The knife in his right hand means that he must cut down
any obstacle on the way and the skull in the left hand means that he must always
take the lead in order to succeed. The *Ikenga* must be carved straight and rigid,
because straightness is the sign of exactitude and rigidity means perseverance. In
some places an *Ikenga* may be owned in common by a whole community, in which
case it may be carved in a more elaborate style.

THE RITUALIZATION OF THE *IKENGA* IMAGE (*MMACHA*)

The *Ikenga* image carved by the artist is only a piece of wood. The image has to be
transformed into a ritual object by consecrating it, *Mmacha*. The owner, let us
call him Okafor, asks the head, *Onyi Isi*, of his minimal lineage to come and

consecrate his *Ikenga*. He also invites one of his age-mates who has an *Ikenga* similar to his own. The lineage members congregate in the house or in the front of the domestic temple, *Obu*, of the owner of the *Ikenga*. The owner produces some yams, a cock, two gallons of palm wine, two gallons of tombo wine and two kola-nuts.

The *Onyi Isi* takes the kola-nut and makes the offering, *Igǫ Ǫji*, praying as follows.

> *Ikenga Okafor ta ǫji.*
> *Ikenga Okafor ya ka ana amacha ta.*
> *Ǫ, ki mali na Okafor abatagǫ na akai ta.*
> *Ka ife ǫma si ta bataba.*
> *Okafor si na ya nụ nwanyi, ya nyei ebunu.*

> *Ikenga* Okafor accept this offering of kola-nut.
> We are consecrating Okafor's *Ikenga* today.
> Understand that today Okafor is under your guidance.
> May good things begin to flow in from today.
> Okafor promises to give you a he-goat if he gets married.

The *Onyi Isi* takes the cock and kills it, pouring the blood on the *Ikenga*. He removes the feathers of the cock and sticks them on the *Ikenga*. He repeats the above prayer while he is doing this.

The cock is cut into pieces and used for making soup. The yam is cooked and pounded into yam foofoo. The *Onyi Isi* takes four lumps of pounded yam and places them on the *Ikenga*. He takes the head of the cock and places it on the four lumps of yam, praying:

> *Ikenga Okafor ya ka ana macha.*
> *Wete li Okafor Ife oma, ahṇ ǫma, akụ, nwunye.*

Those present answer: *Ise, Ise.*

> It is Okafor's *Ikenga* we are consecrating.
> Bring to Okafor good things, health, wealth, wife.
> May it be so.

The head and feet of the cock are given to the children, who are hanging around waiting to eat. The *Onyi Isi* takes the femur and the neck of the cock. The wing and the waist are given to Okafor, the owner of the *Ikenga*, and the remaining parts are shared among those present.

The *Onyi Isi* next pours a libation of palm wine and tombo wine on the *Ikenga*, praying:

> *Akụ, awele, ya ka anyi na chǫ.*
> *Ikenga kwụ ǫtǫ ka anyi na chǫ.*

> Wealth, good fortune are what we are seeking for.
> We are searching for an upright *Ikenga*.

The remaining wine is shared and drunk by those present. The *Onyi Isi* takes the *Ikenga* and hands it over to Okafor, saying: '*Ikenga yi di ile.*' (May your *Ikenga* be effective.)

Okafor takes his *Ikenga* and places it in his ancestor shrine, *Iru Ndüchie*, in his compound. The *Ikenga* is no longer a piece of carved wood. It is now a ritual object, a vehicle of communicating with the forces of achievement. Okafor, by directing his strength, *Ike,* can go ahead, *Ga,* undaunted by the fluctuating fortunes of business in this world. *Ikenga* therefore means 'My strength must go ahead'. If the owner is successful in his business he proudly displays his *Ikenga* in the shrine of his *Ndiichie* for people to see and he offers to it a cock or a he-goat proportionate to the magnitude of his success. If his business is unsuccessful the *Ikenga* is given kola-nut. If his efforts are always fruitless, he removes his *Ikenga* from the shrine and hangs it up in a corner until things improve. The *Ikenga* is therefore a ritual object through which individuals express their emotions of joy and frustration. It is said: '*Ikenga adi ile ọta ba sọ ọji*' (an ineffective *Ikenga* eats only kola-nut); '*Ikenga di ile oli be nni*' (an effective *Ikenga* eats food).

MYSTICAL CONFLICTS AND SOCIAL PROGRESS
The *Ikenga* is closely related to *Uho, Iru, Ụkwụnaije* and *Ụmụ Ọkụ,* and all these are related to *Chi* which is that aspect of God in man which enables him to procreate himself. If one's *Chi* is active, one's energy and actions are fully directed and integrated into achieving success with a minimum of misfortune, and it is then only that one's *Ikenga, Uho, Iru, Ụkwụnaije* and *Ụmụ ọkụ* can be effective.

A person makes progress by acquiring wealth, which in order to be of any social value or significance has to be transformed into social status by the taking of titles, *Echichi.* Thus by a graded and systematic 'destruction' of accumulated economic wealth, carried out by a socio-ritual process of public sacrifice and consumption, economic achievement is transformed into social status as indicated in the graded title system and associations characteristic of Igbo society.

Conflicts in the mystical world are generated by the *Alụsi,* called *Agwụ,* and by the misbehaviour of men. *Agwụ* is ambivalent and unpredictable and its actions can be constructive or destructive. In its destructive form *Agwụ* causes confusion, *Mkpasa. Agwụ* can take the place of a person's *Chi* and misdirect the person. In such a case the person's energy and actions are misdirected and so his efforts will yield no fruit. Here the person's *Ikenga* cannot be effective and the person cannot achieve material success. On the other hand, if a person's *Chi* is undisturbed by *Agwụ,* his energy and actions will be well directed and integrated, and his efforts will yield maximum dividends. Here his *Ikenga* is effective.

Nri people do not tolerate the mystical conflict generated by *Agwụ.* During the *Ọnwa Asatọ* of the Nri lunar calendar, the symbols of the forces that stop evil, called *Abanaba* and *Egbo,* are erected at the doors leading into compounds, to stop *Agwụ* in its destructive form, as well as other agents of confusion and violence, from gaining access to the homes and lives of people.

THE *IKENGA*: THE CULT OF INDIVIDUAL ACHIEVEMENTS AND ADVANCEMENT
The forces of dynamism and individualism characterized by the Igbo love of adventure and risk-taking are based on the ritual concepts of Nri theology. The *Ikenga* cult is the most widely distributed.

The *Ikenga* cult is the cult of the right hand, with which people make their livings, make savings, take titles, and bear the responsibilities of living in society.

Ikenga is doubly symbolic because it symbolizes the right hand which itself symbolizes the forces that control individual efforts, achievements and advancement.

When a man dies his *Ikenga* is split into two during his mortuary rites and thrown outside. It then becomes ordinary wood. The owner has ceased to exist in human form. He played his role when he was alive. Now dead, he ceases to have a human personality.

THE *IKENGA* AND SOCIAL CHANGE

Today only traditional Igbo men have ritualized *Ikenga*. Some Igbo élite, out of a desire to uphold tradition, keep *Ikenga* images in their homes, but *Ikenga* has lost its mystical significance to them. Many people nowadays do not know about *Ikenga*.

The concept of *Ikenga* however still pervades Igbo attitudes towards life, especially towards the notion of individual effort. Igbo children are taught to use their right hands in eating, serving kola-nuts and drinks, and handing things to people. They are discouraged from using the left hand except for toilet purposes and removing dirt. Children are socialized to be independent within a communal context and they are discouraged from begging or hanging on others. They are also encouraged to work hard and to be industrious in whatever they are doing.

At a social gathering a person greets his equals by crossing right hands in mid-air, *Ina Aka*. This symbolic Igbo greeting is an acknowledgement of achievement.

In the different fields of human endeavour Igbo men work very hard, with the stubbornness of a ram, to get to the top. They look on almost everything as a status symbol: church marriages, educational qualifications, owning houses, cars and property, belonging to different associations, and holding important jobs.

Nowadays, however, Igbo men are no longer content with these modern status symbols only. Many of them are taking the traditional titles, especially the *Ọzọ* title, though this is frowned upon by some of the Christian sects as heathen practice.

Title-taking is an expression of the Igbo concept of individual effort and achievement. To suppress this urge will be to destroy the dynamic aspect of Igbo personality, and will generate unnecessary conflict and unrest. It should be a major concern of those administering the Igbo peoples to evolve ways of directing and canalizing these personality forces into constructive directions in order to generate progress and advancement in the area.

BIBLIOGRAPHY

SECTION I

Works consulted

DURKHEIM, E. *The Elementary Forms of the Religious Life*, translated by J. W. Swain (New York: Collier, 1961)

EVANS-PRITCHARD, E. E. 'The Meaning of Sacrifice among the Nuer', *J.R.A.I.* (1954), 84

FORTES, M. '*Pietas* in ancestor worship', *J.R.A.I.* (1961), 91

GOODY, J. R. *Death, Property and the Ancestors* (London: Tavistock; Stanford, California: Stanford University Press, 1962)

—— 'The mother's brother and the sister's son in West Africa', *J.R.A.I.* (1959), 89

LOISY, A. F. *Essai historique sur la sacrifice* (Paris: 1920)

Suggestions for further reading

ARINZE, F. (Bishop) *Sacrifice in Ibo Religion* (Ibadan: Ibadan University Press, 1970)

COLSON, E. 'Ancestral Spirits and Social Structure among the Plateau Tonga', in *Cultures and Societies of Africa*, S. and P. Ottenberg (eds.) (New York: Random House, 1960)

FORDE, D. 'Yakö Funeral Ceremonies', in *Essays on the Ritual of Social Relations*, M. Gluckman (ed.) (Manchester: Manchester University Press, 1962)

FORTUNE, R. *Manus Religion* (London: Oxford University Press, 1936)

TYLOR, E. B. *Primitive Culture* (London: Murray, 1871)

SECTION II

Note

The material used in this chapter is drawn from my fieldwork notes.

Suggestions for further reading

BRADBURY, R. E. 'Ezomo's *Ikegobo* and the Benin Cult of the hand', in *Benin Studies*, P. Morton-Williams (ed.), (London: Oxford University Press, 1973)

ONWUEJEOGWU, M. A. 'The Political Organization of Nri, South-Eastern Nigeria' (Chapter 3), M.Phil. thesis (London University, 1974)

CHAPTER 22

Some Patterns of Thought

I *An Analysis of Myth: the Hopi of North America*

The Hopi Indians who live in villages in north-east Arizona had a population of 5000 around 1927. The oldest of the villages is Oraibi which is supposed to have been founded in the twelfth century. Each village is politically independent, having its own chiefs each assigned to the conduct of independent ceremonials and rituals. They are agriculturalists, living in a country where long periods of drought are common; this causes constant anxiety.

Their social and political organization is such that they prefer kin and clan ties to village or tribal unity. The chiefs are peace-makers. Each settlement is faced with the ever-present threat of collapse due to instability and lack of adequate cohesion.

The lack of rain, problems due to crop failure, internal fission and the high frequency of illness and death, combine to make the whole cosmos a big challenge to their existence.

Each village has to carry out an annual rite under the head man of the village. Also each clan has its ritual objects and appoints its own officers. Ceremonies and rituals take place in underground chambers called *kivas*. There are between two and eight *kivas* in each Hopi village. Qualified men officiate in these *kivas*. Members of each *kiva* work or play together; thus the *kivas* function both as churches and club houses.

The village is organized into secret societies, each of which is responsible for the performance of a single ceremony. Children are first initiated into the *Katcina* cult, then later into other various societies. All major rituals last for nine days. The first eight days are devoted to esoteric exercises held in the *kivas* and the ninth day is used for public dancing. Celebrants must observe taboos forbidding them to eat salt and fats, or to have sexual intercourse four days prior to, during, and four days after the ritual.

The Hopi believe in the continuity of life after death. This is made clear in their myth which recounts the emergence of mankind from an underground home on to the surface of the earth. Life in the underground world is pictured as a replica of life on earth. There the dead grow the same crops and live the same life as people here, although they differ in that they do not possess the same solid bodies, wear material clothes, and eat like the people of this world. They can also float in the sky like clouds and bring rain, which is one of their chief concerns. A witch introduced the first death. But even with death, the dead and living were in constant and easy communication. Later, a mischievous *coyote* threw a stone over the *kivas'* opening and blocked the passage leading to the underworld. However, the spirits of the dead do occasionally visit the living.

The people did not emerge out of the underground world all alone; they came out with deities who were their friends called *Katcinas*. Whenever the Hopi settled down and planted crops the *Katcinas* performed the rain dances. The Hopi were

254

attacked by their enemies who killed the *Katcinas*. Their souls returned to the underworld where they mingled with the other spirits. The myth goes on to narrate how the *Katcinas* left their masks, costumes and other paraphernalia behind. The Hopi, missing their good friends and in the hope of retaining some of the benefits they had bestowed, established the *Katcina* cult, in which they wear sacred paraphernalia and attempt to bring down rain by impersonating the gods.

A wide range of variations and innovations is permitted within the *Katcina* complex, and there is also an open and closed season for *Katcina* events. Masked impersonation is permitted only between the months of November and June. During the other part of the year the *Katcinas* are supposed to remain in the underworld.

At Oraibi, *Katcina* activities begin in late November, when activities in the *kivas* are carried on in an atmosphere of conviviality. In February the major ritual is performed which involves the secret growing of bean and corn in highly heated *kivas*. Before the end of the ceremony the fresh sprouts are distributed to the people both as a mimetic device to promote good crops and to prove the secret society's supernatural powers which enable it to grow food in winter.

During the months of May and June the *Katcina* dances are held outdoors. They are usually sponsored by people who have just recovered from illnesses and others who wish to celebrate events such as a child's birthday.

Other rituals are those of the solar and tribal initiations. In the solar ceremonies the Grey and Blue Flute societies assemble to give offerings and prayers to the sun at the solstices. The Snake and Antelope societies hold their rituals biennially in mid-August. The Snake societies collect snakes which are baptized in the *kivas*; they are used for public ceremonies and finally released at shrines with prayers for rain, crops and good health. The Snake and Antelope ceremonies are not focused around a single theme but include several rites concerned with rain, crops, the relation between the dead and the living, war and sun worship.

An adolescent is expected to go through the tribal initiation ceremony before marriage. This is held in November. It marks the passage from boyhood to adulthood. The performance is observed by four societies. Initiates are made to behave like immature birds for the first four days. On the fourth day the spirits of the dead are invited to visit the village and to participate in the ceremony. That night the initiates are spiritually 'killed' and are 'reborn' as men. Each initiate receives a new name and disowns his boyhood name. The various parts of this ceremony serve to dramatize the myth of the emergence from the underworld and the continuity of life after death. Two of the societies perform actions designed to stimulate fertility and germination, and the actions of the other two are concerned with war and hunting. The initiates are taught the secrets of the other world and the stories connected with the tribe's origin.

Another rite called the *Soyer* rite is only performed by those who have undergone tribal initiation and enlisted in the *Wumwutian* society. This rite occurs at the time of the winter solstice in December, and its aim is to speed the sun on its northward course.

Women are allowed to take part in some of the men's rituals and ceremonies. But they also have their own feminine societies. The women's rites parallel the men's. They are also owned by particular class and are performed partly in *kivas* and partly in public.

It is possible to isolate the chief characteristics of myths. First, a myth is a narrative of events; this trait distinguishes myth from cosmological ideas. Secondly, a myth has a sacred quality which is communicated in a symbolic form; this distinguishes myth from legend and folktales. Thirdly, some of the events and the objects that occur in myth are not really found in our world; this differentiates myth from history. Fourthly, the narrative refers to origins, transmutations and transformations in dramatic form. Since every culture has myths, I shall examine the work of some leading exponents of myth.

Frazer and Tylor consider myth to be a form of explanation. Muller and Cassirer regard myth as a form of symbolic statement that reflects a type of thought. Freud treats myth as an expression of the unconscious, a kind of daydream. Durkheim sees myth from its functional aspect of creating and maintaining social solidarity. Malinowski sees myth as a charter that sanctions social institutions. Edmund Leach treats it as a form of symbolic statement about social structure. Lévi-Strauss sees it as a device of mediating contradictions or oppositions. Cohen sees the function of myth as that which 'anchors the present in the past' and so provides 'a point of reference in the past beyond which one need not go'.

Further examination of these opinions will help to elucidate what kind of explanation can be given to Hopi myth and other myths, with special reference to African myths.

Malinowski holds the view that rituals, ceremonies and social organization are usually regarded as the results of mythical events. Myth is therefore a warrant or a charter, and often also a practical guide to the activities with which it is connected. He maintains that myth does not necessarily explain, but it validates. Hopi myth and cosmological ideas fit in with these theories. But it seems that their myth and ritual, as well as their cosmological ideas, also seek to explain some natural phenomena. This theory has been propounded by Dr. Kaberry, although she does not specify the kind of explanatory value that can be attributed to myths. She simply says: 'Myths do in part provide an explanation of certain phenomena for the native and also have a relevance for him in relation to the present.' Professor Forde pointed out that the limitations of knowledge makes primitive technological people tend to seek an explanation of 'why a particular chain of events should occur to particular people at a particular time'. But the Hopi material shows that the explanatory value is more important than this. The secret growing of beans and corn in the heated *kivas* in the *Katcina* cult shows that the Hopi have found out the scientific truth that heat is vital for germination, thus establishing beyond doubt why crops do not grow in winter. But instead of using this explanation in order to explore the possibility of growing winter crops, it is diverted to the reaffirmation of their old belief. Thus by a ritual 'experiment' the natural order is empirically explained, but the explanation is used symbolically to reaffirm the supernatural order which the elders and chiefs manipulate to maintain a sense of order and control in their social order.

The Hopi fully realize that clouds cause rain, and yet they still call clouds *Katcina* spirits. When there is a drought, the Hopi resort to rituals to appease the cosmic spirits. The Hopi impersonator gives a ray of hope to his Hopi audience by providing a type of symbolic explanation.

Leach suggests that the models that people have of their own society are expressed in myth and ritual. What is striking about the Hopi cosmological ideas and myth is that the model they create is simply a replica, a picture of their own society. The Hopi have avoided any idealization. Death is not regarded as a loss to the society; on the contrary, a dead person goes to the underworld, and as a spirit can be counted upon to provide rain. Leach also suggests that myth is the 'counterpart of ritual and that myth implies ritual and ritual implies myth, they are one and the same', but this does not seem to apply to the Hopi. The Hopi rituals are seasonal and are only allowed to be performed at certain times of the year, between November and June, while the myths can be recounted at any time of the year. Myths are not sacred, but the rituals are. Furthermore, not every aspect of the myths is regarded as important, and not every aspect appears in rituals. Thus not every aspect of their ritual has a myth.

Firth followed Malinowski's views about the effects of religious belief and practices on the individual. The Hopi religion emphasizes in rituals the function of the individual, who by impersonating spirits is converted from man to spirit. In this way he is able to secure for himself a meaningful view of the universe. Thus he applies cosmological ideas to resolve the puzzles and contradiction in his physical and social universe.

A most dramatic approach in the study of myth is that put forward by Lévi-Strauss, who has stated that myth is language functioning on a special level. Every myth is structurally reducible to a formula of the type A:B::X:Y, that is as A is to B so is X to Y, and the main function is to mediate 'contradictions' and 'oppositions'. Following Lévi-Strauss's method Hopi myth is attempting to resolve the contradictions of life and death, and rain and drought, by focusing on the relationship between the interchangeable individual characters in the segments of the myth.

Hopi myth does have some explanatory values. The rituals which enact some of the myths are real experiments into the validity of natural law. But on the other hand the Hopi also see the cosmic order as fully under the control of spiritual forces that can only be influenced through the drama and symbolism of rituals and myths.

II *The Context of Witchcraft: the Azande of Central Africa*

The Azande, who are of Negro stock, live on the Nile–Congo divide in Central Africa. Those in the southern Sudan live in savannah forest, while those near the Congo live on the threshold of the tropical rain forest. They are cultivators of eleusine, maize, manioc, groundnuts, etc., and they also hunt, fish and collect wild fruits, roots and insects. In addition they are famous as smiths, potters, wood-carvers and in several other crafts. Many of these arts and crafts are seasonal occupations usually associated with magical rituals and the notion of witchcraft.

The Azande are split into a number of kingdoms, each founded by princes who have carved out small domains for themselves. A kingdom is divided into provinces, administered by a king's younger brothers and sons and some wealthy commoners. Thus the society is stratified into classes: that of the aristocrats who are of the royal class and the conquerors; and that of the commoners who are the conquered. Each king rules over a tribe and keeps peace within his kingdom. He has a court, an oracle and other machinery for enforcing peace and order. Each kingdom is separated from the next by a fringe of unpopulated bush.

The whole area is dotted with homesteads, but the dwellings of single families are often widely separated from each other by cultivated land and stretches of forest. This dispersal is necessary both for economic reasons and as a security measure against witchcraft which operates effectively at close quarters. A homestead is made up of a man, his wife or wives, children and his neighbours, who are generally related to him by bonds of kinship or marriage.

Evans-Pritchard recorded the inferiority of the women, but there is some evidence in his account that shows that whatever superiority men have over women, it is seriously challenged by custom and usage. For example, men are always concerned about their wives and family in the oracular seances. Women can end a family argument by briefly exposing a secret part of her body to her husband, which is considered evil. Women usually initiate divorces.

Communal life is fully expressed in the Azande political system rather than in their clan organization, which has become worse through migration and the development of the royal houses.

According to Evans-Pritchard, witchcraft is a supposedly psychic emanation from the witchcraft substance which is believed to cause injury to health and prosperity. The witchcraft substance is a material substance in the bodies of certain persons. It is discovered by autopsy in the dead and is supposed to be diagnosed by oracles in the living.

Witchcraft is inheritable, for it is transmitted unilineally from parent to child. Male witches transmit it to their sons only, while female witches transmit it to their daughters only. Thus if a man is accused of witchcraft, his close paternal kinsmen are suspected. If public opinion stamps the kin of a guilty man as witches, a post-mortem in which no witchcraft substance is discovered clears his paternal kin of suspicion. If, on the contrary, witchcraft substance is found in the stomach the paternal kin can go to the lengths of denying that the man was ever a member of the clan. They will say that he was a bastard and that the mother conceived him in adultery; if the mother is alive she may be forced to confess. It is also believed that some people have inactive witchcraft, which can be activated by malice.

Members of the ruling class are not accused of witchcraft. Although it is believed secretly that some are witches, nobody ever consults the oracles about them. This may be because the ruling class controls the major oracle for detecting witches. The rich and the court nobility are also immune from witchcraft. Only neighbours who live together often accuse one another of witchcraft, because only neighbours can envy one another or contrive evil to harm each other; and only those who are in close contact do quarrel. Thus women only accuse women and men accuse men. It is suspicious for a woman to accuse a man of witchcraft, and vice versa. If it does happen, which is rare, attempted adultery may be suspected; and the witchcraft accusation may be dropped and damages for adultery demanded in the court.

A witch does not immediately kill his victim. If a man becomes suddenly ill he may be sure of sorcery, and not witchcraft, for the effects of witchcraft lead to death by slow stages. When a person falls ill, first attempts are made to treat him with herbs; when this fails, a relative consults the oracle and finds out who is the witch who caused it. Names of suspects, who are usually people who have had quarrels with the victim, are placed before the oracle. Then an appeal is sent to the witch to desist. If the patient gets better the matter is closed; but if he dies the matter is sent to the prince who consults his oracle for confirmation; if it is in the affirmative, he grants the party authority to get compensation or vengeance by killing the witch.

The Azande believe that witchcraft tampers with individual security. They have several ways of finding out witchcraft, such as witch-doctors who locate witches during seances, the use of the poison oracle, the rubbing board oracle. These oracles are used in the royal courts and are indispensable pieces of equipment.

It is very important to point out that other sources of evil are recognized by the Azande, such as the witch-cats believed to be operated only by women, bad teeth, bad magic, some animals, and worst of all sorcery, which frightens even powerful kings.

14 *Wooden figure* (*Azande, Central Africa*)

At this stage it is necessary to examine the validity of Evans-Pritchard's social interpretations of witchcraft. Here are some quotations from his work.

> Thus a man who suffers a misfortune knows that he has been bewitched, and only then does he seek in his mind to find out who wishes him ill and might have bewitched him. . . . Hence, even a prince will sometimes accuse commoners of witchcraft, for his misfortunes must be accounted for and checked, even though those whom he accuses of witchcraft are not his enemies.

> In our society only certain misfortunes are believed to be due to the wickedness of other people. Disease or failure in economic pursuits are not thought by us to be injuries inflicted on us by other people. If a man is sick or his enterprises fail he cannot retaliate upon any one, as he can if his watch has been stolen or he has been assaulted. But in Zandeland all misfortunes are due to witchcraft, and all allow the person who has suffered loss to retaliate along prescribed channels in every situation because the loss is attributed to a person. In situations such as theft or adultery or murder by violence there is already in play a person who invites retaliation. If he is known he is sued in the court, if unknown he is pursued by punitive magic. When this person is absent notions of witchcraft provide an alternative object. Every misfortune supposes witchcraft, and every enmity suggests its author.

> We have seen how misfortunes are expressed in stereotyped idiom, and being attributed to persons. The feelings that accompany this action are also influenced by custom, which in harmony with Zande notions of witchcraft imposes anger rather than fear, resentment rather than resignation.

This theory of misfortune and frustration expressed and canalized in witchcraft does not cover the whole society, because the aristocrats and wealthy commoners are not involved in the practice. Also society has other ways of canalizing the fear of misfortune, one of which is sorcery, surprisingly described by Evans-Pritchard thus: 'The concept of sorcery appears to be redundant' – possibly an attempt to brush sorcery aside in order to allow himself to develop his theory of misfortune and frustration. The Azande in fact fear sorcery far more than they fear witchcraft. This may be partly due to the serious symptoms of sickness it produces, and partly to the absence of adequate machinery of control.

Marwick advocated a sociological approach to witchcraft. He treated Cewa witchcraft under two headings: as an index of social relations; as forces supporting the system of values. He says that competition will tend to occur between persons in a social relation if their relative statuses are not ascribed by the social structure, and that this competition will develop into tension and conflict. If the desire for the object or status competed for is intense and/or if the social structure does not eliminate or regulate the competition, this tension will tend to be projected into belief in witchcraft and subsequent conflicts. The weakness of this argument is that it does not say why particularly witchcraft is used in Cewa society, which has many other methods of expressing conflict.

His argument that Cewa belief in witchcraft tends to sustain the system of values, and so the social system, is cogent and needs no further elaboration. But he also tries to show how witchcraft accusations are related to tensions which are related to the lineage segmentation. For example, A believed that he was bewitched by his mother's sister's daughter. He later died and was succeeded by his mother's sister's son. Marwick's conclusion is that witchcraft is a means of rupturing a social relation when it has become unbearably tense and there is no other way of doing so, that is, witchcraft sustains the system it also tends to disrupt.

Nadel, in his comparative works on the Nupe and Gwari, Korengo and Mesakin, maintains that witchcraft accusations act as a releasing mechanism for tensions inherent in the system of social relations. He talks of child training and of the hostility between the sexes: 'The concrete hostilities are canalised in the sense that they are directed against a few scapegoats rather than against more numerous victims.' This theory of conflict does not fully explain the function of witchcraft. Other more turbulent societies with conflicts and hostilities do not have beliefs in witchcraft, and yet do not have other means either. Also other mechanisms of expressing hostility and conflicts do exist hand in hand with witchcraft beliefs. Hostility, and conflict are vague, rather undefined notions having a very wide range of meanings.

Paul Bohannan (in a paper on extra-processual events in Tiv political institutions) described witchcraft as above and beyond institutionalized political force and a result of subject–object confusion. This power the Tiv called *Tsav*, translatable as witchcraft power, and usable for good or for bad.

The Rev. H. Debrunner in his discussion of witchcraft in Ghana concluded: 'Witchcraft is only one of the ways in which the African reacts to his upsetting challenge . . . missionaries all over Africa are teaching a religion which puts out fear, but economic and social changes have so shattered tribal institutions and moral codes . . .' His explanation was based on the reaction due to change. But the Christian religion has put new fears into the Africans – the fear of everlasting punishment after death. Ghana has always been a changing society, and European contact really accelerated the changes. Reaction to European culture cannot explain witchcraft as an institution.

The main function of witchcraft belief in any society may be delineated. Every society, primitive or advanced in technology, has ideals set out for its members. These ideals are set out in legal or moral, written or unwritten codes. In England, for example, there is the legal code comprising the criminal, civil and common laws. If A kills B, he is punished for doing it, but if Z contrives in his mind or wants to kill D, it is not an offence because no one knows of it until he commits the offence or attempts to do so physically.

The Azande have conceptualized the ideal man in an ideal society, and no matter how diffused this concept is, their aim is to attain to it; if successful, harmony will obtain in the society. But man is weak and may never achieve this ideal. He either commits an offence openly or wishes to commit one. If he commits it openly and is caught he is punished accordingly. But what of a person who wishes or who plots to upset and disturb his neighbours, and so society? In most modern advanced technological societies it is not a crime to think evil of a neighbour without expressing it in action. But in some primitive technological societies it is anti-social to think evil of one's neighbour even without expressing it in action. Such a person deserves to be punished, because he is considered more dangerous than a person who comes out in the open to act. Such society feels itself too small and precious to tolerate animosity. Therefore all hidden animosities which are really inimical to relationships must be detected. There are several ways of detecting such 'crimes' and there are several ways of committing them. Witchcraft, sorcery, bad magic are just a few of the ways of expressing these 'crimes', while dreams, witch-doctors and oracles are methods of detecting them. These systems are further complicated by the religious concepts of the societies.

Thus in these societies wicked intentions may be regarded as 'crimes', which are expressed in several mystical idioms of which witchcraft is one. Such 'crimes' and 'criminals' are detected by using mystical instruments. Once found the criminals are brought to physical trial. Witchcraft is a symbolic machinery of upholding the morals and legal codes of a society at a mystical level. Some societies use it, others do not, while still others use other techniques. The Azande use not only witchcraft but also sorcery. Sorcery in Azande deals with specially hidden types of 'crimes' which witchcraft does not concern itself with. The analogy in an 'advanced' society is that detectives deal with ordinary crimes, while specialized detectives deal with the more obscure ones. Specialized detectives are not redundant, and neither is sorcery among the Azande. Witchcraft and sorcery among the Azande are serving the same purpose, but they differ in the degree of mystical and symbolic codes employed.

Since witchcraft belief is still prevalent in Africa and is changing in form and content, more work has to be done before its real character and nature are fully understood. But, at present, it is clear that it is a system of belief which may or may not have anything to do with reality and yet conditions the mind and behaviour of people.

BIBLIOGRAPHY

SECTION I
Works consulted

CASSIRER, E. *The Logic of the Humanities,* translated by C. S. Howe (New Haven: Yale University Press, 1961)

COHEN, P. S. 'Theories of Myth in Man', *J.R.A.I.* (1969), 4, 3

DURKHEIM, E. *The Elementary Forms of Religious Life,* translated by J. W. Swain (New York Collier; London: Allen & Unwin, 1961)

FIRTH, R. W. 'Religious Belief and Personal Adjustment', in *Essays on Social Organisation and Values* (London: Athlone Press, 1964)

FORDE, D. 'Hopi and Yuma in the American Descent,' in *Habitat, Economy and Society* (London: Methuen, 1964)

FORDE, D. (ed.) Introduction to *African Worlds* (London: Oxford University Press, 1954)

FRAZER, J. G. *Folklore in the Old Testament* (London: Macmillan 1918) Vol. 1

FREUD, S. *The Interpretation of Dreams,* translated by James Strachey (London: Allen & Unwin, 1955)

KABERRY, P. M. 'Myths and Ritual: Some Recent Theories', *Bulletin of the Institute of Classical Studies* (1957)

LEACH, E. R. Introduction to *The Political Systems of Highland Burma* (London: G. Bell, 1954)

LÉVI-STRAUSS, C. 'The Structural Study of Myths' in *Structural Anthropology,* translated by C. Jacobson and B. G. Schoepf (London: Allen Lane, Penguin Press, 1963)

MALINOWSKI, B. 'Myth in Primitive Psychology,' in *Magic, Science and Religion and Other Essays* (Glencoe, ill.: Free Press; London: Allen & Unwin, 1948)

STEWARD, J. S. 'Notes on Hopi Ceremonies in Their Initiatory Form in 1927–28', *American Anthropology* (1931), 33

TITIEV, M. *Old Oraibi,* Papers of the Peabody Museum (1944), 22, 1

TYLOR, E. B. *Primitive Culture* (London: Murray, 1871)

SECTION II
Works consulted and suggestions for further reading

BOHANNAN, P. 'Extra-Processual Events in Tiv Political Institutions', *American Anthropologist* (1958), 60

DEBRUNNER, H. W. *Witchcraft in Ghana* (Kumasi: 1959)

EVANS-PRITCHARD, E. E. *Witchcraft, Oracles and Magic among the Azande* (London: Oxford University Press, 1937)

GLUCKMAN, M. 'The Logic in Witchcraft', in *Custom and Conflict in Africa* (Oxford: Blackwell, 1970)

MARWICK, M. J. 'The Social Context of Cewa Witchcraft', *Africa* (1937), 22

NADEL, S. F. 'Witchcraft in Four African Societies', *American Anthropology* (1952), 54

WILSON, M. 'Witch Beliefs and Social Structure', *American Journal of Sociology* (1951), 56

CHAPTER 23

Rituals of Social Relationships

I *The Sociological Significance of Initiation Ceremonies: the Bambuti Pygmies of the Central Ituri Forest (Zaire)*

The Bambuti are pygmies of the Central Ituri Forest. They are nomadic hunters and gatherers. They practise communal hunting with nets, which necessitates the cooperation of a fairly large group.

Their neighbours are Negroes who live in the open country at the fringe of the forests. Each pygmy hunter is attached to a certain Negro 'patron'. In the eye of the Negro the pygmy hunts for him and in return receives products from his patron's plantation. The pygmies do not regard their attachment in the same way. They change their affiliation to patrons at will and easily, and since they can do without the plantain they get from them, the attachment can be considered to be a very loose alliance.

The Bambuti pygmies have adopted the Negro languages and customs; of these, the initiation and circumcision ceremonies are of great importance.

The initiation ceremony *Nkumbi* is organized and supervised exclusively by the Negroes. The pygmies are only spectators in a ceremony in which their children are the initiates. Boys are selected from both the pygmies and Negroes. The pygmy children are sponsored by their fathers' Negro 'patrons'. The ages of the children range from nine to twelve years. The circumcision is performed by Negro operators with the same knife. During the long period of seclusion they are taught various aspects of Negro tribal life, its history, folklore, and songs, and they are subjected to various ordeals and privations. They are forbidden to eat certain food and told to avoid certain things and certain meals.

One of the ceremonies (recorded by Turnbull) is described below. The preparations are marked by the making of an extensive collection of food and palm-wine in the Negro village where it is stored. Pygmies from neighbouring villages come in and occupy the extreme edge of the village clearing. Dancing among the Negroes starts in the evening. On the same day the initiation dance is organized. The dancers imitate the jerky movements of a bird and act like spirits.

Masked dancers parade round the villages driving the children and women into the houses, and then the initiates are secluded and housed separately in a site between the village and the river.

The Negroes take all this very seriously, while the pygmies ridicule the whole idea in secret. They accept that the children are made strong by the initiation ordeals, but cannot see it from the ritual point of view as the Negroes do. At times they even protest when they think that the Negro officers become unduly harsh to the children. The first integration ritual was marked by the initiates going into the villages, breaking up groups of young girls, and lashing them with whips.

After the ceremony of the 'net blessing' which the pygmies regard as a farce, a hunting expedition is organized by the fathers of the initiates, in which they are allowed to participate. At this point there is considerable argument between the pygmy parents and the Negro officers as to whether it is right or wrong for the initiates to go hunting. On this matter of procedure, the pygmy parents are allowed to have their own way.

The last ordeal called the 'bow and arrows' ordeal is performed. The initiation camp is burnt down and the initiates are washed in the river: purification. The last ceremony of tattooing is performed in the village, during which the initiates are presented with gifts by the general public. With this the initiation ends.

The initiated Negro boys become entitled to certain privileges in their society. The pygmy boys seem to have undergone no change of status. Their relationships with other pygmies and with Negroes seem to be the same as before, except that when they are in the Negro village they speak more familiarly with the Negroes and enter their 'baraza' more freely.

The chief characteristics of the Negro initiation are as follows. It is a period of a large distribution of food and drink; also of gift giving and receiving, and of mutual cooperation between peoples of two different cultural backgrounds. The Negroes, whose custom it is, take it as a 'sacred' duty in which every item must be fully adhered to, while the pygmies look at it as a 'farce' from the ritual point of view. There is always considerable disagreement between the Negroes and pygmies over procedures involved or over the significance of the ritual and the value and meaning of the initiation. The stages of separation, transition and incorporation (as postulated by Van Gennep) can be distinguished.

It has been pointed out that the pygmies take the Negro initiation lightly. However, they are more interested in 'initiation' into their own associations, the *Lusumba* and the *Alima*, exclusively for males and females respectively.

The Negro initiation does not qualify the pygmy boys for membership in the *Lusumba*. To be a member one has to be a hunter. Entry into the *Lusumba* association depends on a combination of physical growth and power. A boy must be big enough to hunt alone and kill real game such as antelope. When he has performed his first kill he is admitted into the *Lusumba* association. The feat is usually accomplished at the age of fourteen or so. Once a member, he is fully fledged, for within the association there is no hierarchy. There is no ritual to be performed before entry. Every one plays the same part in the meetings, save one who is chosen to play the *Lusumba* horn. The choice falls on the best performer present regardless of age or other qualities.

The association is called out in times of crisis such as bad hunting, illness and death. It is vested with the power to communicate with the God of the Forest, who is the source of all good and bad in the pygmy world. The means of communicating with the God is by special songs sacred to the association, sung by initiates only, and echoing far into the forest with the sound of the *Lusumba* horn. The God is roused to mediate by the repetition of his name and recitation of his qualities.

All adult women are members of the *Alima* association and all come to the meetings. They communicate with the forest God by means of special songs sacred to the *Alima*. The *Alima* is called out on occasions of major concern to women, such as birth, arrival at puberty, marriage and death.

Initiation into the *Alima* is more formal than initiation into the *Lusumba*. Girls when they reach puberty are secluded in a special hut adapted for that purpose. They remain there under the care of one of the old women for about a month between their first and second periods. While in the hut they are taught all the things a woman ought to know and the *Alima* songs. A girl may invite her lover to visit her, but he has to fight his way through all the women of the camp, who

15 *Bronze 'anklet'* (*Igbo-Ukwu, Nigeria*)

gather around the hut to protect it. The lover is supported by the menfolk and a 'battle' is staged between the *Alima* and the *Lusumba*. If the lover succeeds he enters the hut and meets his girl, who may or may not sleep with him.

The *Lusumba* and *Alima* have the following characteristics. They are both religious associations, concerned chiefly with the 'supernatural' and with the ordering of man's relationship with the spiritual world. They both lack the elaborate ceremonies characteristic of the Negro initiation, *Nkumbi*. Entry into the *Alima* has some features of the initiation ceremony, such as the separation, transition and incorporation. The *Lusumba* is a religious association whose entry qualification is killing game, and whose internal structure and organization reflect the non-stratified pygmy society. The two associations reflect the dichotomy between male and female in pygmy society. The conflict, antagonism and harmony between the sexes are 'ritually' dramatized in the rites of the *Alima*.

The initiation ceremony shows two peoples between whom contact is inevitable but whose fundamental differences in values are expressed in their religious beliefs.

Why do the pygmies subject themselves to the initiation of the Negroes and yet do not accept it as a standard in their forest culture? Turnbull maintains that its most important function is: 'the establishment of common values which enable neighbouring tribes to move within each other's society'. He attempts to explain the relationship between the pygmies and the Negroes by referring to history and legend, according to which the Negroes invaded the Bambuti pygmies' forest and used them as guides, scouts and mercenary soldiers in the fight against other Negro immigrants, and also as agents during the time of the ivory trade. After the end of these wars and the advent of control of the ivory trade, the pygmies became redundant and returned to their nomadic existence. They have ceased to rely on the Negroes for food, but the old relationship is kept up in the patron–client relationship. It may be suggested that the initiation ceremony is a symbolic expression of the patron–client relationship.

Here in fact what we are dealing with is the *rite de passage*. Van Gennep gave a general interpretation of it. He said that its function is to reduce the disturbances caused in social relations or changes of status. Gluckman says that *rites de passage* help to differentiate roles in a society where people play many roles. The rituals provide mystical sanctions which help to check the spread of conflict inherent in this sort of society. He suggests that people believe in a causal linkage between the social and the natural order. Thus a disturbance in the social order generates a disturbance in the natural order. To avoid this the natural order is assured by ceremonials in which the social order is re-enacted and symbolically adhered to.

Horton postulates that in Africa each corporate group of people is defined in terms of personal beings who are supposed to support the activities of their members and keep the group going. Since membership of the group implies being under the control of these beings, it will also involve the procedure of being put under their control which is carried out by rituals on the occasions of change of status.

Meyer Fortes, in developing the full implications of Van Gennep's ideas, holds that initiation ceremonies are 'the means of divesting a person of his status as a child in the domestic domain and of investing him with the status of actual or potential citizen in the politico-jural domain'.

The scholars cited above all agree on at least one point, that all initiation ceremonies (*rites de passage*) mark a change of status. In fact this is only true of one type of initiation ceremony in particular societies; for example, Meyer Fortes had the Tallensi in mind, Horton the Ijo.

If one were to accept Meyer Fortes' view *in toto*, it would be difficult to explain the *Nkumbi* initiation, because pygmies regard it as farcical, and pygmy boys gain nothing in their own society. Could one call the pygmy world the 'domestic domain' and the Negro world the 'politico-jural domain' in order to make Fortes' thesis workable? The pygmies have their own 'quasi-initiation' into the *Lusumba* association, but this is ritual and its concern is to reflect and cater for the problems of the hunt, health, death and the environment.

Another problem which is not solved by Fortes' theory is why the pygmy boys undergo the same initiation ceremony as the Negro boys, since they operate in different societies. Why should the Negro boys undergo the 'net blessing' and hunting ordeal when their adult occupation is agriculture? Hence as stated earlier, this type of initiation ceremony can only be explained in terms of its symbolic significance.

The pygmy women initiation ceremony does seem to fall in line with Meyer Fortes' theory. But it is difficult to demarcate, in the lives of pygmy girls, which is the 'domestic domain' and which is the 'politico-jural domain'. Re-phrasing Fortes' remark might make it more acceptable: 'Initiation ceremonies are the means of divesting a person of his status as a 'child' and of investing him with the status of actual or potential citizen.' This still leaves some problems unsolved, such as the lack of initiation among the male pygmies; and yet there is a definite changing over from a 'child's' status to an 'adult' status.

The significance of the pygmy initiation is their concern over the spirits; it offers them an explanation for the wonders of life – living, growing and dying – of which change of status is only a part. It is therefore important to conclude that the initiation ceremony as a social phenomenon is multi-functional. It can be a means of changing status or a symbolic method of explaining the nature of certain types of relationships or dramatizing the life cycle of a group of individuals.

II *Religious Movements that Sanction Politico-Economic Aspirations: the Zulu of South Africa*

Millenarianism is characteristic of all known world religions, except perhaps Hinduism where the caste system is inhibiting. The term 'millenarianism' has been used by Worsley to describe those movements which expect, and prepare for, the coming of a period of 'supernatural or natural bliss' in the distant future or even here and now. In Melanesia the bliss is to come in the form of goods from their ancestors; these goods are called 'cargo' in the local pidgin English.

Millenarianism is active or passive. In the active movement the millennium is expected to come soon. The people therefore occupy themselves in preparing for the coming of the blissful day, and so its procedures are marked by great emotional outbursts. In the other type the millennium is regarded as a remote event and the movement is usually passive in character and non-revolutionary. The people are resigned and dedicate themselves to their beliefs and expectations of future salvation either in this world or in the world to come. In this category falls the religion of many people, but the germ of active millenarianism is there. The term 'cargo cult' to describe one sort of millenarianism is a misnomer, because the 'cargo' is never worshipped. It is expected to come either from the ancestors or by spiritual intervention. In the former case, therefore, the religion remains virtually an ancestor cult, using new techniques gained from Christian rituals and material goods obtained from Europeans in order to placate their ancestors to come and bring the 'cargo'.

Here the Zulu, who are agriculturalists and pastoralists, will be discussed. (For a general description of the Zulu, see Chapter 5, Section II.) They have adopted the patrilineal principle in their social organization, although they were once organized into a centralized kingdom. One of their greatest rulers was Chaka, under whom the kingdom was run on a military basis with an age-set regimental system and barrack life for those in active service. Long before the Zulus had come into effective contact with Europeans, the society had undergone various changes. Chaka's war and the social changes had a great influence upon the society. These influences are strongly imprinted upon the Zulus' attitudes towards the past, and their concepts of independence and leadership.

Zulu religion emphasizes the existence of a supreme God as well as other lesser supernatural beings, but the ritual which permeates their daily lives is the ancestor cult. The ancestors are believed to be the guardian spirits of their descendants which is how they validate their principle of agnation. All major human misfortunes are attributed to the ancestors' discontent and they are appeased in various ways, among which sacrifices are the most important. The spirits of the chiefs and royal ancestors are more important than those of commoners. They are the source of communal well-being and prosperity. The royal ancestors keep in touch with the Zulu people largely through the king whose principal function is to be the head priest in the various rites. The king was formerly the only great medicine man and also the greatest rain maker.

Ancestors usually express their wishes through diviners who are expected to be possessed by spirits. These diviners are important in social life. When they become 'troublesome' Chaka did all he could to eliminate them by execution. However they have emerged as 'prophets' in the new religious movements.

The Zulu nation became unsettled as a result of rearrangements in their social structure, the movements of people and the constant wars. Later the British defeated them and handed them to the South African whites, who governed them as a subject people. Thus, having been a conquering race, they were subjected to humiliation – a thing the Zulu never forget.

The new masters, the white South Africans, believe that the black South Africans, including the Zulu, are born to be water-carriers and wood-cutters for the whites, that white and black are not created equals. In order to achieve and maintain this the whites employ a vast battery of political, economic, social and religious instruments. At first they supported their principle by referring to biblical texts; the Dutch Reformed Church has become the chief bulwark and exponent of the policy of racial segregation.

Other religions, such as the Catholic, Baptist and Anglican, do not fully support the policy, although they tacitly practise segregation, since laws were passed by the government to enforce it. There is racial discrimination in the appointment to positions of leadership in the higher orders of the churches, which is resented by Africans. Furthermore, the different denominations are in constant doctrinal rivalry with one another, as well as not practising what they preach.

The attitudes of the churches are fully comprehended by the Zulu – at least in their own way. Some of them feel that the Christian churches are the white men's churches. It is not surprising that Zulu religious life, which had already undergone changes as a result of Chaka's innovations, has become still more chaotic as a result of the new Christian doctrines.

Political, economic and social freedom has been denied the Zulu. They have been prevented from participating in the country's political life, moved into reserves and restricted from entering certain areas or using freely the public services, such as buses, trains, lavatories and shops. Some areas and shops are clearly marked: 'For Europeans only', 'For blacks only'. Laws have been passed excluding them from the ownership of land in certain areas. Thus ten million people own and live on one-tenth of the country's land. The population has increased, but the supply of land has remained almost constant. The Zulu have been forced into the factories and gold mines, where again laws forbid them from holding certain jobs and limit their earning capacity. They are forbidden to form effective labour movements, so that they are left at the mercy of their employers.

The impact has been far-reaching. The old tribal life is now restricted to the reserves; the movements of people have again disarranged the social structure. In the reserves a new system of administration has been introduced in which the Zulu play a secondary role in decision-making. Land for pasture and farming has been limited. These rapid changes have taken place within a generation. Tension has grown high, but each revolt or expression of strain has been ruthlessly suppressed by the government.

The only escape route remaining is through religion. The frustrations and tensions are expressed in the new religious movement which has sprung up during the long period of these social changes.

As early as 1872, attempts were being made within various tribes to found a national or tribal religious organization or movement distinct from denominational or inter-tribal churches. These breakaway tribal churches were supported by tribal chiefs. One of them was the Tembu Church, founded by Nehemail Tile, who was one of the prominent African leaders in the Wesleyan Mission Church. The cause of his secession was not only his opposition to European control but also his desire to make the church adaptable to Tembu tribal ideals. For the latter reason he made the paramount chief of Tembu its head.

The major break from the Wesleyan Church came in 1892 when Makona, a Wesleyan minister, opposed what he regarded as racial segregation in the church's leadership. This new church appealed to many tribes in the Rand, and it was named the 'Ethiopian Church'. Several secessionist groups gained inspiration from Ethiopia and from American Negroes. As segregation laws were intensified, and as the political and economic situation deteriorated, new churches sprang up.

By the beginning of the twentieth century, two main types of churches could be distinguished: the Zulu Congregational Church and its offshoots, and the African Congregational Churches and their offshoots. As regards Christian doctrine, some of the new churches ran parallel with the mother churches, while others developed in an opposite direction. These were two main types of churches, the 'Ethiopian' and the 'Zionist'.

The Ethiopian independent churches seceded from the mission churches chiefly on racial grounds. Other churches in their turn seceded from the Ethiopian independent churches for quite different reasons. The issues at stake were leadership, prestige, power and church property. Generally the Ethiopian types of churches have adopted the Protestant mission churches' interpretation of the Bible, but their slogan is 'Africa for Africans'. They have also incorporated the Zulu ranking system and some of their rituals.

The other group, the 'Zionist', have their historical roots in 'Zion City', Illinois, USA. Theologically, however, the 'Zionists' are Bantu movements, with healing, speaking tongues, purification rites and taboos as their main articles of faith. Their attitude towards the heritage of the white missions is different from that of the Ethiopian churches, because they maintain that the whites are ritually unclean. They oppose the Zulu diviners but adopt in full the old Zulu religion. They have recast the whole doctrine of the Bible. The Zionist churches have become the bridge across which Africans are brought back to the old Bantu religion whence they once started.

The sociological implications of the development of these churches can best be inferred from their fissiparous tendencies, the nature of their leadership and followers, and their systems of worship.

By 1945 there were over 800 independent churches in South Africa with up to 40 000 adherents in the biggest ones and only seven in the smallest ones.

It has already been pointed out that the chief cause of splitting from the mission churches is racial discrimination and the desire to be free from the white men's institutions. Why, then, are there further splits in the independent churches? Here are three important factors involved: leadership, the distribution of church property, and most important (which Sundkler fails to point out), the 'inherent' nature of Zulu social organization which is incorporated into the new religious movements.

The Zulu notion of leadership is based on Chaka's model: leaders of military regiments hierarchically arranged under the king. This system was adopted by the new churches. Each church has a chief leader, and under him are other leaders who are almost independent in their activities. Apart from these leaders, there are male and female prophets who can at any time claim divine inspiration and appeal for the purification of the church. This generally means the expulsion or disciplining of one or more leaders. The chief leader lacks any effective mechanism for controlling the other leaders or even the prophets. And serious friction, and there are some, ends in a split.

The South African government has allowed these churches to grow, realizing that they act as a safety-valve. It only intervenes when it is thought to be wise. Some of the churches are allowed to own land and build on it. Each new church, therefore, wants to be recognized by the government because recognition means owning land, very scarce wealth to black South Africans. Land, money, cattle are also obtainable from chiefs who support a particular church, and money and other goods can be obtained from members. For the leaders the church is therefore one of the easiest ways of accumulating wealth. Quarrels over the allocation and distribution of this wealth lead to litigations and division.

Another reason for the splits in the new churches is the introduction of Zulu social organization, that is, the Zulu system of marriage, the patrilineal system, the notion of the role of women and tribal differentiation, 'tribalism'. The question whether a church should adopt polygamy or monogamy has often been a deciding factor for or against secession. Some leaders may wish to adhere to the Christian precepts, while others may want their church to adopt polygamy. The latter support their desire by quoting from the Old Testament, maintaining that the New Testament is a white man's addition. This theological dispute usually ends in a split, and thus we see the old social order in direct conflict with the new.

The leaders of most of the churches wish to make the leadership of the church pass from father to son, adopting the patrilineal system if possible. Others might wish it to be elective; others, still, gained by merit and service. Here again the result may be a split, and here again, it is the old social order that comes into conflict with the new.

In the past the Zulu were a conquering people, domineering and proud. Other peoples who were once under the Zulu were not ready to accept a humble position. Splits are therefore inevitable in those churches where the leader fails to maintain a fair democratic balance between the Zulu and others.

The principle of lineage segmentation is mirrored in the organization of the churches. A hierarchy is built with segments under leaders linked upwards and downwards in the 'brotherhood' of Christ. Lineages and clans are represented in the churches. These become structurally the greatest weakness, combined with the churches' loose hierarchical ordering of its officials. Fission is easy once an ambitious leader emerges to take advantage of the structural weakness.

The most irritating thorn in the flesh of all the leaders is the position of women in the new churches. In the Zulu traditional religion women play an active part in the cult of the hoe and in 'spirit possession', and Chaka executed some of them to avoid a revolt. Now there is no Chaka, and the women have climbed to the pinnacle of authority in some of the churches as 'prophets' or 'sister ministers'. They make fission or even fusion easy.

Among the Zionist churches a completely new system of worship has been adopted. The coming of their ancestors to restore the old order of things is stressed, and the 'God of Africa', who is coming to redeem them from the whites, has been named. Some moderates preach that the whites have not followed the Bible properly because they have preached one thing and done the opposite, and so only blacks shall see the Kingdom of Heaven. Another feature of Zionist worship includes healing and purification, an emphasis on the whole concept of rebirth and a new morality. The social order is to be transformed by radical political and economic changes, but the new order must have a new morality.

The religious movements in South Africa are emotionally charged with political aspirations. They may be psychologically interpreted as a method of readjustment. They are also movements in which the political as well as the economic and social aspirations which are denied them are not only expressed but also symbolically achieved and experienced in the 'daydream' and 'make-believe' world of religion.

BIBLIOGRAPHY

SECTION I
Works consulted
VAN GENNEP, A. *The Rites of Passage*, translated by M. B. Vizedom and G. L. Caffee (Chicago: University of Chicago Press, 1961)
GLUCKMAN, M. (ed.) *Essays on the Ritual of Social Relations* (Manchester: Manchester University Press, 1963; New York: Humanities Press, 1963)
HORTON, R. 'Ritual Man in Africa', *Africa* (1964), 34, 2
TURNBULL, C. M. 'Initiation among the Bambuti Pygmies of the Central Ituri', *J.R.A.I.* (1957), 87

Suggestions for further reading
RICHARDS, A. I. *Chisungu: a Girl's Initiation Ceremony among the Bemba of Northern Rhodesia* (London: Faber, 1956)
VANSINA, J. 'Bushong Initiation', *Africa* (1955), 25, 2

SECTION II
Works consulted
CARTER, G. M. *The Politics of Inequality: South Africa since 1948* (London: Thames & Hudson, 1958)
SUNDKLER, B. G. M. *Bantu Prophets in South Africa* (London: Oxford University Press, 1948)
WORSLEY, P. *The Trumpet Shall Sound* (London: MacGibbon & Kee, 1957)

Suggestions for further reading
HOGBIN, H. J. *Social Change, with Special Reference to Melanesia* (London: C. A. Watts, 1959)
HUNTER, M. *Reaction to Conquest: the Effect of Contact with Europeans on the Pondo of South Africa* (London: Oxford University Press, 1961)
MALINOWSKI, B. *The Dynamics of Culture Change* (New Haven: Yale University Press, 1946)
WILSON, G. and H. *The Analysis of Social Change, Based on Observations in Central Africa* (Cambridge: Cambridge University Press, 1968)

EPILOGUE

The 'Faceless' versus the 'Face'

In 1968, Mr X, an Igbo man, told me the story which I recount here. It was a true story in which he was one of the *dramatis personae*. I have verified this story from others who were also participants and they confirmed it. The story is as follows.

1. IN 1925

Around 1925 when X was about ten years old and about fifteen years after the British and the missionaries were effectively established in the heart of Igbo land in Nigeria, there lived a woman called Mgbafo.

Mgbafo was a great lover of children. In the evening all the children of the big compound and other neighbouring ones always gathered in front of her house talking and exchanging views with her. She was loved by the children because she told them traditional stories and sang traditional songs for them. Mgbafo was also expert in traditional hairdressing and body decoration, which she took delight in doing on the young girls.

One moonlight night, the children gathered round as usual and the following discussion occurred between Mgbafo and the children. (This is a close translation of the discussion.)

CHILDREN *(all screaming)*: Mgbafo! Come! Our mother come! and tell us
  stories. Come and sing for us.
MGBAFO *(talking from the inside of her house)*:
  Have patience my children
  I shall soon come.
  (Mgbafo comes out and the children yell with delight.
  They all sit around her.)
  Well, my children, you must first tell me one by one what you did today before
  I tell you stories.
(Mr X, who is a child, talks first.)
MR. X: I went to the school belonging to the Reverend Fathers. Our teacher
  was hard on us. He caned us, because we went to the forest of Idemmili to trap
  rats. He said we must not enter the forest of Idemmili, because it was pagan
  forest. He also caned us because we played at masquerades. He said it was a pagan
  thing.
    So when my father said I must go trapping this afternoon I refused. Father
  beat me and when I came to you, you had gone to the stream.
MGBAFO: It is a pity you had a nasty day at school and at home. As a man you
  must learn how to make and use traps, to make and use nets, to carve on wood
  and to make shrine images. You can also be a blacksmith and make knives and
  hoes and iron staffs for title-taking.
    You must learn to sing the songs we sing during different periods of the year.
    If all these things are things of the pagans, they are also our things. If you
  leave them all to learn only the things of the white man, you will be like Ifili, the

273

spirit who lived in the land of the spirits and who in his great desire to look his best, transformed himself into a 'faceless' spirit.

CHILDREN: Please, our mother, tell us about Ifili.

MGBAFO: (*Sings the song associated with the folk tale and the children sing the refrain after her.*)

My story moves to a long time ago when the world of men and the world of spirits were separated by seven forests, seven rivers, seven deserts.

In the land of the spirits, there was a young spirit called Ifili. Ifili thought that his face was not handsome enough and deliberately lost his eyes, nose, mouth, jaw, ears and hair. He became a 'faceless' spirit. When he discovered his folly, he made attempts to find the parts, but failed. So whenever there was a festival in the world of human beings Ifili had to borrow these missing parts from other spirits who were going and fit them on before he could attend.

One day there was a festival in the land of men. As usual Ifili went and borrowed all the parts of his face. Generally he borrowed beautiful ones, so that after the fitting he looked very handsome and attractive.

On arrival at the festival, Ifili beheld a very beautiful girl who was fond of refusing suitors. Ifili approached the girl and offered to marry her. The girl admired the handsome young man and without haste agreed.

Ifili went to the parents of the girl to persuade them to agree not only to his marrying the girl but to his taking her away immediately to his home. The parents reluctantly yielded, because the girl insisted on going and because they were fed up with the past behaviour of their daughter with regard to refusing suitors.

Ifili took his wife home. On the first day, Ifili returned the hair he borrowed for his face to the owner, and so was suddenly bald. On the second day he returned the ears, on the third day he returned the nose, on the fourth day he returned the mouth, on the fifth he returned the jaw, on the sixth he returned the eye. He became 'faceless' again. The girl was disgusted and decided to run away, because each time Ifili returned the part he borrowed he made up an excuse to her why that part was missing from his face. Indeed Ifili was a spirit without personality and character.

Early one morning, the girl started her flight from the land of the spirits. But she was pursued by Ifili. She ran nine days and nine nights and at last came to her father's home. The door was locked and Ifili was close behind her. She sang:

IGBO:	*A je belim ije di*	*Mgbafụli (Refrain)*
	Nuta di ifile	*Mgbafụli (Refrain)*
	Ifili enwe anya	*Mgbafụli (Refrain)*
	Ifili enwe imi	*Mgbafụli (Refrain)*
	Mmanụ ifili	*Mgbafụli (Refrain)*

ENGLISH:	I went to marry	I have run out (*Refrain*)
	I married a 'faceless'	I have run out (*Refrain*)
	A faceless without eye	I have run out (*Refrain*)
	A faceless without nose	I have run out (*Refrain*)
	I will not marry a 'faceless'	I have run out (*Refrain*)

IFILI sang:

IGBO:	*Ọgo nwanyi Akpọyepune*	*Mgbafụlifụli (Refrain)*
	Ọga nuto Akpọyepune	*Mgbafụlifụli (Refrain)*
	Fụ di okweli Akpọyepune	*Mgbafụlifụli (Refrain)*

ENGLISH: O my mother-in-law, do not open   For the runaway (*Refrain*)
    She must go on with the marriage   For the runaway (*Refrain*)
    She who sees a husband at sight, and marries him   For the runaway (*Refrain*)

The door did not open and so the girl ran to her mother's patrilineage, to her mother's brother. Again the door was locked and she sang the song. Before the 'faceless' spirit could sing his song, the mother's brother roasted a coco-yam and threw it at the face of the 'faceless' spirit. The spirit ran back to spirit land to live his 'faceless' existence, while the girl remained in the world of humans and lived an existence with a face.

So, my children, there I leave the 'faceless' spirit in the spirit land.

Those who leave their traditions and customs for others are like the 'faceless' spirit. Your teacher is like the 'faceless' spirit. Do not listen to them. In such matters listen to your fathers and mothers.

2. AROUND 1935

By 1935, Mgbafo had died and many of those children had become adults. Some remained in their home town and never travelled beyond the neighbouring towns. Others left for the towns. Mr X was one of those who left home; he joined the Nigerian police force. He served at Kaduna, Lagos, Minna, Sapele and Calabar. He retired after over thirty years of service on a pension of about £4 per month. During those thirty years he visited his home town about eight times, staying not more than two weeks for each visit.

During X's period of service in the police force, he had many children who were brought into direct contact with European technology, ideologies and knowledge. One of his children is now an engineer, another a lecturer, and another a nursing sister.

On retiring, X took the Igbo title of *Ozo*. He deplored and also praised the many changes that took place in his lifetime. He died in 1972.

3. IN 1972

The grandchildren of X, the children of the engineer, the lecturer and the nursing sister, came home with their parents to perform the traditional burial ceremony for him. I happened to live next door to them and so had the opportunity to observe and interview them as well as those living at home on certain specific issues. Here are some of the more important comparisons and observations that were made. All the children of the lecturer, the engineer and the nursing sister could sing: 'Ba, ba, black sheep', but not one of them could sing any of the traditional rhymes. All the local children could sing the traditional rhymes and a few European rhymes. The new élite parents said that it was not important to know the traditional rhymes, but the parents of those at home thought it was important to know both. The children of the new élite did not know that the teapots and teacups which they were using were made of clay, while all the local children knew this. Indeed, some of them helped their parents to make clay pots and cups and fire them. The children at home could name all the trees around, and talked about the palm trees, banana and yam, while the children of the new élite knew nothing about them. They ate them and that was all. The children from the urban area talked about aeroplanes, television, hotels, birthday parties, fine dresses and shoes. Those at home talked about masquerades, wrestling on the sand, making traps and fishing.

However, all the children talked and played ball together. Those at home could talk freely and express themselves in Igbo, while those from the towns spoke little Igbo and more English. In English they could not express themselves as quickly, briskly and effectively as the local children spoke Igbo.

4. SOCIAL CHANGE:
INDUSTRIALIZATION AND MODERNIZATION

The changes that have occurred within the three generations described in the story above have been tremendous. Some changes were accepted and others rejected. Mgbafo was a typical example of someone who effectively resisted some of the changes. Her folktale may have had a lasting effect on the minds of some of the children. We noticed how the mission school aided in eroding the traditional small-scale primitive domestic technology, without replacing it with something positive and creative, although such schools played a major role in introducing Western education in this part of the world.

Mr X learnt to read and write the European script and became a policeman. However he lost the skills of the primitive domestic technology he had acquired while young, and so was not able to transmit them to his children. His grandchildren did not even know how the teacups they were using were made, although they could sing European rhymes designed to meet the requirement of the European environment, and talked about shoes and fine dresses.

Anthropologists call this type of change social and cultural. It can be progressive as well as regressive. Of course African societies were not static, but the changes that have occurred since 1850 have been far-reaching, because African cultures characterized by a domestic technology have been brought into contact with the cultures and industrial technology of Europe, America and Japan. African domestic technology has been swept away and replaced by dependence on Western and Japanese technologies.

This has probably resulted in an erosion of self-confidence among the African élite. To most of them technology means those big machines in Europe. The whole process of technology involves its intellectual aspects. It has to be clearly appreciated that European advanced technology was the child of European primitive technology. If one cannot appreciate the degree of empirical science involved in the manufacture of a simple clay pot, the smelting of iron ore for the making of a simple hoe, the moulding of a bronze vessel and the making of a simple twig trap, one cannot evaluate the technological attainments of the makers of the Igbo–Ukwu, Ife and Benin bronzes or the builders of what are now the Zimbabwe ruins. The destruction of African primitive technology created a technological hiatus in the cultural advancement of Africa.

I do not believe that modern Europeans, Americans, Japanese, or Russians, all of whose civilization is based on technology and militarism, will teach Africans or Asians the secrets of advanced technology. There is clear evidence that what is being done in the name of industrial development is to teach African consumers how to maintain their machines. The deep secret of technology is in the making of machines that make machines. When one compares the amount of cars imported into Africa and the amount of tools and manufacturing machines imported into Africa from Europe, Japan and North America, this argument will seem valid. At present, the relationship between Europe and Africa in terms of technology and economy is similar to the patron–client relationship. Some writers refer to it as neo-colonialism.

Not only technological changes are taking place in Africa, but ideologies are changing too. The European concepts of theism, atheism, capitalism, communism, democracy, socialism, are being brandished around Africa. In the past thirty years much of the African élite has been chanting versions of these ideologies.

The traditional African concepts of theism, polytheism, individualism, democracy, political freedom, social welfare, social discipline, communalism, alliance have all been thrown abroad by the African élite in the names of modernization and industrialization, without much effort being made to study their value.

How can Africa achieve modernization and industrialization? What do these words mean? If by industrialization is meant the use and maintenance of machines, then it is understandable why the first stage in the so-called industrialization programme in most African countries is the installation of soft-drink, cigarette and beer factories. However, if by industrialization the making as well as the using of tools and machines are implied, Africa seems far away from it. It is alarming to observe that rural farmers, on whose cash crops and food crops modern Africa depends, lack the simple primitive tools which are adapted for dealing with African soil and its particular problems of erosion and leaching. The lack of tools is due to the fact that there are fewer traditional blacksmiths who make them. The cutlasses and the hoes they now use are generally imported ones, and there are no smiths around to repair them. Where these tools are manufactured in Africa, the iron ore used is generally imported.

Bulldozers, heavy tractors and mechanized ploughs have been introduced in some parts of Africa, but they have created more problems. The forest is hewn down, the top soils are exposed to the torrential rains. The disasters of heavy leaching and erosion follow and a new struggle of erosion control begins. This is the case in southern Nigeria. Most of these giant machines are beyond the reach of the common farmer, and most of them are not adapted to the agronomic needs of African ecology.

It will be better for African governments to manufacture simple mechanized hoes and wheelbarrows and sell them cheaply to the rural farmers, than to buy more jet bombers, aircraft, Japanese and British transistor radios and cars, or to build beer and cigarette factories.

The reason why they do the latter rather than manufacture a simple mechanized hoe is that the manufacturing process needs a completely different system of organization from the ones used in building a beer factory or using a transistor radio. African agricultural engineers should meet the challenge not by ordering new bulldozers and tractors but by thinking out ways of designing and making new machinery so that it will be suitable for African ecological and manpower needs. This is what I envisage as an aspect of the African Industrial Revolution.

Let us examine the meaning of modernization. One fact that is striking is how African traditional arts, music and political systems have added some vigour to European arts, music and politics. Some European artists, like Picasso, have been influenced by African traditional art forms. These are all aspects of modernization in European art forms.

Modernization is a dynamic process. It is a movement that has two interdependent facets. First it is a movement from 'primitive' forms to 'advanced' forms. Such movement is generally purposive and planned and so it involves research work. It is also a process of transformation which uses past and contemporary patterns to build new patterns.

Whilst African cultures are influencing other cultures, other cultures are also influencing African cultures. As Africa moves into the later part of the twentieth century, she is faced with the problem of finding a lasting place in the world of advanced technology. Here the wisdom in Mgbafo's story of the 'faceless' spirit seeking for a wife with a beautiful face becomes pertinent.

Africans should look for those parts of their 'faces' lost during the colonial days. Those parts may still be found in African traditions and cultures. Having found them, they will also discover new inspiration, new imagination, new creativity, new confidence to face the problems of industrialization and modernization. This is what the universities, colleges and schools in Africa should strive to achieve. Indeed the message of this book is that in African cultures there is a very rich mine of knowledge which if properly understood and applied may provide a firmer foundation for modern advancement.

If the reader has faithfully read through this book, I hope he will begin to appreciate more deeply the implications and the crucial roles of African cultures and societies in terms of what are now called industrialization and modernization.

BIBLIOGRAPHY

Suggestions for further reading
AMIN, S. *Neo-Colonialism in West Africa* (Harmondsworth: Penguin, 1973)
BRETTON, H. L. *Power Politics in Africa* (Harlow: Longman, 1973)
DAVIDSON, B. *Which Way Africa? The Search for a New Society* (Harmondsworth: Penguin, 1964)
—— *The Africans: An Entry to Cultural History* (Harmondsworth: Penguin, 1969)
KIBY, P. *Industrialization in an Open Economy: Nigeria 1945–1966* (Cambridge: Cambridge University Press, 1969)
——*Who Controls Industry in Kenya?* (Nairobi: East African Publishing House, 1969)
RODNEY, W. *How Europe Underdeveloped Africa* (London & Tanzania: Bogle-Louverture Publications, 1972)

Signs Used by Anthropologists for Describing Models of Kinship

Social anthropologists use certain signs to record and describe models of kinship. In this section are set out the basic signs which would help the reading of anthropological material.

 Living male or man

Living female or woman

 Dead male or man

Dead female or woman

A living man who is married to a living woman

Two living brothers and a dead sister (also called siblings)

 A living man married to a living woman. They have had three children, two males, living, and one female, dead. This model is a combination of the two above

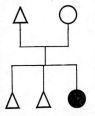

FIGURE 10   *A set of basic anthropological signs*

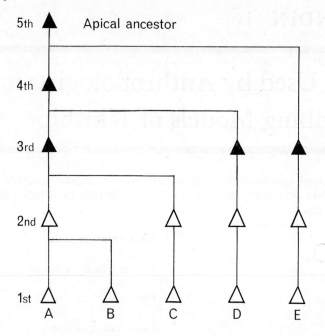

FIGURE 11   *A genealogical tree of five generations showing a patrilineal descent group*

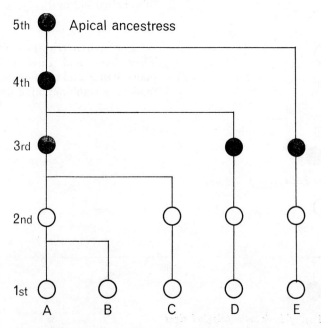

FIGURE 12   *A genealogical tree of five generations showing a matrilineal descent group*

FIGURE 11

This is a genealogical tree of five generations. The persons represented as A, B, C, D, E, called agnates, have a common ancestor and are linked through males, that is, it is a patrilineal descent group. C is marked Ego. This is a Latin word meaning 'I', used by anthropologists to refer to the person whose genealogy is under discussion or who is being referred to. The whole unit may or may not have a name. It is generally named after an apical ancestor. The lines to A, B, C, D and E are called lineages. These lineages are segments of the whole tree. They differ in depth and span.

FIGURE 12

This is a genealogical tree of five generations showing a matrilineal descent group. The persons represented as A, B, C, D, E, have a common ancestress and are linked through females. They are called uterines. The whole unit may or may not have a name.

FIGURE 13

The descendants of A and B counting descent through males as well as females belong to a stock. A stock is ancestor-centred, that is, reckoning is downwards through males and females, starting from a man and his wife.

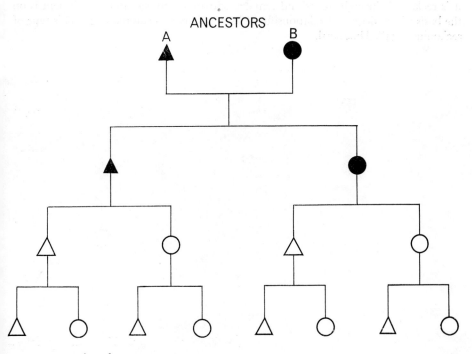

FIGURE 13   *A stock*

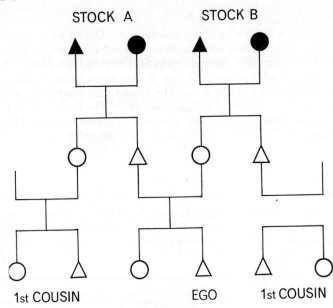

FIGURE 14 *A bilateral system – cognative descent*

Stock A and Stock B are ego's kindred, socially defined as two ascending generations from ego, or first cousin range. Ego or any of his siblings can generate cooperative activity in the mother's set and the father's set. Kindred is ego-centred, that is,
it is reckoned through males and females, starting from ego and recruitment is on
the basis of the degree of relationship of its members to a common ego. This type of
reckoning is called bilateral.

APPENDIX 2

Terms Used by Anthropologists to Describe Social Organization Based on Kinship

Kin

Agnates: Kin in which descent is reckoned through males.

Cognates: Kin that includes agnates and uterines as well as other kin.

Cousins: Children of two siblings of either sex.

Cross-cousins: Children of two siblings of opposite sex, that is, the children of a man and of his sister.

Kindred: A set of cognates of an individual recognized for social purposes. Kindred is Ego-centred and is reckoned through both male and female links.

Kin: A relation in which one person is descended from another, or both persons are descended from a common ancestor or ancestress.

Kinship: A socially recognized relationship traced through parent–child relations.

Kinship system: A model of recognized relations between persons and groups related through parentage and marriage.

Kinship terminology: Terms used by a people to describe types of relationships in their kinship system. For example, the terms father, mother, son, etc., are types of the kinship terminology in the English kinship system.

Parallel cousins: Children of two siblings of the same sex, that is, the children of two brothers or of two sisters.

Siblings: Full siblings are persons of either sex having the same father and the same mother. Persons who are the children of the same father and different mothers are called paternal half-siblings. Persons having the same mother and different fathers are maternal half-siblings.

Stock: All the descendants of a man and wife counting descent through males as well as females (according to Radcliffe Brown). It is ancestor-centred and not Ego-centred. It is not a set of cognates but consists of all ascendants.

Uterines: Kin in which descent is reckoned through females.

Descent

Bilateral: Term describing the tracing of filiation through both parents. For example, kindred is a bilateral grouping.

Ambilateral: Term describing the tracing of filiation through either parent according to certain social or cultural circumstances.

Ambilineal: Term describing a non-unilineal descent group in which membership is through either parent. It is ancestor-based and lineally organized. Some anthropologists are reluctant to classify this type as a descent group because membership is determined by other criteria as well as that of descent.

Clan: A unilineal descent group believed to have had a single founding ancestor; within it specific genealogical connections with an ancestor and between members are not traced.

Complementary filiation: The link between a person and the kin of that parent who does not determine descent group membership.

Descent: A socially recognized link between a person and his forebears or ancestors. Descent may be patrilineal, matrilineal, double unilineal, ambilineal or bilateral.

Descent group: A corporate kin group in which descent is the important criterion for membership.

Double unilineal: Term describing descent reckoned exclusively through males for certain purposes, and exclusively through females for other purposes.

Filiation: The socially recognized relation between a child and a parent and through that parent with his or her kin. Filiation is bilateral.

Lineage: A descent group in which the successive genealogical connections are assumed and traced between living members and the founding ancestor. A lineage may be patrilineal, that is, a patrilineage, or matrilineal, that is, a matrilineage. The span of a lineage indicates the range of kin included. The depth describes the genealogical distance of the ancestor.

A lineage may be segmented (subdivided) into smaller groupings, once or more, for different activities. Each segment is then a unit in a system of segments and each is a corporate group.

Matrilineal (uterine) descent: Unilineal descent, reckoning exclusively through females. (Mater = Mother).

Moiety: One of two divisions of a society, descent groups, to one of which every member must belong. Two such groups exchange women.

Patrilineal (agnatic) descent: Unilineal descent, reckoning exclusively through males. (Pater = Father).

Phratry: One of three or more divisions of a society, to which the groups descent groups belong. It is composed of clans and sub-clans. It may or may not be exogamous, and may or may not be corporate.

Unilateral: Term describing the tracing of descent through a parent of one sex only. As well, the descent may be patrilateral, that is, reckoning through the father; or matrilateral, that is, through the mother.

Marriage

Affinity: The relation between a person and his or her spouse's kin; for example, the relationship between a man and his wife's brother.

Concubinage: The cohabitation of a man and a woman who are not married or the cohabitation of a married man and a woman who is not married.

Cousin marriage: Marriage with a cross-cousin or parallel cousin. It may either be preferred or prescribed.

Endogamy: The rule or practice which insists that a person should marry within his or her own group.

Exogamy: The rule or practice which prohibits a person from taking a spouse within his or her own group. The exogamous group may be a lineage, clan, local community, moiety, phratry, etc.

Ghost marriage: A marriage arranged between a woman and a dead man who is regarded as the *pater* of any children she may subsequently bear. The mate of the woman is usually the dead man's brother, another kinsman, or a stranger.

Incest: Sexual intercourse between individuals who are related within a socially defined degree of prohibition. This degree varies from society to society. In some societies sexual intercourse may be allowed between kin who are forbidden to marry. Incest and marriage prohibitions may or may not coincide.

Levirate: The custom whereby a kinsman of a dead man is allowed to care for and mate with his widow and beget children in the dead man's name. The dead man is regarded as the *pater* of the children and the living man the *genitor*.

Marriage: The union between a man and a woman in which their relationship to one another is jurally defined, and which establishes the legitimacy of the children born to the woman. In most societies, marriage also entails jural obligations between certain classes of the spouse's kin.

Marriage prohibitions: Rules forbidding marriage with specific categories of persons.

Monogamy: The custom or law, and also the fact, of having one socially recognized spouse at a time.

Polyandry: The custom or law by which a woman is allowed to have more than one husband at a time.

Polygyny: The custom or law by which a man is allowed to have more than one wife.

Polygamy: A general term covering both polygyny and polyandry.

Preferred marriage: The preference for marriage with a particular category of relative.

Prescribed marriage: The custom which enforces marriage with a particular class of relative.

Residence at marriage: When a couple marry, the types of residence may be as follows:

(i) *Virilocal*, where the woman goes to live in her husband's abode.

(ii) *Uxorilocal*, where the husband goes to live in his wife's abode.

(iii) *Patrilocal-virilocal*, where the woman joins her husband who lives near his father.

(iv) *Avunculocal-virilocal*, where the woman joins her husband who lives near his mother's brother.

(v) *Patrilocal-uxorilocal*, where the husband joins his wife who lives near her father.

(vi) *Bilocal*, where the couple spend some time with the wife's group and some time with the husband's group.

(vii) *Neolocal*, where the couple move to a new home away from their respective kin.

(viii) *Duolocal*, where the spouses reside separately. The residence pattern at marriage has bearings on patterns of authority, property rights and the stability of marriage.

Sororate: The custom whereby a woman's kin are allowed to provide her husband with another wife (who may be her sister), should she die, prove barren, or bear only daughters.

Widow inheritance: The custom whereby a widow is bound or expected to marry a kinsman of her husband. The new husband will be both the *pater* and *genitor* of the children.

Widow concubinage: The custom whereby a widow cohabits with another man or men; the rights in and over the children borne by the widow are retained by the dead man or his kin.

Woman-to-woman marriage: A marriage arranged between two women. One of the women has the rights of a *pater* over any children borne by the other woman, who cohabits with a lover or lovers. The children belong to the kin group of their female *pater.*

Family

Compound family: There are three types of compound family:

(i) The polygynous compound family, which is made up of a man and his wives and their children.

(ii) The polyandrous compound family, which is made up of a woman and her husbands and their children.

(iii) A group made up of a remarried widow or widower who has children by a former marriage.

Domestic group: A group which occupies a single homestead or part of it, and cooperate for some purposes of production and consumption. A domestic group is therefore, more or less, an economic unit and may correspond in whole or part to a simple, compound, or joint family with additional relatives or attachments. The domestic group often undergoes a developmental cyclic process.

Elementary, nuclear, or simple family: Common names for the group that is made up of a man and his wife and children.

Extended family: This is composed of a number of joint, compound and elementary families, occupying separate but near-by homesteads. Each has a degree of jural and economic independence, but all are subject to a common head. Simple, compound, joint and extended families are often stages in the developmental cycle in domestic groups.

Family of orientation: The family in which Ego is a child.

Family of procreation: The family in which Ego is a parent.

Joint family: The group formed when two or more closely related kinfolk, usually of the same sex, together with their spouses and children, occupy a single homestead and are jointly subject to the same head. There are four well-known types:

(i) The patrilineal joint family, which consists of a man, his wives and children, and his sons' wives and children. Married daughters may be included.

(ii) The matrilineal joint family, which consists of a woman and her husband and their children, and her daughters' husbands and children. Married sons may be included.

(iii) The fraternal joint family, which consists of two or more brothers with their wives and children.

(iv) The avunculocal joint family, which consists of a man and his wife, unmarried daughters and young sons, and his married sisters' sons and sisters' married sons with their wives and children. This type occurs in some matrilineal societies where boys, at a certain age, join the household of one of their mother's brothers.

Association and Age-Sets

Association: A socially recognized, self-recruiting group organized for the pursuit of an interest or set of interests. The most common criteria for membership are age, sex, rank, locality, individual experience, payment of a fee, or a combination of these. Membership may be voluntary or compulsory.

Associations have been classified according to the following criteria:

(i) Their main activity, for example, ceremonial, ritual, recreational, military, economic, political, social.

(ii) The possession of special knowledge and paraphernalia; for example, secret societies (freemasonry), monasteries, convents.

(iii) The possession of a privilege. Membership involves taking a title. Example: title or honorific societies.

(iv) The character of membership. For example: a body of men, called a fraternity; a body of women, called a sorority; a body of people of the same age, called an age-set (not all age-sets are associations).

Age-grade: One of a series of stages through which age-sets pass. These stages may be named. The grade represents the status reached.

Age-set: A formally organized, usually named group of persons within a given age span. Each set may pass through a series of stages known as age-grades.

Terms Used in Analysing Systems of Kinship and Marriage, Descent, Associations

Corporate: 'A group may be spoken of as "corporate" when it possesses any one of a certain number of characters: if its members, or its adult members, or a considerable proportion of them, come together occasionally to carry out some collective action, e.g. the performance of rites; if it has a chief or council who are regarded as acting as the representatives of the group as a whole; if it possesses or controls property which is collective, as when a clan or a lineage is a land-owning group' (Radcliffe-Brown). It should be noted that the property may be incorporeal, such as an exclusive common name or an exclusive cult. Some anthropologists only use the term 'corporate' for a property-owning group.

Inheritance: The transmission, following certain recognized rules, of a dead person's property, to another person or persons.

Jural relationship: A relationship which involves binding rights and obligations sanctioned morally, ritually, or legally (or a combination of these).

Succession: The process by which a dead person's statuses, rights, and obligations are transmitted to another person or persons.

ACKNOWLEDGMENT

These terms are compiled from various sources but are mainly based on the definitions current in the Department of Anthropology at London University between 1961 and 1966. Since I have re-phrased some, I am solely responsible for any errors.

INDEX

The names of peoples are given in brackets after topics in the index, wherever possible.

Production, and consumption—*contd.*
  status (Tolowa Titutni, Ponapeans, Tiv and Lele), 203–6
  systems of, and patterns of distribution (Perak and Selangor), 216–17
Prostitution, 105
Psychic powers, 248, *see also* Sorcery; Witchcraft
Purdah system, 23–4, 25, 103
Pygmies, 117, 264–8

Qgbolia (Yakö headmen), 117

Racism defined, 58–9
Radcliffe-Brown, 3–4, 11–12, 16–18, 31, 95, 98, 115, 129–30, 231
Raja, meaning of, 146
Raja Muda, office of, 146
Rajas (Malay States), 215–16
Ram's horns, carving of, and sacrificial cults, 249
Relativism, 233–4
Religion, and initiation (Bambuti), 266; and science, origin and character of thoughts in, 221–5; and magic and morality, 225–6; and culture, related to moral code, 227–31; Comanche, 164
Religious movements sanctioning politico-economic aspirations (Zulu), 268–72
Residences: (Comanche), 160; (Mayombe, Bemba and Yao), 87–8
Resources and patterns of distribution (Perak and Selangor), 214
Richards, Audrey, 146
Ritual concepts (Igbo), 182
Riyom settlement (Borom), 136
Rock paintings (Sahara), 30
Role, concept of, *see* Social Structure, concepts of
Role differentiation (Tajore and Hausa-Fulani), 152–8
Roles: An Introduction to the Study of Social Relations (Banton), 19

Sacrifices to ancestors (LoDagaa) 240–8; (Malaita), 81, *see also* Ancestor cult
Sahlin, 10, 15, 31, 160
Sai Abdulkerim, King, 107
Salmond, J. W., 190
Sapir, Edward, 10, 16
Schapera (or Shapera), 19, 129
Satellite towns (Igbo), 184–5
Science and religion, origin of thoughts on, 221–5

Seances to detect witchcraft, 258
Secret societies, 22, 254
Segmentation, nature and level of, 99, 116–17, 124
Selangor peoples, 142–6, 214–17
Seneca tribe, 140
Serer language, 29
Sex (Hausa-Fulani), 103
Shapera (or Schapera), 19, 129
Shaw, Professor, 38, 41
Shrine organization (ancestor cult), 242–8, *see also* Ancestor cult
Sibling relationship, 57–61; (Nuer) 64–5
Skill and ability (Hausa-Fulani), 106, *see also* Achievement
Slave group (Hausa-Fulani), 103
Smith, M. G., 32, 98, 101, 106, 108, 109, 110, 156, 164
Social change, industrialization and modernization, 276–8
Social groupings and kinship terminology, 57–61; and unilineal systems, 63–76; relationship patterns (Nuer), 63–9; (Lele), 69–74; (Yakö), 74–6; and non-unilineal systems, 77–83; bilateral system and double unilineal system contrasted, 77–80; ambilineal system (Malaita), 80–3
Social inequality (Tajore and Hausa-Fulani), 152–8
Social organization in economic activities, 176–89, *see also* Environment
Social progress and mystical conflicts, 251
Social relationships, 264–72; initiation ceremonies (Bambuti), 264–8; religious movements sanctioning politico-economic aspirations, (Zulu), 268–72
Social structure, concepts of, 15–25; survey of functional and structural approaches, 15–17; functional significance explaining an institution, 17–18; status and role, 18–20; education of non-literate societies, 21–3; women's status in tribal and small scale societies, 23–5; and landholding, *see* Production and consumption, patterns of; and morality, and morality, 233–9; Iroquois, 138–9
Societies:
  with states, 136–50; descent groups (Birom), 136–7; factors in development of, (Iroquois), 137–42; kingship and royal descent, (Perak and Selangor), 142–6; eligibility for